Ulrich Bonnell Phillips

Ulrich Bonnell Phillips. Photo courtesy of Hargrett Rare Book and Manuscript Library, University of Georgia.

ULRICH BONNELL PHILLIPS

*A Southern Historian
and His Critics*

Edited by **John David Smith**
and **John C. Inscoe**

Studies in Historiography, Number 1

GREENWOOD PRESS
New York • Westport, Connecticut • London

Library of Congress Cataloging-in-Publication Data

Ulrich Bonnell Phillips : a Southern historian and his critics /
  edited by John David Smith and John C. Inscoe.
     p. cm.—(Studies in historiography, ISSN 1046-526X ; no. 1)
  Includes bibliographical references.
  ISBN 0-313-26814-2 (lib. bdg. : alk. paper)
     1. Phillips, Ulrich Bonnell, 1877-1934.   2. Southern States—
  Historiography. I. Smith, John David, 1949-   II. Inscoe, John
  C., 1951- .   III. Series.
  E175.5.P47U47   1990
  975′.007202—dc20   89-26040

British Library Cataloguing in Publication Data is available.

Library of Congress Catalog Card Number: 89-26040
ISBN: 0-313-26814-2
ISSN: 1046-526X

First published in 1990

Greenwood Press, 88 Post Road West, Westport, CT 06881
An imprint of Greenwood Publishing Group, Inc.

Printed in the United States of America

The paper used in this book complies with the
Permanent Paper Standard issued by the National
Information Standards Organization (Z39.48-1984).

10 9 8 7 6 5 4 3 2 1

Richard Hofstadter, "U.B. Phillips and the Plantation Legend," *The Journal of Negro History* (April 1944) and Ruben Kugler, "U.B. Phillips's Use of Sources," *The Journal of Negro History* (July 1962) are reprinted by permission of *The Journal of Negro History*.

John David Smith, " 'Keep 'em in a Fire Proof Vault'—Pioneer Southern Historians Discover Plantation Records," is reprinted with permission from *South Atlantic Quarterly*, 78:3. Copyright 1979 by Duke University Press.

Robert W. Fogel and Stanley L. Engerman, *Time on the Cross: The Economics of American Negro Slavery*, (Boston: Little, Brown and Company, 1974), p. 223-232 is reprinted by permission of Robert W. Fogel, Stanley L. Engerman, and W. W. Norton & Company, Inc.

Louis Filler, "Ulrich B. Phillips: A Question of History and Reality," Introduction to U.B. Phillips, *Georgia and State Rights* (1968 edition), p. v-xiv is reprinted by permission of Antioch Publishing Co.

Excerpts from the Herbert Anthony Kellar Papers of the McCormick Collection at the State Historical Society of Wisconsin is reprinted courtesy of the State Historical Society of Wisconsin.

Every reasonable effort has been made to trace the owners of copyright materials in this book, but in some instances this has proven impossible. The publishers will be glad to receive information leading to more complete acknowledgments in subsequent printings of the book and in the meantime extend their apologies for any omissions.

For Kirby—who taught me the meaning of loyalty
—J.D.S.

For Meg and Clay
—J.C.I.

Contents

Preface   *xiii*

Acknowledgments   *xv*

A Chronology of Ulrich Bonnell Phillips's Life and Career   *xvii*

**Introduction: The Place of Ulrich Bonnell Phillips
in American Historiography**   1
John David Smith

I. THE SOUTHERNER   15

1. **The Experts**   17
   W. E. B. Du Bois

2. **Ulrich B. Phillips: Historian of Aristocracy**   19
   Wendell Holmes Stephenson

3. **U. B. Phillips: A Southern Mind**   29
   John Herbert Roper

II. THE PROGRESSIVE   35

4. **Ulrich B. Phillips: Progress and the Conservative
   Historian**   37
   William L. Van Deburg

5. **A Case of Forgotten Identity: Ulrich B. Phillips as a
   Young Progressive**   47
   John Herbert Roper

6. **Rewriting Southern History: U. B. Phillips, the New
   South, and the Antebellum Past**   57
   W. K. Wood

III. THE RACIST   79

7. Reviews of *American Negro Slavery*   83
   W. E. B. Du Bois, Carter G. Woodson, and Mary White Ovington

8. The Historian and Southern Negro Slavery   91
   Kenneth M. Stampp

9. Racial Inferiority as the Basic Assumption   103
   Stanley M. Elkins

10. Introduction to *Life and Labor in the Old South*   109
   C. Vann Woodward

11. Race and Class in Southern History: An Appraisal
   of the Work of Ulrich Bonnell Phillips   113
   Eugene D. Genovese

IV. THE SCIENTIFIC HISTORIAN   129

12. U. B. Phillips and the Scientific Tradition   131
   Sam E. Salem

13. U. B. Phillips's Use of Sources   143
   Ruben F. Kugler

14. "Keep 'em in a fire-proof vault"—Pioneer Southern
   Historians Discover Plantation Records   153
   John David Smith

15. U. B. Phillips, Unscientific Historian   169
   W. K. Wood

V. THE SOCIAL AND ECONOMIC HISTORIAN   183

16. U. B. Phillips and the Plantation Legend   185
   Richard Hofstadter

17. The Enigma of the South   199
   David M. Potter

18. Ulrich Bonnell Phillips as an Economic Historian   203
   Eugene D. Genovese

19. Toward an Explanation for the Persistence of the
   Myth of Black Incompetence   207
   Robert William Fogel and Stanley L. Engerman

20. Ulrich B. Phillips: The Old South as the New   215
   Daniel Joseph Singal

VI. THE POLITICAL HISTORIAN

VI. THE POLITICAL HISTORIAN   235

21. U. B. Phillips on Southern Politics, Politicians,
    and Civil War Causation   237
    Wendell Holmes Stephenson

22. Ulrich B. Phillips: A Question of History and Reality   241
    Louis Filler

23. U. B. Phillips: Revisionist of the 1930s   249
    Merton L. Dillon

BIBLIOGRAPHIES

The Major Writings of Ulrich Bonnell Phillips   255

Historical Analyses of Ulrich Bonnell Phillips
and His Work, 1934-1989   259

Index   267
About the Contributors   273
About the Editors   277

Preface

Ulrich Bonnell Phillips (1877-1934) ranks among the most important and controversial historians of the American South. Although hundreds of historians have written about slavery and the plantation regime, relatively few have earned the lasting place in American historiography that Phillips has. As early as 1937, for example, Phillips was honored, along with such historians as George Bancroft, Francis Parkman, and Frederick Jackson Turner, in *The Marcus W. Jernegan Essays in American Historiography*, edited by William T. Hutchinson. Phillips, a white Georgian, was trained in the era of "scientific" historical methodology and Jim Crow race relations. He employed his resourcefulness—and connections among the gentry—to become a pioneer in locating and using plantation materials as sources. Despite Phillips's racial and class bias, he continues to loom as an almost larger-than-life figure among students of Afro-American slavery and the plantation South. His two famous books, *American Negro Slavery* (1918) and *Life and Labor in the Old South* (1929), stand as classic studies in the historical literature. Even his most severe critics—and they are numerous—acknowledge Phillips's pathbreaking efforts. His contributions, both positive and negative, still serve as the starting place for many scholars. No historian of slavery can ignore Phillips's insightful contributions to the topics of master-slave relations and the profitability of slavery. To a significant degree, he defined the issues that later generations of students would investigate. Phillips's work, especially on the social and economic aspects of slavery, provides an important link between what James Harvey Robinson termed the "New History" in the early twentieth century, and the "new" social and economic history of today. Phillips, then, remains an important influence, if only behind the scenes, for much of the present scholarly debate on slavery and the South.

Phillips's importance to southern historiography can be measured by the surprisingly large volume of critical scholarly interest devoted to his writings. No other historian of the region—past or present—has attracted such attention. Aside from book reviews, Phillips has been the subject of almost seventy articles or chapters in books, including two full-length biographies (as the bibliography at the end of this volume attests). Other studies on the scholar and his work are still in progress. Convinced that the great interest in Phillips has become an important theme in itself, the editors of this anthology have assembled a work that chronicles the major issues of debate and the range of topics concerning Phillips and his writings.

The anthology consists of twenty-six essays or excerpts from larger works—all published between 1913 and 1986—that assess in some way Phillips's writings or career. Because of the varying critical responses to his work, this volume is arranged thematically. Phillips's background, his training, his regional and racial prejudices, his ideology, his methodology, and the historical genres in which he worked are analyzed by recognized authorities. A brief interpretive introduction prefaces each section and a chronological listing of the extant critical literature on Phillips completes the volume. Taken collectively, the historical criticism of Phillips reflects the vast scope of his contributions. It also suggests the various ways in which this Georgia native influenced the field of southern history in general, and slavery studies in particular. Indeed, despite the flaws that mar his work, Phillips remains a past master of his craft. Subsequent scholars need not agree with Phillips's conclusions, but they would be negligent and short-sighted to ignore them.

As editors, we have silently corrected and systematized spelling, punctuation, grammar, capitalization, and minor factual errors in the essays herein. We have used brackets for any insertions made within the text. All footnotes appear as endnotes and have been left in their original format, with minor alterations made only to achieve consistency within each article. For those essays made up of non-continuous selections from a larger work, breaks have been indicated.

Acknowledgments

The editors gratefully acknowledge permission to reprint the materials on U. B. Phillips from the journals and books in which they originally appeared. Sharon Darden expertly typed several drafts of the manuscript. Joe Inscoe generously shared his expertise. Sylvia A. Smith and Jane Inscoe offered timely encouragement and valuable suggestions that have strengthened the final product. A grant from the College of Humanities and Social Sciences Research Committee, North Carolina State University, assisted with administrative expenses. The Departments of History at North Carolina State University, Rice University, and the University of Georgia provided generous financial support for expenses involved in the long-distance collaboration of the editors. The Copywright of Richmond, Virginia designed and typeset the book.

A Chronology of Ulrich Bonnell Phillips's Life and Career

1877 — Born in La Grange, Georgia, November 4

1893 — Completed curriculum at Tulane Preparatory School
— Entered University of Georgia

1897 — Awarded A.B. degree by University of Georgia

1898 — Attended University of Chicago summer term with Frederick Jackson Turner

1899 — Awarded A.M. degree by University of Georgia
— Enrolled at Columbia University

1902 — Elected president of the Federation of Graduate Student Clubs
— "Georgia and State Rights" awarded Justin Winsor Prize and published by American Historical Association
— Appointed instructor at University of Wisconsin

1903 — Proposed to reform Georgia Historical Society
— Taught at the Summer School of the South at Knoxville, Tennessee
— Assessed the public records of Georgia for the American Historical Association

1904 — Began campaign to reform education and agriculture on Wisconsin model
— Joined Richard T. Ely's American Bureau of Industrial Research, University of Wisconsin
— Received grant from Carnegie Institution of Washington
— Taught summer school at University of Georgia

1907   – Promoted to assistant professor at the University of Wisconsin
        – Taught summer school at the University of Kansas
        – Appointed visiting professor at Tulane University

1908   – Published *A History of Transportation in the Eastern Cotton Belt to 1860*
        – Promoted to associate professor at University of Wisconsin
        – Appointed chairman of the Department of History and Political Science at Tulane University

1909   – Published *Plantation and Frontier Documents, 1649-1863*

1911   – Married Lucie Mayo-Smith, February 22
        – Appointed professor at University of Michigan

1913   – Published *The Correspondence of Robert Toombs, Alexander H. Stephens, and Howell Cobb*
        – Published *The Life of Robert Toombs*

1914   – Elected to executive council of American Historical Association

1917   – Joined staff of YMCA at Camp Gordon, Georgia

1918   – Published *American Negro Slavery*

1924   – Appointed visiting professor at University of California

1925   – Taught summer school at Harvard University

1927   – Published (with James David Glunt) *Florida Plantation Records from the Papers of George Noble Jones*

1928   – Awarded book prize from Little, Brown & Company
        – Presented "The Central Theme of Southern History" at American Historical Association annual meeting

1929   – Published *Life and Labor in the Old South*
        – Awarded Albert Kahn Foundation Fellowship
        – Appointed professor at Yale University
        – Elected to executive council of the American Historical Association

1930   – Toured Africa

1931   – Invited to conference of southern writers meeting at University of Virginia
– Attended rural education conference at Tuskegee Institute, Alabama

1932   – Delivered series of lectures at Northwestern University
– Taught summer school at the University of California

1934   – Died in New Haven, Connecticut, January 21

1939   – *The Course of the South to Secession* published

Ulrich Bonnell Phillips

INTRODUCTION:

The Place of Ulrich Bonnell Phillips in American Historiography

John David Smith

"The ghost of U. B. Phillips haunts all of us," wrote John W. Blassingame in 1978.[1] Ulrich Bonnell Phillips—the very sound of his name conjures up historical bogies for many scholars. By the 1960s Phillips had come to symbolize the reactionary and racist strains in southern historiography in general and of the historiography of slavery in particular. Phillips was condemned for ignoring the agony of the slaves. He was *the* classic apologist for an inhumane, brutal, and exploitative system. Professors rarely assigned Phillips's books to their students. When they did, they offered them as case studies in flawed historical scholarship. Phillips not only asked the "wrong" questions, his critics charged, but his conclusions were made ludicrous by overt elitism, extreme antipathy toward blacks, and methodological imbalance and imprecision.[2] To this generation of scholars, Phillips exemplified the many evils of racist white historiography of an earlier day.

Phillips died in 1934. Had he lived, the criticism of the 1960s and 1970s would have dumbfounded him. During the first three decades of this century Phillips had reigned as the master of slave historiography. His nine books and more than fifty-five articles had established him as the most thorough, systematic, and resourceful student of plantation slavery.[3] Phillips's work dominated the literature on slavery until the 1950s. During the last three decades, however, the pioneer historian has been dethroned and, according to some critics, all but repudiated. The rise and fall of Phillips as a historian of slavery provide an essential backdrop for a third phase of the historiographic cycle: the resurgence of interest in his work in recent years. Several scholars have looked at Phillips anew and—while strongly critical of his racial and class bias—paint a more positive image of the man and his contributions.

When analyzing Phillips's writings on slavery, students usually focus on his two landmark books, *American Negro Slavery* (1918) and *Life and Labor in the Old South* (1929). Attention, however, also should be given to a number of pathbreaking essays that he published in the decade and a half after completing his doctorate in 1902. In these early articles Phillips introduced many of the themes and utilized most of the manuscript and plantation sources that he developed and used in his two famous books.[4]

Phillips described slavery as a necessary and successful mode of racial control. He equated the plantation with both the modern factory and the social settlement houses of the Progressive Era. In his view the plantation served a vital social function: it created a controlled environment in which the master and slaver lived in peace and harmony.[5] Slavery, then, was a benign, paternalistic institution. The blacks received adequate housing, food, and clothing. Slave laws were enforced only casually and, "except in emergencies," masters rarely sold slaves. The planters' "dominating consideration was not that of great profit," wrote Phillips, "but that of comfortable living in pleasant surroundings, with a consciousness of important duties well-performed." Considerable give and take, argued Phillips, characterized labor relations on the plantation. Masters, out of self-interest and genuine kindness, were benevolent patriarchs. "The slaves," Phillips explained, "had many leverages, and oftentimes... ruled their masters more than the masters ruled them." And life under this "paternalistic despotism" also included an educational component. The plantation, in his opinion, was a school that trained "ignorant," "unenterprising," "barbaric," "childlike and credulous" Africans in the ways of civilization. Phillips concluded that slavery offered "the most efficient method ever devised for the use of stupid labor in agriculture on a large scale."[6]

Despite its importance in ordering southern society Phillips judged slavery an utter economic failure. He even predicted that had the Civil War not intervened, financial considerations would have led to its disestablishment in some peaceable way. Phillips criticized slavery for what he termed "capitalizing the prospective value of the labor of each workman for the whole of his life."[7] Although varied and flexible as a social system. It locked up and exported too much scarce capital, thereby retarding industrialization and making the section susceptible to financial crises. Slavery further discouraged the immigration of wage-earning whites into the South, limited crop diversification, and wasted the fertility of the soil. "It was only in special industries," wrote Phillips in 1905, "and only in times of special prosperity, that negro slave labor was of such decided profit as to escape condemnation for its inherent disadvantages."[8]

Phillips refined and elaborated these themes in *American Negro Slavery*, his magnum opus, and the first systematic analysis of slavery in the entire South.[9] This volume thrust Phillips into the role of the unexcelled authority on the peculiar institution. It eclipsed in scope and detail prior books on North American slavery and has influenced virtually all subsequent works on the subject. His chapters on West African culture, the slave trade, Caribbean slavery, and slavery in the North actually added little to previous scholarship. But his use of the comparative method to examine slavery in the West Indies offered a fresh perspective to American historians. He also made penetrating observations regarding the mechanics of plantation agriculture, the plain folk of the South, and overseers.[10] Even so, Phillips focused predominantly on the masters and their slaves.

He identified a sense of fellowship between the two, a relation characterized by "propriety, proportion and cooperation." Through years of living together, Phillips maintained, blacks and whites developed a rapport not between equals, but of dependent unequals. Under slavery the two racial groups became interdependent—the blacks "always with the social mind and conscience of the whites, as the whites in turn were within the mind and conscience of the blacks." Though masters controlled the privileges that the slaves enjoyed, Phillips considered blacks "by no means devoid of influence." Foreshadowing Eugene D. Genovese's work by a half-century, Phillips interpreted slavery as a labor system "shaped by mutual requirements, concessions and understandings, producing reciprocal codes of conventional morality" and responsibility.[11]

In *Life and Labor in the Old South,* Phillips's award-winning social history, he did not revise his interpretation of slavery to any significant degree.[12] In fact, the basic arguments—the duality of slavery as an economic cancer but a vital mode of racial control—can be traced back to his earliest writings. He modified neither his view that blacks were inherently inferior nor his belief that they retained few of their African cultural traits after enslavement. "The bulk of the black personnel," explained Phillips, "was notoriously primitive, uncouth, improvident and inconstant, merely because they were Negroes of the time."[13] Less detailed and presented in a more attractive literary style than *American Negro Slavery,* his *Life and Labor* was a general synthesis rather than a monograph. His racism consequently appears less pronounced in *Life and Labor* because of its broad scope. Fewer racial slurs appeared in 1929 than in 1918, but Phillips's overt prejudice remained.[14]

Most white historians greeted Phillips's two books with praise. They complimented the breadth, lack of partisanship, fairness, and factual accuracy of *American Negro Slavery.* Several noted Phillips's use of new sources—plantation records, letters, and diaries. According to the white southern historian Philip Alexander Bruce, "The work is a monument of research, and equally so of fair and discriminating presentation. I venture to assert that you have said the final word."[15] *Life and Labor* enjoyed an even more enthusiastic reception. J. G. de Roulhac Hamilton described the publication of the book as "a real event in American historiography." Because of its broad portrait of southern culture, another reviewer considered *Life and Labor* a prime example of James Harvey Robinson's "New History."[16] Others argued that Phillips's analysis of slavery in *Life and Labor* surpassed that of his earlier work. Henry Steele Commager spoke for many of his fellow historians when he judged the later Phillips book "perhaps the most significant contribution to the history of the Old South in his generation."[17]

The writings of Phillips on slavery impressed not only his white contemporaries but scores of later historians as well. In the years after his death a "Phillips School" of state studies on slavery appeared. These incorporated the essential organization, sources, and interpretation of *American Negro Slavery*.[18] Even his severest critics have often embraced the source materials, method, and topics that Phillips popularized. According to Herbert G. Gutman, many historians of slavery still use Phillips's "model of slave socialization." They tend to approach "slave belief and behavior as little more than one or another response to planter-sponsored stimuli." Repeating Phillips's essential premise, they ask: "What did enslavement do to Africans and their Afro-American descendants?"[19]

Despite the generally favorable responses to Phillips's writings, black historians leveled serious criticism at them as early as 1913. In that year W.E.B. Du Bois attacked Phillips's proslavery attitude, specifically his argument that since emancipation the productivity of southern black laborers had declined, while that of their white counterparts had increased. Phillips, Du Bois wrote bitterly, "is white and Southern, but... has a Northern job and... knows all about the Negro." Du Bois struck a more devastating blow at Phillips five years later, in his review of *American Negro Slavery*. He faulted Phillips for writing a "curiously incomplete and unfortunately biased" economic history of American slaveholders—without focusing on the slaves or consulting slave sources. Phillips was so insensitive to blacks as persons, that "the Negro as a responsible human being has no place in the book." Du Bois considered *American Negro Slavery* a blatant "defense of American slavery—a defense of an institution which was at best a mistake and at worst a crime—made in a day when we need sharp and implacable judgment against collective wrongdoing by cultured and courteous men."[20]

Others mirrored the criticisms of Du Bois. Carter G. Woodson faulted Phillips for ignoring evidence of slave rebelliousness and for not comprehending "what the Negroes have thought and felt and done." Objecting to Phillips's denial of slave-breeding, white historian Frederic Bancroft admittedly was "looking for someone to give him his deserts."[21] Other white reviewers chided Phillips for approving, seemingly endorsing, slavery as the best mode of race relations. A Michigan journalist quipped that "Prof. Ulrich seems rather to ignore the fact" that "freedom, in itself, counts for something." Mary White Ovington disagreed with Phillips's tolerant spirit toward slavery. In contrast to Bruce's statement, she feared that "unless the descendant of the slave writes an exhaustive book from his standpoint this might be the last word on the subject."[22]

Life and Labor also received considerable criticism. Again blacks led the way in reproving Phillips. William M. Brewer attacked him for ignoring slave artisans. Phillips, charged Brewer, erroneously grouped all slaves together as a monolith. This, he explained, "is still the policy of white Americans in thinking of Negroes and prescribing a place for them." Brewer cogently described Phillips as "a disciple of the color line and a staunch defender of the faith of the South." Frederic Bancroft dubbed Phillips "Sir Oracle of Southern History" and accused him of failing to recognize in his own evidence proof of large-scale slave breeding from which the planters earned immense profits. Either Phillips was an apologist for slavery, said Bancroft, or he was terribly naive in underplaying the extent and harshness of the slave trade.[23]

These criticisms by pioneer black historians and a few white scholars indicated just how vulnerable Phillips was to the forces of revisionism. During the thirties and forties historians continued to chip away at Phillips's major themes. Lewis C. Gray disagreed with the economic indictment of slavery by Phillips. Gray found slavery a highly profitable business enterprise but conceded that the institution had pernicious effects on the economy of the region. In Gray's opinion, Phillips misread the fluctuations in slave prices. Over-capitalization was "at most only a temporary phenomenon," and for the entire antebellum period "there was a considerable reduction in cost of producing cotton."[24] Other economic historians added to Gray's critique. Robert R. Russel absolved slavery from several charges made by Phillips. He blamed the attractiveness of staple agriculture for the backwardness of the antebellum economy of the South. Thomas P. Govan and Robert W. Smith questioned Phillips's bookkeeping methods. The pioneer historian calculated as plantation expenses items which were in reality profits. And he erroneously used appreciated values of bondsmen as capital investment in figuring profit.[25] Through the years Phillips's work on plantation economics has fared poorly. Today few subscribe to his belief in the unprofitability of slavery.[26]

Nor have historians withheld criticism of Phillips's method. As early as 1944 Richard Hofstadter impugned his use of inadequate and misleading data, the records of large plantations. Influenced strongly by Frank L. Owsley's researches on the plain folk of the Old South, Hofstadter faulted Phillips for slighting small slave units, where many of the bondsmen lived. Further, Hofstadter accused Phillips of holding "certain preconceptions which disposed him to throw out materials that showed the institution in a less favorable light."[27] Another critic identified examples of "unbalanced selection, misquoting and inaccurate paraphrasing" which, he said, "raise a strong doubt in regard to the objectivity of Phillips' works."[28] Recently students have uncovered inaccuracies in Phillips's slave price data for New Orleans and occupational records from the 1848 Charleston census. For years unsuspecting historians have relied upon these sources.[29]

Phillips's racism, however, has always been his most vulnerable weakness. Innumerable historians have objected to his racial slurs. In 1943, for example, Herbert Aptheker pointed out that Phillips's racism prevented him from identifying large-scale resistance on the part of the bondsmen.[30] But among mainstream, "establishment," white historians, Phillips's reputation remained intact until the 1950s.[31] White Americans in general, and white historians in particular, simply were unaware of how anti-Negro prejudice had clouded their writings of the past. It was not until the post-World War II years, in the midst of Third World revolutions abroad and a black revolution at home, that white American intellectuals became ripe for a complete repudiation of Phillips. Racism, while still very much a part of American life, then came under fire.

Kenneth M. Stampp led the assault on Phillips. While mindful of his predecessor's significant accomplishments, Stampp reproved Phillips for ignoring slave life on small plantations and farms, for "loose and glib generalizing" about slavery, and for failing to view the institution "through the eyes of the Negro." In treating slavery, explained Stampp, Phillips overemphasized the "mild and humorous side and minimized its grosser aspects." Because Phillips was incapable of taking blacks seriously, Stampp concluded that he had lost his relevance for Americans of the 1950s. Summarizing the best anthropological thought of his day, Stampp wrote: "No historian... can be taken seriously any longer unless he begins with the knowledge that there is no valid evidence that the Negro race is innately inferior to the white, and that there is growing evidence that both races have approximately the same potentialities."[32] To underscore his commitment to racial equality, Stampp assured his readers that "I have assumed that the slaves were merely ordinary human beings, that innately Negroes *are*, after all, only white men with black skins, nothing more, nothing less."[33]

That statement, of course, has come back to haunt Stampp. Much like Phillips's books, Stampp's excellent work, *The Peculiar Institution* (1956), has undergone revisionism of its own.[34] In retrospect Stampp was remarkably restrained in his criticism of Phillips. But historians of the 1960s used Stampp as a symbol. His work represented a victory over those evils in American life—racism, elitism, proscription—so conveniently identified with Phillips. Unconsciously many historians may have "scapegoated" Phillips. By focusing upon his racism—projecting onto him their own racial ambivalence—they could keep their feelings safely outside of themselves, and all the while justify their self images as liberals.[35] By the mid-1960s it was easy—even stylish—to abhor U. B. Phillips.

Then came Eugene D. Genovese. More than any other historian, Genovese is responsible for the resurgence of interest in Phillips. According to historian Charles B. Dew, in these years Genovese was "engaged in a one-man crusade to focus scholarly attention on Phillips's work instead of his anti-Negro bias."[36] In 1966 he read a revisionist paper on Phillips before the American Historical Association and wrote an interpretive foreword to the paperback edition of *American Negro Slavery*. Two years later he edited a collection of Phillips's articles. "Phillips," wrote Genovese, "came close to greatness as a historian, perhaps as close as any historian this country has yet produced." Admitting that Phillips's racism "prevented him from knowing many things which he in fact knew very well," Genovese praised Phillips because he "asked more and better questions than many of us still are willing to admit, and he carried on his investigations with consistent freshness and critical intelligence."[37]

Genovese's rise as a Phillips booster paralleled his climb as an authority first on the planter class, then on the slaves. The radical historian seemed to delight in shocking liberal historians with his overly zealous defense of the arch-racist Phillips. Genovese chided Stampp, for example, for failing in *The Peculiar Institution* to attain the objectivity that Stampp had found so wanting in Phillips. Yet he also was annoyed at Phillips because he "failed to draw the necessary conclusions from his extraordinary lifetime efforts."[38] Put another way, Phillips fell short of his admirer's own perception of the Old South as a quasi-feudal, pre-bourgeois, pre-industrial society under the thumb of the master class. Yet Genovese undervalues his own intellectual debt to Phillips. Even though he credits blacks with transforming plantation paternalism "into a weapon of resistance," the Marxist's use of the paternalism construct is strikingly similar to that first espoused by Phillips.[39]

Genovese's favorable assessments of Phillips legitimized study of the historian and his work, especially among liberal scholars. Genovese thus provided a crucial model, one that has enabled investigators to go beyond simply denouncing Phillips's racism. In addition, scholars following Genovese's lead have been free to examine Phillips's contributions critically without a hint of defending Phillips's racial or class ideology. As a result, today Ulrich Bonnell Phillips ranks as a legend in the historiography of slavery and southern history. A virtual mystique surrounds him. Never before has interest in the man and his writings been so widespread. Studying Phillips has become a cottage industry of sorts. Since 1969 more than thirty-five articles have appeared on Phillips, viewing his life and work from a variety of perspectives.[40] At one point in the early 1980s, at least four historians were writing biographies of the man. So far two of these studies have made their way into print.

In 1984 John Herbert Roper published a valuable intellectual portrait, *U. B. Phillips: A Southern Mind*, a book that places Phillips's ideas within the context of twentieth-century American thought.[41] Roper pioneered much of the research on Phillips conducted in the 1970s, especially by interviewing Phillips's Yale University contemporaries, the transcripts of which are now part of the Southern Oral History Collection at the University of North Carolina at Chapel Hill. Again and again Roper unselfishly led fellow historians to the primary sources on Phillips at Chapel Hill, New Haven, and Ann Arbor. In 1976 he published an important article on Phillips's early labors as a young progressive.[42]

In his monograph, a far-ranging interpretive work, Roper wove Phillips's ideology into the warp and woof of his narrative of the historian's life. Roper focused keenly on Phillips's essential optimism, his sense of historical continuity in his native South, and his identification with the traditions of his section's antebellum past. In his study Roper traced the evolution of Phillips's life and work through the prism of such broad ideas as scientism and progressivism. He interpreted Phillips as a forward-looking conservative—an elitist whose search for order and community cohesion reinforced the southerner's traditional sense of place.

Like historian Daniel J. Singal before him, Roper deftly placed Phillips's metamorphosis within the context of New South ideology. "Phillips *was* the New South," wrote Roper, "even though he studied the Old South, and despite the fact that others... more self-consciously identified themselves that way. Because he never forgot the past, Phillips more than his contemporaries knew where the South was really going." Like other recent students of Phillips, Roper sympathized with and admired his subject. He praised Phillips's attainments and complimented the usefulness of his writings to contemporary scholars. Much in line with other Phillips scholars, for instance, Roper commended the historian's "pioneering, even herculean, work in collecting and preserving manuscripts, his trustworthy scholarship, and his contribution as a teacher who trained superb historians." Roper credited Phillips as being a master of his craft, one who wrote with artistry and power.[43]

But, according to Roper, Phillips's writings hold even more importance. The Georgia scholar drew heavily on his own background for insight into the history of his beloved state and region. And in Roper's opinion, these insights generally served Phillips well. His essential description of the Old South as an evolving hierarchal, elitist, and racist society was on the mark. "Although many prefer to believe other interpretations of the Southern past," Roper wrote, "Phillips's depiction of a society with leaders more dedicated to order than to opportunity, more interested in harmony than in justice, and frankly opposed to egalitarianism, is historically more accurate than the history written by his detractors." Though he regretted Phillips's "smiling acceptance, even celebration of that past," Roper acknowledged "the validity of the past as he [Phillips] described it." To be sure, Roper thoroughly exposed Phillips's blatant racism. But he placed Phillips's determination that whites should reign supreme over blacks within the context of Phillips's own time and place, not ours. Roper, then, concluded that despite Phillips's flaws, historians continue to owe him a tremendous debt. Roper reminded us that Phillips's racism was not unique to him, but rather "betrays the sin of an entire age."[44]

While Roper's book broadly analyzed Phillips's ideas, Merton L. Dillon's *Ulrich Bonnell Phillips: Historian of the Old South* focused more minutely on Phillips's life.[45] An exemplary biography, more detailed but no less analytical than Roper's study, Dillon's book signaled the high-water mark of Phillips studies. No one has examined Phillips's life or the extant source materials more carefully than Dillon. While Dillon adhered more closely to the facts than Roper, he nonetheless also presented important interpretations of Phillips's life and work. In Dillon's opinion, Phillips envisioned southern history as a "seamless web." Stressing continuities from the antebellum to the postbellum periods, Phillips observed fewer turning points in his region's past than did historian William E. Dodd. And like Roper, Dillon obviously admired his subject. Phillips, he explained, "is one of the century's great professorial success stories.... His was a career distinguished by a rare blending of mission, intellect, and ambition." He rose to the top of his profession by determined hard work, by the force of his important writings.[46]

But, Dillon added, Phillips's success depended heavily on other powers as well—his driving personality, his ability to calculate, manipulate, and plan, and his wide cultivation of acquaintances both within and beyond academe. According to Dillon, Phillips "took for granted that he was important within his sphere, and he persuaded others to accept him as such. Deserving his positions of authority, expert, and leader, he comported himself in a manner calculated to win common consent that these indeed were his legitimate roles. In due time the image became reality."[47]

Similarly, Dillon identified flaws in Phillips's racial outlook. Unlike C. Vann Woodward, who argued that Phillips's racism grew milder over time, Dillon identified continuity in the Georgian's racial ideology. Too confident that he understood blacks, Phillips never questioned white stereotypes nor investigated the conditions of contemporary Negroes. He never lost sight of the fact that Phillips lived at a time when even the most "advanced" thinkers subscribed to theories of racial inferiority. Still, Phillips's blatant racism colored every word he wrote about slavery and the plantation South.

In the end, Dillon interpreted Phillips as a forward-looking southern conservative. The product of his day, not ours, Phillips viewed history, as well as contemporary life, through the prism of the gentry. "He believed in hierarchy of peoples and of principles. He valued a moral code in which responsibility, duty, sacrifice, and sublimation predominate. In short, he adhered to much in principle and behavior that is now recessive." Like antebellum Georgia politician Robert Toombs before him (Phillips published a biography of Toombs in 1913), the historian recognized imperfections in southern life but resisted all proposals to change them. Phillips's pervasive racism, his aristocratic ethos, and his deterministic view of the past represent one scholar's response to the changing world around him.[48]

Does Phillips deserve all this attention? Unquestionably yes. Ironically today's historians of slavery owe a tremendous debt to this racist, white southern historian. Although we may not wish to admit it, Herbert G. Gutman was correct: Phillips continues to dictate the manner in which many historians approach the study of slavery. His works remain standards against which we judge the new scholarship on slavery. Writing in the era of Jim Crow, not civil rights, Phillips focused squarely on the complex interrelationship of class and race in southern history. He was the first historian systematically to evaluate slavery as a social system and to measure the effect of its social role. For him the peculiar institution was as much a mode of interracial adjustment and control as a system of organizing labor. Phillips also possessed an uncommonly broad conception of slavery as an economic institution. He pioneered the examination of slavery on a cost basis. Anticipating much recent work, Phillips recognized the importance of comparative slave studies. In articles he identified the value of comparing Caribbean and North American slavery. Through Phillips's innovative use of various plantation sources, he further revolutionized the study of slavery, and his analysis of the workaday world of master, slave, and overseer was on a scale unprecedented by his peers. No less a critic than Kenneth M. Stampp has admitted that "In their day the writings of Ulrich B. Phillips on slavery were both highly original and decidedly revisionist." "He was about as objective as the rest of us," asserted Stampp at the meeting of the Southern Historical Association in 1982, "and that's not very much."[49]

From the vantage point of the three historiographic cycles presented here, Phillips's contributions to the study of slavery clearly outweigh his deficiencies. Neither saint nor sinner, he was subject to the same forces—bias, selectivity of evidence, inaccuracy—that plague us all. Descended from slave owners and reared in the rural South, he dominated slave historiography in an era when Progressivism was literally for whites only. Of all scholars, historians can ill afford to be anachronistic. Phillips was no more a believer in white supremacy than other leading contemporary white scholars.[50] That his anti-black bias did not prevent him from becoming the foremost student of slavery is less an indictment of American historical scholarship than an indicator of how completely he represented white American racial attitudes of his day.

But why have historians been so attracted to Phillips's life and work? In studying him we learn much not only about southern history, but about intellectual life in America in the first half of the twentieth century. All historians, concluded Merton L. Dillon, "write for a time;... they write to reflect the concerns of their day and, it follows, for a period that inevitably is itself a part of history."[51] Students find Phillips so compelling because he represents the most and least attractive sides of professional historical scholarship in America in the early twentieth century. Trained in the scientific historical method to allow documents to speak for themselves, Phillips went on to break fresh analytical ground in economic, social, and political history. He mastered the available sources in southern history and uncovered rich new collections of plantation materials for later generations of scholars. And through all of his work Phillips consistently wrote with style and charm. Nevertheless, Phillips's genteel racism, his condescension toward blacks, and his elitism remain his foremost legacy. Fortunately, in Phillips's case, a historian's writings seldom outlast the ethos of their age.

Notes

1. Blassingame, "Redefining *The Slave Community:* A Response to the Critics," in Al-Tony Gilmore, ed., *Revisiting Blassingame's* The Slave Community (Westport, Ct., 1978), 158.

2. See, for example, Bruce E. Steiner, "A Planter's Troubled Conscience," *Journal of Southern History*, 28 (August, 1962), 343; Sterling Stuckey, "Remembering Denmark Vesey," *Negro Digest*, 15 (February, 1966), 33; John Henrik Clarke, ed., *William Styron's Nat Turner: Ten Black Writers Respond* (Boston, 1968), 7, 10, 16, 57; Edward F. Sweat, review of Ralph B. Flanders, *Slavery in Georgia*, in *Journal of Negro History*, 53 (January, 1968), 82; Jane H. Pease, "A Note on Patterns of Conspicuous Consumption Among Seaboard Planters, 1820-1860," *Journal of Southern History*, 35 (August, 1969), 381-382; Herbert Aptheker, *Afro-American History: The Modern Era* (New York, 1971), 9, 21, 81-83, 94, 175; William W. Nichols, "Slave Narratives: Dismissed Evidence in the Writing of Southern History," *Phylon*, 32 (Winter, 1971), 403; Charles Crowe, "Historians and 'Benign Neglect': Conservative Trends in Southern History and Black Studies," *Reviews in American History*, 2 (June, 1974), 164-168; Brenda L. Jones, "'Time on the Cross'": A Rallying Cry for Racists!" *Freedomways*, 15 (1975), 30-31; Melvin Drimmer, "Thoughts on the Study of Slavery in the Americas and the Writing of Black History," *Phylon*, 36 (June, 1975), 127-128, 136-137; A. Leon Higginbotham, Jr., "To the Scale and Standing of Men," *Journal of Negro History*, 60 (July, 1975), 350; Randall M. Miller, "When Lions Write History: Slave Testimony and the History of American Slavery," *Washington State University Research Studies*, 44 (March, 1976), 14-15; Peter Kolchin, "The Sociologist as Southern Historian," *Reviews in American History*, 5 (March, 1977), 22; Aptheker, "Commentary," in Vera Rubin and Arthur Tuden, eds., *Comparative Perspectives in New World Plantation Societies* (New York, 1977), 493; Earl E. Thorpe, "*The Slave Community:* Studies of Slavery Need Freud and Marx," in Al-Tony Gilmore, ed., *Revisiting Blassingame's* The Slave Community, 42; William L. Van Deburg, *The Slave Drivers: Black Agricultural Labor Supervisors in the Antebellum South* (Westport, Ct., 1979), 32-35.

3. See Fred Landon and Everett E. Edwards, "A Bibliography of the Writings of Professor Ulrich B. Phillips," *Agricultural History*, 8 (October, 1934), 196-218, and David M. Potter, Jr., "A Bibliography of the Printed Writings of Ulrich Bonnell Phillips," *Georgia Historical Quarterly*, 18 (September, 1934). 270-282. Neither bibliography is complete.

4. These articles are analyzed in John David Smith, "The Formative Period of American Slave Historiography, 1890-1920" (unpublished Ph.D. dissertation, University of Kentucky, 1977), 269-283.

5. Phillips, "The Economics of the Plantation," *South Atlantic Quarterly*, 2 (July, 1903), 233, 235, 236; "Making Cotton Pay," *The World's Work*, 8 (May, 1904), 4792; "The Plantation as a Civilizing Factor," *Sewanee Review*, 12 (July, 1904), 264; "Conservatism and Progress in the Cotton Belt," *South Atlantic Quarterly*, 3 (January, 1904), 7, 8, 3.

6. Phillips, "The Slave Labor Problem in the Charleston District," *Political Science Quarterly*, 22 (September, 1907), 437; "Black-Belt Labor, Slave and Free," University of Virginia, Phelps-Stokes Fellowship Papers, *Lectures and Addresses on the Negro in the South* (Charlottesville, 1915), 30; "Racial Problems, Adjustments and Disturbances," in Julian A. C. Chandler and others, eds., *The South in the Building of the Nation*, 12 vols. (Richmond, 1909), IV:200; "The Economics of the Plantation," 231; "Racial Problems, Adjustments and Disturbances," 226,223; "The Origin and Growth of the Southern Black Belts," *American Historical Review*, 11 (July, 1906), 805.

7. Phillips, "Conservatism and Progress in the Cotton Belt," 8; "The Economic Cost of Slaveholding in the Cotton Belt," *Political Science Quarterly*, 20 (June, 1905), 261.

8. Phillips, "The Economic Cost of Slaveholding in the Cotton Belt," 260.

9. Phillips, *American Negro Slavery: A Survey of the Supply, Employment and Control of Negro Labor as Determined by the Plantation Regime* (New York, 1918).

10. For an analysis of these themes and others, see Smith, "The Formative Period of American Slave Historiography, 1890-1920," 283-295.

11. Phillips, *American Negro Slavery*, 296, 327, 322.

12. Phillips, *Life and Labor in the Old South* (Boston, 1929).

13. Phillips, *Life and Labor*, 199-200. In 1929 Phillips's book was selected as the best nonfiction work from among those submitted in a competition sponsored by Little, Brown and Company. His manuscript was published and he received a large cash prize.

14. For a differing opinion, see C. Vann Woodward's "Introduction" to the paperback edition of *Life and Labor in the Old South* (Boston, 1963), v.

15. Bruce to Phillips, 11 March 1919, Ulrich Bonnell Phillips Collection, Sterling Memorial Library, Yale University.

16. Hamilton, "Interpreting the Old South," *Virginia Quarterly Review*, 5 (October, 1929), 631; Allen Tate in *The New Republic*, 59 (10 July 1929), 211.

17. Commager in New York *Herald Tribune*, 19 May 1929.

18. Stanley M. Elkins and Bennett H. Wall identify nine state studies on slavery (1924-1963) that bear the Phillips stamp. See Elkins, *Slavery* (New York, 1963 [1959]), 15, and Wall, "African Slavery," in Arthur S. Link and Rembert W. Patrick, eds., *Writing Southern History* (Baton Rouge, 1967 [1965]), 185n.

19. Gutman, "The World Two Cliometricians Made," *Journal of Negro History*, 60 (January, 1975), 58-59, 220, 219, and *The Black Family in Slavery and Freedom* (New York, 1976), 21, 21, 259, 554.

20. Du Bois, "The Experts," *The Crisis*, 5 (March, 1913), 239-240; in *American Political Science Review*, 12 (November, 1918), 722-726.

21. Woodson in *Journal of Negro History*, 4 (January, 1919), 102-103; in *Mississippi Valley Historical Review*, 5 (March, 1919), 480-482; Bancroft to James Ford Rhodes, 14 December 1918, Frederic Bancroft Papers, Butler Library, Columbia University.

22. Detroit *Saturday Night*, 19 April 1919; Ovington in *The Survey*, 40 (28 September 1918), 718.

23. Brewer in *Journal of Negro History*, 14 (October, 1929), 535-536; Bancroft to Harrison A. Trexler, 17 October 1931, Bancroft Papers; Bancroft, *Slave Trading in the Old South* (New York, 1969 [1931]), 24, 80, 208, 234n, 235n, 283. Also see Charles H. Wesley's review in *Opportunity*, 7 (December, 1929), 385.

24. Gray, *History of Agriculture in the Southern United States to 1860*, 2 vols. (Gloucester, Mass., 1958 [1933]), I: 476 and *passim*.

25. Russel, "The Economic History of Negro Slavery in the United States," *Agricultural History*, 11 (October, 1937), 308-321; Govan, "Was Plantation Slavery Profitable?" *Journal of Southern History*, 8 (November, 1942), 513-535; Smith, "Was Slavery Unprofitable in the Ante-Bellum South?" *Agricultural History*, 20 (January, 1946), 62-64.

26. Eugene D. Genovese is a notable exception.

27. Hofstadter, "U.B. Phillips and the Plantation Legend," *Journal of Negro History*, 29 (April, 1944), 109-124; Hofstadter to Frank L. Owsley, 18 May 1944, Frank L. Owsley Papers, Joint University Libraries, Nashville.

28. Ruben F. Kugler, "U.B. Phillips and the Plantation Legend," *Journal of Negro History*, 47 (July, 1962), 167.

29. Robert W. Fogel and Stanley L. Engerman, draft of manuscript on U.B. Phillips's slave price data [1973-1974], unpublished paper in possession of the author; Anne W. Chapman, "Inadequacies of the 1848 Charleston Census," *South Carolina Historical Magazine*, 81 (January, 1980), 25.

30. Aptheker, *American Negro Slave Revolts* (New York, 1970 [1943]), 13. In his preface to the 1969 edition, Aptheker described Phillips as "a devout white supremacist who was as incapable of writing truthfully of what it meant to be a Negro slave... as it would have been for Joseph Goebbels to have written truthfully of what it meant to be a Jew." Reprinted in 1970 edition, p. 2.

31. This resulted in part from the many sympathetic appraisals of Phillips and his work. See, for example, Wood Gray, "Ulrich Bonnell Phillips," in William T. Hutchinson, ed., *The Marcus W. Jernegan Essays in American Historiography* (Chicago, 1937), 354-373; Fred Landon, "Ulrich Bonnell Phillips: Historian of the South," *Journal of Southern History*, 5 (August, 1939), 364-371; Philip C. Newman, "Ulrich Bonnell Phillips—The South's Foremost Historian," *Georgia Historical Quarterly*, (September, 1941), 244-261; Wendell Holmes Stephenson, *The South Lives in History* (Baton Rouge, 1955), 58-94; Sam E. Salem, "U.B. Phillips and the Scientific Tradition," *Georgia Historical Quarterly*, 44 (June, 1960), 172-185.

32. Stampp, "The Historian and Southern Negro Slavery," *American Historical Review*, 57 (April, 1952), 615-620.

33. Stampp, *The Peculiar Institution* (New York, 1956), vii.

34. For an exhaustive critique of Stampp's book, see Fogel and Engerman, *Time on the Cross: Evidence and Methods* (Boston, 1974), 218-246.

35. On the theories of "scapegoating" and "projection," see Irving L. Janis and others, *Personality: Dynamics, Development, and Assessment* (New York, 1969), 165-166, 376-377. I am indebted to Leslie Smith Rousell for sharing with me her insights into the possible use of psychoanalytic theory in historical criticism.

36. Dew, review of Genovese, ed., *The Slave Economy of the Old South*, in *Louisiana History*, 10 (Spring, 1969), 183.

37. Genovese, "Ulrich Bonnell Phillips & His Critics," *American Negro Slavery* (Baton Rouge, 1966 [1918]), vii-ix.

38. Genovese, "Race and Class in Southern History: An Appraisal of the Work of Ulrich Bonnell Phillips," *Agricultural History*, 41 (October, 1967), 354.

39. Genovese, *Roll, Jordan, Roll* (New York, 1974), 7. Responding to this criticism, Genovese insisted that "Phillips' notion of paternalism was... radically different from my own." Genovese to John David Smith, 28 June 1978, in possession of the author.

40. For an enumeration of scholarship on Phillips since 1934, see the bibliography that accompanies this volume.

41. Roper, *U.B. Phillips: A Southern Mind* (Macon, Ga., 1984).

42. Roper, "A Case of Forgotten Identity: Ulrich B. Phillips as a Young Progressive," *Georgia Historical Quarterly*, 60 (Summer, 1976), 165-175.

43. Roper, *U.B. Phillips: A Southern Mind*, 1, 4.

44. *Ibid.*, 167, 4.

45. Dillon, *Ulrich Bonnell Phillips: Historian of the Old South* (Baton Rouge: Louisiana State University Press, 1985).

46. Dillon, *Ulrich Bonnell Phillips*, 116, 2-3, 4.

47. *Ibid.*, 3.

48. *Ibid.*, 167.

49. Stampp, "Slavery—The Historian's Burden," in Harry P. Owens, ed., *Perspectives and Irony in American Slavery* (Jackson, Miss., 1976), 160; *The Imperiled Union: Essays on the Background of the Civil War* (New York, 1980), 200; comment at Southern Historical Association annual meeting, 5 November 1982, Memphis, Tennessee.

50. I.A. Newby, *Jim Crow's Defense: Anti-Negro Thought in America 1900-1930* (Baton Rouge, 1965); and John David Smith, *An Old Creed for the New South: Proslavery Ideology and Historiography, 1865-1918* (Westport, Ct., 1985).

51. Dillon, *Ulrich Bonnell Phillips*, 167.

I

THE SOUTHERNER

Among the themes pervading almost all assessments of U. B. Phillips is the impact of his own southern identity on his writings. The mixture of Georgia planter and yeoman stock in his ancestry, his birth and boyhood in LaGrange, Georgia, and his education in a New Orleans preparatory school and at the University of Georgia have been universally recognized as integral factors in shaping his interest in and interpretation of southern history. Yet his critics have been deeply divided as to whether Phillips's southern roots proved more a negative or a positive influence on his version of his region's past. Much of the range of that debate is reflected in the following three selections (and to varying degrees throughout the rest of the volume as well).

In the first published critique of Phillips's work, preceding by five years the publication of his *American Negro Slavery*, the black scholar W.E.B. Du Bois challenged Phillips's claim that current free black labor in the South was incapable of matching the agricultural production levels of slave labor. This first of many biting attacks on Phillips by Du Bois would fit just as appropriately into several other sections of this anthology. It is included here not solely because of its chronological significance, but also because Du Bois began his indictment of Phillips's views by pointing out that Phillips was "white and Southern." In so doing, Du Bois thereby introduced what would become a major trend in criticism of Phillips—drawing a causal link between the Georgia-born historian's coming of age in the post-Reconstruction South and the blatantly racist (if paternalistic) assumptions that characterized so much of his work.

The other two selections included here offer far more sophisticated and balanced analyses of the relationship between Phillips's background and his writings. Both Wendell H. Stephenson and John Herbert Roper, in excerpts from, respectively, the first historiographical treatment and the first book-length study of Phillips's work, acknowledged that the Georgian's racism, along with a sectional defensiveness, colored his historical perspective. But they also pointed out the extent to which Phillips's familiarity with his region's geography and his insights into its society contributed much to the quality and validity of his work. Both Stephenson and Roper underscored Phillips's zealous commitment to correct the distortions and misconceptions about the South and its past through his unprecedented use of indigenous sources—particularly plantation manuscripts and local government records. Each concluded (and many other historians represented here would have concurred) that had Phillips not been a "descendant of the Old South," he neither could nor would have emerged as one of its most productive or influential chroniclers.

1

The Experts

W. E. B. Du Bois

For deep insight and superb brain power commend us to Dr. Ulrich B. Phillips, of the University of Michigan. Phillips is white and southern, but he has a northern job and he knows all about the Negro. He has recently been talking to the students of the University of Virginia, and he disclosed some powerful reasoning faculties. Consider this, for instance:

"To compare Negro efficiency in cotton production before and since the war, it is necessary to select districts where no great economic change has occurred except the abolition of slavery—where there has been no large introduction of commercial fertilizers, for example, and no great ravages by the bollweevil. A typical area for our purpose is the Yazoo delta in Northwestern Mississippi. In four typical counties there—Tunica, Coahonia, Bolivar and Issaquena—in which the Negro population numbers about 90 per cent. of the whole, the per capita output of cotton in 1860 was two and one-third bales of 500 pounds each, while in 1910 and other average recent years it was only one and one-half bales per capita. That is to say, the efficiency of the Negroes has declined 35 per cent. A great number of other black-belt counties indicate similar decline.

"On the other hand, the white districts throughout the cotton belt, and especially in Texas, Oklahoma and Western Arkansas, have so greatly increased their cotton output that more than half of the American cotton crop is now clearly produced by white labor. Other data of wide variety confirm this view of Negro industrial decadence and white industrial progress."

We are delighted to learn all this, for in the dark days of our college economics we were taught that it was labor *and* land, together, that made a crop; and that worn-out land and good labor would make an even poorer crop than rich land and poor labor. It seems that we are grievously in error. This is apparently true only of *white* labor. If you wish to judge *white* labor, judge it by the results on rich Texas and Oklahoma prairies, with fertilizers and modern methods; if, on the other hand, you would judge *Negro* labor, slink into the slavery-cursed Mississippi bottoms where the soil has been raped for a century; and be careful even there; pick out counties where there has been "no large introduction of commercial fertilizers," and where debt peonage is firmly planted under the benevolent guardianship of Alfred H. Stone and his kind. Then, rolling your eyes and lifting protesting hands, point out that, whereas the slave drivers of 1860 wrung 1,200 pounds of cotton from the protesting earth, the lazy blacks are able ("with no large introduction of commercial fertilizers") to get but 700 pounds for their present white masters. Hence a decline in efficiency of "35 per cent." Why, pray, 35 per cent.? Why not 50 or 75 per cent.? And why again are these particular counties so attractive to this expert? Is it because Issaquena County, for instance, spends $1 a year to educate each colored child enrolled in its schools, and enrolls about half its black children in schools of three months' duration or less?

Astute? Why, we confidently expect to see Phillips at the head of the Department of Agriculture if he keeps on at this rapid rate. Not that it takes brains to head our Department of Agriculture (perish the assumption!), but that it *does* call for adroitness in bolstering up bad cases.

And the bad case which the South is bolstering to-day must make the gods scream. Take this same State of Mississippi, for instance, where Negroes are so futile and inefficient: the property which they own and rent was worth $86,000,000 in 1900. In 1910 it was worth $187,000,000!

"That, of course," says the *Manufacturers' Record*, of Baltimore, being strong put to it to nullify such ugly figures, "is a merely flat statement and takes no account of the character of holdings, whether burdened with mortgages or otherwise, and no account of what is being done with the holdings, especially land."

And then this masterly sheet bewails the fact that "Intrusion, in the guise of special care for the Negroes, of influences bitterly hostile to the whites of the South, loosened the ties of sympathy and interest of the Southern whites and the Negroes and alienated the second generation of both races from each other. In that the Negroes lost much of the advantages their fathers had in close contact with the directing minds of the South, and the results must be considered in studying Negro progress."

The late William H. Baldwin, Jr., used to affirm that a few more generations of that "close contact with the directing minds of the South" would have left the whole South mulatto! But the *Record* ends with this master stroke: "Another point to be borne in mind in measuring progress is the fact that the property of nearly 12,000,000 Negroes in the United States to-day has a value less than half the value that 3,954,000 of them in slavery, or 90 per cent of their total number in the country, represented in 1860, at an average value of $600 each."

Frankly, can you beat that?

2

Ulrich B. Phillips: Historian of Aristocracy

Wendell Holmes Stephenson

"Southern history is almost a virgin field, and one of the richest in the world for results. The history of the United States has been written by Boston, and largely written wrong. It must be written anew before it reaches its final form of truth. And for that work... the South must do its part in preparation. New England has already overdone its part. There have been antiquarians and chroniclers at work in the southern field, but few historians—few thinkers—and thought is the all-essential. I have only begun to dabble in the edge of it; but the results are already quite surprising. A study of the conditions of the Old South from the inside readily shows an immense number of errors of interpretation by the old school of historians.... What must be sought is the absolute truth, whether creditable or not. My lectures on the history of slavery, with an economic interpretation; on the plantation system; and on political parties and doctrine in the South, are received as little short of revelations by men who have thought that they knew American history. I am not rushing these things into print, because it is necessary to study them further to guard against errors of fact or interpretation."

When Ulrich B. Phillips penned this analysis of a problem and his ambition to contribute a solution, he was a youthful instructor of twenty-six at the University of Wisconsin, just out of his doctorate at Columbia. At the moment he was concerned with a movement to invigorate the state historical society of his native Georgia; but underneath wise counsel to reformers in Savannah lay a deep conviction that history had dealt unjustly, through neglect and distortion, with the southern region. Where exordium existed, he would amplify; where misconception prevailed, he would revise. Other scholars native and adopted accepted the same responsibilities, but no historian of the first third of the twentieth century contributed so large a measure of expansion and revision. His thirty-two productive years yielded some forty-eight hundred printed pages, most of them relating to the Old South. His writings were significant, but he suffered the usual fate of revisionists, for some of his conclusions wore an impress of southern tradition. Thanks to his poised and prolific pen, the pendulum was nearer equilibrium in 1934 than it had been at the turn of the century.

If Phillips's memory served him well in 1926, and mine has not erred in the interim, two books stimulated his interest in the South's history; two others prompted a belief that northern historians perverted it. Before entering the University of Georgia he read Susan Dabney Smedes' idyllic memoir of her father, *Memorials of a Southern Planter*, and Daniel R. Hundley's *Social Relations in Our Southern States*, an able analysis of classes in ante-bellum society that refuted partisans from another section with a show of surface irritation. As an undergraduate at the university he studied the early volumes of James Ford Rhodes and John Bach McMaster. A chapter on slavery in the first volume of the *History of the United States from the Compromise of 1850* was a strange medley of truth, half-truth, and error, of uncritical use of prejudiced sources and reliance upon valid evidence, of generous understanding of the South's problems and wholesale repudiation of her means of solving them. McMaster's presentation of slavery in his *History of the People of the United States* differed only in degree; perhaps he wore his irritation just as visibly. These works, whether by northern or southern writers, seemed unreal to the young Georgian who had already developed the habit of thought, and they stirred a desire to search for the truth. Did it not lie somewhere between southern romanticism and northern nescience?

Born in 1877, Phillips was a product of the Old South as well as the new. The year marked the technical end of Reconstruction, for home rule was restored a few months before his birth at La Grange, Georgia, on November 4; but the problem of maintaining "white supremacy"—a commanding desideratum of almost universal acceptance among white southerners of Phillips's generation—still remained. Other remnants of the Old South persisted. Cotton culture and Negro labor dominated the agricultural or industrial enterprise, but the fundamental concepts of southerners yielded slowly to innovations. Adjustments had been made since 1865, and were still in the making; but habits of life and thought were not transilient. Accelerated industrialization was hardly as important as agrarian protests against "redeemer" governments.

Phillips's ancestry and early life remain nebulous themes despite a search for records and correspondence with contemporaries. He once wrote to Roland M. Harper, a classmate at the University of Georgia, that he was uninterested in genealogy, and Harper concluded that Phillips was "not proud of some of his ancestors." He did not mention his father, Alonzo Rabun Phillips, in his letters; but he often wrote affectionately of his mother, nee Jessie Elizabeth Young, who taught in a girls' school in Milledgeville and directed dressmaking and needlework in the Industrial College at Greensboro, North Carolina. Poor health soon terminated the Greensboro appointment; she joined her son in Madison [Wisconsin]; and in 1906 he recorded her death. Only twenty years his senior, she had been a "boon companion." Several of Phillips's maternal ancestors, including his mother, died comparatively young, which may explain some of his own physical weaknesses. He improved his health considerably as a student at Athens; daily laps around the Lumpkin Street reservoir conditioned him to set a new college record for the mile race in the spring of his senior year.

Choice bits of autobiography were recorded with literary artistry in *Life and Labor in the Old South*. "In happy childhood I played hide-and-seek among the cotton bales with sable companions; I heard the serenade of the katydids while tossing on a hot pillow, somewhat reconciled to the night's heat because it was fine for the cotton crop.... Later I followed the pointers and setters for quail in the broom-sedge, the curs for 'possums and 'coons in the woods, and the hounds on the trail of the fox." At the home of a great-uncle, with whom he visited in vacation time, "the backyard, shaded and sandy, was vocal with the joys of sorrows of white and black children." When eyestrain interrupted his college career, he planted, plowed, and chopped a crop of cotton, "gaining more in muscle and experience than in cash." As a boy he "had picked cotton for short periods as a diversion. But the harvest of this crop of my own brought pain of mind and body. My hands, cramped from the plow-stock, made no speed in snatching the fluffy stuff, and my six-foot stature imposed a stooping intolerable in its day-long continuance." By this time a desire for practical experience was appeased, a Negro woman and her children were employed to complete the task, and Phillips returned to college convinced "that none of the work was beyond the strength of a stripling, and the sunshine, though very hot, was never prostrating."

Other "recollections from a barefoot age" yield observations on rural life in upland Georgia. Phillips occasionally attended camp meetings at Warm Springs and Flat Rock in Meriwether and Heard counties, but his own county of Troup had outgrown primitive assemblages. At home the family attended Asbury Chapel on circuit-rider Sundays and enjoyed "a specially copious dinner" prepared "against the 'coming by' of a crowd of guests." Perhaps he participated in the annual "all day singing with dinner on the ground" as Methodists assembled to clear weeds and underbrush from graveyard and grove. "These customs had held on from preceding genera-tions, along with the murmur of 'studying aloud' in the schoolhouse, whose session still avoided the months in which the children were needed to pick cotton."

To supplement local schools young Phillips attended the Tulane preparatory department in New Orleans. Then followed seven years at the University of Georgia, as undergraduate, graduate student, fellow, tutor, and assistant librarian, before he transferred at the turn of the century to study for the doctorate at Columbia University. His record at Tulane High

School, where he graduated in 1893, and at the University of Georgia, where he received the bachelor of arts degree four years later, did not reveal unusual aptitude for history or foretell a career as a scholar. High-school marks were on the whole superior, with highest attainment in Greek; but an examination grade of 73 in junior history discouraged enrollment for another year in that subject. Performance as a freshman at Georgia reversed the ratings, for a grade of 93 in history and a perfect score in botany compensated for low marks in Latin and Greek, algebra and geometry, and English composition. His senior average of 93 indicated considerable improvement. A poor student of Latin until his fourth year, he did superior work in three years of French and two of mental science, and he also performed creditably in the biological and physical sciences. He made the honor roll in several classes, including history, although he never rated higher than sixth in his class in that subject.

The history offerings of Franklin College, the liberal arts division of the University of Georgia, were quite standard for that period. Under the direction of John H. T. McPherson, doctoral graduate of Johns Hopkins, the department prescribed general history and historical geography, political and constitutional history of England, United States history, and political economy with a presentist emphasis and an application of principles to American economic history. Phillips's ambition and McPherson's encouragement led the student to continue as a candidate for the master's degree, with courses in French and German, English constitutional history, readings in history and historiography, and federal and state constitutions. As a tutor in history, 1898-1900, Phillips taught a freshman class in general history and also the sophomore course in English history. According to McPherson, "He acquitted himself most creditably. His presence and manner in the class-room are good; he was at all times diligent, progressive, willing, cheerful, and self-controlled under the trials that oft beset a young teacher." During Phillips's last year at Georgia, he served as assistant librarian as well as tutor; his interest in library work was sufficient to stimulate a desire to seek appointment as librarian after he acquired the doctorate, a post to which the chancellor was willing to appoint him.

In the midst of his work for the master's degree, Phillips attended the 1898 summer session at the University of Chicago, a fateful event in his career, for Frederick Jackson Turner was temporarily a member of the faculty. The Georgia student enrolled in courses with Benjamin S. Terry and Ferdinand Schevill as well as in Turner's seminar on American colonial institutions. He also had opportunity to attend Turner's lectures on the history of the West. Phillips had already begun a study of ante-bellum Georgia politics as a master's thesis, later expanded into a dissertation at Columbia University and published as *Georgia and State Rights*. In its preface he wrote that "a very suggestive lecture by Dr. F. J. Turner upon American sectionalism" set him "to work some years ago to study the effect of nullification upon Georgia politics." A critique of Phillips contributed to *The Marcus W. Jernegan Essays in American Historiography* says that "[William A.] Dunning's primary concern with political and constitutional problems" at Columbia "failed to arouse any responsive enthusiasm in his pupil." Rather, incentive was provided by the Turner lecture on American sectionalism which was Phillips's "light on the road to Damascus. It furnished him with the key to the subject with which he had been struggling in his dissertation." As the incentive had been provided "some years" before, the conclusion that the doctoral candidate, in the midst of his dissertation, found Dunning unsatisfying must be discarded. Despite Turner's stimulating lecture in 1898, Phillips went to Columbia to work with Dunning rather than to Wisconsin to study with Turner.

During his two years of residence at Columbia, Phillips worked with eminent scholars in history, economics, and international law. In American history he studied the colonies in the seventeenth and eighteenth centuries with Herbert Levi Osgood, from whom "he derived almost nothing"; political and constitutional history of the United States with John W. Burgess, who failed to impress Phillips favorably; and American political philosophy and the United States during the Civil War and Reconstruction with Dunning. He took several courses in the European field with James Harvey Robinson and William M. Sloane. In other departments Phillips studied the history of political economy and railroad problems with Edwin R. A. Seligman and diplomatic history with John Bassett Moore.

❖ ❖ ❖ ❖ ❖

A few historians used plantation records sparingly before Phillips became their chief consultant; he was the first scholar to make them a major source of information. New Orleans residence gave access to the tens of thousands of slave bills of sale in the notarial records office, to ship manifests in the customhouse, and to agricultural records in the lower Mississippi Valley. Whether at Madison, Ann Arbor, or New Haven— where he spent nine-tenths of his postdoctoral years—Phillips made frequent foraging expeditions into the South to press his quest for plantation diaries, journals, account books, correspondence, rare imprints, and a medley of miscellany.

Historians who have sought some hidden key to Phillips's interest in planters and plantations are unaware of a basic principle which motivated his own research and served as admonition to neophytes: the scholar should exploit whatever sources are readily available. He did not ignore the problem motive—a more accurate portrayal of the South—but it is highly probable that the existence of documentary collections was as important in suggesting the problem as in providing the answer. The accessibility of great collections of plantation records, a few in public depositories but most of them still in private possession, incited a thrill of discovery and a sense of preservation as well as a desire for exploitation.

Zest as a researcher did not wane as Phillips accumulated thousands of note cards and acquired stature as a historian. His personal letters attest the eagerness with which he sought new evidence and solicited lecture engagements to defray the cost of travel. They yield copious evidence of cordial reception by southern families who opened their cellars of wines and garrets of manuscripts, or put him on the trail of other planters' descendants who gave access to historic treasures. To Wymberley Jones DeRenne's "two tables," Phillips wrote in reviewing his benefactor's published catalogue of holdings, "the one enriched from an ancestral cellar of sherries and madeiras, the other laden at command with manuscripts and rare pamphlets, he welcomed friends and students, as I can warmly testify." Supplementing a quarter century of research, he devoted the greater part of another year to examining records in most of the southern states before penning *Life and Labor in the Old South.*

A study of Phillips's personal and professional career leads inevitably to the conclusion that he knew much of the human and physical geography of the South firsthand. Like Francis Parkman he sought the open road that led to human understanding as well as to physical remains; unlike Parkman, Phillips was "born and bred in the briar patch," a nativity with some handicaps as well as many advantages. A traveling companion on a month's tour of Virginia from Tidewater to Valley witnessed Phillips's enthusiastic participation in community life to acquire authentic knowledge of southern thought and culture. He "was no cloistered scholar," a Canadian historian observed. "He lived and moved among men and knew that from the humblest and most illiterate there might come some illumination of the life of the past which he was seeking to interpret." Educational service to Negro troops at Camp Gordon during World War I and a sojourn in Africa as an Albert Kahn traveling fellow in 1929-30 provided other "human documents, as important for a true understanding of his subject as the most authentic letters and diaries and account books."

While a knowledge of the human geography of Phillips's South was an asset in recapturing the atmosphere of the past, the written record was a more tangible indication of its life and labor. Phillips recognized the superiority of unconscious evidence; hence his esteem for contemporary writings that were not intended for the public eye. In selecting *Plantation and Frontier* documents, three qualities were determinative: "rareness, unconsciousness, and faithful illustration." An unpublicized participant would adhere more exactly "to facts and conditions" than a witness who wrote for posterity. Phillips returned to this theme in *American Negro Slavery.* Statutes "described a hypothetical regime, not an actual one"; court records seldom penetrated to "questions of human adjustment" and "decisions were... largely controlled by the statutes." But "the letters, journals and miscellaneous records of private persons dwelling in the regime and by their practices molding it more powerfully than legislatures and courts combined" provided "intimate knowledge."

Unlike plantation records, unconscious in motive and continuous in design, travel accounts were defective in that they recorded "jottings of strangers likely to be most impressed by the unfamiliar, and unable to distinguish what was common in the regime from what was unique in some special case." Travelogues and other writings for the press embodied propaganda, yet Phillips used such "indispensable" sources to good effect. He classified Frederick Law Olmsted and William H. Russell as "expert observers." As to Olmsted, Phillips quoted, paraphrased, and cited him two dozen times in *American Negro Slavery,* less often in *Life and Labor in the Old South.* With few exceptions, Phillips used the traveler's books approvingly although his dissent was considerably more pronounced than his selections would indicate. The historian knew the South more accurately and more thoroughly than Olmsted; hence he rejected many statements in his travel accounts. One censor's observation that the southern historian distrusted the traveler because of a supposed "uncontrollable animus against the South" should be balanced against Phillips's classification of Olmsted as an "expert." The critical observation, "I believe that a fuller and more accurate knowledge of the late antebellum South can be obtained from the volumes of Olmsted than from Professor Phillips's own writings," has sensational appeal, but it demonstrates shallow knowledge of Olmsted, Phillips, and the South.

We have seen that a crusading spirit prompted Phillips to write southern history because he believed it had been neglected and distorted in nineteenth-century works. As northern historians had a near monopoly upon historical productivity, the standard histories set a pattern which would endure until less prejudiced accounts corrected it. One-sided presentation of controversial issues was not solely attributable to absence of objectivity, however, for a dearth of primary sources at institutions where history was written, Phillips said, resulted in substitution of "conjecture for understanding," as in Henry Adams's inadequate treatment of southern Federalists. Except for "mere surface politics," Phillips thought, the Old South was "largely an unknown country to American historians."

In common with other young southern historians, Phillips readily admitted that the South must share the responsibility for the inadequacy of its recorded history. There were apologias aplenty from the pens of partisans, but the South had done little during the last third of the nineteenth century to provide correct information on the Old South or the new. A correct picture could not be presented, Phillips believed, until southerners, trained in scientific method, delved into the records and made the truth available to anyone who sought a dispassionate concept of the South's positive role as one of the nation's sections. Eventually historians from other regions and countries might criticize, supplement, and correct the writings of native southerners, but for the present "the great need seems to be that of interpretation of developments in the South by men who have inherited southern traditions."

This conviction—that southern history should be written by southerners—was not peculiar to Phillips as he surveyed the problem at the opening of the twentieth century. It was shared by [William E.] Dodd and [Walter L.] Fleming and, indeed, by most historians of the South who began their labors in the first quarter of this century. They were wrong, of course; and they were also right. Historians who "inherited southern traditions" could advance revision but they could hardly attain an ultimate. American history in 1900 was unbalanced: the West as well as the South was still subordinated to the East. Both "sections" found spokesmen before the turn of the century, however, for Turner at Wisconsin and Dunning at Columbia were already changing the course of historiography. Virginia-born Woodrow Wilson and other southerners trained in the [Herbert B.] Adams seminar at [Johns] Hopkins were laboring to the same end. A beginning had been made, but only a beginning.

The problem of the South was greater than that of the West, for eleven southern states had played truant in the sixties and many southerners in the border states had defied authority in that decade. More than that, white southerners had held Negroes in bondage in an age of enlightenment, and some of them had defended the practice. The Civil War had settled that issue, but southerners persisted in their nonconformity: their race problem seemed so insuperable that they continued the white-supremacy rationale beyond the point of contrary proof. Westerners were Americans—more Americanized than Easterners, Turner thought. Sons of the South were different. An Ohio River ferryman said so whenever he approached the northern bank: "We are nearing the American shore."

A critical appraisal of Phillips's writings should be predicated upon an awareness of the historian's own concept of his task as well as upon imperfections in attaining it. Acknowledging an appreciative letter which voiced a single criticism of *Life and Labor*—that modesty prevented the author from expressing his own views—Phillips replied that even the lament was pleasant, "for it says what I want my readers to gather—that I am not an authority primed with opinions but a student seeking to attain and to spread understanding." Many years earlier he put the matter strikingly in discussing slave codes of ante-bellum years. The "frankly repressive" regulatory laws "permit no apology," he asserted, "yet they invite explanation, for they were enacted and reenacted by normal representatives of normal American citizens, commonplace, acquisitive, fearful of disorder, resentful of outside criticism, and prone to cherish accustomed adjustments even if they put to scorn their own eloquence on each Fourth of July." If outsiders doubted that southerners were "normal American citizens," he would remind them that slavery was not always a "peculiar" southern institution: that in the eighteenth century, certainly an age of enlightenment, it was a hemispheric legality; that it existed in all the eastern commonwealths from Maine to Pennsylvania; that moral scruples did not in the early period prevent ancestors of abolitionists from holding human beings in bondage. His interest in slavery therefore transcended the limits of the South with the view of putting the institution in proper perspective.

To accomplish his purpose, Phillips directed attention to the existence of slavery in the North, to the presence of a race problem wherever Negroes lived, to the relative ease with which northern states could solve the simple social and economic problem attending the emancipation of a few slaves, and to the insuperable parallel problem of effecting that desideratum wherever Negroes were a strong minority or an actual majority of the population. He admitted the evils of slavery and balanced the contributions of the institution to the advancement of the Negro with illustrations of protests against the enforced regime and admissions of slavery's shortcomings as a civilizing factor. In his early writings irritation occasionally came to the surface; as Phillips developed into a quiet patrician he acquired the ability to submerge annoyance beneath a tolerant understanding of sectional variation.

Speaking of New Englanders in general, he observed normal attitudes in the colonial period: "Shrewd in consequence of their poverty, self-righteous in consequence of their religion, they took their slave-trading and their slaveholding as part of their day's work as part of God's goodness to His elect." While Massachusetts laws "were enforced with special severity against the blacks" in the late ante-bellum period, the colony's policy "merits neither praise nor censure; it was merely commonplace." Climate, economy, and poverty kept Negro slavery "negligible" in Plymouth and New Haven, Maine and New Hampshire. In New Jersey, where the code approximated New York's, the leader of an "alleged conspiracy" received capital punishment; "his supposed colleagues [lost] their ears only." Slaves guilty of ordinary crimes were often sentenced "to burning at the stake," with neighbors turning "honest shillings by providing faggots for the fire." An abundance of advertisements for absconding slaves in Pennsylvania newspapers indicated severity, but this impression was partly nullified by travelers' accounts which stressed a kindly regime. "The spirit not of love but of justice and the public advantage" terminated bondage in northern commonwealths. With perspective established, Phillips narrowed his interest in slavery to the southern commonwealths and especially to Virginia and the Cotton Kingdom.

❖ ❖ ❖ ❖ ❖

After residing alternately in the South and the North, Phillips regarded himself as "a somewhat denatured Southerner"; actually he had lost little of his southernism. He was grateful when Negro students enrolled in his classes; twentieth-century southerners should, in their own interest, emulate the example set by masters and mistresses of ante-bellum plantations—"'catch them young and bring them up in the way they should go.'" He regretted the racial chasm that had developed. Intelligent Negroes of his generation had no desire to destroy civilization. But the great mass of Negroes, though "not without likeable and admirable traits," were not ready for "full fellowship of any sort in a democratic civilized order." They were unprepared to exercise the right to vote effectively and intelligently.

A descendant of the Old South was speaking, and much that he said was true; but it was not the whole truth. Phillips was spokesman for the dominant class of the South; a mellowed intellectual patrician who saw the Negro through the eyes of a kindly master, understood his weaknesses, and appreciated his faithfulness and loyalty; who stressed lack of talent rather than lack of opportunity as explanation of inferior status; and who minimized the Negro's quest for freedom and civil rights. He was essentially a historian of aristocracy, incidentally of slavery. His primary interest was the plantation system of which slaves were an integral part. But the system was organized and to some extent dominated by an economic and social aristocracy, and its historian was as handicapped in viewing the pyramid from its base as a captain of industry would be in writing a balanced history of the factory system. Phillips, like the business magnate, could fathom the laborer's mind as far as vocal expressions and surface reactions permitted but not to the depths of inner consciousness.

Historically speaking, Phillips's central theme of southern history was correct, for white southerners from colonial days to the twentieth century advocated white supremacy. The theory was not peculiar to the South: the white race everywhere found it a convenient and acceptable explanation of progress and enlightenment on the one hand, of quiescence and illiteracy on the other. But before Phillips's generation closed, a new scholarship repudiated racial inferiority and found other accounting for the economic, social, and cultural backwardness of nonwhite people. Unfortunately for Phillips, all of his basic views were the product of his early research of thought; within a decade after he attained the doctorate his concepts were formulated. The next twenty years of research and writing lacked dynamic quality; they were devoted to amplifications and refinements of ideas already expressed. Despite imperfections and imbalance, the static view was a contribution, for it presented aspects of southern history theretofore unexploited and it relegated to limbo much that had passed for history of the South in the preceding generation.

3

U. B. Phillips: A Southern Mind

John Herbert Roper

Let us begin by discussing the weather, for that has been the chief agency in making the South distinctive.[1]

—*Ulrich Bonnell Phillips*

This is the story of a Georgian who was an important historian and a useful citizen of the modern Republic between the ending of the Civil War and the coming of the New Deal. Although he fell short of the greatness he sought, he accomplished much, leaving behind scholarly works of significance and a cadre of hard-working scholars of no less significance. More important, the story of his life and the study of his thought are informative, since this man spoke for many. Phillips *was* the New South, even though he studied the Old South, and despite the fact that others—the Clark Howells and Henry Gradys—more self-consciously identified themselves that way. Because he never forgot the past, Phillips more than his contemporaries knew where the South was really going; because he was not "selling" or "boasting" or otherwise advertising, he left a more useful record of his day.

As Phillips is quoted above, to understand the South it is best to start by inquiring about the weather. In this sense, however, it is the intellectual and cultural weather, a figurative climate that interests us rather than the literal climate to which Phillips refers. For him, the sun was shining brilliantly as clouds were dispersed by a gulf stream; as he noted in a letter to his daughter, the postbellum South "felt" right, both literally and figuratively. An optimist who believed deeply in progress, Phillips was the very embodiment of a new age; yet, ironically, he always insisted on the continuity, the sameness, as he put it, "the central theme" running through southern history. The climate he so loved was not witness to a new day dawning, he felt, but only a happier hour in the same day after a terrible storm. The central unifying theme that pleased Phillips was racism, the white will to superiority over the black race. It was this white will, this white determination, that "felt" so right when he traveled in his homeland, whether he traveled there by train, automobile, or more frequently, by the mental conveyance of the archival manuscript.[2]

Phillips saw no contradiction between this blatant, if genteel, racism and the Progressive politics of reform in which he enthusiastically participated. Furthermore, he interpreted southern history as a story of class as well as race, and he felt as comfortable with an elite dominance as he did with white rule. This too fit his assumptions about the Progressive movement, a social reformism that he considered elitist, conservative, and perfectly congruent with southern traditions that preferred order to opportunity, community cohesion more than individual rights, peace over mobility, a sense of place on an immutable hierarchical chain of being instead of a sense of destiny beckoning a rendezvous.[3]

❖ ❖ ❖ ❖ ❖

The boy Ulysses, the boy Ulrich.

The professor, Phillips, saw to it that both boys remained mysteries. Born 4 November 1877, only months after the last Federal troops marched out of the South to end Reconstruction, Phillips was originally named "Ulysses," apparently to honor the attending physician who delivered him. Eventually, in the next decade, the boy would tire of the name Ulysses because of its connection with the Yankee general and president Grant, and he would change it to "Ulrich." This was the first of several changes in identity and status that Phillips effected, and it pointed up some of the baffling complexities of his life. The only son of an only son, he was the child of a mother, nee Jesse Elizabeth Young, who came from a slaveholding planter family of some standing before the Civil War, and of a father, Alonzo Rabun Phillips, who hailed from "plain folk." With two names and with legacies from two classes, Phillips became a man of the New South who celebrated the continuing tradition of the Old South. For all his success at illuminating the present by the light of the past, however, Phillips managed to shroud his own childhood, both as Ulysses and as Ulrich, in obscurity.

The young Phillips came through a tumultuous, complicated day in history, the turning of the century in Georgia. It was a time of dirt-poor depression and penury, of political strife, and of racial violence that rent the fabric of society at the very moment when it sought to deal with industrialization, a new materialism, and global materialism. Once back on the path to progress, it was small wonder that some minds would tend to forget the bad days. Those who came through all this were later uncertain of their individual experiences and could only guess at those of their neighbors. Any latter-day recounting of their feelings must proceed from a humble acknowledgment of ignorance. It is especially difficult to recreate the aura of Phillips's childhood because he took such pains to close from future scrutiny the facts of his early days. Still, no discussion of the professor, the historian, the political animal, the father—ultimately, the man—makes sense without at least an estimation of the patterns of his youth.

❖ ❖ ❖ ❖ ❖

A brief consideration of Phillips's writing style will help to show how far he came in developing a history of realism. The evaluation shows as well how far he did *not* come: an essay on Phillips the ironist or Phillips the tragedian would not be very long. In many ways he reflected the Progressives—the Progressive that he had been and the Progressive that his colleagues remained—in his little-developed sense of irony. This is not to repeat Richard Hofstadter's critique of [Frederick Jackson] Turner, when he claimed the Wisconsin giant was little concerned with the tragedy or the comedy of history. On the contrary, Phillips wrote with a well-developed sense of humor and he dealt with more issues in a way Turner did not.[4] Still, Phillips saw and reported southern life from a basically defensive stance; again and again he noted injustice, but always as a quality balanced by redemptive justice. Moreover, he stood in a posture upholding conservatism against attack from radicals and extremists both within and outside the South. That left him little opportunity to note the elements of irony in the South. Instead he had to disregard the ambiguities and the inconsistencies, the many, many square pegs forced into round holes by the great conservative theory of life. Like most conservative intellectuals of his day, Phillips found his southern world a good one, especially after the definitive defeat of the extremist racists, the Tillmans and the Vardamans, by 1928.

But it is exactly in 1928 that Phillips began to fail, the same kind of failing one finds in William Alexander Percy. For after 1928 the extremist threat was virtually gone, and there was then time and space enough to grow intellectually, to come out from behind the intellectual barricades and recognize the imperfections, the inconsistencies, the special problems of a South one could still love for all its wrongs. Yet Phillips and Percy, and others of this generation, remain in their defensive crouch, elbows tucked in and heads low to ward off the Tillmans and the Vardamans. It was almost as if they had been born that way. It would take another generation, one less influenced by the nadir of race relations, to face up to the flaws in Dixie's fabric.

Thus much of Phillips's failure is the failure of his generation, to borrow Alfred North Whitehead's chestnut once more. Again, however, Phillips's failure is qualitatively different. Consider for a minute Percy, who suffered from the same generational flaw of excessive defensiveness about the South. For all that, Percy's poetry and his autobiography, *Lanterns on the Levee,* are much richer literature than Phillips's equally stylish history. A deep sense for fallibility, for ambiguity, for inconsistency in humanity is in Percy and it enables him to offer this final ironic prayer:

Of the good life I have learned what it is not and I have loved a few who lived it end to end. I have seen the goodness of men and of things. I have no regrets. I am not contrite. I am grateful. Here among the graves in the twilight I see one thing only, but I see that thing clear.... On the tower of the rampart stand the glorious high gods, Death and the rest, insolent and watching.... As one comes beneath the tower, the High God descends and faces the wayfarer. He speaks three slow words: "Who are you?" The pilgrim I know should be able to straighten his shoulders, to stand his tallest, and to answer defiantly: "I am your son."[5]

That is an affirmation full of knowledge of wrong and of injustice and failures, but an affirmation all the same. As such, it aligns Percy in contrast to Phillips, who wrote his own affirmation:

The olden times had prevailed but a hundred years in the Virginia Piedmont and half as long in most of the cotton belt; but that was ample to hallow them in the minds of those who found them congenial. The scheme of life had imperfections which all but the blind could see. But its face was on the whole so gracious that modifications might easily be lamented, and projects of revolution regarded with a shudder.[6]

Both affirmations are moving, but Percy's expresses a greater knowledge of life, a poet's knowledge, something that makes Phillips by contrast almost pedantic. Of course, historians are seldom poets, and it is testament to Phillips's craftmanship that he tempts us into comparison with an artist. But the very unfairness of the comparison reveals the limits of his style. His final, lasting contribution, then, was not so much style as substance: he stood in a new place and asked questions about race and about the South; mastered the techniques of Scientism and Progressivism; blended them artistically, creatively in a rich and powerful history.

Although many prefer to believe other interpretations of the southern past, Phillips's depiction of a society with leaders more dedicated to order than to opportunity, more interested in harmony than injustice, and frankly opposed to egalitarianism, is historically more accurate than the history written by his detractors. Much as one could regret his smiling acceptance, even celebration, of that past, one cannot deny the validity of the past as he described it. His history and his teaching had considerable truth for his time, and his life, and that of his people. As he built so much of his history in the end upon his own past, those historians who succeeded him have built, finally, so much of their own history upon him.

Notes

1. Ulrich Bonnell Phillips, *Life and Labor in the Old South* (Boston: Little, Brown, 1929), 4.

2. Ulrich Bonnell Phillips to [Mabel Elizabeth Phillips] That Same Sometimes Darling Daughter, 9 February 1927; letter in possession of Mabel Phillips Parker and used with her permission. Ulrich Bonnell Phillips, "The Central Theme of Southern History," *American Historical Review* 34 (October, 1928), 30-43.

3. This interpretation is developed in Roper, *U. B. Phillips, A Southern Mind*. The sources of its inspiration are discussed in the critical bibliography.

4. Richard Hofstadter, *The Progressive Historians: Turner, Beard, Parrington* (New York: Random House, 1968), 3-164.

5. William Alexander Percy, *Lanterns on the Levee, Recollections of a Planter's Son*, intro. Walker Percy (Baton Rouge: Louisiana State University, 1968), 348.

6. Phillips, *Life and Labor*, 366.

II

THE PROGRESSIVE

Writing in 1971, William L. Van Deburg began an important historiographical reassessment of U.B. Phillips by focusing on Phillips's efforts at social and economic reform. While others reexamined Phillips's works in terms of class and race, Van Deburg sought to evaluate Phillips within the highly charged social and intellectual context of his day. Van Deburg argued that by Phillips's own definition (as presented in the *South Atlantic Quarterly* in 1904) he favored the tenets of "conservative progress." On the one hand, Phillips's conservative, though not reactionary, racial views were in line with those of many of the Progressive Era's leading social, political, and economic theorists. On the other hand, Phillips, under the influence of Frederick Jackson Turner and other Progressives at the University of Wisconsin, espoused forward-looking reforms. He argued, for instance, in favor of a progressive extension of education in Georgia, and recommended major reforms in the South's economy—agricultural diversification, planning, and industrial development. The reestablishment of the plantation system, said Phillips, without slavery but under the direction of efficient planter-capitalists, held the key to southern economic growth. Ironically, Van Deburg rehabilitated Phillips's reputation—crediting him with being a Progressive—at the very moment when most liberal scholars cast him off as the arch white racist of southern historiography.

Five years later John Herbert Roper, following Van Deburg's lead, added much detail to the emerging portrait of Phillips as Progressive. Also employing Phillips's 1904 definitions of conservative, progressive, and reactionary, Roper detailed Phillips's controversial campaigns to reform Georgia's education system as well as the South's agricultural system. Enamored of the broad community-based, service-oriented mission of the University of Wisconsin, Phillips urged Georgians to devote money and other resources to transform the University of Georgia into an institution of similar renown. In submissions to Georgia newspapers, Phillips also championed large-scale agricultural planning, crop diversification, and the introduction of manufacturing in the South. Specifically, Phillips proposed that Georgians establish a cotton cartel, setting a production quota of 10,000,000 bales for 1904. This proposal generated debate in newspapers throughout the South. Ultimately Phillips's plans for agricultural reform, like his earlier dreams of educational change, had limited impact on his native state or the South. In no way, however, concluded Roper, do these failures lessen the importance of Progressivism to Phillips's thought.

Like Daniel Joseph Singal in a later selection in this volume, W. K. Wood recognized the link between Phillips's attitudes toward the New South and his historical interpretation of the Old South. Wood, however, more so than Singal, credited that connection to Phillips's Progressive views. So influential in fact was Progressivism, according to Wood, that Phillips's "new South-progressive" ideology—his determination to reform and reunify the South—undercut and distorted the historian's view of the past. Influenced strongly by the turn-of-the-century New South movement and the "new" history and economics of his day, Phillips came to write history aimed indirectly at attaining progress, prosperity, and modernity for his native region. In keeping with his polemical efforts urging crop diversification, railroad development, and efficiency, Phillips in his historical writings depicted an antebellum South made up of forward-looking planter-capitalists, the originators of the plantation system. As each of the contributors to this section point out, Phillips blamed slavery, not the plantation, for inhibiting economic progress in the Old South. Wood identified a contradiction in Phillips's historical synthesis—a conflict between his hopes for the New South and his allegiance to the Old South. By explaining away differences between North and South and ignoring basic ideological conflicts, Phillips misread the forces that led to civil war. In Wood's opinion, Phillips "did as much to obscure as to reveal the antebellum past," and in the process "created a South that never really existed."

4

Ulrich B. Phillips:
Progress and the Conservative Historian

William L. Van Deburg

Ulrich Bonnell Phillips's interpretation of antebellum southern history retains a prominent, but threatened position in American historiography. The Georgia-born and educated professor contributed both important new methods and significantly revised viewpoints to the study of nineteenth-century economic and social history. Phillips's use of plantation documents and original manuscripts, many of which were personally gathered, was a pioneering step in the study of southern agriculture. His interpretation of the antebellum South meaningfully altered the works of James Ford Rhodes and John Bach McMaster by asserting that plantation slavery was not a totally immoral and retrograde institution.[1]

The dignified and measured tone of his lectures and seminar questions at Wisconsin, Tulane, Michigan, and Yale was indicative of a classroom composure stemming from subject area mastery, a competence that was made available to a much wider audience through the publication of over fifty of his books and articles. Phillips's 1899 University of Georgia M.A. thesis was expanded into *Georgia and State Rights* at Columbia University. The Ph.D. dissertation was awarded the prestigious Justin Winsor prize by the American Historical Association. In 1928, *Life and Labor in the Old South* won the $2,500 Little, Brown and Company award for the best unpublished work on American history. His *American Negro Slavery* is still considered to be the most intensively researched study of the chattel labor system.

Phillips's election to the presidency of the Agricultural History Society and to the American Historical Association executive council, his chairmanship of the Beveridge Memorial Fund, and his receipt of an Albert Kahn Foundation Fellowship further illustrate the esteem in which the former Troup County, Georgia, farmboy's work was held by his colleagues.

Phillips's position in American historiography has, however, been threatened by extensive changes in race relations and historical interpretations since 1930. No longer does his view of the plantation as a school for racially inferior, irresponsible, and acquiescent Negroes remain unchallenged in the American historical profession. His belief in the repressibility of the Civil War, the paternalism of the southern planters, the declining profitability of ante-bellum slavery, as well as his presumption of the northern abolitionists' inimical effect on southern society, the meagerness of African cultural retentions among the slaves, and the social as opposed to the economic importance of the chattel system have been challenged by the new generations of historians.[2]

This more recent scholarship has been greatly influenced by the more liberal racial attitudes of the last half of the twentieth century. Compared to the newer works, Phillips's books are now viewed as being filled with erroneous, inaccurate, and dangerous preconceptions about the Negro in America. The research techniques that he perfected are seen as evidence of his narrowness and lack of insight because they were focused primarily on one section of the country.[3] This portrayal of Phillips as a reactionary tends to obscure the fact that his interpretation of ante-bellum southern history was accepted by the early twentieth-century Progressive social reformers and historians, that he championed innovative agricultural reforms, and that he considered himself to be a "conservative progressive" in economic and social matters. In sum, it must be recognized that although Phillips can quite justly be called a conservative in racial matters, it is not true that these attitudes totally dominated his thoughts on other issues.[4]

The acceptance of Phillips's interpretation of the race issue by Progressive social reformers and historians in the early twentieth century shows that he was not as estranged from Progressive thought and ideals as his critics have led us to believe. Naturally, not all Progressives were conservatives on racial questions. Oswald Garrison Villard was a founder of the N.A.A.C.P., Charles Edward Russell glorified Filipino leaders in denouncing the Philippine war, David Graham Phillips made a Jewess the heroine of one of his novels. Nevertheless, as Louis Filler has written, it is difficult to find "any movement anywhere which was wholly composed of angels who loved to fly around and do nothing but good."[5]

A large number of Progressives held anti-Negro views or were indifferent to the plight of the blacks. Many were just as callous toward the needs of the "innately inferior" immigrant groups. In a recent study of these attitudes among the social reformers, David W. Southern noted that the majority of northern Progressives had acquired a racial philosophy akin to that of the Negro-baiting politicians of the South. The only difference was that the racism of the northern Progressives was often more circumspect, more subtle.[6]

Historians and journalists were not immune to this conservatism on the question of race. It is only necessary to look at the work of Frederick Jackson Turner and Ray Stannard Baker to ascertain that Phillips's views were accepted by the Progressive writers. Turner, popularizer of the "frontier thesis," believed western expansion to be more important than slavery in explaining American development. When he did speak of the chattel system it was with the Phillips, not the Rhodes tone. In *The United States, 1830-1850,* he noted that the southern slave "was sufficiently fed, with a coarse diet, adequately clothed, but poorly housed (though not to such a degree as to produce discontent in the slave's mind), and allowed opportunity for expressing the natural joyousness of the African temperament...."[7]

Baker's *Following the Color Line* is perhaps the best example of the fusion between Progressive journalism and conservative racial attitudes. Holding to Booker T. Washington's Tuskegee system as opposed to W.E.B. Du Bois's more aggressive education program, it was easy for Baker to accept Phillips's paternalism and to transform it into an even more benevolent sympathy for the downtrodden, if inferior, Negro. Nevertheless, Baker concluded his book by championing the Jim Crow laws and by asserting that the "Great Teacher never preached the flat equality of men, social or otherwise."[8]

Phillips was greatly influenced by the Progressive thought of the era. Even as he studied under William Archibald Dunning at Columbia, the conservative scholar who, between 1886 and 1922, trained a generation of historians to write southern history with an anti-Negro bias, Phillips came to respect the Progressive historical techniques of Frederick Jackson Turner.[9] It was Turner's influence that led him to study the South primarily as a "section" and only incidentally from a national viewpoint. Phillips's emphasis on economic history and his use of maps and charts was also derived from his respect for Turner and the infant "school" of Progressive historians who attempted to discredit their historiographical predecessors' belief that historical writing could be as "objective" as the sciences. In an *Agricultural History* article published after his death, Phillips asserted that Turner's inspiration was as "a ripple which, though it must lessen in the lapse of time and the spread of space, never quite reaches an end." To the end of his life Phillips avowed his indebtedness to Turner.[10]

The influence of the Progressive "school" on Phillips was most clearly evident in the preface to *Life and Labor in the Old South.* He made clear his belief in the relativity of historical scholarship by noting, "Every line which a qualified student writes is written with a consciousness that his impressions are imperfect and his conclusions open to challenge."[11]

It must not be assumed that Phillips held to the Progressive historian's tenets exclusively. After all, he was considered Dunning's "most distinguished" student.[12] While he did account for Georgia's political divisions by examining economic cleavages based on soil fertility in *Georgia and State Rights,* a framework based on Progressive history concepts, he really intended the work to be a "scientific" treatment of Georgia politics. "I have made little use... ," he noted in the preface, "of the historical imagination. The method is that of the investigator rather than the literary historian."[13]

Later in life, Phillips still held to many of the precepts of the old "scientific" history. In a 1931 address he told a group of Yale students that "a historian must abide by the records," thereby refraining from imposing unscholarly personal opinions into historical scholarship.[14]

Just as his writing style had both Progressive and scientific characteristics, Phillips's social views contained elements of liberalism as well as his better known, and perhaps over-emphasized conservatism. Conservative thoughts did, indeed, dominate much of his writing. He held what we would today call illiberal or racist views regarding the Negro. The "great mass" of "ordinary" blacks supposedly created peculiar social and economic problems in the South because they reasoned and acted in "distinctly negro-like ways." There were "exceptional" Negroes who had acquired a greater amount of "civilization" than their less educated brothers, but they had done so by borrowing from the white man's culture and not through any originality of their own. To say that this educated black man was a greater source of guidance for the "average" Negro than the white man was "to argue that the reflected light of the moon is brighter and more effective than the direct rays of the sun."[15]

To Phillips, the Negro in slavery was a trusting, obedient, musical, and subservient member of society. Slave labor tended to be slothful "because the negroes were slaves, and also because the slaves were negroes...." These traits were largely carried over into the twentieth century. After observing life at an army camp in 1918, Phillips wrote that Negroes "show the same easygoing, amiable, serio-comic obedience and the same personal attachments to white men, as well as the same sturdy light-heartedness and the same love of laughter and of rhythm which distinguished their forbears."[16]

Disfranchisement of the bulk of southern blacks was supported by Phillips both as a Progressive reform to cleanse the electoral process of Bourbon corruption and as a means to lessen irritation within the white electorate. Today, we cannot interpret this stand as forward looking. Phillips's lamentation of the gulf between the "better" elements of the two races, his advocacy of suffrage for educated blacks only, and his belief that the great mass of Negroes "have yet to show, indeed yet to begin to suggest, that they can be taken into full fellowship of any sort in a democratic civilized order" illustrated both his twentieth-century paternalism and his regressive views on suffrage extension.[17]

Phillips also displayed his conservatism in relation to certain types of social change in a 1931 address at Virginia Polytechnic Institute. Noting that order is the product of custom and religion and that law is essential to "security, serenity, and harmonious life," he inveighed against legislation which "imposes a drastic change in social adjustments." This type of action was more likely to bring "confusion, dislocation, and disorder" than was "informal trial and error and trial again by ten thousand individuals...."[18]

Despite these conservative tendencies, Phillips did hold more liberal views on a number of important issues. As a college student in 1899, he championed a progressive extension of education in Georgia. He wrote, "The impetus to education must extend from above downward, from the State University to the public schools of the State. In order to lessen the proportion of illiterates in her population, she must begin by increasing the proportion of those who have the higher learning."[19]

Agricultural diversification and industrial development of the southern economy was also supported. Phillips saw slavery as an institution of racial control and not as a profitable economic system. Thus, he could write that slavery and an over-dependence on a few agricultural staples hampered southern progress and prevented the economic independence of the section. The modern South needed to overcome this legacy by planting "more orchards and vineyards and broad fields of varied crops." He urged farmers to raise the "best sorts" of grasses and forage crops, and to "cover the land with lowing herds and thrifty creameries."

The benefits of industrial development would be of a cumulative nature. Phillips believed that an increase in the number of manufacturing towns would mean greater demand for truck farm items and dairy supplies, which in turn would increase the opportunities for educational improvement and enlarge "the opening for progressive spirit."[20]

Phillips's more forward-looking views coalesced around a plan for southern agricultural reform that appeared somewhat regressive on the surface. He advocated the re-establishment of the plantation system. While recognizing that the plantation of the nineteenth century "had imperfections which all but the blind could see," he also asserted that plantation society "was on the whole so gracious that modifications might easily be lamented...." The system was not economically sound but it was, after all, less a business than a life. It made "fewer fortunes than it made men" and it did at least as much as any possible nineteenth century system toward adapting the Negroes to civilized life.

Phillips saw the planter as a "captain of industry" who would undoubtedly have made a better industrial manager than most of the men actually supervising American industry in the early part of this century. On the ante-bellum plantation there was, he noted, "little of that curse of impersonality and indifference which too commonly prevails in the factories of the present-day world... where the employers have no relations with the employed outside of work hours, where the proprietors indeed are scattered to the four winds...."[21]

The land tenure system on which Phillips wanted to graft the resurrected plantation was dominated by inefficient tenant farming. In 1890, 53.5% of Georgia's farms were operated by tenants. By 1930 the percentage had risen to 68.2%. The farms were decreasing in acreage as the number of tenants grew. In 1890, the average Georgia farm consisted of 147 acres. In 1920, the average was 82 acres. Only 47% or 63,000 of the tenants were white in 1900.[22]

The "new plantation" would re-establish units of agricultural production large enough to justify increased investment in machinery, yet small enough to enable the managers to have close personal contact with and control over the predominately Negro laborers. The managers would have to be "men of constructive leadership" who would formulate programs and set sound examples for the people to follow. They would be progressive and dynamic men, who, previously, would have emigrated to the North in order to make use of their supervisory talents. The institution of a profitable agricultural system would create opportunities for such men to ply their trade in the South.[23]

Phillips saw the "new plantation" as a means of affording the "ignorant" and "improvident" blacks a source of much needed guidance. It would "give the negroes a renewed association with the best of the southern people (always the negroes' best friends) and enable them to use their imitative faculties and make for further progress in acquiring the white man's civilization." The southern Negro would be saved from the miseries of tenancy and segregation—conditions which, if continued, could cause him "to lapse back toward barbarism." The black laborers, by earning a money wage while being closely supervised by a farm manager, would help to bring "order out of existing chaos" in southern agriculture. The capable mulatto and even the "exceptional Negro" could hope to advance from hired plowman status to plantation overseer or owner.[24]

The combination of Negro labor and paternalistic white management was seen to be capable of ridding southern agriculture of the tenant system's inefficiencies while increasing agricultural output and lowering production costs. The "new plantation" would enable the South to produce a greater amount of its food and would induce a spirit of sectional thrift through market competition. The revitalized system would offer increased opportunities for engineers, carpenters, millers, and blacksmiths. A premium would be placed on ability and enterprise.

Thus, while Phillips's plan contained many aspects and preconceptions of the nineteenth-century slave system, it did advance a large enough selection of modern agricultural ideas and techniques such as increased farm size, use of labor saving machinery, and efficient management to add some credence to his belief that initiation of the plan would be "a movement of progress" from economic stagnation "toward a more effective system for the future."[25]

Phillips's tendencies toward Progressivism must be viewed in the light of his personal philosophical system. He held a strong belief in "conservative progress," a policy which based it contentions "upon the best features of the Old South," urging the preservation of "everything which will tend toward restoring and maintaining the graciousness and charm of the ante-bellum civilization..." while increasing economic efficiency, southern resources, and the condition of the Negro. Conservative progress demanded that the "present generation stand upon the shoulders of the ones that have gone before" and give to the future a legacy of intertwined historic and contemporary values.

Phillips saw this philosophy as an alternative to both Bourbonism and Radicalism. Conservatism "need not be of the Bourbon type, never learning and never forgetting; the spirit of progress need not be exaggerated into radicalism." The fusion of Conservatism and Progressivism accepted or rejected nothing because it was old or new, but because it was good or bad, wise or unwise. He urged the South to spread education and encourage freedom of thought under the banner of his all-inclusive philosophy. Every detail of southern political, industrial, religious, and educational policy should be "regulated upon sound principles of conservative progress."[26]

Any interpretation of Phillips's work which fails to take into consideration his belief in progress, conservatively interpreted, his relationship to the early twentieth-century Progressives, and his innovative plan for southern agriculture is unjustly dishonoring the Georgia historian's place in American historiography.

Notes

1. Thomas J. Pressly, *Americans Interpret Their Civil War* (Princeton, N.J., 1954), 238. See also James Ford Rhodes, *History of the United States from the Compromise of 1850 to the Final Restoration of Home Rule at the South in 1877* (7 vols., New York, 1893-1906), I; John Bach McMaster, *A History of the People of the United States from the Revolution to the Civil War* (8 vols., New York, 1883-1913), VII.

2. See Arthur C. Cole, *The Irrepressible Conflict, 1850-1865* (New York, 1934); Kenneth M. Stampp, *The Peculiar Institution* (New York, 1956); Alfred H. Conrad and John R. Meyer, "The Economics of Slavery in the Ante-Bellum South," in *Journal of Political Economy*, LXVI (April, 1958), 95-130; Martin Duberman, ed., *The Anti-Slavery Vanguard* (Princeton, N.J., 1965); Melville J. Herskovits, *The Myth of the Negro Past* (Boston, 1958); Eugene D. Genovese, *The Political Economy of Slavery* (New York, 1967), for major re-interpretations of Phillips's views.

3. Wood Gray, "Ulrich Bonnell Phillips" in *The Marcus W. Jernegan Essays in American Historiography*, ed. by William T. Hutchinson (Chicago, 1937), 370-71.

4. For an interesting discussion of Phillips's "Liberalism" see Eugene D. Genovese, "Race and Class in Southern History: An Appraisal of the Work of Ulrich Bonnell Phillips" and comments by David M. Potter, Kenneth M. Stampp, and Stanley M. Elkins in *Agricultural History*, XLI (October, 1967), 345-72.

5. Louis Filler, "Ulrich B. Phillips: A Question of History and Reality," introductory essay in Ulrich B. Phillips, *Georgia and State Rights* (Reprint edition, Antioch Press, 1968), xii.

6. David W. Southern, *The Malignant Heritage: Yankee Progressives and the Negro Questions, 1901-1914* (Chicago, 1968), 2. See also Gabriel Kolko, *The Triumph of*

Conservatism (Glencoe, Ill., 1963) for further economic and social consequences of this conservatism; and Rayford W. Logan, *The Betrayal of the Negro* (New York, 1969) for an excellent picture of the Negro in the Progressive era.

7. Frederick Jackson Turner, *The United States, 1830-1860* (New York, 1935), 167; Staughton Lynd, "On Turner, Beard and Slavery," in *Journal of Negro History*, XLVIII (October, 1963), 237.

8. Ray Stannard Baker, *Following the Color Line* (New York, 1964), 292-307.

9. I. A. Newby, *Jim Crow's Defense* (Baton Rouge, 1968), 65-67. See also William A. Dunning, *Reconstruction, Political and Economic, 1865-1877* (New York, 1962).

10. Ulrich B. Phillips, "The Traits and Contributions of Frederick Jackson Turner," in *Agricultural History*, XIX (January, 1945), 21; James C. Bonner, "Plantation and Farm: The Agricultural South," in Arthur S. Link and Rembert W. Patrick, eds., *Writing Southern History* (Baton Rouge, 1965), 162; Gray, "Phillips," 357.

11. Ulrich B. Phillips, *Life and Labor in the Old South* (Boston, 1963), vii.

12. Pressly, *Civil War*, 233.

13. Phillips, *Georgia and State Rights*, 5-6.

14. *New York Times*, March 29, 1931, p. 7.

15. Ulrich B. Phillips, *American Negro Slavery* (New York, 1952), viii, 291; Ulrich B. Phillips, "Plantation as a Civilizing Factor," in *Sewanee Review*, XII (July, 1904), 265.

16. Ulrich B. Phillips, *American Negro Slavery* (New York, 1952), viii, 291; Ulrich B. Phillips, "Plantations with Slave Labor and Free," in *American Historical Review*, XXX (July, 1925), 741.

17. Ulrich B. Phillips, "Conservatism and Progress in the Cotton Belt," in *South Atlantic Quarterly*, III (January, 1904), 9; Ulrich B. Phillips, "The Historic Civilization of the South," in *Agricultural History* XXI (April, 1938), 149. See also Ulrich B. Phillips, "The Central Theme of Southern History," in *American Historical Review*, XXXIV (October, 1928), 42-43.

18. Phillips, "The Historic Civilization of the South," 147.

19. Wendell Holmes Stephenson, *Southern History in the Making* (Baton Rouge, 1964), 171.

20. Phillips, "Conservatism and Progress in the Cotton Belt," 3-4; Ulrich B. Phillips, "The Overproduction of Cotton and a Possible Remedy," in *South Atlantic Quarterly*, IV (April, 1905), 154, 158; Phillips, *American Negro Slavery*, 35.

21. Phillips, *Life and Labor in the Old South*, 366; Phillips, *American Negro Slavery*, 307, 343, 401; Phillips, "Conservatism and Progress in the Cotton Belt," 8; Phillips, "The Economics of the Plantation," in *South Atlantic Quarterly*, II (July, 1903), 232.

22. Willard Range, *A Century of Georgia Agriculture, 1850-1950* (Athens, Ga., 1954), 89, 283, 285.

23. Gray, "Phillips," 365; Phillips, "Black-Belt Labor, Slave and Free," 35; Phillips, "The Economics of the Plantation," 233.

24. Phillips, "Conservatism and Progress in the Cotton Belt," 8; Phillips, "The Plantation as a Civilizing Factor," 258, 263, 266; Phillips, "The Economics of the Plantation," 232, 235.

25. Phillips, "The Plantation as a Civilizing Factor," 256-57; Phillips, "The Economics of the Plantation," 235. Phillips was not alone in his advocacy of the

"new" plantation system. One of the most extensive plantation plans was drawn up by Enoch Marvin Banks in 1905. Aspects of Phillips's system were still being discussed as progressive agriculture reforms in the 1960's. See Enoch M. Banks, *The Economics of Land Tenure in Georgia* (New York, 1905), and Stephen J. Brannen, "Structural Change of the Individual Farm" in *The Structure of Southern Farms of the Future,* ed. by Charles R. Pugh (Raleigh, N.C., 1968), 25-38.

26. Phillips, "Conservatism and Progress in the Cotton Belt," 2, 7-9.

5

A Case of Forgotten Identity: Ulrich B. Phillips as a Young Progressive

John Herbert Roper

Between 1900 and 1934 the Georgia historian Ulrich B. Phillips established himself as the pioneer in the systematic examination of the Old South and the slave system. Since the Second World War there has been an inevitable, and necessary, reassessment of Phillips's work. During this period of revisionist historiography, critics correctly labeled Phillips as conservative, romantic, and racist. Indeed, Phillips was a conservative who feared and resisted political change and a romantic who idealized the plantation system. Also, there was no denying his basic racial assumptions. Clearly, the Georgian considered blacks inferior to whites and insisted on a racial hierarchy with a limited place for the Negro. Furthermore, as he pointedly stated, this racial relationship was "the central theme," the distinguishing characteristic of his adored South.[1]

To grant these facts, however, is to tell less than the whole story. The man lived in an era of tremendous racial strain and his views reflected the times. Nevertheless, he adopted a full and complex political philosophy which was often rather far-looking in the context of thought in those times. Beyond race Phillips held firmly to what he considered true conservatism, or conservatism willing to change to meet new conditions. Those in the South who refused to acknowledge post-Civil War economic and political realities Phillips called Bourbon reactionaries. Of, course, Phillips's conservatism also ruled out radicalism, or the attempt to create an entirely new social order. In short, this political schema demanded a highly trained, flexible elite which could constantly adapt to pressing social needs without producing a revolution.[2]

At the turn of the century Phillips found a place for such conservatism in the Progressive movement. Without debating the actual political direction of that diffuse and variegated phenomenon, one must understand that Phillips saw no contradiction between his conservatism and Progressivism.[3]

As a young graduate student at the University of Georgia and later at Columbia University, Phillips idolized the work of Frederick Jackson Turner. The famous Progressive offered advice and direction to the doctoral candidate who at that time intended to follow the line of the frontier thesis to interpret the South. In 1902, after taking his doctoral degree at Columbia, Phillips joined Turner at Madison, accepting a position as Instructor in History at the University of Wisconsin. There Phillips enthusiastically embraced the Progressive educational project which infused the university community. Moreover, he dreamed of extending into Georgia the Wisconsin system of practical service to the state economy coupled with abstract intellectual contemplation of society.[4]

With the energy of youth the dreamer sought to make real the vision. His vehicles for expression were the presses of Georgia, and he filled the columns of the newspapers back home with his proposals. In particular, a series of public articles in the Atlanta Constitution and private correspondence with its editor Clark Howell reveal the essence of Phillips the young Progressive.[5]

"Let us Georgians," exhorted the Madison resident to readers of the Constitution in 1905, "have long pull and a strong pull, and a pull altogether." No southern state university matched Wisconsin in 1905, he asserted; but, with a determined pull Georgia could reach that lofty goal in time.[6]

The enthusiasm and personal involvement implied in this exhortation represented the height of his active participation in Georgia educational reform. Although a thousand miles from his alma mater in Athens, Phillips kept in touch through the pages of the Constitution. At this time Wisconsin employed him only as a part-time instructor and the young man hoped to build a career rejuvenating both the Georgia Historical Society in Savannah and the university in Athens. The plan never materialized in the end, but throughout his stay at Madison Phillips looked to Georgia for his future as well as his past.[7]

He told his history classes about the University of Georgia, calling it the first state university in the nation. The mid-western students learned that the university was a noble experiment, a grand dream. They learned, too, that a "spirit of individualism," a good characteristic in many ways, injured the experiment: individualists were not apt to cooperate in a collective educational enterprise. Moreover, the pupils heard that there was a "spirit of democracy, independence, and even turbulence in the college, and, in fact, the students were in many cases the masters of the situation." Where Progressive politics served Madison, Phillips implied, Athens served Georgia politics. Continuing this comparison, the lecture took up the subject of the 1862 Morrill federal land grants to state schools: with them and with subsequent funding Wisconsin built one great state campus while Georgia spread its money out thinly over several branches of its college system.

Finally, he concluded the lecture with the story of the post-Civil War rise of the denominational colleges and the demand by sectarians for the limited resources left in the South.[8]

Obviously Clark Howell knew of and approved what Phillips said about university reform. In November of 1904 Howell and thirty-nine other Georgians traveled to Madison to tour the northern campus. The distinguished group included Governor Joseph M. Terrell, University of Georgia Chancellor Walter B. Hill, judges E. H. Galloway of Atlanta and Hamilton McWhorter of Athens, and educational benefactor George F. Peabody. The Badger welcome committee was equally stellar, including Governor Robert LaFollette and University President Charles R. Van Hise. Of course, Phillips alone did not arrange this remarkable interstate exchange; with such heavyweights on the scene he probably did not even play the dominant role. On the other hand, it seemed that he was a lynch pin for the two groups, a Georgian already in Wisconsin, the one person with first hand experience at both schools and the one in communication with both state presses. Not only the Atlanta *Constitution*, but also the Madison *Democrat* relied on the instructor for background information and for articles concerning the trip.[9]

Even as the southerners headed home, Phillips began work on a long article at the request of someone from the *Constitution*, probably Howell. Carefully he drew around him the mantle of his homeland, swearing that Georgia's people remained foremost in his affection and scholarly interests. Although proudly southern, there was nothing to hold back Phillips's praise for the great midwestern universities at Minnesota, Michigan, and Wisconsin, of which Wisconsin was "the most progressive." Part of the Madison success Phillips attributed to the outstanding leadership typified by the current president, Van Hise. Another large part of the credit accrued to the agricultural experts, Stephen M. Babcock, William A. Henry, and Harry L. Russell.[10]

But the crucial sources of greatness lay in the state's attitude toward reform and toward education. Like Georgia, Wisconsin was rural and peopled with a rich variety of denominational sects. Unlike southern schools, nevertheless, "at no time has the university had to fight for the affections of the state." The difference was that Madison offered visible gifts to the populace: its faculty and graduates entered "every hamlet" bearing practical instruction on the latest agricultural techniques. As a result the citizens "have appreciated the invincible force which collective effort exerts."[11]

Having made a powerful case for the Wisconsin program in the dairy land, Phillips sought to draw parallels for the land of cotton. Already, he asserted, manufacturers had brought progress to the South, offering an economic impetus for improvement in all areas of industry and agriculture. "Georgia must awake," proclaimed the Progressive. It must "equip the university" to serve the people; it must build its own Madison campus at Athens.[12]

Reaction from the readers of the *Constitution* was sudden and sharp. The article had committed a major tactical error by appearing antagonistic to denominational colleges, and, by extension, antagonistic to the different Protestant sects in the South. The "Bible Belt" certainly included the Georgia Piedmont and the region's devout were quick to defend religious-oriented higher education. Rembert Smith of Oxford College, a Methodist school affiliated with Emory, typified the response: Phillips was blaming denominational colleges for the state university's slow growth. By contrast, Smith claimed good will for the public schools, but he felt Phillips "wants to build up his alma mater over the ruins of the destroyed denominational colleges." Increased taxes for the University of Georgia could only hurt the private schools: Christian wage earners, giving money to Athens, would have nothing left for other causes.[13]

In trying to mollify such critics Phillips claimed that the editor's "blue pencil and editing misrepresented" what he said. His draft of the letter contained the qualifying phrase that antagonism between state and private sectors "is more apparent than real." Furthermore, this advocate of the public system expressed friendship for the faculties at Mercer and at Emory. He ended his letter with the urgent appeal that Georgia copy Wisconsin by giving generous financial gifts to the university.[14]

As a matter of fact Rembert Smith did come close to the truth, for Phillips was not enthusiastic about sectarian schooling. Oxford and Mercer and others siphoned off money desperately needed for laboratory equipment, experiments, faculty salaries, graduate training, and other decidedly secular pursuits. Never religious in a church-going sense, Ulrich Phillips was constitutionally unable to tolerate denominational debates, particularly when the debate stood in the path of reform. A member of the broadly Protestant Young Men's Christian Association, Phillips eventually became a nominal Episcopalian, but never became a sectarian. Late in life he turned down a dissertation proposal because it dealt with theological issues of no interest to him.[15]

Stubbing his toes on this aspect of the college debate Phillips still had reason for some encouragement. Chancellor Walter Hill seemed to him an energetic reforming administrator who protected intellectual freedom on campus. More importantly the Georgians who made the trip north remained active in educational reform, especially George F. Peabody, a warm correspondent and friend. With these positive feelings of accomplishment Phillips turned to a broader reform, agriculture. The time had come, he declared, for scientific planning, for a well managed and diversified farming system in the South.[16]

His reform dealt with the Cotton Belt's continuing historic problem as he saw it. The problem was an unprofitable plantation system, a major thesis of his later publications. Antebellum cotton culture, the historian said, had tied up liquid resources in slaves and land, preventing southern investment in other industries. Furthermore, cotton depleted the soil rapidly, causing planters to migrate constantly, monopolizing the best land. Finally, the reliance on slave manual labor perpetuated a general inefficiency and a backward technology.[17]

Freedom for slaves in 1865 presented a great opportunity for the whole region. At long last the planters could plant something besides cotton: now they could raise other crops and bring a healthy diversification to the stagnant economy. Unfortunately, the destruction from the Civil War and the confusion of Reconstruction prevented growth in the 1870s; and severe political strife between "radical" Populists and "reactionary" Bourbons stunted economic growth in the 1880s and 1890s. Then, a severe economic depression further injured the South. Now, however, the twentieth century was bringing economic recovery and political peace. Manufacturers were coming south and prices for all farm products were rising. There were tremendous opportunities, if only southerners would act. It was the intricacies of his plan for action which Phillips discussed in newspapers across his native state from the summer of 1903 to the winter of 1905.[18]

The specific proposal which Phillips set forth was an organized cotton cartel in Georgia to set quotas on production. With demand for cotton on the rise, there was a seller's market. If there were less cotton available, then the price of this limited commodity would increase. Such large-scale planning and cooperation already characterized farmers in the upper midwest, a region prosperous because of scientific organization. By cooperating to constrict cotton acreage the Georgia farmers could sell their product at a real profit, insuring themselves against the inevitable lean years. In the meantime farmers could plant their fields with other crops, thus enjoying the benefits of diversification.[19]

Clark Howell gave Phillips much exposure in his editorial page, reprinting the reformer's article from the *South Atlantic Quarterly* of June, 1903. Howell continued in August with a story favorable to the plan of reform. In April of 1904 the young professor returned to the fray with a specific proposal that Georgians limit total production to 10,000,000 bales of cotton. He included a graph to demonstrate that 10,000 bales would command a high price per pound. Conversely, 12,000,000 bales or more would produce a surplus, a buyer's market, lowering the price to a nickel a pound. Thus, there was more money to be made per farm by holding down acreage.[20]

By 1904 there was much talk among editors and correspondents about the details of Phillips's plan for an informal cartel. The Savannah *News* was frankly unappreciative, inferring that the cartel was a dream and no more. Southern editors had tried to get farmers to limit production for years and the *News* supported the theory. Unfortunately there remained the problem of enforcement, the means of keeping independent farmers from flooding the market "the first time the price of cotton goes back up after a previous decline." The *News* sketched a gloomy scenario: there would be too much cotton, prices would fall drastically, and then Phillips would crow "I told you so." If Phillips tried to say "I told you so," the *News* would never accept that attitude: "you told us nothing," but a pipe dream.[21]

This time Howell did not completely agree with his scholar friend. On the broad issues of scientific planning and diversification Howell continued to fight alongside Phillips; but on the specific issue of production limitation by cartel or other arrangement, Howell broke ranks. Southern farmers "have learned their lessons," the newsman pointed out, "there will be no more gambling or speculation on cotton prices," and hence, no need for a formal program. A few days later the *Constitution* carried stories of a boll weevil plight in Texas, with the implication that Georgia should step into the breech left by Lone Star State cotton. Hugh T. Inman, a reader, wrote a letter urging record Georgia production to meet the opportunity, rejecting cooperative limits. Under Inman's letter Howell noted "we can only concur." Near the end of April Howell strengthened his new stance: overproduction was simply not an issue for Georgia in 1904.[22]

If the cartel lost because of Texas boll weevils in 1904, thought Phillips, then it could still win in 1905. Thus he again wrote in favor of lower production for 1905, this time setting a limit of 12,000,000 bales. To make a stronger case the analyst employed more sophisticated economic data, offering a graph showing seven-cent cotton on 12,000,000 bales, nickel cotton above 13,000,000 bales. A Decatur planter, Pironus H. Bell, was first to answer the professor; Bell approved the goal but not the means. No trusts, not cotton trusts nor others, vowed Bell; trusts looked as sinful as the tariff which he disparaged at great length. The historian countered that he, too, disapproved tariffs; but tariffs were a fact, a fact producing higher prices and the only possible response to the tariff was a cotton coalition.[23]

At this point the planner went on the offensive, placing a strongly worded article in the Savannah *Morning News*. The press, charged Phillips, served its readership badly by confusing the issues of the cooperative effort at crop limitation. Newspapers had encouraged planters "to plant like crazy" in 1904 and the "the bottom fell out" of prices. He went further: "The only ultimate remedy is education because it is ignorance that has hurt us before." And popular education must come through the news media, a task still to be met in 1905. On this occasion the Savannah paper showed more sympathy: its contributor was on "solid ground" in the call for popular education about diversification and scientific planning. As for the proposed limits, the journal suggested, the Wisconsin plan ran against the grain of human nature; anybody would plant more cotton when prices improved, cooperative agreements notwithstanding.[24]

Despite such complaints, Georgia planters did hold back some of their cotton and the price did rise. J. J. Conner of Cartersville wrote a triumphant letter, thanking all cooperative planters and sympathetic journalists. Into Phillips's scrapbook went this letter, an indication that intellectuals could communicate with practical men in the South as well as in the midwest.[25]

Thus, Phillips could be pleased that his political activism had been a part of two trends which he approved, university expansion and agricultural planning. There was clear reason for him to continue his proselytizing in the editorial pages of Clark Howell's publication. Instead, the agricultural quota campaigning was Phillips's last activist foray in the South. Soon afterward, complaining bitterly that "the editor's blue pencil" did damage to an article, Phillips retired from the pages of the *Constitution*.[26]

In fact, Howell's editing was not the central point of dispute between the two. The real problem was politics and, in a deeper sense, social philosophy. Howell was then drawing closer to President Theodore Roosevelt, a man Phillips refused to support. The historian's animus for Roosevelt dated to October, 1901, when the executive sat down to dinner with black leader Booker T. Washington. Privately Phillips wrote a statement in protest of the incident which revealed a curious ambivalence: he continued to profess respect for Washington but he denounced Roosevelt harshly. By bringing a Negro into the dining room, the president was giving encouragement to radical ideas of integration, the very ideas which inspired violent white reaction in the South. Thus, Phillips, by his definition of conservatism, could not vote for Roosevelt, the tool of radicalism. As for Washington, Phillips supported the Tuskegee leader with no evident qualms about inconsistency: the president had taken the initiative in the matter and his visitor had suffered only an uncharacteristic, forgivable, "lapse."[27]

In the fall of 1905 Phillips wrote an article, much of which criticized Roosevelt's growing executive power and federal usurpation of local prerogative. Howell, not wanting to serve political enemies in Georgia, cut from the article the passages critical of Roosevelt. Within the context of agricultural reform the incident was minor; but Phillips needed a rational way out of his tacit alliance with Howell and, by extension, with the "radical" Roosevelt. At this point the editorial blue pencil gave Phillips his opportunity: writing a strong letter of protest against Howell's editing the critic "lamented that yellow journalism prevails in a high degree in the State." With that Phillips wrote off his once vigorous letter-to-the-*Constitution* career.[28]

As with all things, the demise of this Phillips-Howell political cooperation seems much more clear in retrospect. Phillips, the intellectual situated in Madison, Wisconsin, could find Progressive alternatives to Roosevelt and thus insist on his point of honor. By contrast, Howell faced at close hand a bitter gubernatorial struggle, involving, among others, Hoke Smith, a contest in which the editor greatly needed Roosevelt's support. The wonder, then, was that Phillips and Howell could cooperate on any project for any length of time. After all, the sources of their differences existed before Phillips wrote his first article for Howell. Yet the two did work together for over two years to produce some tangible, if slight, results.[29]

Phillips, then, was surely conservative, racist, and a romanticizer of the past. On the other hand he had another identity which this series of letters and articles serves to illustrate: young Progressive of Georgia and Wisconsin.

Notes

1. Eugene D. Genovese has dealt with Phillips in a complex and fascinating discussion in *In Red and Black, Marxian Explorations in Southern and Afro-American History* (New York, 1971). For this essay, however, the Marxist interpretation seems irrelevant. Ulrich Bonnell Phillips, "The Central Theme in Southern History," *American Historical Review*, XXXIV (October, 1928), 30-43.

2. Phillips, "Conservatism and Progress in the Cotton Belt," *South Atlantic Quarterly*, II (January, 1904), 1-10.

3. *Ibid.*

4. Frederick Jackson Turner to Ulrich Bonnell Phillips, April 15, 1899, with enclosed critique; and Ulrich Bonnell Phillips Scrapbook, 1903-1908, Ulrich Bonnell Phillips Collection, Manuscript Division, Yale University Library (hereafter referred to as Scrapbook).

5. Scrapbook, 1903-1905.

6. Phillips, "The Development of the University," *Constitution* (Atlanta), June 29, 1905, clipping in Scrapbook.

7. Phillips to George J. Baldwin, February 23, May 2, 9, June 8, 16, 1903; the Ulrich Bonnell Phillips Papers in the Southern Historical Collection of the University of North Carolina, Chapel Hill. Wendell Holmes Stephenson, *Southern History in the Making: Pioneer Historians of the South* (Baton Rouge, 1964).

8. "Georgians Reach Badger Capital," *Democrat* (Madison), November 22, 1904, pp. 1-2.

9. *Ibid.*

10. Phillips, "Wisconsin University Object Lesson for Georgia," *Constitution*, December 4, 1904, p. 5.

11. *Ibid.*

12. *Ibid.*

13. "University of Georgia and Dr. Phillips' Suggestions," *Constitution*, December 4, 1904, p. 5.

14. Phillips, "Georgia's Colleges and Universities," *Constitution*, December 8, 1904, in Scrapbook.

15. Interview, Ralph H. Gabriel, New Haven, Connecticut, March 13, 1975; Interview, Mabel Phillips Parker, Cheshire, Connecticut, July 16, 1974; Phillips to James B. Browning, October 17, 1931, Phillips Collection, Yale.

16. Phillips, "A Plea for Tolerance," in Scrapbook, 1905; see the Phillips-George Foster Peabody correspondence in the Phillips Papers, Southern Historical Collection; Phillips, "The Economic Cost of Slaveholding in the Cotton Belt," *Political*

Science Quarterly, XX (June, 1905), 257-75; Phillips, *Life and Labor in the Old South* (Boston, 1928).

17. "The Economic Cost of Slaveholding in the Cotton Belt," 257-75; "Conservatism and Progress in the Cotton Belt," 1-10.

18. Phillips, "The Economics of the Plantation," *South Atlantic Quarterly*, II (June, 1903), 231-36; "Phillips on Cotton," *Constitution*, December 28, 1903, in Scrapbook.

19. Phillips, "Plantation Economics," *Constitution*, August 24, 1903; and Phillips, letter to the editor, *Constitution*, September 6, 1903, in Scrapbook.

20. Phillips, "Plantation Economics," *Constitution*, August 24, 1903; Phillips, "Cotton Supply and Demand," *Constitution*, April 11, 1904, p. 6 in Scrapbook.

21. "Staple Industry and Policy," *News* (Savannah), April 11, 1904, p. 6.

22. Phillips, "Cotton Supply and Demand;" "The Eternal Cotton Crux," *Constitution*, April 15, 1904; and "Mr. Phillips on Cotton Economy," *Constitution*, April 24, 1904; in Scrapbook.

23. "Phillips on the Cotton Crop," *Constitution*, December 28, 1904; "Georgia's Part in Growing Cotton," *Constitution*, January 12, 1905, in Scrapbook.

24. Phillips, "The Duty of Southern Newspapers," *Morning News* (Savannah), January 15, 1905; and "The Education the Farmer Needs," *Morning News*, January 15, 1905, in Scrapbook.

25. U.S. Department of Commerce and Labor, *Statistical Abstract*, 1906, p. 552; J. J. Conner, "Captain Conner Appeals to the Cotton Planter," *Constitution*, February 19, 1905, in Scrapbook.

26. Phillips to Clark Howell, November 4, 1905, Phillips Collection, Yale.

27. Phillips, "The Southern Situation in 1903," unpublished ms. on microfilm in Phillips Collection, Yale.

28. Phillips to Clark Howell, November 4, 1905, Phillips Collection, Yale.

29. C. Vann Woodward, *Tom Watson, Agrarian Rebel* (New York, 1938), 372-82.

6

Rewriting Southern History: U. B. Phillips, the New South, and the Antebellum Past

W. K. Wood

U.B. Phillips's contributions to and influence upon the writing and interpretation of southern history are well known. Not only was he the author or editor of nine major historical works, but also he contributed numerous articles to professional journals, biographical-encyclopedic collections, and larger multivolume histories. It would not be incorrect to state that Phillips deserves to be included as one of the founding fathers of the modern study of the South with his pioneering researches into such subjects as transportation, politics, and slavery not to mention his efforts to uncover primary source materials and bring them to light in the form of documentary publications. In his own lifetime Phillips would become regarded as a recognized expert on southern history particularly with regard to slavery and the plantation system.[1]

It is the thesis of this study that for all of his writings on the South, Phillips did as much to obscure as to reveal the antebellum past. He did so, as suggested here, because of his own desire to rewrite southern history and demonstrate that there was a basis both for reform and reunification after the Civil War. Indeed, overcoming the burden of southern history was an important first step in the creation of the New South mentality and toward that end Phillips (like other liberal southern historians of the postbellum era) created a South that never really existed and which embodied "traditional Yankee virtues." In effect, the Old South in Phillips's analysis became the New South of his own day and time. No longer was there to be a "Cavalier myth" of gracious, indolent southerners who were opposed to progress and the "cash-nexus" basis of society or even a "Lost Cause" that upheld states' rights and slavery at the expense of more modern ideas.[2]

How Phillips actually accomplished this reconstruction of southern history, and its consequences for later interpretations of the Old South, are the concerns of this article.[3] As will be seen, Phillips first turned the Old South into a liberal-progressive society by imparting to it more modern ideas about politics and economic progress in general. Thus, not only were planters nascent capitalists, but also they shared the original egalitarian philosophy of the Revolutionary generation. On the other hand, and to explain the course of the South to secession as well as its failure to develop like the North, Phillips placed the blame not on southerners themselves but rather on the institution of slavery which inhibited capital formation and otherwise attracted men of talent into plantation management. In other words, there was hope for the future economic development of the South after all since southerners had desired to industrialize from the beginning. In similar fashion, sectional reunification was possible since most southerners had opposed secession only to be persuaded by "fire-eaters" to withdraw from the Union as a means of preserving the historic white civilization of the Old South.[4]

The key to this important new insight into Phillips's writings is to be found in his own New South-progressive origins and beliefs. As Eugene D. Genovese has noted so perceptively, "Phillips's interpretation of the Old South was informed by his vision of a New South in a Progressive America." Far from looking back nostalgically "to a romantic age of moonlight and magnolias," Phillips "did not pine away over the loss of the golden age of slavery, much less desire in the slightest its restoration. Phillips accepted without hesitation the industrial-commercial civilization of the [postbellum] United States and sought actively both as a journalistic reformer and a historian to ease the South toward it." In this sense, he adds, "his sympathetic and appreciative portrayal of the plantation regime must be understood not as a defense of slavery but as an appeal for the incorporation of the more humane and rational values of prebourgeois culture into modern industrial life." Phillips's great achievement, writes Daniel J. Singal, was to show that the "antebellum period could be interpreted within the framework of the New South values" and in his own works, "although he surely had no such intention," he represented the first major intellectual challenge to "the Cavalier myth."[5]

Phillips was very much the product of the New South. The year of his birth, 1877, marked the traditional end of Reconstruction in the South; his formative years coincide with emergence of such liberal spokesman as J.L.M. Curry, Henry Grady, Daniel A. Tompkins, and Henry Watterson and the rising belief in general that a new era was dawning. Reinforcing this widespread optimism were the rapid strides being made in the construction of new rail lines, the establishment of manufacturing centers, and the growth of urban areas. As Phillips himself described this new spirit:

> The political outlook is still overcast, but rifts are breaking through the clouds. Dominated by Bourbons, the South has long esteemed its political solidity.... But men of the South of late have begun to think on these things.... A divine discontent is working, and results must

come in time. The path of progress out of the slough of political solidity and mental bondage and intolerance is visible only a step at a time, but the steps are being taken.... When the zealots of the school of Charles Sumner and Thad Stevens shall have subsided in the North, the Bourbons must lose their control of the South, and give way to the moderate-liberals of the school of Henry Grady and J.L.M. Curry.

Writing to John N. Parker of New Orleans, Phillips stated that "the South has entered, since a dozen years ago upon a period of prosperity and development which bids fair to eclipse all previous ones in her history. Whatever the causes of this good fortune, the southern community ought to see to it that the resources and opportunities shall be utilized in the soundest possible advantage to the country in the long run...."[6]

As a graduate student of Columbia University (1900-1902) and as a member of the faculty at the University of Wisconsin (1902-1908), Phillips was exposed to some of the most advanced thinking of the early twentieth century including the new economics and the new history. Unlike classical economies, which held to a strict laissez faire policy with market forces determining the best good for all, the new economics emphasized moral concerns and social reform. In Edwin R. A. Seligman's words, economics "correctly conceived, adequately outlined, [and] fearlessly developed,... is the prop of ethical upbuilding, it is the basis of social progress." Economics was another way to improve society. To quote Seligman again, "economic theory, therefore, has a progressively important role to play in the future. With the commanding significance of the economic life in its influence on social forces, economics in pointing out exactly what is, will inevitably concern itself with what ought to be."[7]

Just as the new economics pointed to the relevance of social science study to the problems of society, so did the new history. Taking exception to the old view that history was past politics with events being determined singly by political developments, practitioners of the new history assumed that historical events had multiple causes and the diligent inquirer had to be concerned with a combination of factors—economic, social, geographical, and political—to understand the past fully. If the study of history required a broad, interdisciplinary approach, it also had a more practical value, namely, demonstrating the mistakes of the past and thus pointing the way to a better future. "The tendency to catalogue mere names of persons and places," wrote James Harvey Robinson, ". . . is too common to require further illustration." History was more than that. While it enabled people to see themselves in the light of the past, it provided a guide to the future as well. As he explained it in *The New History*:

Society is today engaged in a tremendous and unprecedented effort to better itself in manifold ways. Never has our knowledge of the world and of man been so great as it now is.... The part that each of us can play in forwarding some phase of this reform will depend upon our understanding of existing conditions and opinions, and these can be explained... by following more or less carefully the processes that produced them.

History, he added, was not "a stationary subject" and its study should play a positive role in the advancement of society. The end of historical study, declared Frederick Jackson Turner, should be "to let the community see itself in the light of the past, to give it new thoughts and feelings, new aspirations and energies."[8]

Significantly, both James Harvey Robinson and Edwin R.A. Seligman taught Phillips at Columbia University, the former instructing him in European history and the latter in political economy and railroad problems. Turner, whom Phillips first met in 1898 at the University of Chicago, made a lasting impression with his theories of the frontier and sectionalism as well as his broad concept of history. Turner was equally impressed with Phillips and specifically recruited him to teach southern history at Madison. Two other liberal thinkers who served with Phillips at Wisconsin were Richard T. Ely and John R. Commons. Ely had arrived there in 1892 from Johns Hopkins and "helped to build Wisconsin into perhaps the most liberal university in the nation." Commons, a graduate of Oberlin College, was Ely's assistant at Hopkins and joined his mentor in Madison in 1904. Commons and Ely served as directors of the American Bureau of Industrial Research (founded in 1904) which sponsored the publication of Phillips's "Plantation and Frontier" as part of *A Documentary History of American Industrial Society.*[9]

Phillips's New South-progressive orientation is further evident in both his philosophy of history and his efforts to put the South on the path toward progress, prosperity, and modernity. "The lessons of the past," he stated, "should be applied for the betterment of the future." "Her [the South's] leaders should study the economic, political, and social history of the South, and guide the South of today to profit by its former successes and its former failures." On a practical level, Phillips urged farmers to raise more grasses and forage crops, and to plant more orchards and vineyards in order to free the South from its dependence upon staple crops. Phillips also favored larger units of production which would allow for efficient management including the use of labor-saving machinery. To complement this diversification in agriculture, Phillips advocated industrial development as a good end in itself, and because it would lead to a greater demand for agricultural products.[10]

In common with other New South prophets, Phillips favored the construction of a modern rail system. Railroads held the key to the region's economic development. In addition to providing basic transportation services, railroads also "paved the way for massive investments in other industries and enterprises" given their own demand for coal, iron, machinery, and other manufactured goods. Above all, railroads served as a "purposeful agent of interregional communication and intraregional unification." As Phillips expressed this belief, "transportation is not an end in itself, but, when rightly used, is a means to the end of increasing wealth, developing resources and strengthening society." "Transportation facilities," he added, "play a large part in the life of any modern people, and the study of this theme of development along with many others is an essential for thorough historical understanding."[11]

To speak of a New South was one thing. To realize it in actuality was another matter, especially in view of the history of the Old South and its discouraging record of economic achievement and political reaction. As Phillips was well aware, the region had noticeably lagged behind the North in industrial and urban development. "The antebellum South," he wrote in "The Decadence of the Plantation System," "achieved no industrial complexity and its several interests were deprived of any advantage from economic interdependence and mutual gain from mutual satisfaction of wants." Thus, "whereas the settlement of Ohio proved of great benefit to New York and Pennsylvania extending the demand for their manufactures and swelling the volume of their commerce, the settlement of Alabama yielded no economic benefit to Virginia...." At the same time, southerners themselves seemed to lack those qualities—efficiency, energy, and enterprise—which were deemed crucial to the establishment of modern, industrial society. In fact, the Old South had been characterized by a debilitating "cult of leisure" that disdained progress and the profit motive altogether. As a rule "the planters... relished and even exalted their calling." In the words of James Henry Hammond (quoted by Phillips), "planting in this country is the only independent and really honorable occupation.... The planters here are essentially what the nobility are in other countries." The plantation system dominated "the whole industrial life of the South" and "attracted nearly all the men of capacity into agricultural management."[12]

As one illustration of the South's backwardness, Phillips referred to the rail network of the antebellum South which, really, was no system at all. It was "made up of heterogeneous parts, working together with more or less efficiency of the common end." Although the South "had come to be equipped with at least the skeleton of a well-planned system" by the end of the antebellum era, "that system was a source of weakness and a failure." "In contrast with the North, the cotton belt railroads did not greatly increase the local productive resources; nor... did they vastly increase the volume of commerce." To the contrary, "the building of railroads led to little else but the extension and intensifying of the plantation system and the increase of the staple output. Specialization and commerce were extended, when just the opposite development, towards diversification of products and economic self-sufficiency, was the real need." The railroads of the South "proved less to be trade makers than trade catchers."[13]

Phillips's solution to this problem of discontinuity in southern history was to rewrite the history of the region to demonstrate that there was a basis for both reform and reunification after the Civil War. As his own researches had shown, or so he thought, "the Old South did not deserve its stigma as a land of industrial slackness." He noted, planters were really "captains of industry," the "big businessmen of their era." The planter, he observed:

> owned the land... planned the work of the year... and... saw to it that the work was done. His problem was to lay out the fields for the best return, to keep his laborers profitably at work in all seasons, and to guard against the overworking of his laborers or his mules, and to watch receipts and expenditures with an eye for economy. If the planter failed in any of these requirements, he lost his wages of superintendence. If he allowed expenditures to exceed receipts, he lost first his profits, then his rent, and finally his capital.

The plantation itself "was the application of manufacturing methods to agricultural production." Far from being "a latter-day version of the feudal manor," it was "a highly efficient economic unit comparable to a factory."[14]

As Phillips was quick to emphasize, southerners also shared the same liberal-democratic values of the Revolutionary generation. "The statesmen of the South," he wrote in "Conservatism and Progress in the Cotton Belt," "have been as a rule far from retrogressive, except in certain instances where slavery was concerned." "In promoting sentiment leading to the Declaration of Independence, the formation of the Union, and the declaration of war in 1812," he added, "men of the South were among the most progressive and powerful leaders." As further proof of this assertion that southerners were really liberals (and nascent capitalists as well), Phillips pointed to the southern frontiersmen who "accomplished the conquest of the trans-Allegheny wilderness, opened the Southwest for cotton production" and in the process "called the Northwest into being" to supply foodstuffs. The South also "set a mighty precedent in educational lines" by establishing public state universities and for many years "led New England and the Middle states in railway development (a forgotten fact but true)." "In all these matters," he concluded, "the governing class in the South showed strong progressive spirit."[15]

As for the sources of this liberal-progressive spirit, Phillips (following Frederick Jackson Turner) traced them to the influence of the frontier on the development of the South. The South was originally a frontier and its history, "like all social history," was "the record of the adjustment of men to their environment." "The frontier performed its mission in one area after another, giving place in each to a more complex society which grew out of the frontier regime and supplanted it. By this process the whole vast region of the United States, within the limits where the rainfall is sufficient for tillage, has been reduced to occupation in a phenomenally rapid process." As in the West, "the frontier had a lasting influence... in its giving a stamp of self-reliance and aggressiveness to the character of the men." Unlike the West of which Turner wrote, the frontier in the South did not lead to the same desired results. Instead of urbanization and industrialization, there emerged only the system of slavery and the production of staple crops. Instead of democracy, the South fostered an aristocracy of slaveowners who controlled the wealth and politics of the region. Instead of nationalism, a sense of separateness and local allegiance prevailed. Finally, there was secessionism as southerners endeavored to preserve their "peculiar institution."[16]

The explanation for these failures, Phillips argued, was the introduction of slavery and the plantation system. As he explained it in "Plantation and Frontier":

The influence of the plantation system... was more local and lasting [than the frontier]. The system gave a tone of authority and paternalism to the master class, and of obedience to servants. The plantation problems, further, affected the whole community; for after the close of the seventeenth century the plantation problem was mainly the negro problem, and that was of vital concern to all members of both races in all districts where negroes were numerous. The wilderness and the Indians were transient; the staples and the negroes were permanent, and their influence upon the prevailing philosophy became intensified with the lapse of years. It eventually overshadowed the whole South, and forced the great mass of the people to subordinate all other considerations to policies in this one relation.[17]

Once established, the plantation system dominated the entire society of the Old South, all for the worse. "Slave labor proved to be a type of labor peculiarly unprofitable to its employers in a multitude of cases, and peculiarly burdensome in the long run to nearly all the communities which maintained the system." Given the capitalization of labor, "wealth from the prosperous districts" was exported outside the region "for the purchase of recruits to the labor supply," a process that not only drained capital from an area but that "excluded or discouraged most of the population save masters and slaves from sharing or endeavoring to share in large-scale industrial affairs." Moreover, "slavery... tended to devote the great bulk of negro labor incessantly to the production of the staple crops. This fixed the community in a rut and deprived it of the great benefits of industrial diversification."[18]

If slavery turned circulating capital into fixed capital and inhibited economic diversification, it also "militated in quite positive degrees against the productivity of several white classes." Among the "well-to-do it promoted leisure by giving rise to an abnormally large number of men and women who... did little to bring sweat to their brows." At the other end of the social scale, the poor whites were affected by the "limitation upon their wage-earning opportunity which the slavery system imposed." For the middle-class, it limited capital and provided the "temptation of an unsound application of earnings," that is, the purchase of slaves. Slavery and the plantation system also caused the South to spoil the market for its distinctive crops by producing greater quantities than the world could buy at remunerative prices. Still another "influence of the plantation system was to hamper the growth of towns" especially since "the capital which might otherwise have been available for factory promotion" went into the purchase of slaves and the fact that planters dealt primarily with distant wholesalers and patronized "the local shopkeepers only for petty articles."[19]

Slavery was more of a social than an economic institution. "It was less a business than a life" and "it made fewer fortunes than it made men." Its purpose, strictly speaking, was to control and train "the unintelligent negro laborers" since "as a rule they were inefficient for any tasks but those of crude routine." "In plantation industry with unfree, unwilling, stupid, and half-barbarous laborers, a premium was of necessity put upon routine. A negro, once taught to do so simple tasks to any degree of satisfaction, was encouraged to continue performing the same work to the end of his days." Hence, "the plantation system... was highly excellent for its primary and principal purpose of employing the available low-grade labor supply to serviceable ends." For that matter, "the five great southern staples became plantation staples because each of them permitted long-continued routine work in their production."[20]

What Phillips was really doing here was making the South more alike than different from the North. Put another way, the South really wanted to develop like its rival region but because of slavery was unable to do so. As Phillips lamented again and again, "the slaveholding regime kept money scarce, population sparse and land values accordingly low; it restricted opportunities of many men of both races, and it kept many of the natural resources of the southern country neglected." "The great fault of the antebellum system of plantations," he reiterated, "lay in its exclusive devotion to the staple crops, and in its discouragement of manufacturing, and other forms of industry." "The great obstacles to a general diversification," he wrote in *A History of Transportation*, "were the dependence upon negro labor and the maintenance of slavery as a system for its control." "In virtually every phase, after the industrial occupation of each area had been accomplished," he added in *American Negro Slavery*, "the maintenance of the institution [of slavery] was a clog upon material progress."[21]

By thus blaming slavery for the failure of the South to progress economically, and not the southern people as a whole or their character and spirit, Phillips was able to establish that continuity which was so crucial to the inauguration of a newer and modern South. Once the South would rid itself of the "peculiar institution" the nascent entrepreneurial and industrial talent that southerners possessed would emerge and pave the way to a New South.[22]

> In the great system of Southern industry and commerce, working with seeming smoothness, the negro laborers were inefficient in spite of discipline, and slavery was an obstacle to all progress. The system may be likened to an engine, with slavery as its great fly-wheel—a fly-wheel indispensable for safe running at first, perhaps, but later rendered less useful by improvements in the machinery, and finally becoming a burden instead of a benefit. Yet it was retained, because it was still considered essential in securing the adjustment and regular working of the complex mechanism. This great rigid wheel of slavery was so awkward and burdensome that it absorbed the momentum and retarded the movement of the whole machine without rendering any service of great value.... To be rid of the capitalization of labor as a part of the slaveholding system was a great requisite for the material progress of the South.

Significantly, Phillips was careful to distinguish here between slavery and the plantation system. The former, Phillips emphasized, was "a means of domesticating savage or barbarous men, analogous in kind and in consequence to the domestication of the beasts of the field." The latter, on the other hand, "formed... the industrial and social frame of government in the blackbelt communities" and in "its concentration of labor under skilled management made [it], with its overseers, foremen, blacksmiths, carpenters, hostlers, cooks, nurses, plow hands and hoe hands, practically the factory system applied to agriculture." Its economic strength "depended in large degree upon the ability of the planters to direct the energies of the laborers... to better effect than each laborer could direct his own energies in isolation."[23]

Unfortunately, during the antebellum period "the plantation system was in most cases not only the beginning of the development, but its end as well.... If a large number of planters had customarily educated a large proportion of their laborers into fitness for better things than gang work, the skilled occupations on the plantations would have been glutted and the superior ability of the laborers in large degree wasted. This was the fault of slavery as well as the plantation system." "Slavery... was... responsible for the calamitous fact that the antebellum planters were involved in a cut-throat competition in buying labor and selling produce." In turn, "these shortcomings impaired the industrial efficiency of the southern com-munity, and, at the same time, prevented the community from securing the full normal earnings from such productive efficiency as it did achieve."[24]

In this fashion, Phillips was able to advocate the revival of the plantation system (without slavery) as a means of curing the South's agricultural ills (i.e., the prevalence of small farms and the system of sharecropping). "The most promising solution for the problem," he wrote, "is the re-estab-lishment of the old plantation system, with some form of hired labor instead of slave labor." As he noted, "the whole tendency of American industry is toward organization for more efficient management" and such a system "was necessary to bring southern industry in agriculture as well as in manufacturing to a modern progressive basis." "When the plantation comes to be re-established," he added, ". . . it will bring order out of the existing chaos. By introducing system in place of haphazard work, it will lower the cost of production, increase the output, and enable the South to produce a greater amount of its food and other needed supplies. It will infuse a spirit of thrift into the southern community, for the competition of plantation managers for the market will not permit intolerance." With these improvements the plantation would offer "profitable work for blacksmiths, engineers, millers, carpenters, and other artisans. As in a factory or a great business concern, the system when thoroughly developed, will put a premium upon ability and enterprise" while "capable men will be promoted to responsible positions."[25]

Phillips's effort at reconstructing the antebellum past can also be seen in his interpretation of secession and the Civil War in which he took exception to the traditional Confederate view of these events as the end result of a long-standing controversy between two different societies with constitu-tional principles being in the forefront of their disagreement. To admit that there were any deep-seated differences between sections or that southerners espoused the right of revolution or secession was to deny the possibilities of reunification or reform after the Civil War. Hence Phillips's emphasis upon the similarities between North and South (there were really no differences) and his focus upon the more immediate origins of the Civil War, primarily the events of 1854 and after. Hence, too, his view that secession was really a "crisis of fear" in which southerners, blinded to their true interests by the abolitionists' agitation, were persuaded by radical "fire-eaters" to undertake a course of action they really did not support.[26]

As Phillips elaborated this theme in *The Course of the South to Secession,* there were in the beginning of the nation no differences between the North and the South:

> Prior to the Revolution there were plentiful quarrels within the several colonies and between neighboring jurisdictions; but as to regional [sectional] interests the sole conflict arose over the molasses trade.... Each community tended to its own affairs with a minimum of neighborly contacts.... As to contrasts other than economic, there were not many to be found. Negro slavery was a matter of course in every colony, differing in volume but not essentially in law.

Although "seeds of sectional antagonism" sprouted in the early national period over the ratification of the Constitution, the ban on the importation of slaves, the rise of Quakerism and its anti-slavery tendencies, and the formation of the American Colonization Society, these issues did not rend the Republic (thanks largely to the Revolutionary generation of leaders who, unlike their successors, "genuinely cherished and exemplified moderation, good-will, and patriotism without limit of region"). "As yet... the South as a conscious entity was emergent only now and then, here and there. It had no prior coherence, no constitutional status, and seemingly no cogent occasion to procure specific establishment." Nor was there a unified North.[27]

Beginning with the Missouri Compromise, matters changed considerably. Then, for the first time, "so sharp a sectional alignment appeared" that "the repercussion did not die." From that point on, the debate over slavery, the precipitating issue, only intensified with each new crisis giving rise, in turn, to successive groups of "fire-eaters" who calculated the value of the Union. While the Compromise of 1850 brought a temporary surcease in agitation and defense, the "fateful Kansas-Nebraska bill" of 1854 only refueled the whole sectional controversy. Combined with increased radical abolitionist activity in the 1850s and John Brown's raid, southerners became more fearful than ever both about their "peculiar institution" and their position in the Union. With the election of Lincoln and the triumph of the Republican party in 1860, the worst fears of southerners were realized. With "congressional mathematics" working against them and Republicans resisting compromise on the issue of slavery in the territories, the "fire-eaters" now preached secession and separate nationality before the strength and resolve of the North could grow stronger "and be consolidated for crushing purposes."[28]

The difference between 1860 and other periods of crisis, Phillips observed, was that the cry of the wolf had been heard once too often. "The value of the Union," he reiterated, "had been actively calculated from time to time by sectional spokesmen and doctrinal propagandists ever since the achievement of American independence." Yet, "the partial failure of each of its [the South's] earlier campaigns... made the crisis of 1860 all the more acute." By that time, "great numbers of the people [in the South] had come to endorse this position [secession]." Most of the North "refused to believe before secession was an accomplished fact that anything of earnest was contained in the Southern threats of disunion."[29]

The real issue at hand was race or, more precisely, "the threat of Africanization." This racial issue, which Phillips would label the "central theme of southern history" (that "common resolve indomitably maintained... that [the South] shall be and remain a white man's country"), was by no means a new one. "It arose as soon as the negroes became numerous enough to create a problem of race control in the interest of orderly government and the maintenance of a Caucasian civilization." Slavery, after all, had been instituted "to provide control of labor" as well to assure "a system of racial adjustment and social order." When this system was threatened, "it was defended not only as a vested interest, but with vigor and vehemence as a guarantee of white supremacy." How else, he maintained, would nonslaveholders be so "fervid" for secession and why the "eager service of thousands in the Confederate army."[30]

If Phillips believed secession to be a "crisis of fear," he viewed the Civil War itself as a "needless conflict." "If the abolition agitation had never arisen in its violent form to blind the Southerners to their own best interests," he wrote, "it is fairly probable that within the nineteenth century slavery would have been disestablished in some peaceable way in response to the demand of public opinion in the South." In the first place, Phillips argued, slavery had reached its "natural limits" having in "the middle of the nineteenth century" entered Texas, "its last available province." In the second place, great improvements had been made within the "peculiar institution" in "the two centuries and more of industrial-slaveholding in English America" when "conservative readjustment was interrupted by the clash of war...." In this sense, he concluded, the war could be viewed as a regrettable occurrence that delayed the emergence of a New South by inhibiting progressive reforms already at work in the Old South.[31]

In his desire to make the history of the Old South more relevant by placing it in the "vanguard of progress," Phillips nevertheless overlooked or denied aspects of the antebellum past that conflicted with his central theme of continuity. Phillips paid little attention to southern "individualism and conservatism" which he admitted had a debilitating effect upon "joint undertakings and new enterprises." Phillips also neglected southerners' attachment to the land and their agrarian outlook which formed an integral part of their inheritance of republicanism from the Revolutionary generation. At the same time, Phillips gave short shrift to the critique of capitalism, industrialism, and urbanism that was inherent in the proslavery argument and which underscored the South's basic opposition to the "isms" of the day. The same can be said for the doctrine of states' rights which, as Phillips realized, formed such an important part of southern political philosophy. "The principle of close construction of the Constitution," he stated in "Georgia and States Rights," was "held by all Georgians at all times" from the adoption of the Constitution. Moreover, the people of Georgia "adopted the Constitution in the capacity of the people of a sovereign State, delegating certain specified powers [only] to the central government in order to increase efficiency, but reserving to themselves and to their previously existing State government all rights and powers... not expressly delegated...." As for the idea of secession, it was "as old as the federal Constitution itself."[32]

There is a fundamental and debilitating contradiction in Phillips's analysis of the Old South. On the one hand, he believed that the South really represented a different civilization from that of the North. "The conditions, the life, the spirit of its people were so different from those which prevailed and still prevail in the North," he wrote in 1907, "that it is difficult for Northern investigators to interpret correctly the facts which they are able to find." Yet, on the other hand, he assumed that the South should have developed like the North and even faulted it for not doing so. In a larger sense, this contradiction is itself symbolic of the conflict in Phillips's mind between his New South-progressive ideals and his allegiance to the old regime. As a native southerner, Phillips could not agree that the plantation regime was wholly evil. As a New South advocate, Phillips had to believe that southerners wanted a more progressive economy and society and were actually capable of achieving that goal. The problem was to combine his progressive hope with his ancestral allegiance and to explain that the demise of a peculiar but noble way of life had not been all for naught and actually for the better, which is precisely what Phillips did by creating a new synthesis of southern history that rationalized or explained away the less progressive aspects of the pre-Civil War South.[33]

If the analysis presented here portrays Phillips in an entirely new light by reminding us that he was not really a defender of the Old South and more properly belongs to the liberal school of postbellum historians, it also suggests that there is perhaps more to the agrarian image of the Old South and the "Lost Cause" than historians have heretofore been willing to admit. As southern spokesmen reiterated again and again both before the Civil War and afterwards in their apologia, the South was indeed different from the North. In the words of Louis T. Wigfall:

We are a peculiar people, Sir! You don't understand us, and you can't understand us, because we are known to you only by Northern writers and Northern papers.... We are an agricultural people; We are a primitive but civilized people. We have no cities—we don't want them. We have no literature—we don't need any yet.... We do not require a press, because we go out and discuss all public questions from the stump with our people. We have no commercial marine—no navy—we don't want them.... We want no manufactures; we desire no trading, no mechanical or manufacturing classes.

Or, as Avery Craven noted many years ago, "the South lacked some things in the Northern pattern because her values and ideals had been taken from rural England. Southerners did not always want a diversified economic life or a public school system or a great number of larger cities. The South often deliberately chose rural backwardness."[34]

❖ ❖ ❖ ❖ ❖

Ironically, for one whose purpose was to write a true account of the Old South, Phillips perpetuated the "myth of democracy" with its extreme nationalist bias. In this sense, his works are not so old-fashioned as generally assumed but are in keeping with the mainstream of modern opinion regarding the South and its history. Phillips as much as anyone has influenced recent scholars' emphasis upon slavery and race with his focus on southern fears regarding their "peculiar institution" and the debilitating impact of slavery upon antebellum southern economic development. It is hoped that the analysis presented here will not only lead to a better understanding of Phillips's life and works, but also will remind us that American history (including the South) has more often than not been interpreted from the standpoint of what happened after 1865, all of which is to say that there is another version of the American past and perhaps it is time to give it serious consideration particularly with the recent "emergence of an understanding of republicanism" and its implications for American history between the Revolution and the Civil War.[35]

Notes

1. See Wood, "Ulrich Bonnell Phillips," in Clyde N. Wilson, ed.,*Dictionary of Literary Biography: Twentieth Century American Historians* (Detroit, 1983), 350-63. According to Eugene D. Genovese, Phillips's most important latter-day enthusiast, "his work, taken as a whole, remains the best and most subtle introduction to antebellum Southern history and especially to the problems posed by race and class...." (*In Red and Black: Marxian Explorations in Southern and Afro-American History* [New York, 1971], 275, 276). "Much of what Phillips wrote," declared C. Vann Woodward, "has not been superseded or seriously challenged and remains indispensable." (Introduction to the paperback edition of *Life and Labor in the Old South* [Boston, 1963], v.) In the words of Bennett H. Wall, "it was Phillips who was the real pioneer and formative scholar...." ("African Slavery," in Arthur S. Link and Rembert W. Patrick, eds., *Writing Southern History: Essays in Historiography in Honor of Fletcher M. Green* [Baton Rouge, 1965], 185.)

As Phillips admitted to Yates Snowden of South Carolina, "I have been diligently exploring for material for four or five years...." (Phillips to Snowden, Washington, D.C., 20 September 1904, Yates Snowden Papers, South Caroliniana Library, University of South Carolina). Writing to Rion J. McKissick from Ann Arbor, Michigan, on 6 February 1926, Phillips mentioned once again going on the "Southern circuit, from New Orleans to Washington, to get further materials for a projected history of the South." (McKissick Papers, South Caroliniana Library, University of South Carolina.)

2. The term "traditional Yankee virtues" is quoted from Daniel Joseph Singal, "Ulrich B. Phillips: The Old South as the New," *Journal of American History* 63 (March 1977), 873. "Almost without exception," writes Paul M. Gaston, "New South historians wrote as confirmed nationalists and interpreted southern development within the context of national trends. Reconciliation and conversion to national ways were central to their histories." (Gaston, "The 'New South'," in Link and Patrick, eds., *Writing Southern History*, 322.) Referring to the studies by Phillip A. Bruce, Broadus Mitchell, Paul H. Buck, and Holland Thompson, Sheldon Hackney states that their principal theme "was that of sectional reconciliation and the casting off of the dead hand of the past." ("*Origins of the New South* in Retrospect," *Journal of Southern History* 38 [May 1972], 192.) For similar comments about Woodrow Wilson, William P. Trent, John Spencer Bassett, Edwin Mims, William Garrott Brown, and William E. Dodd, see Thomas J. Pressly, *Americans Interpret Their Civil War* (New York, 1954, 1962), 186-95. Significantly, Pressly does not include Phillips in this group of liberal historians. Rather he classifies him with Charles Ramsdell, Frank Owsley, and E. Merton Coulter as examples of "The New Vindication of the South." (*Ibid.*, 165-87.)

3. See below notes 10-30. Although Phillips scholars are now beginning to appreciate his New South-progressive beliefs, they do not describe the actual process by which he accomplished his reconstruction of southern history. Nor have they fully realized the extent to which his liberal persuasion affected his research as well as his basic approach to and understanding of the antebellum past. See Wood, "U.B. Phillips, Unscientific Historian: A Further Note on His Methodology and Use of Sources," *Southern Studies* 21 (Summer, 1982), 146-62.

4. According to Thomas J. Pressly, "dissatisfaction with traditional Confederate explanations of the coming of the war was widespread by the 1890s among trained southern historians" and much of the focus of their criticism "centered upon the institution of slavery and the movement for secession." (*Americans Interpret Their Civil War*, 186-87, 189.) See also John M. Cooper, Jr., *Walter Hines Page: The Southerner as American* (Chapel Hill, 1977). As he notes, "the idea that slavery had perverted a humane, democratic development was one that Page repeatedly advanced in his career as a southern spokesman." This view "later became the hallmark of critical, reformist thinking among southern whites during the first half of the twentieth century." (*Ibid*, 54.)

5. Genovese, *In Red and Black*, 290, 293; Singal, "Ulrich B. Phillips: The Old South as the New," 873. See also John H. Roper, "A Case of Forgotten Identity: Ulrich B. Phillips as a Young Progressive," *Georgia Historical Quarterly* 60 (Summer, 1975), 165-75; John David Smith, "DuBois and Phillips—Symbolic Antagonists of the

Progressive Era," *The Centennial Review* 24 (Winter, 1980), 88-102; William L. Van Deburg, "Progress and the Conservative Historian," *Georgia Historical Quarterly* 55 (Fall, 1971), 406-16; and Wood, "Ulrich Bonnell Phillips," in the *Dictionary of Literary Biography*. Important in this respect are Phillips's nonslavery studies which provide direct clues to his New South-progressive orientation as well as his critical attitude toward the antebellum past. For the most part, historians have chosen to focus upon his slavery studies with the result that they have presented a one-sided view of Phillips as a defender of the Old South. See Richard Hofstadter, "U.B. Phillips and the Plantation Legend," *Journal of Negro History* 29 (April 1944), 109-24; Kenneth M. Stampp, "The Historian and Southern Negro Slavery," *American Historical Review* 57 (April 1952), 613-24; Stampp, *The Peculiar Institution* (New York, 1956); and Stanley Elkins, *Slavery: A Problem in American Institutional and Intellectual Life* (Chicago, 1959); John David Smith, "The Historiographic Rise, Fall, and Resurrection of Ulrich Bonnell Phillips," *Georgia Historical Quarterly* 65 (Summer 1981), pp. 138-53.

6. Phillips, "Conservatism and Progress in the Cotton Belt," in Eugene D. Genovese, ed., *Ulrich Bonnell Phillips, The Slave Economy of the Old South: Selected Essays in Economic and Social History* (Baton Rouge, 1968), 80; Phillips to John Parker, New Orleans, 21 January 1911 (Phillips Papers, SHC/UNC). Parker had earlier sent Phillips a copy of a program describing a southern commercial convention at Atlanta. For biographical information about Phillips, see Wood Gray, "Ulrich Bonnell Phillips," in William T. Hutchinson, ed., *Marcus W. Jernegan Essays in American Historiography* (Chicago, 1937; New York, 1955), 350-74; Stephenson, *The South Lives in History* and *Southern History in the Making: Pioneer Historians of the South* (Baton Rouge, 1964); Harvey Wish, *The American Historian: A Social-Intellectual History of the Writing of the American Past* (New York, 1960); and Wood, "Ulrich Bonnell Phillips." On the New South movement in general, see Gaston, "The 'New South'," in Link and Patrick, eds., *Writing Southern History*; and C. Vann Woodward, *Origins of the New South* (Baton Rouge, 1951). See also Richard H. Edmonds, *The South's Redemption: From Poverty to Prosperity* (Baltimore, 1890) and *Facts About the South* (Baltimore, 1902); Alexander K. McClure, *The South: Its Industrial, Financial and Political Condition* (New York, 1886); Holland Thompson, *The New South* (New Haven, 1919); Phillip A. Bruce, *The Rise of the South* (Philadelphia, 1905); and Raymond B. Nixon, *Henry W. Grady: Spokesman of the New South* (New York, 1943).

7. Edwin R.A. Seligman, *Essays in Economics* (New York, 1925), 303. See also his *The Economic Interpretation of History* (New York, 1907). According to Richard T. Ely, "the principles of self-interest, of adjudging ends by a pleasure-pain calculus, of the free market-place as the mechanism for bringing the best good to all, held true for all time and places." In his view, laissez-faire or "hands off" was a complete negativism. See Benjamin G. Rader, *The Academic Mind and Reform: The Influence of Richard T. Ely in American Life* (Lexington, Kentucky, 1966), 44, 45.

8. James Harvey Robinson, *The New History* (New York, 1912, 1965), 5, 23, 25; Turner, "The Significance of History" (quoted from Harvey Wish, Introduction to *The New History*, xxiii.) See also Ray Allen Billington, *Frederick Jackson Turner: Historian, Scholar, Teacher* (New York, 1973). As he notes, Turner was guided by two beliefs: (1) that historical events had multiple causes and (2) society could be

understood only by getting at the forces underlying political behavior. (*Ibid.*, 477.) While Turner adopted the methodology of the new history, he did not necessarily regard history as a specific tool for "bringing about specific social, political, or economic reforms." (Wilbur R. Jacobs, *The Historical World of Frederick Jackson Turner* [New Haven and London, 1968], ix, 125.)

9. See Stephenson, *The South Lives in History*, 63-65; Rader, *Richard T. Ely*, 167; Billington, *Frederick Jackson Turner*, 244; Gray, "Ulrich Bonnell Phillips," 356-57; and Russell B. Nye, *Midwestern Progressive Politics: A Historical Study of Its Origins and Development, 1870-1958* (New York, 1959), 139-41. Although Phillips studied under William A. Dunning at Columbia University, he did not care for his master's narrow political focus; nor did he share his enthusiasm for Reconstruction. See Wood, "Ulrich Bonnell Phillips." Phillips specifically acknowledged his debt to Turner in "Plantation and Frontier": "A deepening appreciation of the historical significance of the plantation and of the preceding frontier regimes I owe to Dr. Frederick Jackson Turner... whose constant disciple I have been since 1898." (Ibid., I: 103.) See also U.B. Phillips, "The Traits and Contributions of Frederick Jackson Turner," *Agricultural History* 19 (January 1945), 21-23.

10. Phillips, "Conservatism and Progress in the Cotton Belt," in Genovese, ed., *The Slave Economy of the Old South*, 78, 81. According to Wendell Holmes Stephenson, Phillips "contributed communications to sundry newspapers on these and related subjects" and actually "sought to influence policy in the South by advocating a reduction in cotton acreage, adjustment of the labor problem, an application of modern business methods, and a return to the plantation system." (*The South Lives in History*, 140-41.) See also Phillips's articles in the Atlanta *Constitution*, 24 August 1903 ("Economics of Plantation"); 6 September 1903 ("Plantation System is Strongly Favored"); 10 September 1903 ("More Talk About Cotton and the Supply of Labor"); 3 April 1904 ("Planting for 12,000,000 Bales"); and 28 December 1904 ("Phillips on Cotton Crop"). For Phillips's views on the revival of the plantation system to remedy the inefficient system of small farms and tenancy that had developed in the South after the Civil War, see "Conservatism and Progress in the Cotton Belt," "The Plantation as a Civilizing Factor," "The Decadence of the Plantation System," and "Plantations with Slave Labor and Free," in Genovese, ed., *The Slave Economy of the Old South*, 78, 91, 246, 262-68.

11. Phillips, *A History of Transportation*, vii. The "axiom of indispensability," or the notion that railroads played a key role in economic and social transformation, is described in Robert W. Fogel, *Railroads and American Economic Growth: Essays in Econometric History* (Baltimore, 1964), 1-9. See also Maury Klein, *The Great Richmond Terminal: A Study in Businessmen and Business Strategy* (Charlottesville, Va., 1971), ix; and James A. Ward, "A New Look at Antebellum Southern Rail Development," *Journal of Southern History* 29 (August 1973), 409-20. In the words of Richard H. Edmonds, "railroads of the South have been the most popular factors in the upbuilding of that section. It is largely to their immediate work that the development of the textile industry, lumbering and the iron and coal interests has been due." (*Facts About the South*, 32.)

12. Phillips, "The Decadence of the Plantation System," in Genovese, ed., *The Slave Economy of the Old South*, 248; Phillips, "Plantations with Slave Labor and Free,"

in *ibid.*, 257; "Transportation in the Ante-Bellum South: An Economic Analysis," in *ibid.*, 159. Note in this context Phillips's description of Milledgeville, Georgia as "a fairly typical unprogressive village...; a town in the midst of a region where town life was overshadowed by the plantation system. The merchants and innkeepers and perchance the lawyers twirled their thumbs or whittled soft pine throughout the spring and summer, until the arrival of autumn when the planters began to drop in and market their cotton...." ("Historical Notes of Milledgeville, Ga.," in *ibid.*, 176.)

13. Phillips, *A History of Transportation in the Eastern Cotton Belt to 1860* (New York, 1908, 1968), 19-20, 388. This same theme can be found in *Life and Labor in the Old South*: "In the main the railroads prospered but modestly because... their main-haul traffic was not great and their back-hauls were very light.... For the time being the railroads had as their main effect the broadening of the plantation area and the intensification of staple agriculture." (*Ibid.*, 148.)

14. Singal, "Ulrich B. Phillips: The Old South as the New," 873; Phillips, "The Economics of the Plantation," in Genovese, ed., *The Slave Economy of the Old South*, 66; Phillips, "Plantations with Slave Labor and Free," in *ibid.*, 258. See also *Life and Labor in the Old South*, 197. Interesting in this regard is Phillips's statement that "the chronology of the antebellum South, like that of every other *modern capitalistic community* [italics added], is filled with a succession of industrial expansions and contractions." ("Financial Crises in the Antebellum South," in Genovese, ed., *The Slave Economy of the Old South*, 147.)

15. Phillips, "Conservatism and Progress in the Cotton Belt," in Genovese, ed., *The Slave Economy of the Old South*, 73-74. To Edgar Gardner Murphy, "the Old South was the real nucleus of the new nationalism." (*Problems of the Present South*, 11.) The southern people, emphasized Thomas Nelson Page, were "naturally as capable as any part of our population" and "they are now slowly but surely working out their own destiny; and that destiny is a democratic order." As he added, "there is no undemocratic trait in the Southern people that is not directly accounted for by slavery and by the results of slavery." (*Old Commonwealths*, 138, 153.) This view is also evident in works by William E. Dodd and William P. Trent, who present southern history in terms of a "Great Reaction" in which southerners turned their backs on the egalitarian ideas of the Revolution and embraced states' rights as well as proslavery doctrines. See Dodd, *Expansion and Conflict* (Boston, 1915); and William P. Trent, *Southern Statesmen of the Old Regime* (New York, 1897).

16. Phillips, "Plantation and Frontier," I:69, 70-71, 94. "The frontier," Turner wrote, "promoted the formation of a composite nationality for the American people." As it advanced from the coast, it led to more "diversified agriculture" and the growth of "seaboard cities like Boston, New York, and Baltimore" which engaged in "rivalry for what Washington called 'the extensive and valuable trade of a rising empire.'" "The most important effect of the frontier," however, "has been in the promotion of democracy here and in Europe" since "the frontier is productive of individualism." ("The Significance of the Frontier," in the *Annual Report of the American Historical Association for the Year 1893*, 215, 217, 221.)

17. Phillips, "Plantation and Frontier," I: 94.

18. Phillips, "The Economics of Slave Labor," in Genovese, ed., *The Slave Economy of the Old South*, 132-33, 137. In Thomas Nelson Page's view, "the Southern people

were deflected from their natural development," (*Old Commonwealths*, 153.) "It is useless to speculate upon what might have been, but if the profitableness of cotton-growing with slave labor had not concentrated the capital and energy of the South... the industrial growth... would doubtless long before the war made the South, instead of New England and the Middle States, the manufacturing center of the country." (Edmonds, *Facts About the South*, 9.)

19. Phillips, *American Negro Slavery*, 338-40, 398; "The Economic Cost of Slaveholding in the Cotton Belt," in Genovese, ed., *The Slave Economy of the Old South*, 121. Comparing the North and South, Phillips stated that the former region "was annually acquiring thousands of immigrants who came at their own expense... worked zealously for wages... and... possessed all the inventive and progressive potentialities of European peoples. But aspiring captains of industry in the South could as a rule procure labor only by remitting round sums in money or credit which depleted their working capital and for which were obtained slaves fit only for plantation routine, negroes of whom little initiative could be expected and little contribution to the community's welfare beyond their mere muscular exertions." (*American Negro Slavery*, 395-96.)

20. Phillips, *American Negro Slavery*, 401; "The Economic Cost of Slaveholding in the Cotton Belt," in Genovese, ed., *The Slave Economy of the Old South*, 121; *A History of Transportation*, 388; "The Decadence of the Plantation System," in Genovese, ed., *The Slave Economy of the Old South*, 247. As Phillips reiterated, "the bulk of the black personnel was notoriously primitive, uncouth, improvident and inconstant, merely because they were Negroes of the time...." (*Life and Labor in the Old South*, 199-200.) As such, "and to make him play a valuable part of it [civilized life], strict guidance and supervision were essential." ("The Economic Cost of Slaveholding in the Cotton Belt," in Genovese, ed., *The Slave Economy of the Old South*, 129.) See also *American Negro Slavery*, 339.

21. Phillips, *American Negro Slavery*, 395, 401; "The Economics of the Plantation System," in Genovese, ed., *The Slave Economy of the Old South*, 70; *A History of Transportation*, 388. In Henry Grady's words, the Old South "was a slave to the system. The old plantation, with its simple police regulation and its feudal habit, was the only type possible under slavery." (Quoted in Nixon, *Henry Grady*, 347.) See also Page, *Old Commonwealths*, 121.

22. Phillips, "The Economic Cost of Slaveholding in the Cotton Belt," in Genovese, ed., *The Slave Economy of the Old South*, 135. "After suffering and prostration it [the South] has been relieved of its great incubus [slavery] and is becoming more and more able to hold its own with other sections in trade and manufacturing." (Edmonds, *Facts About the South*, 1.) The South of 1850 was "a region of immense potentiality. Its great waterfalls might run the wheels of many thousand industrial plants, if Southerners ever turned their minds in the direction of manufacturing." (Dodd, *The Cotton Kingdom* [New York, 1919], 22.) As Henry Grady put it in 1886, "the shackles that held her [the South] in narrow limitations fell forever when the shackles of the negro slave were broken." (Quoted in Nixon, *Henry Grady*, 347.)

23. Phillips, *American Negro Slavery*, 344; "The Decadence of the Plantation System," in Genovese, ed., *The Slave Economy of the Old South*, 245-47. See also "Plantation with Slave Labor and Free," in *ibid.*, 250-68. "Every plantation of the

standard Southern type was, in fact, a school constantly training and controlling pupils who were in a backward state of civilization." (*American Negro Slavery*, 342.)

24. Phillips, "The Decadence of the Plantation System," in Genovese, ed., *The Slave Economy of the Old South*, 248.

25. Phillips, "The Economics of the Plantation," in *ibid.*, 68, 70. See also "The Decadence of the Plantation System," in *ibid.*, 245-49. If no cataclysm of war and false reconstruction had accompanied the displacement of slavery," Phillips wrote in 1910, "the plantation system might well have experienced something of a happy further progress with free wage-earning labor." (*Ibid.*, 248.) Phillips's belief in the revival of the plantation system was reinforced by his study of large-scale farming in California while serving as a visiting professor at the University of California at Berkeley. The plantation system, he observed, "now flourishes in California, in the West Indies and the East Indies; and its introduction even into England is advocated as a means of improvement." ("Plantations with Slave Labor and Free," in Genovese, ed., *The Slave Economy of the Old South*, 268.)

26. See in general *The Life of Robert Toombs, The Course of the South to Secession;* "The Southern Whigs, 1834-1854," in *Essays in American History Dedicated to Frederick Jackson Turner* (New York, 1910, 1951); and "The Literary Movement for Secession," in *Studies in Southern History and Politics Inscribed to William Archibald Dunning* (New York, 1914). As Phillips summarized this viewpoint, "to the leaders of the South, with their ever present view of the possibility of negro uprisings, the regulation of slavery seemed essential for safety and prosperity. And when they found themselves about to become powerless to check any legislation hostile to the established order of the South, they adopted the policy of secession, seeking as they saw it, the lesser of the evils confronting them." ("The Economic Cost of Slaveholding in the Cotton Belt," in Genovese, ed., *The Slave Economy of the Old South*, 134.)

27. Phillips, *The Course of the South to Secession*, 2, 59, 81, 90-95.

28. *Ibid.*, 95-97, 114-15, 129-36, 145-49, 156; *Life of Toombs*, 56, 116, 193; "Georgia and State Rights," 159-60, 194.

29. Phillips, *Life of Toombs*, 194. Phillips endeavored "to use his [Toombs'] career as a central theme in describing the successive problems which the people of Georgia and the South confronted and the policies which they followed in their efforts at solving them." In particular, Toombs, who "was primarily an *American* statesman with nation-wide interests," illustrated the process by which the South became "distinctly *Southern*" and sectional. (*Ibid.*, viii-ix.) As it turns out, Phillips's works do embody a central theme, namely, the all pervading and totally negative impact of slavery upon the South's development. See Wood, "Ulrich Bonnell Phillips." For an outline of Phillips's approach to the study of the South, see his letter to Yates Snowden of South Carolina College, 13 January 1905 (Yates Snowden Papers, SCL/USC).

30. Phillips, *The Course of the South to Secession*, 152-53, 156; "Georgia and State Rights," 153. "The [southern] community had always in contemplation the possibility of social death from negro upheaval and control, as illustrated in San Domingo, and the milder fate of industrial stagnation and decay from premature emancipation, as illustrated in Jamaica." ("The Slave Labor Problem in the Charleston District," in Genovese, ed., *The Slave Economy of the Old South*, 213.) As the

"conflict of interests" between North and South became more accentuated, "it became apparent that the South was in a congressional minority, likely to be overridden at any time by a Northern majority. Ruin was threatening the vested interests and the social order in the South; and the force of circumstances drove the Southern politicians into the policy of resistance." ("The Economic Cost of Slaveholding in the Cotton Belt," in Genovese, ed., *The Slave Economy of Old South,* 117-35.)

31. Phillips, "Conservatism and Progress in the Cotton Belt," in Genovese, ed., *The Slave Economy of the Old South,* 79; *American Negro Slavery,* 337; "Racial Problems, Adjustments and Disturbances," in Genovese, ed., *The Slave Economy of the Old South,* 23. See also *Life and Labor in the Old South.* According to Phillips, southern expansion was limited by the nature of staple crops grown below the Mason-Dixon line. Rice required an "aquatic" habitat while sugar was limited by the tariff. Cotton, which in 1825 surged north to Richmond, retreated southward after "frosts nipped the prospect." While tobacco, wheat and corn had possibilities for expansion, it did not follow "that distinctive Southern pattern of life, in which Negroes were an essential element, was capable of expanding beyond its historic bounds." Indeed, "the South barely hoped to maintain its established borders...." (*Ibid.,* 137, 139.)

32. Phillips, *A History of Transportation,* 9-10; "Georgia and State Rights," 24, 121, 193, 210. The southern critique of northern society is analyzed in C. Vann Woodward, "The Southern Ethic in a Puritan World" and "A Southern War Against Capitalism" in *American Counterpoint: Slavery and Racism in the North-South Dialogue* (Boston, 1971), 13-46, 107-39. As Woodward stated in an earlier study, the South was "traditionally hostile to capitalistic legislation." (*Origins of the New South, 1877-1913* [Baton Rouge, 1951], 24.) See also Wood, "The Union of the States: A Study of Radical Whig-Republican Ideology and Its Influence upon the Nation and the South, 1776-1861" (Ph.D. diss., University of South Carolina, 1978).

33. Phillips, "The Economic Cost of Slaveholding in the Cotton Belt," in Genovese, ed., *The Slave Economy of the Old South,* 117. As Phillips admitted in the preface to *American Negro Slavery:* "For twenty years I have panned the sands of the stream of Southern life and garnered their golden treasure. Many of the nuggets rewarding the search have already been displayed in their natural form; and this [book] now is a coinage of the grains great and small. The metal is pure, the minting alone may be faulty. The die is the author's mind, which has been shaped as well by a varied Northern environment in manhood as by a Southern one in youth." (*Ibid.,* vii.) Phillips dedicated *Life and Labor in the Old South* to Ulrich, Mabel, and Worthington, "three children of the North who their father hopes may learn to love the South." See also "Plantation and Frontier," I:103.

34. Wigfall's quote is from Alvy L. King, *Louis T. Wigfall: Southern Fire-Eater* (Baton Rouge, 1970), 125. For Craven's comments, see *The Coming of the Civil War* (Chicago, 1942, 1966), 90-91.

35. See Wood, "Ulrich Bonnell Phillips," *Dictionary of Literary Biography.* On the revival of interest in Phillips's "central theme," see Robert E. Shalhope, "Race, Class, Slavery, and the Antebellum Southern Mind," *Journal of Southern History* 37 (November 1971), 557-74 and James M. McPherson, "Slavery and Race," in *Perspectives on American History* 3 (1969), 460-73. For "the emergence of an understanding of

republicanism," see Bernard Bailyn, *The Ideological Origins of the American Revolution* (Cambridge, Mass., 1967); Gordon S. Wood, *The Creation of the American Republic, 1776-1787* (Chapel Hill, 1969); Edmund S. Morgan, *American Slavery, American Freedom: The Ordeal of Colonial Virginia* (New York, 1975); William Gribbin, "Rollins's Histories and American Republicanism," *William and Mary Quarterly* 29 (July 1972), 411-22; Edmund S. Morgan, "Slavery and Freedom: The American Paradox," *Journal of American History* 59 (June 1972), 5-29; Lance Banning, "Republican Ideology and the Triumph of the Constitution, 1789 to 1793," *William and Mary Quarterly* 31 (April 1974), 167-88; and J.G.A. Pocock, *The Machiavellian Moment: Florentine Political Thought and the Atlantic Republican Tradition* (Princeton, 1975).

III

THE RACIST

U. B. Phillips, like all scholars, was very much a product of both his time and his region. He came of age in the deep South during the "nadir" of American race relations—the 1890s. Just as Phillips never escaped his identity as a southerner, despite the fact that the latter two-thirds of his life and practically all of his career were spent outside of his native region, so he never escaped the white supremacist views of that background. But because the southern historian's major works on slavery, in 1918 and even in 1929, appeared during an era when most white Americans still shared his views on the inherent inferiority of Negroes, the few contemporary protests to their racist implications so apparent to later generations were voiced primarily by black scholars.

The reviews of *American Negro Slavery* included in this section are by the era's two preeminent black historians, Carter G. Woodson and W.E.B. Du Bois, and by a white New York social worker active in the establishment and leadership of the National Association for the Advancement of Colored People, Mary White Ovington. The three reactions differ considerably in the degree to which they see Phillips's racist assumptions as undermining his scholarly achievement. Not surprisingly, it was Du Bois who lashed out at the book as a defense of slavery that marred much of its potential value. Woodson and Ovington were considerably more restrained in their criticism of Phillips and both found much in the book worthy of praise. And yet they, like Du Bois, took issue with the lack of humanity in Phillips's treatment of his black subjects, accusing him of approaching them in the same "cold-hearted fashion" as did their masters. Woodson went on to point out the factual flaws derived from that misguided assumption, while Ovington bemoaned the system's deplorable realities that so overshadowed Phillips's attempts to stress its "idyllic aspects."

The next critiques are by the first two historians to provide alternatives to Phillips's interpretation through comprehensive book-length treatments of the "peculiar institution." In their 1950s assessments of Phillips's historiographical significance, both Kenneth M. Stampp and Stanley M. Elkins made the Georgia-born historian's racism so integral to his treatment of slavery that it not only discredited his own work, but also set dangerous precedents for much subsequent work in the field. Stampp, in his 1952 essay in the *American Historical Review*, saw his own generation as the first seriously to challenge Phillips and the racist assumptions that so shaped his findings. In his controversial book, *Slavery: A Problem in American Institutional and Intellectual Life* (1959), Elkins introduced his own challenge to Phillips's "genial view" of the institution, explaining its enduring hold as the result of "impressive scholarship" used to validate the "popular ideology" of black inferiority so entrenched in Progressive Era thought throughout the nation.

Phillips's historiographic resurrection generally is credited to Eugene D. Genovese's reassessment of his work through a series of critiques in the mid-1960s. Included here is Genovese's 1966 address before the American Historical Association (AHA), the most influential of those new appreciations. Maintaining that Phillips's defense of the plantation regime did not imply a defense of slavery, Genovese attempted to move his racism out of the spotlight, where, according to Genovese, it had obscured and overshadowed far more basic and valuable findings and conclusions. But Genovese, as he himself acknowledges, was not the first to attempt a restoration of Phillips's reputation. Three years before his "turning point" AHA speech, a southern historian of an earlier generation had made an equally direct and forceful plea for renewed attention to Phillips's work. This was C. Vann Woodward, in an introduction to the 1963 edition of *Life and Labor in the Old South*. He too urged that Phillips's racial views be set in perspective and separated from the large part of his work that "has not [as of 1963] been superseded or seriously challenged and remains indispensable."

Thus the controversy over Phillips's racial prejudices has never been a debate over either their legitimacy or their existence. The fact that he thought of and depicted blacks as innately inferior to whites is one which his critics and his supporters alike readily acknowledge. Rather the debate, as represented here, has always been over the extent to which those prejudices limit, or even negate, the value of Phillips's work as a whole.

7

Reviews of American Negro Slavery

W. E. B. Du Bois, Carter G. Woodson,
and Mary White Ovington

American Negro Slavery. A Survey of the Supply, Employment and Control of Negro Labor as Determined by the Plantation Regime. By Ulrich Bonnell Phillips, Ph.D., Professor of American History in the University of Michigan. (D. Appleton and Company. 1918. Pp. ix, 529. $3.00.)

W. E. B. DU BOIS:

Mr. Phillips's work is not a history of American slavery but an economic study of American slaveholders and their land and crops. As such it gives evidence of wide reading and knowledge of the facts. Two hundred of its five hundred pages are mainly historical, treating of Africa and the slave trade and West Indian and American conditions. Two hundred other pages contain a series of essays on aspects of slavery—the cotton crop, plantation economy, etc. The other chapters are devoted to freedom and crime among slaves and slave codes.

Mr. Phillips was born and lived in earlier life on a Southern plantation (p. 313, note), and bases some of his information on this experience. To this he had added a knowledge of the standard authorities like Helps, Hakluyt, Nieboer, Kingsley and Ellis, and the less well-known Saco and Scelle. He has made wide use of southern newspapers and pamphlets and some manuscript materials, but had done little with any Negro sources, most of which he regards as "of dubious value" (p. 445, note).

The result is a readable book but one curiously incomplete and unfortunately biased. The Negro as a responsible human being has no place in the book. To be sure individual Negroes are treated there and here but mainly as exceptional or as illustrative facts for purposes outside themselves. Nowhere is there any adequate conception of "darkies," "niggers" and "negroes" (words liberally used throughout the book) as making a living mass of humanity with all the usual human reactions.

This intrigues the reader, for a history of slavery would ordinarily deal largely with slaves and their point of view, while this book deals chiefly with the economics of slaveholders and is without exception from their point of view. Its thesis is that slavery was an ordinary human labor problem not unlike that of modern factory labor. It had little to do with humanity, and even its sufferings were not different from the ordinary hardships of laboring people (pp. 52, 181, 182, 307).

This thesis, however, encounters the difficulty that most writers, even of the ultra-economic sort, have regarded slavery as a peculiar sort of labor problem because of its degradation of the laborer and the reflex action of this on the master class. Mr. Phillips sees this difficulty and notes the horrors of the Roman *latifundia* and Cato's code (p. 341); but he surmounts the difficulty by two premises, nowhere clearly stated, but always implicit in his narrative. The unstated major premise is that Negroes were not ordinary slaves nor indeed ordinary human beings. "The heartlessness of the Roman *latifundiarii* was the product partly of their absenteeism... and partly of the lack of difference between masters and slaves in racial traits. In the antebellum South all these conditions were reversed."

Mr. Phillips recurs again and again to this inborn character of Negroes: they are "submissive," "light-hearted" and "ingratiating" (p. 342), very "fond of display" (pp. 1, 291), with a "proneness to superstition" and "acceptance of subordination" (p. 291); "chaffing, and chattering" (p. 292) with "humble nonchalance and a freedom from carking care" (p. 416). From the fourteenth to the twentieth century Mr. Phillips sees no essential change in these predominant characteristics of the mass of Negroes; and while he is finishing his book in a Y.M.C.A. army hut in the South all he sees in the Negro soldier is the "same easy-going amiable serio-comic obedience," and all he hears is the throwing of dice (pp. vii, ix). This Negro nature is, to Mr. Phillips, fixed and unchangeable. A generation of freedom has brought little change (p. ix). Even the few exceptional Negroes whom he mentions are of interest mainly because of their unexpected "ambition" and not for any special accomplishment (p. 432). The fighting black maroons were overcome by "fright" (p. 466), and the Negroes' part in the public movements like the Revolution was "barely appreciable" (p. 116); indeed his main picture is of "inert Negroes, the majority of whom are as yet perhaps less efficient in freedom than their forbears were as slaves" (p. 396)!

Having now rather by innuendo and assumption than by dogmatic statement established these subhuman slaves Mr. Phillips, by similar method, evokes the slaveholding superman.

Slavery, we are told, (p. 401) was "less a business than a life; it made fewer fortunes than it made men." Life among Negro slaves "promoted, and well nigh necessitated the blending of foresight and firmness with kindliness and patience" (p. 287). In fact the slave system was "analogous in kind and in consequence to the domestication of the beasts of the field" (p. 344). With such masters, Mr. Phillips finds the treatment of slaves on the whole excellent. He notes the "interest of the master in the future of his workers" (p. 357). The surviving vestiges of slave quarters prove how comfortably they were housed (p. 298). Planters had to "guard their slaves' health and life as among the most vital of their own interests" (p. 301), and the tradition of the mistreatment of slaves in the southern South were simply spread by border state masters "in the amiable purpose of keeping their own slaves content" (p. 305).

"There was clearly no general prevalence of severity and strain in the regime" (p. 307). "The generality of the Negroes insisted upon possessing and being possessed in a cordial but respectful intimacy" (p. 307). White and black children were playmates; returning masters had their hands and feet kissed; and the result of the whole system was no fatigue or overwork, as the "sturdy sleekness as well as the joviality" of most of the slaves proved (p. 384). Slaves were rarely sold by a master (p. 397), and if hired out their masters were most solicitous for their "moral and physical welfare" (p. 410). Among town slaves there was "much comfort and even luxury" (p. 424).

The author quotes some cases where this idyllic picture seems a bit beside the truth, but he immediately marshals overwhelming witnesses to the contrary. As for instance, on page 251, he gives two inches to Fannie Kemble's picture of a wretched plantation, and follows it with three pages of contradicting testimony. The various severe indictments of certain aspects of slavery Mr. Phillips touches lightly but surely. The breaking up of family by sale is dismissed by the statement that slave owners "deplored" it (p. 202). Breeding for the domestic slave trade is dismissed as "extremely doubtful" (p. 362). Concubinage and illicit intercourse between master and servant receive but passing mention. Fugitive slaves are camouflaged as "truants." As for overwork, "anyone who has had experience with Negro labor may reasonably be skeptical when told that healthy, well-fed Negroes, whether slave or free, can by any routine insistence of the employer be driven beyond the point at which fatigue begins to be injurious" (p. 384).

After having painted this picture of the slave regime, Mr. Phillips is too logical a thinker not to see that he has overshot his mark, for the ugly fact remains that this institution of born slaves, kindly masters, and favorable conditions in crops was a tragic economic failure. Why was this? It was not, Mr. Phillips assures us, because of any especial moral delinquency of the South and he uses the *Tu quoque* argument against New England abolitionists and English philanthropists with inspiring if not convincing keenness, even to the extent of making Oglethorpe "the manager" of the Royal African Company. He finds Cairnes' stinging indictment of the slave barons full of "grotesqueries" (p. 356). He attacks Loria's socialistic explanation of the overvaluation of slaves as a "fallacy;" and finally he, himself, explains the economic failure of slavery as chiefly due to the fact that "the routine efficiency of slave labor itself caused the South to spoil the market for its distinctive crops by producing greater quantities than the world would buy at remunerative prices. To this the solicitude of the masters for the health of their slaves contributed" (p. 398)!

Mr. Phillips elaborates this thesis and also offers other and apparently contradicting explanations; on the whole this is by far the weakest part of the book and leaves the reader much befogged.

The last chapters come as more or less illogical addenda to the main thesis. Under "Town Slaves," the servant problem of the whites is mainly treated. Under "free Negroes," we are told of some slaves who won deserved freedom and of others who tasting freedom returned to the beloved plantation. Slave crime includes the stories of such "criminals" as Denmark Vesey and Toussaint L'Overture; and the treatment of slave codes shows, according to Mr. Phillips, that "the government of slaves was, for the ninety and nine, by men, and only for the hundredth by laws. There were injustice, oppression, brutality and heartburning in the regime—but where in the struggling world are these absent? There were also gentleness, kind-hearted friendship and mutual loyalty to a degree hard for him to believe who regards the system with a theorist's eye and a partisan squint" (p. 514).

On the whole this book, despite its undoubted evidence of labor and research, its wealth of illustrative material and its moderate tone, is deeply disappointing. It is a defense of American slavery—a defense of an institution which was at best a mistake and at worst a crime—made in a day when we need sharp and implacable judgment against collective wrongdoing by cultured and courteous men. The case against American slavery is too strong to be moved by this kind of special pleading. The mere fact that it left to the world today a heritage of ignorance, crime, lynching, lawlessness and economic injustice, to be struggled with by this and succeeding generations, is a condemnation unanswered by Mr. Phillips and unanswerable.

CARTER G. WOODSON:

This book far transcends the limits of most histories dealing with slavery and at the same time falls short of illuminating certain aspects necessary to a complete portraiture of the institution. It is primarily an economic treatise presenting slavery as a commercial enterprise rather than as an evil which so deeply implanted itself in our life that much difficulty was experienced in eradicating it. Several important phases of this history are therefore neglected seemingly with a view to making a successful compilation or digest of numerous facts which have not hitherto been published.

As a history of slavery the book has adequate background in the treatment of the slave trade, the exploitation of Guinea, and the maritime traffic. The work increases in interest in that portion treating of slavery as a factor in the sugar industry of the West Indies and in the tobacco and rice culture of the plantations along the Atlantic. Some attention is given to the influence of the struggle of the rights of man on the betterment of the condition of the blacks, the subsequent change of attitude, and the difficulties involved in the prohibition of the slave trade. In the chapters bearing on the development of the cotton industry and the extension of the domestic slave trade the author has not given much more than has appeared in the works of several other investigators in this field.

He is at best in his treatment of the plantations. No one has hitherto given the public so much information about the management, labor, social aspects, and tendencies of the plantation. Much more, however, could have been said about the contrast between town and country slaves, about free negroes and the relation of those two classes to the poor whites of the south. More space should have been given also to the southern antislavery leaders who opposed slavery because it was an economic evil. While the book therefore is informing, it is for several reasons far from being the last word on its subject.

Among the author's shortcomings are his inability to fathom the negro mind, his failure to bring out the cycles of the history of slavery, and a tendency to argue to the contrary when facts seem to be unfavorable to the slaveholders. The facts of this book, moreover, are so arrayed as to indicate that the institution was in some respects defensible and that the negroes were satisfied with it. How can it be true that the blacks were contented when they from time to time resorted to servile insurrections until the institution become so well established that resistance was suicidal? The author should not have neglected the uprisings which were common around Norfolk, Richmond, Petersburg, Charleston, and New Orleans during the days when slavery was reaching its most cruel form. Furthermore, although the slaves are mentioned as representing both persons and property the treatment lacks proportion in that it deals primarily with slaves as goods and chattels in the cold-blooded fashion that their masters bartered them away. In just the same way as a writer of the history of New England in describing the fisheries of that section would have little to say about the species figuring conspicuously in that industry, so has the author treated the negro in his work.

The book does not clearly show that slavery in America was first of all a patriarchal order which later developed into an economic system. It does not bring out in bold relief that during the eighteenth century when the milder form of slavery obtained the condition of the negroes in this country was decidedly better than it was in the nineteenth century. The author has too little to say about the transition period when the industrial revolution resulting from the multiplication of mechanical appliances like the steam engine, power loom, spinning jenny, and cotton gin gave rise to such a demand for cotton and accordingly for an increase in the slave labor supply as to make slavery throughout the south a system of exploiting one man for the benefit of another. Because of this defect of the book the valuable facts contained therein may establish either the exception or the rule. For example, the statement that the slaves were content may be either true or untrue. It was true to some extent in the eighteenth century when they were well treated, was certainly untrue when slavery was changing from a patriarchal to an economic system, and was apparently true in the nineteenth century,—though in fact it was resignation to fate rather than contentment.

The same may be said about the author's treatment of the plantations. The life portrayed therein was characteristic of one period but not of all, in certain parts but not everywhere. It seems, too, that Mr. Phillips has not exhausted the study of the plantations, for many of the records cited are those of the most enlightened and benevolent slaveholders of the old south such as were never known to be the cruel and inhuman sort of masters who doomed the negroes to torture in the lower south. George Washington, George Mason, Z. Kingsley, Wade Hampton, and Jefferson Davis were certainly not of that class of slaveholders most numerous in the south. Z. Kingsley, for example, was of an unusually benevolent type. In contradistinction to many white men who sold their own flesh and blood in disposing of their offspring by black women, this master recognized his mulatto son, purchased an estate for him in Haiti, and made it the nucleus of a colony to which he sent other emancipated negroes.

The author, moreover, makes certain statements which cannot be easily proved. Referring to the maritime slave trade, he says that "the food if coarse was plenteous and wholesome and the sanitation was fairly adequate." The best authorities do not support this contention. On page 306 he contends that in the actual regime severity was clearly the exception and kindness the rule on the plantation but supports his contention largely with the observations of two travelers, one of whom spoke of what he observed in all the slave states and the other who gave his observation of the situation in Virginia, where slavery was always of a mild form. The author tries also to minimize the prevalence of cases of slave women purchased by white men for purposes of concubinage and supports his contention with the assertion that in scanning thousands of bills of sale they exhibit little or no evidence to this effect (p. 194). An historian should not expect records of this sort to exhibit such evidence. While there were many white men who did not live above this reproach, the standard of morals among the majority was such that no purchaser would make a record of his desire to indulge in such a vice and the auctioneer would not always embarrass him by declaration to this effect. The reviewer has interviewed numbers of women of color, who assert that they were purchased and used for this base purpose.

While this book then is valuable because of the facts it contains, we must expect some other writer interested in this field to use these and other facts to set forth exactly what the institution was in its development from stage to stage and in its final form when it was exterminated by the Civil War.

MARY WHITE OVINGTON:

Mr. Phillips has long been known as an authority on his subject, and this book comes after twenty years of exhaustive work. It is a voluminous study written by a compiler of documents, with lengthy excerpts from diaries of planters, travelers' journals, newspapers, state reports—the many linked together to give a clear and, from the standpoint of the white master, a complete, statement of American slavery. The book opens with the slave trade; to be followed by the picture of slave labor in the tobacco industry, in rice, in sugar, and, last and most important, in cotton. We gain a clear understanding of the management of a plantation, of the growth of large estates, of the building up of the slave system in the western South. There is a chapter on the town slave and another on the free Negro.

The book is written by one who believes that slavery was probably the best labor system that could have been given the savage African and who shows the plantation life in its idyllic aspect, the slaves displaying "a courteous acceptance of subordination," the master and mistress impressed with their responsibilities, "each white family serving very much the functions of a modern social settlement, setting patterns of orderly, well-bred conduct which the Negroes were encouraged to emulate." The reader is told to regard state laws on slavery, often terrible in their severity, as for only the occasional sinner. "The government for slaves was for the ninety and nine by men, and only for the hundredth by laws."

The book is written in a spirit tolerant to the institution of chattel slavery, and yet so accurate and painstaking an historian is Mr. Phillips that one cannot lay it down without a feeling akin to nausea. For there are whole chapters concerned with the economics of the system, with kidnapping in Africa, with the breeding of slave stock in this country, and with the domestic slave trade of the nineteenth century. The relation of the price of a young unskilled, able-bodied slave to the price of cotton in New York is depicted on a graphic chart, and one sees flesh and blood moving with cotton, worth $1,100 a head in 1819, sinking to $700 a head in 1823, to rise to $1,300 in 1837. As capital moved south and west so the slave moved, and the trade was a busy one. Viewed from the business side, the slave took his place with other live stock, and no picture of stable plantation life can remove this inhuman aspect of the system.

One wishes in closing the volume that unless the descendant of the slave writes an exhaustive book from his standpoint this might be the last word on the subject. It is a disgraceful page, in American history, one that the whole country, the slave-trading North and the slave-holding South, must be glad to forget.

8

The Historian and Southern Negro Slavery

Kenneth M. Stampp

A survey of the literature dealing with southern Negro slavery reveals one fundamental problem that still remains unresolved. This is the problem of the biased historian. It is, of course, a universal historical problem—one that is not likely to be resolved as long as historians themselves are divided into scientific and so-called "subjectivist-presentist-relativist" schools.[1] These schools seem to agree that historians ought to strive for a maximum of intellectual detachment and ought not to engage in special pleading and pamphleteering. But whether they are entitled to pass moral judgments, whether they can overcome the subjective influences of their own backgrounds and environments, are still debatable questions—at least they are questions which are still being debated. Yet it must be said that as far as Negro slavery is concerned we are still waiting for the first scientific and completely objective study of the institution which is based upon no assumptions whose validity cannot be thoroughly proved. And as long as historians must select their evidence from a great mass of sources, as long as they attempt to organize and interpret their finds, the prospects are not very encouraging.

This does not mean that everyone who has written about slavery has had the *same* bias, or that some have not been more flagrantly biased than others, or more skillful than others in the use of the subtle innuendo. It most certainly does not imply that further efforts toward a clearer understanding of slavery are futile, or that we are not enormously indebted to the many scholars who have already engaged in research in this field. No student could begin to understand the complexities of the slave system without being thoroughly familiar with the findings and varying points of view of such historians as Ulrich B. Phillips, Herbert Aptheker, Lewis C. Gray, John Hope Franklin, Avery Craven, Carter G. Woodson, Frederic Bancroft, Charles S. Sydnor, John Spencer Bassett, and many others.

Among these scholars, the late Professor Phillips has unquestionably made the largest single contribution to our present understanding of southern slavery. It may be that his most durable monument will be the vast amount of new source material which he uncovered. But Phillips was also an unusually able and prolific writer. Measured only crudely in terms of sheer bulk, his numerous books and articles are impressive.[2] That, taken together with his substantial compilations of fresh factual information, his rare ability to combine scholarship with a fine literary style, and his point of view for which there has been a persistent affinity, explains the deep impression he has made. One needs only to sample the textbooks and monographic literature to appreciate the great influence of Professor Phillips's interpretations and methodology. A historian who recently attempted to evaluate Phillips's investigations of the slave-plantation system arrived at this conclusion: "So thorough was his work that, granted the same purpose, the same materials, and the same methods, his treatment... is unlikely to be altered in fundamental respects."[3]

"There is, however," this historian hastened to add, "nothing inevitable about his point of view or his technique." Rather, he contended that "a materially different version" would emerge when scholars with different points of view and different techniques subjected the slave system to a similarly intensive study.[4] Indeed, he might have noted that a "materially different version" is already emerging. For the most notable additions to the bibliography of slavery during the past three decades have been those which have some way altered Phillips's classic exposition of the slave regime. This revisionism is the product of new information discovered in both old and new sources, of new research techniques, and, to be sure, of different points of view and different assumptions. In recent years the subject has become less and less an emotional issue between scholarly defendants of the northern abolitionists and of the southern proslavery school. It may only be a sign among them to recognize that it is at least conceivable that a colleague on the other side of the Mason and Dixon line could write somthing significant about slavery. For the new light that is constantly being shed upon the Old South's "peculiar institution" we are indebted to historians of both southern and northern origins—and of both the Negro and white races.

One of these revisionists has raised some searching questions about Phillips's methodology. Professor Richard Hofstadter has discovered a serious flaw in Phillips's sampling technique, which caused him to examine slavery and slaveholders on "types of plantations that were not at all representative of the common slaveholding unit." Phillips made considerable use of the case-study method, and he relied heavily upon the kinds of manuscript records kept primarily by the more substantial planters. Therefore, Hofstadter concludes, "In so far... as Phillips drew his picture of the Old South from plantations of more than 100 slaves [as he usually did], he was sampling about 10% of all the slaves and less than 1% of all the slaveholders."[5] The lesser planters and small slaveholding farmers, who were far more typical, rarely kept diaries and formal records; hence they received considerably less attention from Phillips. The danger in generalizing about the whole regime from an unrepresentative sample is obvious enough.

Getting information about the slaves and masters on the smaller holdings is difficult, but it is nevertheless essential for a comprehensive understanding of the slave system. Professor Frank L. Owsley has already demonstrated the value of county records, court records, and census returns for this purpose.[6] Phillips made only limited use of the evidence gathered by contemporary travelers, especially by Frederick Law Olmsted in whom he had little confidence. The traveler in the South who viewed slavery with an entirely open mind was rare indeed, but it does not necessarily follow that the only accurate reporters among them were those who viewed it sympathetically.

How the picture of slavery will be modified when life on the small plantations and farms has been adequately studied cannot be predicted with as much assurance as some may think. The evidence now available suggests conflicting tendencies. On these units there was very little absentee ownership, the proverbially harsh overseer was less frequently employed, and contacts between masters and slaves were often more numerous and intimate. Undoubtedly in many cases these conditions tended to make the treatment of the Negroes less harsh and the system less rigid. But it is also necessary to consider other tendencies, as well as the probability that the human factor makes generalization risky. Sometimes the material needs of the slaves were provided for more adequately on the large plantations than they were on the smaller ones. Sometimes the lower educational and cultural level and the insecure social status of the small slaveholders had an unfavorable effect upon their racial attitudes. There are enough cases in the court records to make it clear that members of this group were, on occasion, capable of extreme cruelty toward their slaves. Nor can the factor of economic competition be overlooked. The lesser planters who were ambitious to rise in the social scale were, to phrase it cautiously, exposed to the temptation not to indulge their slaves while seeking their fortunes in competition with the larger planters. To be sure, as Lewis C. Gray points out, many of these small slaveholders lived in relatively isolated areas where the competitive factor was less urgent.[7] But there still is a need for further investigation of these small slaveholders before generalizations about conditions among their slaves will cease to be highly speculative.

A tendency toward loose and glib generalizing is, in fact, one of the chief faults of the classic portrayal of the slave regime—and, incidentally, of some of its critics as well. This is true of descriptions of how the slaves were treated: how long and hard they were worked, how severely they were punished, how well they were fed, housed, and clothed, and how carefully they were attended during illness. It may be that some historians have attached an undue significance to these questions, for there are important philosophical implications in the evaluation of slavery in terms of such mundane matters as what went into the slave's stomach. In any event, the evidence hardly warrants the sweeping pictures of uniform physical comfort or uniform physical misery that are sometimes drawn. The only generalization that can be made with relative confidence is that some masters were harsh and frugal, others were mild and generous, and the rest ran the whole gamut in between. And even this generalization may need qualification, for it is altogether likely that the same master could have been harsh and frugal on some occasions and mild and generous on others. Some men become increasingly mellow and others increasingly irascible with advancing years. Some masters were more generous, or less frugal, in times of economic prosperity than they were in time of economic depression. The treatment of the slaves probably varied with the state of the master's health, with the vicissitudes of his domestic relations, and with the immediate or subsequent impact of alcoholic beverages upon his personality. It would also be logical to suspect—and there is evidence that this was the case—that masters did not treat all their slaves alike; that, being human, they developed personal animosities for some and personal affections for others. The care of slaves under the supervision of overseers might change from year to year as one overseer replaced another in the normally rapid turnover. In short, the human factor introduced a variable that defied generalization.

This same human factor complicates the question of how the Negroes reacted to their bondage. The generalization that the great majority of Negroes were contented as slaves has never been proved, and in the classic picture it was premised on the assumption that certain racial traits caused them to adapt to the system with peculiar ease. If freedom was so far beyond their comprehension, it was a little remarkable that freedom was the very reward considered most suitable for a slave who rendered some extraordinary service to his master or to the state. It is well known that many slaves took advantage of opportunities to purchase their freedom. Resistance by running away and by the damaging of crops and tools occurred frequently enough to cause Dr. Samuel Cartwright of Louisiana to conclude that these acts were the symptoms of exotic diseases peculiar to Negroes.[8] Though there is no way to discover precisely how much of the property damage was deliberate, and how much was merely the byproduct of indifference and carelessness, the distinction is perhaps inconsequential. Finally, there were individual acts of violence against masters and overseers, and cases of conspiracy and rebellion. If the significance of these cases has been overstated by Herbert Aptheker,[9] it has been understated by many of his predecessors.

This is not to deny that among the slaves only a minority of undeterminable size fought the system by these various devices. It is simply to give proper emphasis to the fact that such a minority did exist. In all probability it consisted primarily of individuals of exceptional daring, or intelligence, or individuality. Such individuals constitute a minority in all societies.

That the majority of Negroes seemed to submit to their bondage proves neither their special fitness for it nor their contentment with it. It merely proves that men *can* be enslaved when they are kept illiterate, when communication is restricted, and when the instruments of violence are monopolized by the state and the master class.[10] In the light of twentieth-century experience, when white men have also been forced to submit to tyranny and virtual slavery, it would appear to be a little preposterous to generalize about the peculiarities of Negroes in this respect. In both cases the majority has acquiesced. In neither case does it necessarily follow that they have reveled in their bondage.

To be sure, there were plenty of opportunists among the Negroes who played the role assigned to them, acted the clown, and curried the favor of their masters in order to win the maximum rewards within the system, sometimes even at the expense of their fellow slaves. There were others who, in the very human search for personal recognition within their limited social orbit, salvaged what prestige they could from the high sales prices attached to them, or from the high social status of their masters.[11] Nor is it necessary to deny that many slaves sang and danced, enjoyed their holidays, and were adaptable enough to find a measure of happiness in their daily lives. It is enough to note that all of this still proves nothing, except that it is altogether likely that Negroes behaved as much as people of other races would have behaved under similar circumstances.

In describing these various types of slave behavior historians must always weigh carefully, or at least recognize, the moral implications and value judgments implicit in the adjectives they use. How, for example, does one distinguish a "good" Negro from a "bad" Negro in the slave regime? Was the "good" Negro the one who was courteous and loyal to his master, and who did his work faithfully and cheerfully? Or was the "good" Negro the defiant one who has sometimes been called "insolent" or "surly" or "unruly"? Was the "brighter" side of slavery to be found in the bonds of love and loyalty that developed between some household servants and some of the more genteel and gentle masters? Or was it to be found among those slaves who would not submit, who fought back, ran away, faked illness, loafed, sabotaged, and never ceased longing for freedom in spite of the heavy odds against them? In short, just what *are* the proper ethical standards for identifying undesirable or even criminal behavior among slaves? There is no answer that is not based upon subjective factors, and the question therefore may not be within the province of "objective" historians. But in that case historians must also avoid the use of morally weighted adjectives when they write about slavery.

The general subject of slave behavior suggests a method of studying the institution which revisionists need to exploit more fully. For proper balance and perspective slavery must be viewed through the eyes of the Negro as well as through the eyes of the white master.[12] This is obviously a difficult task, for slaves rarely wrote letters or kept diaries.[13] But significant clues can be found in scattered sources. The autobiographies and recollections of fugitive slaves and freedmen have value when used with the caution required of all sources. Slaves were interviewed by a few travelers in the ante-bellum South, and ex-slaves by a few historians in the post-Civil War period;[14] but unfortunately the interviewing was never done systematically until the attempt of the Federal Writers Project in the 1930's.[15] The mind of the slave can also be studied through his external behavior as it is described in plantation manuscripts, court records, and newspaper files. For example, there is undoubtedly some psychological significance in the high frequency of stuttering and of what was loosely called a "downcast look" among the slaves identified in the advertisements for fugitives.[16] Finally, the historian might find clues to the mental processes of the slaves in the many recent sociological and anthropological studies of the American Negro. The impact of nineteenth-century slavery and of twentieth-century prejudice and discrimination upon the Negro's thought and behavior patterns have some significant similarities.[17]

This kind of perspective is not to be found in the Phillips version of slavery, for he began with a basic assumption which gave a different direction to his writings. That he failed to view the institution through the eyes of the Negro, that he emphasized its mild and humorous side and minimized its grosser aspects, was the result of his belief—implicit always and stated explicitly more than once—in the inherent inferiority of the Negro race. The slaves, he wrote, were "by racial quality" "submissive," "light-hearted," "amiable," "ingratiating," and "imitative." Removing the Negro from Africa to America, he added, "had little more effect upon his temperament than upon his complexion." Hence "the progress of the generality [of slaves] was restricted by the fact of their being negroes."[18] Having isolated and identified these "racial qualities," Phillips's conclusions about slavery followed logically enough.

It is clear in every line Phillips wrote that he felt no animus toward the Negroes. Far from it. He looked upon them with feelings of genuine kindliness and affection. But hearing as he did the still-faintly-ringing laughter of the simple plantation Negroes, the songs sung in their melodious voices, Phillips was unable to take them seriously. Instead he viewed them as lovable, "serio-comic" figures who provided not only a labor supply of sorts but also much of the plantation's social charm. Thus slavery was hardly an institution that could have weighed heavily upon them.

Now, it is probably true that the historian who criticizes slavery per se reveals a subjective bias, or at least certain assumptions he cannot prove. The sociological argument of George Fitzhugh that slavery is a positive good, not only for the laboring man but for society in general, cannot be conclusively refuted with scientific precision. Those who disagree with Fitzhugh can only argue from certain unproved premises and optimistic convictions about the so-called "rights" and "dignity" of labor and the potentialities of free men in a democratic society. And the historian may run into all sorts of difficulties when he deals with such objective matters.

But to assume that the *Negro* was peculiarly suited for slavery because of certain inherent racial traits is quite another matter. This involves not primarily a subjective bias but ignorance of, or disregard for, the overwhelming evidence to the contrary. Much of this evidence was already available to Phillips, though it must be noted that he grew up at a time when the imperialist doctrine of the "white man's burden" and the writings of such men as John Fiske and John W. Burgess were giving added strength to the belief in Anglo-Saxon superiority. Nor should he be blamed for failing to anticipate the findings of biologists, psychologists, anthropologists, and sociologists subsequent to the publication of his volume *American Negro Slavery* in 1918. It may be significant that he presented his own point of view with considerably more restraint in his *Life and Labor in the Old South* which appeared a decade later.

Nevertheless, it is this point of view which both dates and outdates the Phillips version of slavery. No historian of the institution can be taken seriously any longer unless he begins with the knowledge that there is no valid evidence that the Negro race is innately inferior to the white, and that there is growing evidence that both races have approximately the same potentialities.[19] He must also take into account the equally important fact that there are tremendous variations in the capacities and personalities of individuals within each race, and that is therefore impossible to make valid generalizations about races as such.

An awareness of these facts is forcing the revisionists to discard much of the folklore about Negroes that found a support in the classic portrayal of slavery. Take, for example, the idea that the primitive Negroes brought to America could only adapt to the culture of the civilized white man in the course of many generations of gradual growth. Phillips saw the plantation as "a school constantly training and controlling pupils who were in a backward state of civilization.... On the whole the plantations were the best schools yet invented for the mass training of that sort of inert and backward people which the bulk of the American negroes represented."[20]

This idea would seem to imply that the Negroes could only be civilized through a slow evolutionary process, during which they would gradually acquire and transmit to their descendants the white man's patterns of social behavior. In actual fact the first generation of Negroes born in the English colonies in the seventeenth century was as capable of learning these patterns of social behavior—for they were things that were learned, not inherited—and of growing up and living as free men as was the generation alive in 1865. Indeed many of the Negroes of this Civil War generation were *still* unprepared for freedom; and that fact reveals the basic flaw in the whole Phillips concept. It does not show that the plantation school had not had sufficient time to complete its work but rather that it was capable of doing little more than training succeeding generations of slaves. After two centuries of slavery most Negroes had to learn how to live as free men by *starting* to live as free men. The plantation school may have had some limited success as a vocational institution, but in the field of the social sciences it was almost a total failure.

Other discredited aspects of the mythology of slavery can be mentioned only briefly. Revisionists no longer attempt to explain the origin of the institution with a doctrine of "climatic determinism." Since white men did and still do labor long and hard in cotton and tobacco fields there is little point in tracing southern slavery to the generative powers of southern heat.[21] Nor does it appear that the health of Negroes in the fever-infested rice swamps was as flourishing as it has sometimes been described.[22] And the fact that unfree labor alone made possible the rise of the plantation system proves neither the "necessity" nor the "inevitability" of slavery. For there was nothing inevitable about the plantation. Without this supply of unfree labor southern agriculture would probably have given less emphasis to the production of staples, and the small-farm unit would have prevailed. But the South would not have remained a wilderness. Moreover, Negroes *might* have been brought to America as servants rather than slaves (as the first ones were). Thus, like the white servants, many of them might have become landowning farmers in the period when land was abundant and cheap.

Slavery, then, was the inevitable product of neither the weather nor some irresistible force in the South's economic evolution. Slaves were used in southern agriculture because men sought greater returns than they could obtain from their own labor alone. It was a man-made institution. It was inevitable only insofar as everything that has happened in history was inevitable, not in terms of immutable or naturalistic laws.

And finally, the revisionists have brought some of the classic conclusions about the economics of slavery under serious scrutiny. Was it really a profitable institution? Although Thomas R. Dew and some other pro-slavery writers argued that it was and that it would have been abolished had it not been, there has been a persistent tendency, dating back to ante-bellum times, to minimize the question of profits and to emphasize other factors. It was not that slavery was profitable—indeed many contended that it was actually unprofitable for most slaveholders—but rather it was the race question or the masters' feeling of responsibility for the Negroes that explained its preservation. This was also the conclusion of Professor Phillips who believed that except on the rich and fresh lands of the Southwest, slavery had nearly ceased to be profitable by 1860.[23]

But in recent years there has been much disagreement with this conclusion. Lewis C. Gray, Thomas P. Govan, Robert R. Russel, and Robert Worthington Smith have found evidence that slavery continued to be profitable for the slaveholders as a class down to the very outbreak of the Civil War.[24] Frequently the average money investment in the plantation labor force has been exaggerated; depreciation on this investment has been figured as a cost when the slaves were actually increasing in both numbers and value; and faulty accounting methods have resulted in listing interest on the slave investment as an operational expense. Too often profits have been measured exclusively in terms of staple production, and the value of the natural increase of slaves, of the food they produced for the master and his family, and of the personal services they rendered have been ignored. Many of the debt-burdened planters provided evidence not of the unprofitability of slavery but of their tendency to disregard the middle-class virtue of thrift and to live beyond their means. Nor does slavery appear to be primarily responsible for the crude agricultural methods or for the soil exhaustion that occurred in the South.[25]

Rarely has a group engaged in agriculture earned the returns and achieved the high social status enjoyed by the southern slaveholding class. Certainly no colonial or nineteenth-century farmer could have hoped to reap such fruits from his own labor. The fact that some planters made fortunes while others failed, that the profits were painfully low in times of economic depression, merely demonstrates that the slave-plantation system had many striking similarities to the factory system based on private capitalist production. Is one to generalize about the profits of industrial capitalism from the fortunes accumulated by some, or from the failures suffered by thousands of others? From the high returns in periods of prosperity, or from the low returns in periods of depression? And what is to be made of the oft-repeated argument that the planters got nowhere because "they bought lands and slaves wherewith to grow cotton, and with the proceeds ever bought more slaves to make more cotton"?[26] If this is the essence of economic futility, then one must also pity the late Andrew Carnegie who built a mill wherewith to make steel, and with proceeds ever built more mills to make more steel. The economist would not agree that either Carnegie or the planters were in a vicious circle, for they were simply enlarging their capital holdings by reinvesting their surplus profits.

The revisionists still agree that slavery, in the long run, had some unfavorable economic consequences for the South as a whole, especially for the nonslaveholding whites.[27] And some historian may yet point out that slavery was not very profitable for the Negroes. At least he may question the baffling generalization that the southern whites were more enslaved by Negro slavery than were the Negro slaves.[28] For in the final analysis, it was the *Negro* who had the most to gain from emancipation.

Abolitionists have suffered severely at the hands of historians during the past generation. They have been roundly condemned for their distortions and exaggerations. But are historians really being "objective" when they combine warm sympathy for the slaveholders' point of view with cold contempt for those who looked upon the enslavement of four million American Negroes as the most shocking social evil of their day? Perhaps historians need to be told what James Russell Lowell once told the South: "It is time... [to] learn... that the difficulty of the Slavery question is slavery itself,—nothing more, nothing less."[29] It may be that the most important fact that the historian will ever uncover about the South's "peculiar institution" is that slavery, at its best, was still slavery, and that certain dangers were inherent in a master-slave relationship even among normal men.

Notes

1. Chester McArthur Destler, "Some Observations on Contemporary Historical Thought," *American Historical Review*, LV (April, 1950), 503-29.

2. Phillips's findings and conclusions can be studied most conveniently in *American Negro Slavery* (New York, 1918), and in *Life and Labor in the Old South* (Boston, 1929).

3. Richard Hofstadter, "U.B. Phillips and the Plantation Legend," *Journal of Negro History*, XXIX (April, 1944), 124.

4. *Ibid.*, 122, 124.

5. *Ibid.*, 109-19.

6. Frank L. and Harriet C. Owsley, "The Economic Basis of Society in the Late Ante-Bellum South," *Journal of Southern History*, VI (February, 1940), 24-45. Much information about the treatment of slaves on the small plantations and farms can be found in Helen T. Catterall, ed., *Judicial Cases Concerning American Slavery and the Negro* (5 vols., New York, 1926-37).

7. Lewis C. Gray, *History of Agriculture in the Southern United States to 1860* (Washington, 1933), I: 518, 556-57.

8. Raymond A. and Alice H. Bauer, "Day to Day Resistance to Slavery," *Journal of Negro History*, XXVII (October, 1942), 388-419. For references to some of Dr. Cartwright's unique views see Felice Swados, "Negro Health on the Ante-Bellum Plantations," *Bulletin of the History of Medicine*, X (October, 1941), 462.

9. Herbert Aptheker, *American Negro Slave Revolts* (New York, 1943). Many acts of violence by individual slaves are recorded in Catterall, *Judicial Cases*.

10. The techniques of Negro enslavement are described in Aptheker, *American Negro Slave Revolts*, pp. 53-78.

11. Historians who failed to grasp the psychological significance of such slave behavior have sometimes drawn some unjustifiable inferences from it, for example,

that Negroes were naturally docile and felt no personal humiliation because of their inferior status.

12. John Hope Franklin makes a brief attempt to accomplish this in *From Slavery to Freedom* (New York, 1948), 204-12.

13. Carter G. Woodson, ed., *The Mind of the Negro as Reflected in Letters Written during the Crisis, 1800-1860* (Washington, 1926).

14. See, for example, Harrison A. Trexler, *Slavery in Missouri, 1804-1865* (Baltimore, 1914).

15. Selections from these interviews are published in Benjamin A. Botkin, ed., *Lay My Burden Down* (Chicago, 1945).

16. The present writer was impressed by this while searching through thousands of advertisements for fugitive slaves in various southern newspapers.

17. Especially suggestive is Robert L. Sutherland, *Color, Class and Personality* (Washington, 1942).

18. Phillips, *American Negro Slavery*, 291-92, 339, 341-42.

19. For a summary of the evidence and literature on this subject see Gunnar Myrdal, *An American Dilemma: The Negro Problem and Modern Democracy* (New York, 1944), esp. Chapter VI, including the footnotes to this chapter, pp. 1212-18.

20. Phillips, *American Negro Slavery*, 342-43.

21. Oscar and Mary F. Handlin, "Origins of the Southern Labor System," *William and Mary Quarterly*, VII (April, 1950), 199.

22. Swados, pp. 460-72; J.H. Easterby, ed., *The South Carolina Rice Plantation as Revealed in the Papers of Robert F.W. Allston* (Chicago, 1945), 30; Bennett H. Wall, "Medical Care of Ebenezer Pettigrew's Slaves," *Mississippi Valley Historical Review*, XXXVII (December, 1950), 451-70.

23. *American Negro Slavery*, 391-92.

24. Lewis C. Gray, "Economic Efficiency and Competitive Advantage of Slavery under the Plantation System," *Agricultural History*, IV (April, 1930), 31-47; Thomas P. Govan, "Was Plantation Slavery Profitable?" *Journal Southern History*, VIII (November, 1942), 513-35; Robert R. Russel, "The General Effects of Slavery upon Southern Economic Progress," *ibid.*, IV (February, 1938), 34-54; Robert Worthington Smith, "Was Slavery Unprofitable in the Ante-Bellum South?" *Agricultural History*, XX (January, 1946), 62-64.

25. Gray, *History of Agriculture*, I:447-48, 470; Avery O. Craven, *The Repressible Conflict*, 1830-1861 (Baton Rouge, 1939), Chaps. I, II.

26. Phillips, *American Negro Slavery*, 395-98.

27. Gray, *History of Agriculture*, II:940-42.

28. "In a real sense the whites were more enslaved by the institution than the blacks." James G. Randall, *The Civil War and Reconstruction* (Boston, 1937), 73. "As for Sambo... there is some reason to believe that he suffered less than any other class in the south from its 'peculiar institution.'" Samuel Eliot Morison and Henry Steele Commager, *The Growth of the American Republic* (4th ed.; New York, 1950), I:537.

29. [James Russell Lowell], "The Question of the Hour," *Atlantic Monthly*, VII (1861), 120-21.

9

Racial Inferiority as the Basic Assumption

Stanley M. Elkins

The appearance of Ulrich B. Phillips signified a profound change of phase. The Progressive Era, truly a new age in all things, brought to American history Dunning on Reconstruction and Phillips on slavery. Phillips, who showed the institution through southern eyes for the first time in more than half a century and was at the same time guided by scholarly standards, made an inestimable contribution: he made it possible for the subject to be debated on scholarly grounds. No debate is worth much without a vigorous, knowledgeable, and principled opposition, and the vitality which this debate was to retain for so many years would be due in overwhelming measure to Ulrich Phillips and his followers.

Born in 1877 as the son of a Georgia merchant, Phillips was reared in an atmosphere of reverence for the values and standards of the old planter class. He found it impossible to believe that a society which had produced such values and such standards could have rested on a corrupt and immoral institution. Northerners, in the last analysis, could not really be expected to understand slavery. At the turn of the century Phillips was studying under Dunning at Columbia; he began very early on an intensive study of slavery that would not only challenge the deepest assumptions of Rhodes and Hart but would also make drastic alterations in the views held on that subject by thousands and thousands of American readers. A torrent of articles began flowing from Phillips's pen, and when his major work, *American Negro Slavery*, finally appeared in 1918, it was not a beginning but a grand culmination of nearly fifteen years of steadily growing influence.[1]

The basic assumption in *American Negro Slavery* was that of innate and inherited racial inferiority. There is no malice toward the Negro in Phillips's work. Phillips was deeply fond of the Negroes as a people; it was just that he could not take them seriously as men and women: they were children. His approach to the subject involved the most painstaking and responsible scholarship; it was necessary, he thought, to go to the sources. He gave small weight to legal codes, for they gave little indication of what ante-bellum slavery was actually like; he paid little attention to travelers' accounts, since those accounts were intolerably distorted by antislavery bias. The true sources for the subject—the sources from which the full flavor of plantation life might be evoked—were the actual plantation records. The result was a sympathetic account of the old regime which succeeded (though not in the most obvious polemical sense) in neutralizing almost every assumption of the antislavery tradition.

Phillips found that, in the light of what he saw as the inherent character of the Negro race, plantation slavery was not by any means a cruel and inhumane system. Evidence drawn directly from the records did much to dispose of prior generalizations about inadequate food, clothing, and housing. He showed that earlier stories of cruelty and overwork had been wildly overdrawn. Everywhere in Phillips's pages the emphasis is on the profoundly human relationships between the paternal master and his faithful and childlike blacks. While there may have been "injustice, oppression, brutality and heartburning," as anywhere in the world, there were also "gentleness, kind-hearted friendship and mutual loyalty to a degree hard for him to believe who regards the system with a theorist's eye and a partisan squint."[2] Not only did the institution of plantation slavery maintain a stable labor force for southern agriculture; it functioned as a school. "On the whole the plantations were the best schools yet invented for the mass training of that sort of inert and backward people which the bulk of the American negroes represented."[3] On scholarly grounds alone—scope, depth of research, and use of original sources—*American Negro Slavery* far surpassed anything yet done, and Phillips was easily and beyond question established as the foremost authority on the subject.

The setting in which Phillips worked—and in which his ideas were so well received long before his book actually appeared—was the setting of the Progressive Era. "Progressivism" in the early years of the twentieth century had strong reformist overtones, but the form which the progressive attitude took in this period on matters of race was quite different from that which it would take for later reform generations. Certain streams were by then coming together, making possible a wide acceptance North and South of the essentially tolerant view of Negro slavery which Ulrich Phillips represented.

In the South the muddy and anomalous (so far as the whites were concerned) post-Reconstruction position of the Negro was being systematically liquidated by the turn of the century. (The withdrawal of Federal troops in the 1870's had by no means been followed by the wholesale removal of Negro political and social rights; many of those rights had been maintained until well into the nineties.) But the Populists' organized though abortive efforts to make common political cause with the Negro precipitated an all but unanimous determination, already coalescing throughout southern white society, to eliminate Negroes from politics altogether. The tool whereby liberal white elements, in combination with Populist remnants, might then gain ascendancy in the Democratic party was the formula of a white man's government: the Negro must go. The Negro's by then precarious political status, together with the lukewarm conservatism of the old post-Reconstruction Bourbon element, constituted nothing further in the way of obstacles to the complete triumph of Jim Crow and thoroughgoing Negro disfranchisement. Negro leadership itself— dominated by Booker T. Washington—was quick to see the coming state of things and urged what amounted to full capitulation. This meant not only that the Negro had nothing more in the way of a political future but also that social survival would henceforth require a new form of the old ante-bellum dependency relationship between Negroes and white patrons. The meaning of political Progressivism in the South, therefore, was that civic purity and racial purity would be synonymous.[4]

Progressivism in this sense was not limited to the South: it had its northern counterpart. Imperialism and the white man's burden, ominous hordes of swarthy immigrants in the northern cities, corrupting the bygone simplicity of municipal government and civic life—these things could contribute to, and combine very easily with, the nationwide surge for civil regeneration. In *The Passing of the Great Race* Madison Grant, an old-stock New Yorker and amateur anthropologist, warned that Nordic excellence was being smothered beneath the faster-spawning Mediterranean and eastern European masses. The response to these and related horrors was a tremendous reassertion of Anglo-Saxon vigor in communities everywhere: the strenuous life, the old-time virtues, assaults on civil degeneration. Here too, as with the South, civic purity and racial purity were to a great extent interchangeable, and the southern case in all such matters had virtually ceased to be contested anywhere in the North. Side by side with the muckraking stories in *McClure's* might be found articles by Thomas Nelson Page, giving the "reasonable" version of Negro inferiority.[5]

So far as the writing of history was concerned, these things, together with the fact that Ulrich Phillips had established undisputed and superior claims on the level of scholarship, meant the triumph, North and South, of a view on slavery whose basic premise was racial inferiority. At no time in American history were southern race dogmas so widely accepted throughout the entire nation as in the early years of the twentieth century; and for at least two decades after Phillips left college this was the intellectual climate in which he worked. Phillips's example, moreover, meant the establishment of a school; the intellectual status which he had secured for the southern side of slavery was of untold value as a morale factor in the development of twentieth-century southern historical scholarship. Not only would a number of southern scholars, in special state studies on slavery, be sustained in their work by Phillips's genial view of the institution; southern historians in general could now reach with assurance for an authoritative position on slavery to bulwark the most southern of southern positions on almost any problem of nineteenth-century American history.

The very pervasiveness of Phillips's influence makes that influence virtually impossible to "trace." The coincidence of impressive scholarship and popular ideology gave Phillips's work a special authority for those who followed him, an authority quite noticeable in the state studies on slavery that appeared at intervals for many years after the publication of Phillips's masterpiece. This is not to say that the authors of these monographs were intellectual puppets of the master, for none of them could ever quite match the intensity of Phillips's own conviction of the slave system's essential humanity; this in itself made a great deal of difference. Their reservations, on the one hand, and the reassurance of Phillips's example, on the other, create a fascinating balance which varies this way and that, depending on the individual writer. Charles Sydnor, the most distinguished of the group, concedes in his *Slavery in Mississippi* that "being a slave was not for the every negro a dreadful lot" but lets his story end on a somber note:

> Generally, the chief difference between a slave and a free agricultural laborer lay outside the realm of food, clothing, shelter and work. The difference was the slave was ordered to do his work; his food and clothing were allowanced; his movements were restricted; his every act was watched; he was sometimes punished and he might be sold. How distasteful life was under these conditions depended on two very variable factors: the character of the masters and the desire for freedom in the hearts of the slaves.[6]

In Ralph Flanders's *Plantation Slavery in Georgia* the balance is reversed; Flanders found more cruelty and violence in the system than Phillips had, but his concluding comment is most Phillips-like:

> As a means of social control slavery during the ante-bellum period was invaluable; as a profitable industrial system it was ... profitable in proportion to the progressive spirit and ability of the individual planter; as a training school for the untutored savage it served to a large degree as a civilizing agency.[7]

The moral balance in the work of Phillips's successors, difficult enough to maintain on such a subject anyway and especially through changing times, is thus never quite so firm as the master's own. But the authority of the master's scholarship resolves many a doubt. Moreover, the specific categories of organization—work, food, clothing, shelter, care, police, profitability, and so on—were invariably the same as those Phillips had used, categories which he in turn had taken from Rhodes.[8]

Notes

1. Ulrich B. Phillips, *American Negro Slavery: A Survey of the Supply, Employment and Control of Negro Labor as Determined by the Plantation Regime* (New York: D. Appleton, 1918). Phillips began publishing articles and essays on the subject in 1903 and by 1918 had 28 of them to his credit, as well as having edited the first two volumes of the *Documentary History of American Industrial Society* ("Plantation and Frontier Documents," Vols. I and II [Cleveland: A.H. Clark, 1909]). See David M. Potter, Jr., "A Bibliography of the Printed Writings of Ulrich Bonnell Phillips," *Georgia Historical Quarterly*, XVIII (September, 1934), 270-82; also Everett E. Edwards, "A Bibliography of the Writings of Professor Ulrich Bonnell Phillips," *Agricultural History*, VIII (October, 1934), 196-218. There is an essay on Phillips's life and work by Wood Gray in William T. Hutchinson (ed.), *The Marcus W. Jernegan Essays in American Historiography* (Chicago: University of Chicago Press, 1937), 354-73.

2. *American Negro Slavery*, 514.

3. *Ibid.*, 343.

4. This thesis on the connection between Jim Crow and Progressivism has been developed by C. Vann Woodward. While the post-Civil War suppression of Negro rights did begin with the "Bourbon Restoration" of the 1870s, Professor Woodward emphasizes the not so widely appreciated fact that a new, systematic, and final phase of the Negro's relegation to second-class citizenship was not fully launched until the 1890s, precipitated by the Populist agitation of that decade and completed in a blaze of "reformist" fervor in the early 1900s. See particularly C. Vann Woodward, *The Strange Career of Jim Crow* (New York: Oxford University Press, 1955), 13-95. Varied aspects of the process are treated at greater length in the same author's *Origins of the New South, 1877-1913* (Baton Rouge: Louisiana State University Press, 1951), pp. 321-68.

5. Thomas Nelson Page, "The Negro: The South's Problem," *McClure's Magazine*, XXII (March, April, 1904), 548-54, 619-26; XXIII (May, 1904), 96-102. In the issue which carried the first of Page's three installments there was an article on corruption by Lincoln Steffens, "Enemies of the Republic"; the second installment was accompanied by a chapter of Ida Tarbell's "History of the Standard Oil Company"; and the third by "The Reign of Lawlessness," one of Ray Stannard Baker's exposes of conditions in the Colorado mining districts. These three months of 1904 in *McClure's* give a perfectly consistent index of the enlightened Progressive taste; each of these articles points to a particular form of moral degeneration that must be resisted through a combination of exposure and firm resolve.

6. Charles S. Sydnor, *Slavery in Mississippi* (New York: D. Appleton, 1933), 253.

7. Ralph B. Flanders, *Plantation Slavery in Georgia* (Chapel Hill: University of North Carolina Press, 1933), 299-300.

8. Phillips's work, representing as it did a major turning point in attitude on slavery and the ante-bellum way of life, had an impact which is as difficult to trace as that of Frederick Jackson Turner. His emphasis on the social and economic life of the plantation appears in early monographs such as V. Alton Moody, *Slavery on Louisiana Sugar Plantations (Louisiana Historical Quarterly* reprint, April, 1924) and

Rosser H. Taylor, *Slaveholding in North Carolina: An Economic View* (Chapel Hill: University of North Carolina Press, 1926), and unmistakably in the Flanders and Sydnor studies noted above. One might also include Charles S. Davis, *The Cotton Kingdom in Alabama* (Montgomery: Alabama State Department of Archives and History, 1939), and, with somewhat less assurance, James B. Sellers, *Slavery in Alabama* (University, Ala.: University of Alabama Press, 1950). The list of writers whose thinking was affected by Phillips could be extended indefinitely—to the point where it would begin to lose its meaning. It could include such diverse figures as Edward Channing and Avery Craven. Phillips would have been in excellent company with the "Twelve Southerners" of *I'll Take My Stand* (New York: Harper, 1930)—for instance, with the poet John Crowe Ransom, who in that symposium referred to slavery as "a feature monstrous enough in theory, but more often than not, humane in practice." Philip Newman, asking around in 1939 for opinions about the contributions and influence of Ulrich Phillips, wrote to the Georgia agricultural expert Fred Landon, who replied: "His general conclusions have not as yet been questioned and his influence is seen in the work of his former students and in the constant reference to his writings in the current productions of those working in the same field." See Philip Newman, "Ulrich Bonnell Phillips—the South's Foremost Historian," *Georgia Historical Quarterly*, XXV (September, 1941), 244-61. In short, when an entire attitude on slavery was finally challenged head-on by the revisionism of the 1940's it was just and proper that Ulrich Phillips should be the target. He, more than any other one historian, had been responsible for that attitude, and for the challenge to Rhodes which had kept the debate alive for so many years.

10

Introduction to
Life and Labor in the Old South

C. Vann Woodward

Ulrich Bonnell Phillips's *Life and Labor in the Old South*, first published in 1929, was announced as the first of three volumes on the history of the South that were to sum up a lifetime of work on the subject. It proved to be the only one of the projected series that the historian lived to complete, however, for he died in 1934 at the age of fifty-seven, three years after he moved from the University of Michigan to Yale. The completed volume nevertheless covered those aspects of his field of study—slavery, the plantation, agricultural history—to which Phillips had devoted most of his time since he began to publish in 1902. It may therefore be regarded as the ripest and fullest expression of his thought and scholarship.

Until recent years the work of Phillips was looked upon as the most authoritative treatment of one of the most controversial subjects in American history. Lately, however, much of his writing—particularly that on slavery—has been called into question and subjected to criticism. There are special reasons for this criticism, as we shall see. But it should be noted that it is only part of a general wave of criticism directed at that previous generation of historians, the so-called Progressive generation, of which Phillips was a younger member. They included Frederick Jackson Turner, Charles A. Beard, Carl Becker, and Vernon Louis Parrington, each of whom has been likewise subjected to critical reassessment and fallen into disfavor.

The reasons for Phillips's fall in current favor are clear enough. Born in Georgia in 1877, he grew up in a South dedicated to reviving in a new form the tradition of dependency and subordination the ante-bellum regime had shaped for the Negro. Defense of the new regime was built on a defense of the old, and both rested on the assumption of an inherent inferiority of the Negro race. Phillips fully cherished the values of both the new and old regimes and shared their racial assumptions without imbibing the racial bitterness and malice growing up around him. His attitude was a paternalistic and indulgent affection toward what he regarded as a childlike and irresponsible people with many endearing traits. These attitudes and values were implicit—and often explicit—in what he wrote on the Old South.

Phillips brought a prodigious and unprecedented amount of research in plantation records to the writing of his big monograph *American Negro Slavery* (1918) and more still to his *Life and Labor in the Old South*. Only thus, he declared, could one "get away from the stereotypes." The "stereotypes" he attacked were those that pictured the old regime as one of unmitigated cruelty, baseness, and inhumanity. He could not accept that picture. In fact, he wrote, those who had "known the considerate and cordial, courteous and charming men and women, white and black, which that picturesque life in its best phases produced" would find it "impossible to agree that its basis and its operation were wholly evil." Admitting that there had been "injustice, oppression, brutality and heartburning" in this as in all systems, he emphasized evidence of kindliness, contentment, and "mutual loyalty." Slavery was, on the whole, "a curious blend... of tyranny and benevolence, of antipathy and affection." And plantations were "the best schools yet invented for the mass training... of backward people."

It was no paradox that northern progressives took Phillips to their heart and found his picture of the South acceptable and congenial. Racism was an ingredient of Progressivism and wholly compatible with its brand of reform. That was the generation that took up the white man's burden, acquired an overseas empire of colored people, disfranchised the Negro, preached Nordic supremacy, and deplored and despised the immigrant. Under these circumstances and moods it was easy to conciliate the South, and opposition to its views virtually disappeared.

The contrast between circumstance and mood of that generation and the present one is too striking to require comment. Criticism of Phillips since World War II reflects many of these changes. The most obvious target was the historian's racial assumptions, now no longer tenable. The mainspring of criticism was moral rather than scientific, however, and originated in the new egalitarian demand for Negro rights. On the side of scholarship Phillips was criticized for drawing his evidence too much from large plantations and neglecting smaller slaveholders; for underestimating the profit of slaveholders; for overlooking evidence unfavorable to slaveholders; for blindness to miscegenation, slave breeding, mistreatment, abuse, and cruelty; for mistaking the slave's mask of contentment of happiness for real sentiments; and for playing down evidence of slave discontent and rebelliousness.

The re-evaluation of the work of the previous generation is inevitable and essential to the health of each successive generation of historians. American historians, like American politicians, however, are addicted to a tradition of rather savage abruptness and finality in their treatment of outmoded members of their respective guilds. Once he falls into disfavor the rejected member tends to be cast out of the club completely, unread, unattended, unmourned. His opinion is unsought and his experience and wisdom are disregarded. No comfortable back bench or seat in the House of Lords receives the politician and no comparable office awaits the historian. The books of the latter, worn with constant use, suddenly begin to collect dust on their shelves and disappear from required reading lists. Professors refer to them only to introduce their critics and successors, and students grow up unacquainted with the books that nourished their masters. The result for politics and scholarship alike is an uncivil lack of continuity and a rather halting and jerky flow of ideas.

Granting the validity of much of the criticism of Phillips and the seriousness of it all, what remains to be said for reading him today? As much at least, one might say, as there is to be said for reading a friendly account of the Old Regime in France or the Old Regime in Russia—assuming one of equivalent learning, grace, and elegance could be found. And this quite irrespective of one's hostility or friendliness to the particular old regime involved. Such histories as *Life and Labor* are worth reading, even at the level of polemics, and even its severest critics would concede that the book sustains a higher level than that. For another thing, much of what Phillips wrote has not been superseded or seriously challenged and remains indispensable.

In the Preface that follows this Introduction, Phillips mentions "sundry changes of emphasis and revisions of judgment" that had occurred in his thinking over the previous decade. One clear evidence of change is the degree to which the theme of racial inferiority had been subdued or eliminated. Had Phillips lived out his productive years he might well have revised his views further. "More years of research and reflection would no doubt bring further modification," he wrote. Every line he wrote, he said, was "written with a consciousness that his impressions are imperfect and his conclusions open to challenge." The modern reader would do well to keep in mind that the gulf between him and Phillips is not necessarily one of intelligence or charity or sophistication, but one of time. And if one cannot bridge that gulf he is cut off from a great many worthies who are not his contemporaries.

11

Race and Class in Southern History: An Appraisal of the Work of Ulrich Bonnell Phillips

Eugene D. Genovese

During the last few decades the reputation of Ulrich Bonnell Phillips has swung from an extreme positive to a decided negative. At present he is probably read apologetically and uneasily in much of the South and read not at all in much of the North. The charges are familiar: Phillips was a racist; he concerned himself with the upper classes; he held a nostalgic, latter-day proslavery view of southern history, and of course, unlike the rest of us, he was biased. I would suggest, nonetheless, that his work, taken as a whole, remains the best and most subtle introduction to southern history and especially to the problems posed by race and class, and that his social viewpoint was neither nostalgic, nor reactionary, nor unreconstructed, but was cautiously forward-looking, humanely conservative, and deeply committed to social and racial justice.

One of the earliest and most persistent comments on Phillips's work has described it as being largely free of generalization. Apart from his primitive statements about Negro traits, which were mere assertions, and his interpretative essays on the origins of the secession crisis, he deliberately shied away from drawing conclusions. As he observed in his own special manner, "A lover may generalize his lady, to be startled by her individualization after marriage."[1] Yet, he did generalize about method and content and in so doing provided us with a rich harvest of insights into the history and nature of class rule in the South, as well as into the history and nature of the race problem. In the accents of Frederick Jackson Turner, to whose influence he paid high tribute, Phillips interpreted the history of the Old South as the product of frontier and plantation, which together "shaped the general order of life without serious rival."[2] On a more general plane he asserted in the accents of a historical materialism with which much of Turner's work, like so much of his own, is compatible:

If made inclusive enough, the study of industrial society may touch all phases of human life; but its concern is, primarily, with the grouping and activity of the people as organized in society for the purpose of producing material goods, and secondarily, with the reflex influence of the work and work-grouping upon life, upon philosophy, and upon the internal and external relations of the society.[3]

Phillips opened *Life and Labor in the Old South* by discussing the weather and attributing to it that set of human responses which produced the plantation, staple crops, slavery, regional controversy, and the care question. He carefully avoided treating the plantation regime as a uniform entity but did not shrink from describing its essence as "the matter-of-course habituation of all the personnel to responsible and responsive adjustments between masters and men of the two races."[4]

For him, the Negro constituted an essential element in "the distinctive Southern pattern of life." The regime, he observed in one of his sensitive though infrequent passages on miscegenation, facilitated concubinage "not merely by making black women subject to white men's wills but by promoting intimacy and weakening racial antipathy."[5] Slavery, he conceded, emerged as a system of crass exploitation. "No prophet in early times could have told that kindliness would grow as a flow from a soil so foul, that slaves would come to be cherished not only as property of high value but as loving if lowly friends."[6] Perhaps his saddest failure, which flowed directly from his racist assumptions and sensibilities, was his refusal to develop his most pregnant insight—that the plantation produced a community in which the lives of master and slave became inextricably blended.

Professor Frank Tannenbaum has taken Phillips severely to task for failing to appreciate, in the manner of Gilbert Freyre, that plantation slavery bound master and slave together and made of them a single people with a shared culture to which they both contributed. Tannenbaum's criticism is fully justified, and yet Phillips repeatedly showed his awareness of this process so long as he could discuss it in general terms; only when he had to face its specific implications did his white supremacist sensibilities command a retreat.[7] Thus, he could write of tasks he himself could never even try to accomplish:

"The Negro in American civilization" may some day be the theme of an epic whether in verse or prose. It will involve African folkways and American vestiges thereof, gang labor and slave discipline, abolition chaos and latter-day repression, concubinage, quadroons, and "passing for white," rural isolation and urban congestion, dialects and manners, cast and caste within caste, songs and prayers, sermons and schisms—the nonchalance and bewilderment, the very human hopes and fears, the protests and acquiescence of a somewhat peculiar people through cataclysmic changes in a very complex land.[8]

For Phillips, the nonplantation whites, too, felt the plantation influence in countless, decisive ways. It is not true, as is so often charged, that Phillips ignored the lower and middle-class whites, much less that he showed them no sympathy or understanding.[9] His early work on Georgia politics and on the southeastern transportation system demonstrated considerable awareness and sympathy. If he slighted these classes in his later, more mature work, it was because he correctly saw the plantation regime as having penetrated every part of southern life and consciousness and as having directly commanded much of what it penetrated. The Negro, who never long slipped from his mind, provided an integral part of the regime. For the humbler white men of the black belt and the mountains, he insisted that their economic life, which he saw as of primary importance for their cultural and political life, was ultimately shaped and limited by the plantation regime. Astride society as a whole stood the slaveholders and especially the planters. If he centered his attention on them, it was not so much because they had his heart, although they did, as because they exercised hegemony and, to a remarkable degree, molded the lives of all. For this reason among others, he insisted that the essential features and tendencies of southern society could be most readily grasped through the study of plantation regime where it was most mature.[10]

Phillips began and ended with race relations, which he saw as extruding particular class formations. He affirmed the economic impulse to slavery and to the plantation system, which he considered prior to slavery, but he insisted that, upon establishment of both, social rather than economic considerations prevailed. Specifically, the presence of large numbers of Africans, whom he regarded as primitive, if not savage, required the maintenance of a regime capable of disciplining them and of preserving social order. The plantation proved the best vehicle; slavery served only as the necessary basis for the plantation regime in its early phases. For Phillips, "a realization of the race problem as a persistent and often paramount factor in shaping political orientation is the beginning of wisdom in any general study of the South."[11] The determination of the southern whites to preserve white supremacy constitutes, in this sense, the central theme of southern history and, indeed defines a southerner.[12] Yet, so much of Phillips's work concerns class structure and especially the quality and decisive influence of the ruling class that Professor Stephenson has plausibly, if not altogether convincingly, described him as a historian of aristocracy and only incidentally of slavery.[13]

Phillips opened himself to this criticism by denying that slavery provided the basis of southern identity. A review of his argument reveals it to be surprisingly weak. He began by noting that during the eighteenth century slavery had legal sanction everywhere on the continent but during the twentieth century nowhere. He concluded by maintaining that if slavery, rather than race, had shaped the South, we could not account for the loyalty of the nonslaveholders to the regime. It is, of course, true that slavery was general in the eighteenth century and has been absent in the twentieth, but this observation tells us nothing. Slavery in the North was an incidental arrangement, tangential to society and the economy; slavery in the South was the heart of the regime. The difference lay precisely in the notion of class that repeatedly breaks through Phillips's historical writing, though it is obscured in his specifically theoretical statements. A slave society, not merely slavery, emerged in the South, and it emerged on the basis of the formation of a dominant slaveholding class, which was nowhere to be found in the North, despite considerable occasional slave ownership. Phillips described that class and its society in almost everything he wrote but did not face its ultimate implications.

The loyalty of the nonslaveholders to the regime presents an exceptionally difficult problem of false consciousness within class hegemony. That race played a great role in shaping such loyalty, none would deny, but there were many other forces at work. Phillips, in any case, made the careless error of assuming that lack of class consciousness proves lack of class antagonism, but the advocates of a class view of history and of the doctrine of class struggle are not so naive as to equate consciousness with interests. Phillips simply failed to meet the argument.

Despite this unimpressive excursion he did have something to say on the problem of false consciousness: "For reasons common in the world at large, the Southern whites were not to be divided into sharply antagonistic classes.... Habitat grouping, it is clear, had a cementing force great enough to overcome the cleaving tendency of economic stratification."[14] In this passage he perceived the difference between objective antagonism and subjective response but chose, as always, to emphasize community cohesion and therefore historical continuity, much as he did when he recognized the injustices to and the frustrated aspirations of the slaves, but chose to emphasize their submission. Implicit here is not so much racism nor even upper-class snobbery (although elements of both are present) as a profoundly conservative notion of social change. We shall return to this problem further along. For the moment we may observe that, notwithstanding Phillips's obsession with the race question, he repeatedly returned to the dimension of class. Thus, after referring to the prevalence of slavery among the Greeks and Romans, he added, "In later ages the peoples and powers of Europe... employed other means of maintaining a safely stratified social order."[15]

The duality in Phillips's thought between a primary concern for racial hegemony and the persistent reassertion of a concern for class hegemony does not necessarily imply contradiction but does raise strong suspicions. If slavery, whether or not seen primarily as a means of racial control, threw up a ruling class of the power Phillips described, then the relationship between class and racial hegemony needs to be firmly established; yet, he repeatedly shied away from this confrontation and thereby introduced considerable ambiguity into his work. This ambiguity may be overcome by recapitulating the main line of his analysis with one major alteration: whereas he consistently held the class question to be subsidiary to the race question, we may view the race question as the prevailing social form of the class question. If this procedure alters Phillips's intent, it simultaneously rescues his work from insoluble logical and empirical difficulties without doing violence to its spirit.

From this point of view, the entire body of Phillips's work emerges as the history and sociology of the slaveholding class and of the regime to which it gave rise. In his remarkable early essays—the more remarkable because he was still in his twenties—he laid down several lifelong themes: that the plantation system was a capitalistic enterprise, in the sense of being highly competitive, heavily capitalized, and oriented toward commodity production; that it nonetheless took on the primary characteristics of a paternalistic community; and that it suffered from severe economic disadvantages such as overcapitalization of labor and tendency toward unprofitability.[16] More to the point, he drew attention to "the tendency of slavery as a system of essentially capitalistic industry to concentrate wealth, such as there was, within the hands of a single economic class and within certain distinctive geographic areas."[17] Virtually all of Phillips's economic writings focused on the origins and growth of this class and its regime. Thus, in his splendid book, *A History of Transportation in the Eastern Cotton Belt to 1860*, he combined careful economic and political analysis with remarkable social insight:

> In the larger aspect, that [railroad] system was a source of weakness and failure. Transportation is not an end in itself, but when rightly used, is a means to the end of increasing wealth, developing resources, and strengthening society. And in the South these greater purposes were not accomplished. The building of railroads led to little else but the extension and the intensifying of the plantation system and the increase in the staple output. Specialization and commerce were extended, when just the opposite development, towards diversification of products and economic self-sufficiency, was the real need.[18]

He skillfully demonstrated that the stakes included much more than a dangerously one-sided economic growth and that the economic process solidified an entire social system, which reacted to strengthen the economic one-sidedness and which carried with it grave political implications. The slaveholding class and the regime it spawned traveled those rails and subdued everything in their path. The experience of the Virginia Piedmont was recapitulated in the cotton belt. A social, not merely an economic system conquered the South, a system of class rule, not merely of economic inequality or racial control.[19]

Throughout his life Phillips offered descriptions of and rendered judgments on the quality of the slaveholders and their interaction with other social classes. A typical plantation owner, in his view, had "the faculty of unruffled response to the multitudinous calls of slaves upon the attention and the tolerance of slack service."[20] The slaveholders, he insisted, relished and exalted their calling, and this exaltation fell to the advantage of the slaves, for it reflected a "genuine self-respect, of which an essential ingredient is respect for others."[21]

Phillips attributed these sterling qualities of the ruling class to the plantation, rather than to slavery. Contrary to what even some of his fairest and most professionally scrupulous critics have suggested, he found slavery distasteful; he defended it only as a means of introducing the Negro into the plantation culture but damned it as an increasingly dubious institution once the breaking-in process had been completed. He praised it as a civilizing school but condemned it for failing to produce graduates; he noted with sorrow the unwillingness to provide for the development of the talents of the intelligent and the eager among the slaves; he expressed disgust at the refusal to protect black women against sexual exploitation by masters and overseers; and he commented frequently on the stultifying effects of slavery on economic growth and intellectual freedom.[22] Those southern qualities which he admired he attributed to the plantation way of life, to which slavery was, in his opinion, incidental. The plantation he viewed as a homestead, the spirit of which was neighborliness.

When we reconsider those qualities of personality which he singled out for praise, the emphasis on the plantation rather than on slavery appears more than dubious. The plantation "made for strength of character and readiness to meet emergencies, for patience and tact, for large-mindedness, gentility and self-control."[23] These and other qualities may be attributed to the plantation only in the sense that the plantation housed a series of human relationships. The personal qualities engendered by the system arose from the manner in which men faced men, specifically the manner in which masters faced slaves. When Phillips separated the house from its inhabitants, he offered, implicitly and on occasion explicitly, a vision of other inhabitants. He spoke of plantations with free labor, but it never took him long to get to the point, which was a frank admission of dependent status within a system of paternalistic control. If we use as our model Hegel's extraordinary analysis of the way in which one man comes to self-consciousness through confrontation with a dependent other, then slavery represents the perfect case of the general phenomenon of lordship and bondage. Phenomenologically, Phillips's alternative to slavery appears as an imperfect variation, capable of recapitulating some or perhaps most of the effects of the old regime. Very well. But historically, it was another matter. The plantation and slavery grew up together and "the plantation product of men" of which Phillips spoke so glowingly was, in fact, the slaveholding product of men. Even the postwar plantation largely carried on a regional tradition and preserved a revered sensibility rather than raising an old product on a new soil. When Phillips lamented the threat to the old values and called for their restoration, he refused to place his trust wholly in a restored plantation system: he stressed instead "the impress of the old regime" and hoped that "those who cherish its memory will zealously propagate the qualities it fostered...."[24]

In any case, there can be no dispute over his admiration for the men the regime produced. On the strength of his estimate of their qualities, he penned his striking dedication to *A History of Transportation in the Eastern Cotton Belt*, the opening lines of which read: "To the Dominant Class of the South, who in the piping ante-bellum time schooled multitudes, white and black, to the acceptance of higher standards...."

Phillips's notion of the central theme of white supremacy came most nearly to grief in his discussion of the secession crisis. From the political writings on Georgia and South Carolina with which he began his career, to the interpretive lectures on southern political history with which he closed it, he displayed little patience with the state-rights ideology and insisted that fundamental social questions lay beneath it. In "The Central Theme of Southern History" and *The Course of the South to Secession*, which included that essay, he argued for the primacy of the race question, but his evidence at best raises other possibilities and at worst is irrelevant to his thesis. Phillips quoted Robert Barnwell Rhett and Elijah F. Nuttall to illustrate his point, but their remarks offer questionable support. "A people owning slaves," said Rhett in 1833, "are mad or worse than mad, who do not hold their destinies in their own hands."[25] In 1849, Nuttall replied to Cassius M. Clay by saying: "Kentucky, sir, will be ready for emancipation when she is ready to cut loose all her feelings for the South... then she will be ready to unite with our northern friends, and not until then."[26] These statements are not incompatible with a racial interpretation, but, if anything, they suggest an awareness of a separate southern civilization.

Phillips's resistance to such an interpretation plunged him deep into trouble, as a review of the evidence he arrays will show. He cited an 1822 pamphlet by Edwin C. Holland as evidence of a concern for racial hegemony. The pamphlet urged the expulsion of the free blacks but not of the free mulattoes, "for he said that many of the mulattoes were slaveholders themselves and watchful of slaveholding interests."[27] If this is not a class view, I cannot imagine what would qualify. With noticeable discomfiture Phillips passed rapidly over the work of men like Henry Hughes and George Fitzhugh and finally offered us two clear, well-developed contemporary statements of the sectional question as a race question. The first was by the English-born scientist, Thomas Ewbank, the second by the lawyer and absentee slaveowner, Sidney G. Fisher. Phillips noted, apparently without appreciating the irony, that both men lived in the North. Then he turned to Edward A. Pollard's *The Lost Cause Regained,* which appeared during 1868. In it, Pollard castigated southerners for having defended slavery *per se* instead of having taken a stand on the race question. One wonders what on earth Phillips thought Pollard could or should have said in 1868. It was surely too late to say anything else.

Finally, Phillips dogmatically asserted that the argument for southern rights was nothing more than the demand that the South be left alone to handle the race problem. This view is unworthy of his splendid assessment of the slaveholders and of the plantation's powerful effect on human personality. If, as he never tired of reiterating, the plantation system conditioned all of southern life, and if the slaveholders were its ultimate product, then surely the demand for local and regional autonomy must be understood as the political expression of lordship and as the projection of the plantation ethos into the wider social arena.

The regional divergence on the race question did not, in Phillips's view, have to end in secession and war. Although in his early work he admitted the possibility that the conflict might have been irrepressible,[28] he increasingly spoke of the tragedy of political blundering and sectional insensitivity.[29] Southerners might have conceded the injustices of slavery and the need for a better system of racial control, he argued, had not the abolition agitation pushed them into intellectual and political rigidity.[30] All this is standard fare, which is objectionable not because it is standard, nor because it is intrinsically unworthy of respect, but because it fits so poorly into Phillips's thought.

He asserted that abolition blinded southerners to their own best interests and thereby kept them from disestablishing slavery voluntarily.[31] He held, in general, that the slave system tended toward unprofitability, had reached the limits of expansion, and would have yielded to a system of plantation wage-labor. Having told us, in virtually all his writings, that the southern regime produced men of a special, high-spirited type, he proceeded to insist that their ultimate decisions would flow from economic calculation of the crassest sort. The most serious difficulty with this view is that it does violence to the manner of men we have been offered so lovingly, and that this violence is the worse for its being predicated on a mechanical economic process.

It was one thing for Phillips to insist that the slave economy manifested a tendency toward unprofitability, however defined; it was another for him to assume that the economy was approaching zero profitability. The assumption is palpably absurd and without a hint of empirical verification. If, on the other hand, he meant only to imply that the average rate of profit was falling below the interest rate and that the slaveholders would accordingly wish to switch to free labor, then he would have fallen into another calamitous difficulty. The whole burden of his life's work rejected the idea that the planter could be understood as economic man and affirmed the roles of patriarchal ideology and the achievement of status through slaveownership. The very definition of a planter used by Phillips turned primarily on slaveownership and only incidentally on landownership. Phillips could not have argued that masters bought and sold slaves, when it was economically irrational to do so, in order to do their part in controlling race relations. There are limits to altruism beyond which even the flower of the ruling class of South Carolina could not be expected to go. The only explanation for such behavior, as Phillips repeatedly demonstrated in *American Negro Slavery* and *Life and Labor in the Old South,* is to be found in an ideology of status through the extension of the patriarchal plantation family and its attendant ownership of human labor. Here, as almost everywhere, Phillips's reiteration of the theme of racial hegemony, attractive, enticing and deceptively simple as it was, proved hopelessly encased in a pyramid of dubious assumptions and less useful for historical analysis than would appear at first glance.[32] His uneasiness may be gleaned from his remarks on the fire-eaters, whom he could and often did call reckless extremists but whom he had to accept as "products of plantation life, exalting the system which had bred them... self-chosen guardians of rural gentility... as conservative as any men have ever been."[33]

Phillips's revisionist view of secession flowed from a tenacious commitment to a racial interpretation of southern society and from a faith in history as a process of resolving resolvable antagonisms. The northerners failed to understand the race question because they lacked enough experience with it. Their hostility caused southerners to turn from needed reforms to reactionary intransigence. Yet, Phillips himself demonstrated that southerners gradually did reform their slave practices during late antebellum times. The steady improvement in the conditions of slave life and the steady growth of paternalistic feeling constituted two of the main themes of his magnificent social histories. It was, to say the least, arbitrary of him to decide that abolition agitation barred those reforms which might have compromised the sectional crisis but spurred, or at least did not inhibit, those which intensified it. The history of reform predated and postdated Garrison's onslaught and had one outstanding feature: it displayed a growing tendency to confirm slavery as the Negro's natural and permanent state while making him more comfortable within it. Phillips's racial interpretation offers few clues to this process, but the class analysis implicit in his work offers a solution. This process may properly be understood as part of an ascent by the slaveholders to self-consciousness and to the formation of a slaveholders' world view. George Fitzhugh, not the postwar Edward A. Pollard, presented its logical outcome. Phillips described the slaveholders as a very special kind of men, which they certainly were, and he attributed to them qualities which were anything but bourgeois. If he failed to draw the necessary conclusions from his extraordinary lifetime efforts, we are under no compulsion to follow suit.

To criticize in this way Phillips's notion of the central theme of white supremacy is not to reject it; the thesis contains too much painstaking observation, sound reflection, and good, hard sense for that. The notion of white supremacy as the prime mover of southern history, independent of and superior to all class struggles, breaks down at many points, but its modification into the persistent form of those struggles retains great vitality. All societies are rent by class antagonisms, the depth and violence of which may vary enormously, but southern society has, to a remarkable degree, disciplined its potentially explosive antagonisms in an unusual and, in some respects, unique way. The history of race relations in the South, as Phillips so clearly saw, has been the history of that process.

Phillips's interpretation of the Old South was informed by his vision of a New South in a Progressive America. The most serious error committed by his detractors has been their oft-repeated and widely accepted charge that he looked back nostalgically to a romantic age of moonlight and magnolias. On the contrary, as C. Vann Woodward has pointed out, Phillips's racial attitudes reflected much of the ideology of the Progressive era.[34] This insight might properly be extended to include the whole range of Phillips's social thought. He did not pine away over the loss of the golden age of slavery, much less desire in the slightest its restoration. Phillips accepted without hesitation the industrial-commercial civilization of the United States and sought actively, as a journalistic reformer as well as a historian, to ease the South toward it.

Phillips harshly criticized the Bourbon-inspired agricultural regime of the New South and strongly urged the restoration of the patriarchal plantation. He decried the tendency toward small holdings and hoped it could be reversed. The small farm, especially when worked by tenants and sharecroppers, could only foster economic and cultural backwardness and mediocrity. A restored plantation system, with resident owners and wage-workers, would provide the vehicle for economic rationality and a proper balance between staple-crop production and diversification. He urged a state tax on cotton to drive out marginal producers and the application of the proceeds to encourage industrial and agricultural development.[35]

His social goals may be gleaned from a passage written in 1903, in which he combined an acquiescence in the modern capitalist order with a demand for the preservation and extension of some of the older values: "Any modern system must take a tone from the active, pushing world of today; but in essentials the plantation of old could again look with hope to the system which produced the fine type of Southern gentleman of the old regime."[36] He attacked the impersonality of the modern industrial system and lamented the loss of individual and family interest in the fate of working classes.[37] In a brief but revealing review-essay on *I'll Take My*

Stand, the Mitchells' *Industrial Revolution in the South,* and Odum's *American Epoch,* he noted the persistence of conflict and peacemaking in the "social process" and pitted the Agrarians against the Yankeefying Mitchells. Between the demands of the past and those of the present he yielded to the latter, but his love and flights of lyrical rapture went to those who would preserve from the past what could safely be preserved.[38]

Phillips particularly criticized the agricultural regime of the New South for gravely weakening the relationship between white and Negro. Absentee owners and tenant or sharecropping arrangements divided the races to the cost of both.[39] He drew an analogy between the old plantation and the settlement house, comparing the master and mistress to social workers whose duty was to guide their Negroes toward full participation in American life.[40] A new plantation regime on a free-labor basis would, he argued, train and educate the great mass of the blacks, who must still be subject to racial control. Absentee owners would not do: nothing short of the restoration of a resident planter class and especially the restoration of the prestige and influence of the plantation mistress would do.[41] The patriarchal feature was decisive:

> The average negro has many of the characteristics of a child.... The presence of the planter and his wife and children and his neighbors is required for example and precept among the negroes. Factory methods and purely business relations will not serve; the tie of personal sympathy and affection is essential to the successful working of the system.

The old plantation had molded whites and blacks into one community, and its passing had opened the way for racial antipathy and for a segregation which he deplored.[42]

A new plantation regime would avoid the worst evils of the old. On the economic level it would escape dependence on a one-crop system and would not suffer from the overcapitalization of labor. On the social level it would avoid the most depressing and unjust feature of slavery by providing for the graduation of apt pupils to supervisory positions as well as to industrial and other tasks. In this way the southern ruling class could complete its historic task of bringing the Negro into our national life without the risk of social disorder.[43]

It would not be difficult to criticize this vision on either economic or social grounds. Phillips himself observed, for example, that if the plantation integrated the Negro with the most culturally advanced and socially responsible whites, it simultaneously separated him from the great mass of whites. He did not seem to appreciate that this segregation provided social cohesion under the slave regime only because of the special power of the slaveholders over society, but that it invited social upheaval and terror under a regime from which this special power was removed. The gradual promotion of apt Negroes into such a society would have been, and indeed has been, fraught with all the ingredients of disorder and hatred. Apart from many other problems, it never seems to have occurred to Phillips that an oppressed class or race is not likely to agree to be guided forever by a benevolent paternalism. Those apt Negroes of his were supposed to be grateful for their new opportunities and to help guide their more stupid brethren. What ingrates they have turned out to be! Granted that we have the wisdom of hindsight, Phillips's inability to realize that many of them would use their acquired privileges and culture to lead their people in a more rapid, if disorderly, advance, stemmed from his conservative ideology, not from his historical studies.[44]

The significance of Phillips's vision lies not in the value of his specific political or economic proposals, for he had little influence in those spheres, but in the light it sheds on his historical sensibility. His sympathetic and appreciative portrayal of the plantation regime of the Old South—a portrayal I think largely accurate—must be understood not as a defence of slavery but as an appeal for the incorporation of the more humane and rational values of pre-bourgeois culture into modern industrial life. Those who argue that the United States lacks a conservative tradition stumble badly when they consider the Old South and its heritage. Of course, if one is willing to see only the competitive, capitalistic side of the slave regime, then one is left free to declare it a tortured, guilt-ridden, hypocritical child of bourgeois liberalism and to let it go at that. If, on the other hand, one follows Phillips into an appreciation of the patriarchal and paternalist side of the regime, then one must necessarily follow him into an appreciation of the legitimacy of the world view it engendered. How ironical, therefore, that Phillips should have been betrayed by his own effort—weak and uncertain as that effort was—to prove the Old South a capitalist society. Yet, he had to make it, for how else could he have established an ideological rationale for his defense of its values in the world in which he lived? His effort suggests that he was concerned not with defending the Old South but with reforming the New and with guiding it safely toward a respect for conservative values and racial justice. It suggests also the dilemma of the conservative critics of liberal society, who would restore the world view of a dead world without even the wish to bring the world itself back to life.[45]

The particular difficulty with Phillips's humane vision was that those values and that halting and contradictory start toward racial justice were products not of the plantation *per se* but of the master-slave relationship and were specifically the contribution of the slaveholding class. Every element of paternalism and of the patriarchal ethos necessary to make Phillips's modern plantation function properly would have undercut economic rationality. Many postbellum planters may have tried, even with some local successes, to preserve the older way of life, but for the South as a whole, they were fighting a losing battle. And just where Phillips expected to find enough good bourgeois willing to live down on the farm just to take care of the darkies is beyond my powers of imagination. The old world died with the Confederacy, and if its values and manners have lingered on, they have done so with diminishing force. Phillips, by 1918 at least, began to face this fact and to appeal to ideals and sentiments rather than for the creation of a new material basis in a restored plantation:

> The plantation is largely a thing of the past, and yet it is of the present. We do not live in the past, but the past lives in us. Every man and woman is the product of his or her environment and of the environment of his or her forbears, for we are controlled by tradition. Our minds are the result of the experience of those who gave us birth and rearing; and this plantation regime of which we speak was a powerful influence in the lives of millions of men and women.[46]

This retreat into a fanciful idealism could not save him but might remind us of the extremity of the task facing those who would accept the world of the cash nexus and yet try to defend the ideals of social responsibility, legitimate authority, and a regime of liberating discipline. Toward the end of his sadly shortened life, while he prepared to meet an expected death with a dignity and manliness that would have done honor to most splendid representatives of the old ruling class he so deeply admired, he spoke less (or at least less surely) of the possibilities for a new plantation regime and more of the need to keep the spirit alive. He accepted the industrial order but would not quit the fight for the preservation of something of the older ethos.

We may today reread his work with profit and pleasure for its understanding of slavery as a social system; for its appreciation of the plantation as a community of unlike men trying to live together decently; and for its brilliant descriptions of a proud and tough people who forged themselves into a ruling class and imposed their values as well as their will on society at large. We may consider that his notion of white supremacy as a central theme remains an extraordinary insight, even if it requires modification. And we may profit too from the profound critique of our national culture that informed his life's work. Living as we do amidst a worldwide civil war in which new heights of personal liberty are accompanied by the unspeakable degradation of millions of colored men throughout the world and in which the revolutionary alternative seems incapable of coming to fruition without the crucifixion of whole generations, we might well take heart from his example. He knew he had to make hard choices, and he made them. But he knew too that if much of the old were not preserved, nothing of the new would be worth the battle; that if much of the new were not accepted, nothing of the old could long be endured. Without tears, or pretense, or whining, he demonstrated how one could accept, while refusing to surrender to, that melancholy wisdom so trenchantly offered us by Santayana: "The necessity of rejecting and destroying some things that are beautiful is the deepest curse of existence."[47]

Notes

1. All references are to work by Phillips (unless another author is indicated), *Life and Labor in the Old South* (paperback ed.; Boston, 1964), viii. For a discussion of Phillips as being in the tradition of Ranke, see Sam E. Salem, "U.B. Phillips and the Scientific Tradition," *Georgia Historical Quarterly*, XLIV (June 1960), 172-185. See also Phillips's early claims to eschew historical imagination for "thorough scientific treatment," *Georgia and State Rights*, Annual Report of the American Historical Association for 1901 (Washington, 1902), II: 6.

2. Introduction to *Plantation and Frontier* (1649-1863), Vols. I and II of J.R. Commons, et al., *History of American Industrial Society* (10 vols.; Cleveland, 1909), I: 72.

3. *Ibid.*

4. *Life and Labor*, 304.

5. *Ibid.*, 138, 205.

6. *Ibid.*, 214.

7. Frank Tannenbaum, *Slave and Citizen: The Negro in the Americas* (New York, 1947). For an elaboration of this point, see my "Ulrich Bonnell Phillips & His Critics," Foreword to *American Negro Slavery* (paperback ed.; Baton Rouge, 1966).

8. "The Perennial Negro," review-essay, *Yale Review*, XXI (Autumn 1931), 202.

9. For this viewpoint in the context of a warm and generous critique, see Wendell Holmes Stephenson, "Ulrich B. Phillips, Historian of Aristocracy," *The South Lives in History: Southern Historians and Their Legacy* (Baton Rouge, 1955), 58-94, esp. 93.

10. "The Slave Labor Problem in the Charleston District," *Political Science Quarterly*, XXII (Sept. 1907), 416. How astonishing then that he should choose to study the African not in West Africa, which supplied most of our slaves, but in primitive east-central areas, which supplied few or none. He argued that he wanted to see the Negro in his natural state, where contact with whites had been minimal. It never occurred to him that those particular Africans had never approached the level of pre-European West Africa. See e.g., "Azandeland," *Yale Review*, XX (Winter 1931), 293-313.

11. "A Quest of the Common Man," review of J.T. Adams, *The Epic of America*, in *Yale Review*, XXI (Dec. 1931), 402-403.

12. "The Central Theme of Southern History," originally published in the *American Historical Review*, XXXIV (Oct. 1928), and added as a final chapter to *The Course of the South to Secession*, ed. E. Merton Coulter (paperback ed.; New York, 1964). All references to this article will be from the latter work.

13. Stephenson, *The South Lives in History*, 93.

14. *The Course of the South to Secession*, 155.

15. *Ibid.*, 83.

16. See especially "The Economic Cost of Slaveholding in the Cotton Belt," *Political Science Quarterly*, XX (June 1905), 257-275.

17. "The Origin and Growth of the Southern Black Belts," *American Historical Review*, XI (July 1906), 798.

18. *A History of Transportation in the Eastern Cotton Belt to 1860* (New York, 1908), 19-20.

19. *Ibid.*, 396; *Life and Labor*, 24-25, 110, 111, 148. For Phillips's assessment of the political side of this process, see his *Georgia and State Rights*, and *The Life of Robert Toombs* (New York, 1913), esp. 25-28; "The South Carolina Federalists," *American Historical Review*, XIV (April 1909), 529-540, esp. 531, and XIV (July 1909), 731-743; and *The Course of the South to Secession*.

20. "Plantations with Slave Labor and Free," *American Historical Review*, XXX (July 1925), 744.

21. *Ibid.*

22. See, e.g., "Racial Problems, Adjustments and Disturbances," *The South in the Building of the Nation*, IV: 240; "Conservatism and Progress in the Cotton Belt," *South Atlantic Quarterly*, III (Jan. 1904), 2.

23. "The Plantation Product of Men," *Proceedings of the 2nd Annual Session of the Georgia Historical Association* (Atlanta, 1918), 14-15.

24. *Ibid.*, 15.

25. *The Course of the South to Secession*, 133.

26. *Ibid.*, 110.

27. *Ibid.*, 102.

28. *Life of Robert Toombs*, 102.

29. Some of his strongest statements were made in lectures. For a discussion see Stephenson, *The South Lives in History*, 90.

30. *Life of Robert Toombs*, 51.

31. "Conservatism and Progress in the Cotton Belt," 8; "Plantations with Slave Labor and Free," 748.

32. Phillips criticized William E. Dodd for emphasizing the purely economic rather than social side of the economics of slavery, but whenever he discussed the question with an eye on the larger political issues, he interpreted "social" as racial. See *On the Economics of Slavery*, Annual Report of the American Historical Association for the Year 1912 (Washington, 1914), 151. In his less polemical efforts—i.e., his major writings on slavery—his notion of "social" comes close to the one I am defending here.

33. "Protagonists of Southern Independence," review-essay, *Yale Review*, XXII (March 1933), 643.

34. C. Vann Woodward, Introduction to *Life and Labor*.

35. "The Economics of the Plantation," *South Atlantic Quarterly*, II (July 1903), 231; "The Overproduction of Cotton and a Possible Remedy," *South Atlantic Quarterly*, IV (April 1905), 148-158.

36. "The Economics of the Plantation," 236.

37. "The Plantation Product of Men," 13; "Plantations with Slave Labor and Free," 745.

38. "Fifteen Vocal Southerners," *Yale Review*, XX (Spring 1931), 611-613.

39. "Plantations with Slave Labor and Free," 752.

40. "The Plantation Product of Men," 13.

41. "The Decadence of the Plantation System," *Annals of the American Academy of Political and Social Science*, XXXV (Jan. 1910), 40-41; "The Plantation as a Civilizing Factor," *Sewanee Review*, XII (July 1904), 266.

42. "The Economics of the Plantation," 232; "The Plantation as a Civilizing Factor," 266.

43. "The Decadence of the Plantation System," 38; "The Plantation as a Civilizing Factor," 266.

44. "Origin and Growth of the Southern Black Belts," 815.

45. I am indebted to Professor Warren I. Susman of Rutgers University for an opportunity to study his brilliant paper on the conservative tradition in America. The paper was presented to the first annual Socialist Scholars Conference (1965).

46. "The Plantation Product of Men," 12.

47. George Santayana, *Character and Opinion in the United States* (New York, 1920), 130.

IV

THE SCIENTIFIC HISTORIAN

Much of the historiographical significance and lasting value of U.B. Phillips's work lies in his methodological approach to research and writing. John Herbert Roper has stated that Phillips was the product of "two large intellectual dowries": just as Progressivism provided a ruling ideology that controlled the direction of his research, so scientism shaped the means by which he undertook his historical investigation. Objective conclusions drawn from and limited to primary source materials uncolored by sentimental or ideological preconceptions (and thus at odds with Progressivism) were the basic "scientific" standards laid down for history as a discipline. Its earliest proponents, Leopold von Ranke in Germany and Herbert Baxter Adams in the United States, instilled this rigorous new academic professionalism upon an entire generation of historians in the late nineteenth century. And it was through two of its most committed practitioners, John H. T. McPherson at the University of Georgia and William A. Dunning at Columbia University, that Phillips was introduced to and himself embraced scientism.

As much of this volume makes clear, among the earliest and most persistent aspects of Phillips criticism were questions regarding his objectivity and his choice and interpretation of evidence. The selections included in this section focus specifically on those means by which Phillips adhered—or failed to adhere—to the standards of this aspect of his training. Though in many respects dated and (as reflected by several other pieces in this anthology) debatable, Sam E. Salem's 1960 critique focused on the objectivity in Phillips's work within the context of "scientific" standards, and questioned whether either his southern sympathies or his racism negated any claim to objectivity in his treatment of plantation slavery. Both Ruben Kugler and W. K. Wood took issue with Phillips's use of evidence. The former pointed out specific instances in which he misread or misrepresented the sources that he used; the latter was more concerned with those sources Phillips could have and should have used, but did not. Wood's piece, incidentally, is one of few (and the only one included in this collection) that spotlighted a major, but often forgotten, Phillips work, his 1908 study of transportation in the antebellum South.

Though flawed, perhaps seriously, in his performance as a scientific historian, Phillips, by merely seeking out and utilizing the primary source materials he did, made a significant contribution to furthering scientism within the profession. As John David Smith reminded us in his examination of the early search for and preservation of plantation records for historical use, Phillips rendered an invaluable service to his fellow southern historians—both by the papers he salvaged and by the example he set in their application. Thus in this, as in other facets of his career, Phillips's record was a mixed one, and the question of whether or to what extent he deserves the label "scientific historian," like several of the other labels assigned him here, is one that critics continue and will continue to debate.

12

U. B. Phillips and the Scientific Tradition

Sam E. Salem

Ulrich Bonnell Phillips is a good example of an American historian who tried to write history in the scientific tradition of Leopold von Ranke. Like the German scholar, Phillips apparently believed that the primary duty of the historian was merely to present the facts, allowing the reader to draw his own conclusions. Therefore, in his main works, he shied away from stating opinions and almost completely avoided long-range interpretations. This practice led one reviewer of Phillips's *American Negro Slavery*[1] to remark that "the aim of the author seems to have been to present a great array of facts, and, with but few expressions of opinion, to permit the facts to speak for themselves."[2] Another reviewer described Phillips's *Life and Labor in the Old South*[3] as a ". . . number of detailed snapshots skillfully arranged."[4] And Wendell Holmes Stephenson, who recently has done a penetrating analysis of Phillips as a historian, commented: "He presented particulars; he seldom painted composites. Planters and plantations, overseers and slaves were specifically identified and individually considered.... The more he wrote, Phillips often said, the more reluctant he was to draw conclusions."[5] Perhaps in anticipation of such commentaries, Phillips prefaced his *Life and Labor* with this admission:

> When I read of Howard Odum's Black Ulysses, of DuBose Heyward's Porgy, of Stephen Benet's plantation mammy and her mistress, esteem for their creations is mingled with chagrin that my fancy is restricted by records. The characters portrayed by these writers are as true as the men and women who figure in my pages, though the breath in their nostrils is the ether in which the stars hold their course while mine breathed mundane atmosphere and have long since found rest in earth's bosom. But only when the wind is in a rare quarter would I give rein to Pegasus if I could. In the main I am content to delve rather than try to soar.[6]

Phillips's well-known preference for factual information *sans* broad generalizations and interpretations should be considered in the light of this astute qualifier by Professor Stephenson:

> Evidence, conclusions, and method were so inextricable in Phillips's writings that the reader cannot appreciate the relations of data to consequence without comprehending procedure.... Meager amalgam prevented systematic recital, albeit a parade of particulars in logical sequence stimulated a sense of solidarity and completeness.... Whether he realized it or not, interpretation was accomplished through an intelligible presentation of evidence which could not fail to elicit latent meaning.[7]

The fact that Phillips, perhaps unconsciously, arranged his "snapshots" so as to direct his readers along certain channels raises a question as to whether a historian can write history from the completely objective and detached point of view suggested by von Ranke. Can he relate exactly what happened without at least inadvertently revealing his own personal prejudices and social attitudes? And most important, can he prevent these preconceived ideas from influencing his over-all presentation?

It is the purpose here to examine how successful Phillips was in carrying out the tradition of von Ranke by subjecting the southern historian's writings to two basic questions. First, if he had any social attitudes or personal leanings, were they expressed in his writings? And to what extent? Second, if such ideas were present, did they have any effect in coloring his portrayal of the ante-bellum South? While no effort is made to pass any final judgment on the von Ranke theory of historiography, it may prove interesting to see how the idea worked out in the writings of one man.

As a preliminary, yet relevant, observation it will be remembered that most of Phillips's writings dealt with the ante-bellum South. In all he produced six books, four volumes of edited source materials, approximately 55 articles, and 50 book reviews.[8] His specialty, and the field in which he has had the greatest influence, was American Negro slavery and the plantation system. And his two greatest works in this area were *American Negro Slavery* and *Life and Labor in the Old South*. These observations take on more meaning when one realizes that Phillips himself was a Southerner "bawn and bred." A native of Georgia, he received his bachelor's and master's degrees from the leading university of that state. His mother was related to such illustrious sons of the Old South as William L. Yancey and Joseph E. Brown and was connected with the plantation gentry from the Old Dominion to the Gulf Coast.[9] Thus it would have been truly remarkable had Phillips been able to emerge from his deeply-rooted southern background without having developed certain pre-conceived and traditionally southern notions regarding the ante-bellum South, the Civil War, the plantation system, slavery, and the Negro; and it would have been even more remarkable had Phillips succeeded in being completely impartial in his research.

Another preliminary point is that various writers have differed on the question of social attitudes and personal prejudices in the writings of U. B. Phillips. Most of the contemporary reviewers, although they sometimes criticized him for it, gave this historian credit for being objective and did not see any significant evidence of such sectional feelings.[10] At least one exception, however, was W. E. B. Du Bois, prominent Negro scholar, who subjected Phillips's *American Negro Slavery* to a rather severe treatment. Among other things the reviewer charged that the book had a major premise, nowhere stated but always implicit— "that Negroes were not ordinary slaves nor indeed ordinary human beings."[11] After giving some examples as evidence, he concluded that the work was a "defense of American slavery—a defense of an institution which was at best a mistake and at worst a crime...."[12]

Later writers have also disagreed on this opinion. Wood Gray, who has presented a comprehensive study of Phillips, concluded that, although traces of southern self-consciousness would occasionally appear, "in general he was singularly free from this type of bias." Professor Gray commented that "even less did his social attitudes intrude upon his writings."[13] Richard Hofstadter, to the contrary, took an entirely different view which is more appropriately considered later in this paper.[14]

In the light of these preliminary observations, the first question can be considered: do Phillips's writings reveal any trace of pro-southern feelings or social attitudes? The answer, it appears, must be in the affirmative. True enough, these examples are hard to find—in fact, it is like looking for the proverbial needle in the haystack—but if one reads the historian's works with a scrutinous eye, traces of such attitudes soon begin to appear. Seldom are they obvious, usually they are unconsciously expressed, and often they are only vaguely implied.

Several examples of southern self-consciousness are discernible. Occasionally, when discussing some sectional differences, Phillips would lament that the North failed to understand some particular southern problem. For example, while discussing the tariff controversy of 1832 in his biography of Robert Toombs, Phillips commented: "Partly through wishful ignorance of Southern conditions and purposes, they [the Northerners] failed to see that the South had any actual or prospective grievances, and they considered every Southern measure of defense to be one of unprovoked aggression. They similarly refused to believe before secession was an accomplished fact that anything of earnest was contained in the Southern threats of disunion."[15]

It has been suggested that this sort of thing was particularly true of Phillips's earlier writings. But as late as 1928, only six years before his death and by this time a mature scholar, he made a similar remark. Having advanced the theory that the central theme of southern history has always been the determination of the white man to keep the Negro "in his place," Phillips added: "When California whites made extravagant demands in fear that her three per cent of Japanese might increase to four and capture the business of 'The Coast,' Congress responded as if it were the appendage of the state legislature. But white Southerners when facing problems real or fancied concerning the ten million Negroes in their midst can look to the federal authorities for no more at best than a tacit acquiescence in what their state governments may do."[16]

Although Phillips did at times express his southern self-consciousness in his writings, it would be a grave injustice to say that his works constitute a twentieth-century lament for the lost cause. The examples occur so infrequently and are so hidden, that they are scarcely noticeable unless one is expressly looking for them. The point is, however, that Phillips did not succeed in hiding his bias completely.

Traces of social attitudes towards the Negro also shine through after considerable searching. Examples of these fall into different types. First, there runs through most of Phillips's writings the general impression that the Negroes always were, and still are, just plain lazy. In one article, for example, he advanced the idea of re-adopting some phases of the old plantation system as the "best means of offsetting the ignorance and laziness of the Negro laborers."[17] In his consideration of southern transportation, he mentioned the "aimless shifting of habitation" to which the Negroes are so prone.[18] An article comparing slave and free labor contains the remark that "Negro slackness, along with poor soil, has been the chief cause of [southern] poverty."[19] And in *American Negro Slavery*, while listing prevailing traits of the Negro, Phillips gave special emphasis to the Negroes' "healthy repugnance toward overwork."[20] Largely as a result of this laziness, concluded Phillips, "the most fertile Southern areas, when once converted into black belts, tended, and still tend as strongly as ever, to be tilled only by inert Negroes, the majority of whom are as yet perhaps less efficient in freedom than their forbears were as slaves."[21]

With this idea as a basis for his thinking, Phillips went on to state that the Negro was irresponsible, incapable of taking care of himself, and, therefore, needful of the white man's guidance and supervision. Writing in 1903, he opined that the present system of renting or cropping in the South had not worked out well mainly because under it "the Negro is superintended in but a half-hearted way." "Furthermore," he added, "the average Negro cannot maintain himself as an independent farmer, because his ignorance, indolence, and instability prevent him from managing his own labor in an efficient way."[22] His solution to the problem was as follows:

Laying the question of slavery aside [something which Phillips was sometimes too readily willing to do] the presence of negroes in very large numbers in the population made some system like that of the old plantations essential for the peace and prosperity of the two races. And in view of the still greater proportion of negroes in the black belts of the South of today it appears that a modified form of the old plantation system is the best recourse for agricultural progress and racial sympathy in the present and the near future. It will draw that best element of the Southern whites back into the country, where they will afford the negroes a much needed guidance; it will give the negroes a renewed association with the best of the Southern people (always the negroes' best friends) and enable them to use their imitative faculties and make further progress in acquiring the white man's civilization.[23]

This idea of the Negro's so-called "imitative faculties" is also characteristic of Phillips's social attitudes.

Another theme appearing in Phillips's works is the implication that the Negro, because of his race, was naturally submissive and, therefore, suited for slavery. In his *Life and Labor* he mentioned that slavery was common in Africa, that the African slaveholders conspired with the white sailors to introduce their institution into America, and that "the acquiescence of the slaves themselves made the conspiracy successful."[24] In his *American Negro Slavery*, he argued that "the natural amenability of the blacks... had been a decisive factor in their initial enslavement," and added, "the reckoning which their captors and rulers made of this was on the whole well founded."[25] Earlier in the same work Phillips wrote, "the Negroes furnished inertly obeying minds and muscles."[26] The same idea appears when Phillips compared Roman and American slavery. Placing great stress on race, he declared that, unlike the Roman slaves, the American counterparts were "Negroes, who for the most part were by racial qualities submissive rather than defiant, light-hearted instead of gloomy, amiable and ingratiating instead of sullen, and whose very defects invited paternalism rather than repression."[27] Though willing to admit that occasionally a talented slave would appear, he added: "In the main the American Negroes ruled not even themselves. They were more or less contentedly slaves, with grievances from time to time but not ambition."[28] While describing a group of World War I American Negro soldiers, Phillips wrote: "The Negroes themselves show the same easy-going, amiable, serio-comic obedience and the same personal attachments to the white man...which distinguished their forbears.... It may be that the change of African nature by plantation slavery has been exaggerated. At any rate a generation of freedom has wrought less transformation in the bulk of the blacks than might casually be supposed."[29]

One supposition with which few present-day anthropologists and historians will agree is the suggestion that the black race is naturally inferior to the white. However, such unscientific racialism was common among many writers of Phillips's time. Is such an attitude present in his writings? In no one place does the historian specifically say so, but there are times when he quietly hints that such a thing might be possible. In a sense, his opinions that the Negro was naturally submissive, suited for slavery, and needful of the white man's supervision are suggestive of an opinion that the Negro is below the level of the Caucasian. More direct implications can be found. In one place he mentioned that the southerners feared that the Negroes were likely to prove subversive because of their inexperience and "racial unwisdom."[30] A better example is presented in an article published in 1907:

> Negro slave labor tended to be slothful, because the negroes were slaves and also because the slaves were negroes, imperfectly habituated to a civilized regime. Various devices by way of appeal, reward, or other inducement were utilized in efforts to increase the zeal, energy, and initiative of the laborers; but achievement by the planter was always limited by the quality of the children whom his women chanced to bear, by the inertia implied in slave status, and by any defect in the vigor and finesse of the management.[31]

Further suggestions that the Negro is inherently inferior to the white man can be found in Phillips's references to the free persons of color in the ante-bellum South. His general opinion of this class was that they were "thriftless, inert underlings, content if they could find jobs which no others wanted, and accustomed to live without seeking steady means of support."[32] The suggestion of inferiority came when the writer added, "these were slaves by nature or habit, 'loud laughters in the hands of fate,' who had been cast loose in misguided philanthropy."[33] Phillips was willing to admit that there were some Negroes who proved relatively intelligent, but he was quick to caution that ordinarily these were mulattoes "with far greater intelligence."[34]

The preceding discussion gives the reader an idea of the type of social attitudes and personal prejudices which can be found in the writings of U.B. Phillips if one reads his works carefully. One really has to read carefully for the simple reason that these subtleties are so few and far between. When they do occur they are usually indirectly and unconsciously expressed. Therefore, one may conclude that U. B. Phillips, writing in the tradition of von Ranke, did not succeed completely in keeping out his own preconceived ideas, but that he came pretty close to doing it. These attitudes may be summed up in the following manner: first, he was inclined to be pro-southern in his feelings about the Civil War; second, he felt that the

Negro was and still is lazy, irresponsible, and needful of the white man's constant surveillance; third, he concluded that the black man was naturally submissive and suited for slavery; and finally, he vaguely left the impression that the Negro was naturally inferior to the white man.

The next question is: did Phillips allow these assumptions to influence his presentation of slavery and the plantation system? This point is of extreme importance because, if this answer is also in the affirmative, then the conclusion must be that Phillips failed completely to carry out the von Ranke tradition. Thusfar, all that has been shown is that Phillips slipped in a few (very few) places and let his southern self-consciousness and social attitudes creep into his writings. But if it can also be shown that these ideas colored his overall presentation, then the story is entirely different.

Before considering this question, it may be helpful to recall exactly what sort of picture Phillips painted of the ante-bellum South.[35] His main ideas can be summarized as follows: Originally the Negro was brought to America because of the shortage of white labor and because the Indian failed miserably as a slave. When the invention of the cotton gin made the large scale production of cotton profitable, the importation of the Negroes increased sharply. Because of their barbarism it was necessary to use slavery in order to keep them in check. When the slave trade was shut off, the resulting scarcity of plantation hands increased their price so as to make the system a losing venture. Many plantation owners began to feel that it would be cheaper to use free labor. But they were chained to the maintenance of the existing order because (1) they already had too much money invested in their human property, and (2) they were afraid of racial friction if the great mass of Negroes was suddenly to be freed.

The plantation system was the best means yet devised to get the best out of the Negroes. Some forms of it should be revived in order to pull the Negroes out of the gutter into which they have a natural tendency to fall unless the "best" of the southern whites keep a check on them. The main trouble with the plantation system was that it led to the one crop system, partly due to the limitations imposed by crude laborers. This was bad because it stratified society, restricted those few slaves who were capable of doing better, discouraged nonplanter whites, hindered diversification, and made the South dependent upon the North.

As for slavery:

The government of slaves was for the ninety and nine by men, and only for the hundredth by law. There were injustices, oppression, brutality, and heartburning in the regime, — but where in the world are these absent? There was also gentleness, kind-hearted friendship and mutual loyalty to a degree hard for him to believe who regards the system with a theorist's eye and a partisan squint. For him on the other hand who has known the considerate and cordial, courteous and charming men and women, black and white, which that picturesque life in its best phases produced, it is impossible to agree that its basis and its operation were wholly evil, the law and the prophets to the country not withstanding.[36]

The slaves were not mistreated if only for the reason that they would do better work and would not try to escape.

Such is the general summary of Phillips's impressions of slavery and the plantation system. Now to the question as to whether or not this historian, with scientific objectivity as his aim, allowed his own personal leanings and attitudes to influence his overall presentation. One possible way by which this could have happened was through his selection, use, and organization of source materials. This was the charge made by Professor Hofstadter in his article on Phillips. His main point, and one he proved very conclusively, was that Phillips, in his sampling of documents, restricted himself mainly to the larger plantations which consisted of ten per cent of all the slaves and one percent of all the slaveowners—"the upper crust of the upper crust."[37] Hofstadter went on to charge that Phillips also skipped over and ruled out the testimonials of such critical observers as white southern physicians, that he was especially hasty in his consideration of the record left by Frederick Law Olmsted, and that his casual treatment of the Negroes' resistance to slavery was inadequate. Why did Phillips, who had almost a mania for searching out lost documents, so limit his studies? While admitting that the availability of records for small plantations was an important limiting factor, Hofstadter's main explanations were that, as a native of Georgia, Phillips had a tendency to look upon the Old South as a "haze of romance," that his portrayal of the Negro was characteristically southern, that his works "represent a latter-day phase of the pro-slavery argument," and that he handled rich source materials "in accordance with principles of selection governed by his personal bias."[38]

Professor Hofstadter was too abrupt in his treatment of Phillips. He definitely proved that the late historian depended chiefly on large plantation records, but he did not give sufficient consideration to a number of significant factors when he explained this selectivity and limitation of documents primarily in terms of Phillips's Southernism and personal bias. For one thing, the infrequent, well-concealed, and usually unconscious traces of subjectivity that emerge when one applies a magnifying glass to Phillips's writings are hardly sufficient to warrant the generalization that his works constitute a highly-slanted justification of the Old South. For another, Hofstadter might well have given more attention to the well-known fact that Phillips was the first scholar to use plantation records as a major source of information. More important, Hofstadter was too quick in brushing past his own observations that the sources for bigger units are "much better preserved"[39] and more "readily available"[40] and that "the materials on small plantations and slave farms of sub-plantation size may prove on investigation to be so limited that an adequate historical account of them can never be made."[41] The fact is, much to the dismay of Phillips and other scholars who have delved into the agricultural history of the ante-bellum South, that by and large the man who ran a small farm or plantation simply did not keep any records.

A perusal of Professor Stephenson's more recent, more comprehensive, and more balanced study of Phillips suggests at least two other considerations which may well merit the attention of those who have questioned the reliability of the late southern historian.

First, Stephenson points out that "it would be difficult to prove that Phillips consciously suppressed evidence favorable to the Negro or unfavorable to the slaveholder," and that he "seemed to be ever alert for instances of abscondings, revolts, miscegenation, or any other factors that illustrated maltreatment by whites or protests by blacks." Stephenson goes on to explain that since Phillips "contemplated neither an orthodox synthesis nor a systematic presentation of every facet of slavery, he did not assemble in any one place all the examples that came to his attention, nor did he search all sources for evidences of grievances of them."[42] In short, Phillips did not exhaust the material on racial friction any more than he exhausted all the other aspects of slavery.

Second, Stephenson explains that Phillips's heavy reliance on large plantation records was guided primarily by his conviction that the selection and use of documents should be guided by three determinative criteria: rareness, unconsciousness, and faithful illustration. Hence, according to Stephenson, Phillips felt that such records as plantation journals and overseers' reports to absentee owners were particularly reliable because they were prepared by men who "were totally unaware that their correspondence and journals would be used by historians to reconstruct the life of which they were a part, and one does not therefore have to evaluate their records in terms of subtle meanings or questionable motivations."[43] Quite the contrary, Phillips felt that travelogues and other writings for the press were less reliable because they embodied propaganda and because they recorded "jottings of strangers likely to be most impressed by the unfamiliar, and unable to distinguish what was common in the regime from what was unique in some special case."[44] Nonetheless, Stephenson shows that Phillips considered such records "indispensible" and that he used them to good effect, citing Frederick Law Olmsted two dozen times in his *American Negro Slavery*.

With these considerations, Professor Stephenson went a long way toward tempering the various reproofs of Phillips attributed "to some scholars who shared the field and to some critics who did not."[45] Nevertheless, Stephenson's over-all view was that, in the long run, Phillips was an "historian of aristocracy":

Phillips was spokesman for the dominant class of the South; a mellowed intellectual patrician who saw the Negro through the eyes of a kindly master...; who stressed lack of talent rather than lack of opportunity as explanation of inferior status; and who minimized the Negro's quest for freedom and civil rights.... His primary interest was the plantation system of which slaves were an integral part. But the system was organized and to some extent dominated by an economic and social aristocracy, and its historian was as handicapped in viewing the pyramid from its base as a captain of industry would be in writing a balanced history of the factory system.[46]

This evaluation—coming, as it does, from a sympathetic and well qualified source—leads to the conclusion that Phillips, unconsciously at least, painted a picture of slavery and the plantation system which was too friendly and somewhat unrealistic. Thus, it appears that the late southern historian, writing in the scientific tradition of von Ranke, fell short of that master's ideals. However, one cannot be too critical of Phillips in this respect if one considers that von Ranke also fell short of his own ideals. The fact is that history cannot be written from a pureiy objective and detached point of view. Phillips tried and came surprisingly close to achieving that goal.

Notes

1. Ulrich Bonnell Phillips, *American Negro Slavery: A Survey of the Supply, Employment and Control of Negro Labor as Determined by the Plantation Regime* (New York and London, 1918).

2. Theodore D. Jervey, "Review of *American Negro Slavery*," in *American Historical Review*, XXV (October, 1919), 117.

3. Phillips, *Life and Labor in the Old South* (Boston, 1929).

4. Avery Craven, "Review of *Life and Labor*," in *Political Science Quarterly*, XIV (March, 1930), 136.

5. Wendell Holmes Stephenson, *The South Lives in History, Southern Historians and Their Legacy* (The Walter Lynwood Fleming Lectures in Southern History, Baton Rouge, 1955), Chapter III, "Ulrich B. Phillips: Historian of Aristocracy," 75.

6. Phillips, *Life and Labor*, vii-viii.

7. Stephenson, *The South Lives in History*, 75.

8. For a complete list of all of Phillips's writings see Fred Landon and Everett E. Edwards, "A Bibliography of the Writings of Professor Ulrich Bonnell Phillips," in *Agricultural History*, VIII (October, 1934), 196-218.

9. For the best accounts of Phillips's life see Wood Gray, "Ulrich Bonnell Phillips," in W.T. Hutchinson, ed., *The Marcus W. Jernegan Essays in American Historiography* (Chicago, 1937), 354-73; E. Merton Coulter, "Ulrich Bonnell Phillips," *Dictionary of American Biography*, XXI (Supplement One), 597-98; "Obituary," in *American Histori-*

cal Review, XXXIX (April, 1934), 598-99; "Obituary," in *The New York Times,* January 22, 1934, p. 15; and Stephenson, *The South Lives in History.*

10. Good examples of such reviews are Jervey and Craven, previously cited; Broadus Mitchell, "Review of *Life and Labor,*" in *American Economic Review,* (December, 1929), 655-57; and C.P. Patterson, "Review of *American Negro Slavery,*" in *Political Science Quarterly,* XXXIII (September, 1918), 454-56.

11. W. E. B. Du Bois, "Review of *American Negro Slavery,*" in *American Political Science Review,* XII (November, 1918), 722.

12. *Ibid.,* 725.

13. Gray, "Ulrich Bonnell Phillips," 370.

14. Richard Hofstadter, "U.B. Phillips and the Plantation Legend," *Journal of Negro History,* XXIX (April, 1944), 109-24.

15. Phillips, *The Life of Robert Toombs* (New York, 1913), 195.

16. Phillips, "The Central Theme of Southern History," *American Historical Review,* XXXIV (October, 1928), 43. As though in anticipation of the current integration and civil rights issues, Phillips added: "Acquiescence does not provoke enthusiasm; and until an issue shall arise predominant over the lingering one of race, political solidarity at the price of provincial status is maintained to keep assurance doubly, trebly sure that the South shall remain a 'white man's country.'"

17. Phillips, "The Economics of the Plantation," *South Atlantic Quarterly,* II (July, 1903), 235.

18. Phillips, *A History of Transportation in the Eastern Cotton Belt to 1860* (New York, 1908), 395.

19. Phillips, "Plantations with Slave Labor and Free," *American Historical Review,* XXX (July, 1925), 752.

20. Phillips, *American Negro Slavery,* 291.

21. *Ibid.,* 396.

22. Phillips, "The Economics of the Plantation," 233.

23. Phillips, "Conservatism and Progress in the Cotton Belt," *South Atlantic Quarterly,* III (January, 1904), 8.

24. Phillips, *Life and Labor,* 188.

25. Phillips, *American Negro Slavery,* 454.

26. *Ibid.,* 339.

27. *Ibid.,* 341-42.

28. Phillips, *Life and Labor,* 196.

29. Phillips, *American Negro Slavery,* viii-ix.

30. Phillips, "The Central Theme of Southern History," 42.

31. Phillips, "Plantations with Slave Labor and Free," 741-42.

32. Phillips, *Life and Labor,* 172.

33. *Ibid.*

34. Phillips, "Slave Labor in the Charleston District," in *Political Science Quarterly,* XXII (September, 1907), 419.

35. Particularly helpful in summarizing Phillips's ideas is E. Merton Coulter, ed., *The Course of the South to Secession, an Interpretation by Ulrich Bonnell Phillips* (New York and London, 1939), published posthumously under the direction of the American Historical Association from the income of the Albert J. Beveridge

Memorial Fund, consisting of six lectures presented at Northwestern University in the Spring of 1932, plus a reprinting of "The Central Theme of Southern History." Included here are long-range interpretations absent in most of Phillips's other works. For the best accounts by other writers, see Gray, "Ulrich Bonnell Phillips"; Coulter, "Ulrich Bonnell Phillips"; and Stephenson, *The South Lives in History*.

36. Phillips, *American Negro Slavery*, 514.

37. Hofstadter, "U.B. Phillips and the Plantation Legend," 119.

38. *Ibid.*, 122.

39. *Ibid.*, 110.

40. *Ibid.*, 110.

41. *Ibid.*, 110-11.

42. Stephenson, *The South Lives in History*, 84.

43. *Ibid.*, 74.

44. Phillips's statement, quoted *ibid.*, 78.

45. *Ibid.*, 83.

46. *Ibid.*, 93.

13

U. B. Phillips's Use of Sources

Ruben F. Kugler

Apparently, the debate among historians over the merits of the writings of Ulrich Bonnell Phillips (1877-1934) will continue as long as there is interest in the Civil War and subsequent racial issues. One reason for this debate is that Phillips has been considered the leading authority on slavery and the southern plantation system.[1] Many textbook writers, for example, cite his works as the "standard" and "best" on slavery.[2] Donald Sheehan, who edited a collection of historical writings, wrote in this work:

> Probably Phillips is in no small way responsible for the now common-ly held view that the slaves took kindly to their school [slavery] and that the schoolmasters [slaveowners] were as often fatherly as avaricious and more often indulgent than cruel.[3]

One reason for the authoritative position of Phillips's works is that they reflect extensive research, particularly on plantation records. As will be discussed below, however, recent criticism and findings have thrown doubt on his accuracy and objectivity. Did Phillips follow the scientific method? In one of his first works, he stated that he had attempted to exhaust the sources of his subject:

> It not difficult for one whose native environment is the Cotton Belt to orient himself into antebellum Georgia. I have made little use, how-ever, of the historical imagination. The method is that of the inves-tigator rather than the literary historian. The work is intended to be a thorough scientific treatment of its subject. No pains have been spared in obtaining exhaustive and accurate information.[4]

A decade later he wrote:

The historian who would give a sound exposition of the great issues must be critically cognizant of all the doctrines influential in the period of which he treats; he must view them all as phenomena and be dominated by no one of them.[5]

Toward the end of his career he declared that his "fancy" was "restricted by records."[6]

❖ ❖ ❖ ❖ ❖

This paper will analyze eight examples of Phillips's methods of quoting and paraphrasing sources: the first four touch on conditions of slavery, and the last four concern the Negroes' attitudes toward their bondage. The reader should keep in mind that, inasmuch as this is a limited methodological study, he should not expect a comprehensive analysis of Phillips's interpretation of slavery.

In the first example, Phillips cited sources which did not support the statements which he apparently obtained from them. The second chapter of *American Negro Slavery*, entitled "The Maritime Slave Trade," while admitting some of the deplorable conditions of the slave transport from Africa, painted a brighter picture of that traffic than most historians have done. Phillips wrote, in regard to the slave ships, that "the food if coarse was generally plenteous and wholesome, and the sanitation fairly adequate." He cited as evidence for this paragraph two summaries of a British Parliamentary investigation by W.O. Blake and Thomas Buxton; he did not, however, cite any pages in these two sources.[7] Phillips cited only chapters.

The writer could find nothing in Blake's and Buxton's writings which supported Phillips's generalizations on food and sanitation. As a matter of fact, both works reveal much worse conditions than Phillips described. Buxton quoted Falconbridge, a witness, who testified: "Numberless quarrels take place among them [the slaves] during their meals; more especially when they are put upon short allowance, which frequently happens." Both Buxton and Blake related the testimony of other witnesses who reported the lack of fresh air and other inadequacies resulting in sickness and filthy conditions. Slave-dealers estimated that the average ship lost nearly one-third of its cargo; some ships arrived with only half of the original number of Africans alive.[8] It would seem that Phillips's own opinion of the slave trade prevented his accurate reading of Blake and Buxton.

Another example of such misreading is his use of Fredrika (sometimes spelled Frederika) Bremer's writings. She was a Swedish novelist who visited the ante-bellum South. Phillips wrote in his *Life and Labor in the Old South*: "Frederika Bremer had virtually nothing but praise for the slave quarters she visited or their savory food which she tasted."[9]

While Bremer found that some of the food given to slaves was better than she had expected, Phillips did not quote her description of a planter's provisions for the old and sick:

> Deeper down in the wood I saw a slave village, or houses resembling one, but which had an unusually irregular and tumble-down appearance.... I found the houses actually in the most decayed and deplorable condition, and in one house old and sickly negroes, men and women. In one room I saw a young lad very much swollen, as if with dropsy; the rain and wind could enter by the roof; everything was naked in the room; neither fire-wood nor fire was here, although the day was chilly. In another wretched house we saw an old woman lying among rags as in a dog-kennel.[10]

Elsewhere she saw better quarters, but the complete reading of her book makes it clear that Phillips misread it; rather that "praise" she had virtually nothing but condemnation for the institution of slavery.

By presenting Bremer's observations as he did—incompletely and inaccurately—Phillips gave the reader the incorrect impression that Bremer found that the lot of the Negro under slavery was satisfactory. In her travels she found much she loved about the South, but not its peculiar institution. The effect of the slave-trade upon children horrified her. An overseer told her that masters insisted that overseers whip the slaves in order to force them to work as they "ought." A Mississippi planter admitted that most slaveholders were not good or tender toward their slaves; passion and insanity commonly prevailed in the treatment of bondsmen.[11] Phillips did not quote any of these unpleasant facts observed by Bremer.

Another example of giving the reader an incorrect impression is seen in the manner in which Phillips quoted Frederick Law Olmsted. Olmsted was a northerner who traveled extensively in the South. By quoting Olmsted out of context, Phillips was able to draw a conclusion which supported a pro-slavery interpretation. Phillips wrote:

> With physical comforts provided, the birth-rate would take care of itself. The pickaninnies were winsome, and their parents, free of expense and anxiety for the sustenance, could hardly have more of them than they wanted.[12]

By not quoting Olmsted's complete story, Phillips left an inaccurate impression of the facts. Phillips's version, quoted in the left-hand column, should be compared with the more complete passage as Olmsted himself told it:

Phillips, *Slavery,* p. 298:	Olmsted, *Seaboard Slave States,* pp. 57-58:
[The above quotation from Phillips about slave parents being free from anxiety introduced the following:] A Virginian told Olmsted, 'he never heard of babies coming so fast as they did on his plantation; it was perfectly surprising';[17] and in Georgia, Howell Cobb's negroes increased 'like rabbits.'[18] *[Phillips' 17th citation referred to Olmsted, p. 57; the 18th citation was to another source.]*	But this proportion was somewhat smaller than usual, he [the Virginian] added, 'because his women were uncommonly good breeders; he did not suppose that there was a lot of women anywhere bred faster than his; he never heard of babies coming so fast as they did on his plantation; it was perfectly surprising; and every one of them, in his estimation was worth two hundred dollars, as negroes were selling now, the moment it drew breath.'

Phillips also omitted the further remarks of the Virginian who told Olmsted that he intended to sell his slaves in Louisiana, Texas or California—depending on where he could get the highest price. In Stampp's *Peculiar Institution,* this same passage in Olmsted is cited with the inclusion of the significant words omitted by Phillips. It becomes obvious, after comparing Stampp's and Phillips's use of Olmsted, that the full text in Olmsted supports Stampp's but not Phillips's conclusion therefrom.[13]

Phillips's *Life and Labor in the Old South,* unlike his *American Negro Slavery,* admitted some of the slave-trading activities of planters. In the former work, Phillips wrote:

> The social stigma laid upon them [the slave-traders] can hardly have been so stringent as tradition tells, for many a planter and perhaps most of the general merchants turned a trade on favorable occasion, and sundry citizens of solid worth and esteem can be identified as regular participants.[14]

Life and Labor in the Old South, however, followed *American Negro Slavery* in giving an inaccurate impression of the slave-trading firm of Franklin and Armfield by not quoting a key source completely. Phillips used as his main source of information on this company the work of E.A. Andrews, a northerner who went South to study slavery in behalf of the American Union for the Relief and Improvement of the Colored Race.

In *American Negro Slavery* Phillips devoted almost a page to Andrews's description of the slave pen of Franklin and Armfield. On the whole, it appeared that, according to Phillips, Andrews liked what he saw there. A similar incorrect impression is given in *Life and Labor in the Old South*:

> The clearest account of this traffic at large is by E.A. Andrews, *Slavery and the Domestic Slavetrade* (Boston, 1836), describing particularly the well-ordered assembling house of Franklin and Armfield at Alexandria, Virginia.[15]

Reading the full account in Andrews's work, however, reveals that Andrews did not like what he saw at Alexandria. While Armfield's assistant was telling Andrews about the happy condition of the inmates, one of the slaves looked earnestly at Andrews,

> and as often as the keeper turned away his face, he shook his head, and seemed desirous of having me understand, that he did not feel any such happiness as was described, and that he dissented from the representation made of his condition.[16]

Phillips did not quote the above nor Andrews's statement that the female quarters had a neat and comfortable appearance "for a prison." Andrews wrote:

> In most respects, however, the situation of the convicts at the penitentiary was far less deplorable than that of these slaves, confined for the crime of being descended from ancestors who were forcibly reduced to bondage.

Phillips also failed to quote Andrews's conclusion:

> After resisting myself a few minutes, I took leave of Mr. Armfield and of his establishment, and returned to my lodging in the city, ruminating, as I went, upon the countless evils, which "man's inhumanity to man," has occasioned in this world of sin and misery.[17]

When one reads Andrews's book, it is evident that Phillips failed to inform the reader of the important passages in Andrews. Frederic Bancroft, who cited the same passage in Andrews, quoted the significant lines omitted by Phillips. The full text in Andrews's work supports Bancroft's conclusion; it does not support Phillips's interpretation which gave the incorrect impression that Andrews had a favorable opinion of Franklin and Armfield.[18]

In another case, Phillips omitted a significant phrase from an article by Judge J.B. O'Neall, although he did show the omission with ellipses. This South Carolina judge wrote a legal analysis of slavery published before the Civil War. Phillips quoted him as follows, with the exception of the italicized words:

> Experience and observation fully satisfy me that the first law of slavery is that of kindness from the master to the slave. With that *properly inculcated, enforced by law and judiciously applied,* slavery becomes a family relation, next in its attachment to that of parent and child. [Italics not in Phillips's original.][19]

Without the phrase "enforced by law," the reader is given the impression that the Judge believed that slavery was generally a paternalistic relationship without legal enforcement. If, however, one reads the entire article by Judge O'Neall, it is evident that he held a different opinion.

O'Neall pointed out that South Carolina law required slaveholders to provide their bondsmen with sufficient clothing, housing and food. Then he commented: "I regret to say, *that there is, in such a state as ours,* great occasion for the enforcement of such a law, *accompanied by severe penalties.*" (Italics in the original.) The Judge told of the frequent changes of masters resulting in rending of family ties, he cited laws which did not punish severely enough those who tortured and killed slaves, and he objected to legislation which forbade the education of slaves.[20] None of this is mentioned by Phillips. If he had not omitted from his quotation of O'Neall the phrase "enforced by law" and had summarized the article, this source would then be seen as evidence against his argument that slavery was a patriarchal institution.[21]

Phillips paraphrased inaccurately in his use of another source. In *American Negro Slavery,* the chapter, "Types of Large Plantations," summarized the findings of Fanny Kemble, the English actress who married Pierce Butler, a Georgia planter. Phillips concluded, on the basis of her journal, that she found that the "swarms of negroes were stupid..."[22] Phillips did not cite any pages for this reference. In turning to the source of this information, *Journal of a Residence on a Georgian Plantation in 1838-1839,* one finds instead that Fanny Kemble did not hold the opinion which Phillips ascribed to her. She wrote that, if the laws allowed slaves to read books, they "would seize them with avidity—receive them gladly, comprehend them quickly; and the masters' powers over them would be annihilated at once and forever." She also declared that "if they are incapable of profiting by instruction, I do not see the necessity for laws inflicting heavy penalties on those who offer it to them."[23] It would seem that Phillips allowed his own opinion of the mentality of Negroes to color his summary of Fanny Kemble's experiences.[24]

In another instance of misreading Olmsted, Phillips used a story told to Olmsted by the executor of an estate. The executor related how a lazy slave became energetic when promised that he could buy his freedom by performing extra work. Phillips told only that part of the story in which the freed Negro went North, did not like it there and returned to Virginia. By not completing the tale, Phillips's version made it appear that the ex-slave preferred slavery to freedom. A reading of the complete narrative in Olmsted reveals that the Negro did not return to his ex-master (the executor); actually, he went to a nearby place to work for wages. Compare Phillips's account in the left-hand column with Olmsted's telling:

Phillips, *Slavery,* p. 440:	Olmsted, *Seaboard Slave States,* pp. 103-04:
And at Richmond Olmsted learned of a negro who after buying his freedom had gone to Philadelphia to join his brother, but had promptly returned. When questioned by his former cousin [the executor] this man said: 'Oh, I don't like dat Philadelphy, massa; ant no chance for colored folks dere; spec' if I'd been a runaway de wite folk dere take care o' me; but I couldn't git anythin' to do, so I jis borrow ten dollar of my broder an' cum back to old Virginney.'	*[Phillips' version in the left column is part of the story, but he did not quote the following ending]:* 'But you know [said the executor] the law forbids your return. I wonder that you are not afraid to be seen here; I should think Mr. _____ (an officer of police) would take you up.' 'Oh! I look out for dat, Massr, I juss hire myself out to Mr. _____ himself, ha! ha! He tink I your boy.'

By not quoting the pertinent facts in the beginning of Olmsted's story and by deleting the ending, Phillips minimized this Negro's antipathy toward slavery. Phillips, as shown by the use he made of this story, turned it into an argument against the North in respect to its treatment of Negroes. This may be an example of what psychologists call projection. In addition, he failed to point up Olmsted's sub-title of the account: "Ingenuity of the Negro."[25]

The eighth and last example of subjectivity illustrates one-sided selection of passages. Concerning the feelings of recently enslaved Africans, Phillips wrote in his *American Negro Slavery:* "That by no means all the negroes took their enslavement grievously is suggested by a traveler's note at Columbia,

South Carolina, in 1806." The traveler, Edward Hooker, an attorney, was told upon inquiry of a sixteen year old slave that he saw no injustice in being enslaved.[26]

Phillips did not question the probability that this "bright" Negro replied to the question about his feelings toward slavery in such a manner as to avoid punishment for insubordination. The same page in Hooker contains a report of recent rumors and fears of a slave insurrection, and the killing of a slave who was perhaps falsely suspected of plotting the revolt. Would a bright slave, knowing of such events, complain to a white man about mistreatment? Also it seems that Phillips, by inferring that an appreciable number of Africans saw no injustice in being enslaved, drew an illogical conclusion. The writer found similar examples in which Phillips quoted sources in a one-sided manner.[27] This subjective method revealed a pattern of selection in which he would often cite pro-slavery passages, while ignoring anti-slavery findings related to the same incident sometimes located on the same page.

Allowing for some unavoidable subjectivity, the writings of a leading authority should demonstrate more consistency than Phillips's writings did. Of course, in order to make a definitive judgment on his works, one would need more instances of misused sources than have been presented in this article. The writer believes, however, that the criticisms of the historians cited above, as well as the eight examples of unbalanced selection, misquoting and inaccurate paraphrasing, raise a strong doubt in regard to the objectivity of Phillips's works.

It has been seen that Phillips cited three writers (Blake, Buxton and Bremer) to support an interpretation which their writings did not support. He quoted Olmsted out of context, and he left out a key phrase from a sentence in Judge O'Neall's article. A reading of that article in full reveals the significance of the omitted phrase. In his use of Olmsted, Kemble and Andrews, Phillips left the reader with incorrect impressions regarding their findings and opinions. On the basis of a single incident, which he found in Hooker, he made a sweeping generalization; furthermore, on the same page in Hooker there is contrary evidence which Phillips omitted. Phillips committed another type of methodological error when he used Blake, Buxton and Kemble without citing pages therein. In general, it appears that Phillips did not comply with his own standards of the scientific historical method described at the beginning of this article.

Notes

1. Frederick Jackson Turner, *The United States, 1830-1850; the Nation and Its Sections* (New York, 1935), 149n. Ulrich B. Phillips, *The Course of the South to Secession* (New York, 1939), vii. E. Merton Coulter, the editor of this work by Phillips, wrote: "It is generally agreed that no one had a more thorough knowledge and a keener appreciation of the ante-bellum South than Ulrich Bonnell Phillips."

2. Dumas Malone and Basil Rauch, *Empire for Liberty* (New York, 1960), I: 863. John Hicks, *A Short History of American Democracy* (Boston, 1946), 289n. Leland Baldwin, *The Stream of American History* (New York, 1952), I:170-71. Homer C. Hockett, *Political and Social Growth of the United States* (New York, 1935), 574. In each of seven libraries visited, this writer found additional examples.

3. Donald Sheehan, ed., *The Making of American History* (New York, 1954), I:324.

4. Ulrich B. Phillips, "Georgia and State Rights," *Annual Report of the American Historical Association for the Year 1901* (Washington, D.C., 1902), II: 5-6.

5. Ulrich B. Phillips, "On the Economics of Slavery, 1815-1860," *Annual Report of the American Historical Association for the Year 1912* (Washington, D.C., 1914), 151.

6. Ulrich B. Phillips, *Life and Labor in the Old South* (Boston, 1929), vii-viii. Hereafter referred to as Phillips, *Life and Labor*. Ulrich B. Phillips, *American Negro Slavery* (New York, 1918), 514. Hereafter referred to as Phillips, *Slavery*.

7. Phillips, *Slavery*, p. 37.

8. Thomas F. Buxton, *The African Slave Trade and Its Remedy* (London, 1840), 125, 172-74; W.O. Blake, *The History of Slavery and the Slave Trade...* (Columbus, Ohio, 1859), 126-42.

9. Phillips, *Life and Labor*, 214.

10. Fredrika Bremer, *The Homes of the New World* (New York, 1854), I:293-94. Phillips' citation in Bremer was to "I, 293 *et passim*."

11. *Ibid*, I:366-67, 373; II:188-90. Kenneth M. Stampp, *The Peculiar Institution: Slavery in the Ante-Bellum South* (New York, 1956), 295, quoted Bremer as finding slave quarters "in the most decayed and deplorable condition."

12. Phillips, *Slavery*, 298.

13. Stampp, *Peculiar Institution*, 246. Both Stampp and Phillips cited the same page in Frederick Law Olmsted, *A Journey in the Seaboard Slave States* (New York, 1856), 57.

14. Phillips, *Life and Labor*, 158.

15. Phillips, *Slavery*, 194-95; Phillips, *Life and Labor*, 155n.

16. E.A. Andrews, *Slavery and the Domestic Slave-Trade in the United States* (Boston, 1836), 138.

17. *Ibid.*, 141-43.

18. Frederic Bancroft, *Slave-Trading in the Old South* (Baltimore, 1931), 26n, 55, 59-62, 207.

19. Phillips, *Slavery*, 513, quoting J.B. O'Neall, in J.D.B. DeBow, *The Industrial Resources...* (New Orleans, 1852), II:278.

20. DeBow, *Industrial Resources*, II:276-79. Bancroft, *Slave-Trading*, 200n, quoted a passage from O'Neall about the "rending of family ties...."

21. Phillips, *Slavery*, 306-07, 327, 514. Phillips, "Georgia and State Rights," II:154. Phillips, *Course of the South to Secession*, 125.

22. Phillips, *Slavery*, 251.

23. Frances Anne Kemble, *Journal of a Residence on a Georgian Plantation in 1838-1839* (New York, 1863), 8-9.

24. The following works reveal aspects of Phillips's racial beliefs: U.B. Phillips, "The Economic Cost of Slaveholding in the Cotton Belt," *Political Science Quarterly,*

XX (June, 1905), 257-59; Phillips, *Slavery*, viii, 339-43; and Phillips, *Life and Labor*, 261-66.

25. Olmsted, *Seaboard Slave States*, 103.

26. Edward Hooker, "Diary of Edward Hooker," in *Annual Report of the American Historical Association for the Year 1896* (Washington, D.C., 1897), I: 882. Phillips, *Slavery*, 42n, incorrectly cited the A.H.A. report for 1906.

27. Compare Phillips, *Slavery*, p. 287, with Harriet Martineau, *Society in America* (London, 1837), II:315-17, 320-21; Phillips, *Slavery*, 241, with Estwick Evans, "A Pedestrious Tour...," in Reuben G. Thwaites, ed., *Early Western Travels, 1748-1846* (Cleveland, 1904), VIII:325-26, 332; Phillips, *Slavery*, 324-25, and Phillips, *Life and Labor*, 219, 222-28, with Phillip Vickers Fithian, *Journal and Letters, 1767-1774* (Princeton, 1900), 68-69, 128-32, 248, 279, 287; Phillips, *Slavery*, 129, with Max Farrand, ed., *The Records of the Federal Convention of 1787* (New Haven, 1911-12), II:369-70; Phillips, *Slavery*, 307, with William Faux, "Memorable Days in America...," in Reuben G. Thwaites, ed., *Early Western Travels* (Cleveland, 1905), XI:62, 74, 77, 80, 91ff. Phillips often fell into methodological errors in his unrepresentative selections from Olmsted; random choices from the citations in *American Negro Slavery* will reveal this.

14

"Keep 'em in a fire-proof vault"—Pioneer Southern Historians Discover Plantation Records

John David Smith

Writing in 1910, and again a year later, William Thomas Laprade addressed himself to the problems which faced students of American slavery.[1] The young assistant professor of history at Trinity College urged historians to be innovative in the sources which they employed when examining the peculiar institution. For too long, argued Laprade, writers had depended exclusively on biased travel narratives and accounts to document the history of slavery and the plantation regime. In addition to advocating the use of fresh sources, Laprade suggested that investigators free themselves from the legalistic framework which dominated the historiography of slavery. Critical of the majority of the volumes, Laprade wrote:

> Of making many books on American slavery there does not seem to be any prospect of an end in the immediate future. And if much of the study which has been expended on it has not resulted in a weariness of flesh, this must be due to the perennial interest which seems to attach to the subject rather than to any useful conclusions which have resulted from such study. For in spite of all this work some of the most fundamental questions with regard to slavery in America still await authoritative answers.[2]

Laprade's comments on the literature of slavery written during these years were in the main correct. "Fundamental questions" did remain to be answered; yet "useful conclusions" were reached by historians of slavery who wrote during the Progressive era.[3] Heretofore an emotionally charged issue for Americans North and South, during the Progressive era slavery came to be examined calmly, "scientifically." Whether studied systematically as an institution or mentioned in the context of contemporary racial problems, it emerged in the period 1890-1920 as a major topic of discussion. Not since the late antebellum years had so much attention been devoted to it. Professor Laprade's concern with the sources for the history of slavery was mirrored in the writings, both published and unpublished, of a generation of southern historians and archivists. They recognized the value of a previously unexploited source material—plantation records and manuscripts. And for a number of southerners locating these documents became a major preoccupation.

Both an appreciation of the importance of manuscripts and access to them were necessary before historians could study slavery in what was then considered a "scientific" manner. Southern historians were at a marked disadvantage in this field because of the region's negligence in establishing collections of source materials. True, the southern state historical societies, organized in the nineteenth century, published some official documents and encouraged the study of history. For example, as early as 1818 South Carolina took steps to appropriate money for preserving state records, and by 1856 the state historical society held the papers of Henry Laurens, which were particularly valuable on the history of the slave trade. On the whole, however, according to J.G. de Roulhac Hamilton, the historical societies neglected their "fundamental function," which, he believed, was collecting source materials and making them available to scholars.[4]

Nor did the creation of the Southern Historical Society in 1869 and the Southern History Association in 1896 remedy this defect of inadequate sources on slavery. The Society was almost wholly dedicated to Confederate history. The Association had broader interests, and its *Publications*, which have been called the region's "first modern historical magazine," contained essays on slavery. But the organization did little toward collecting or publishing manuscript sources on the peculiar institution. Unfortunately, too, the meetings of these organizations, which might have stimulated the study of slavery and southern history in general, were attended mainly by affluent nonprofessionals. Few professors attended, most of them being unable to come because of distance and lack of funds.[5]

Scholars were, however, beginning to emphasize the importance of manuscripts. In 1887 Justin Winsor of Harvard urged the American Historical Association (AHA) to seek a national repository for manuscripts "before it is too late." By the turn of the century, according to Wendell Holmes Stephenson, southern historians had begun recognizing the historical significance of plantation records, including diaries, journals, and account books. As early as 1892 William P. Trent made extensive use of over 1,000 manuscript letters in his biography of William Gilmore Simms. Three years later, Trent, who like Laprade was trained at the Johns Hopkins University, emphasized the historians' need for the collection of sources such as old letters, plantation account ledgers, and files of newspapers. Unfortunately, the South's first great collector of primary materials, North Carolina's Stephen B. Weeks, became discouraged with the regional apathy toward his work. "If I had studied Egyptian history in Idaho as thoroughly as I have N.C. history," he wrote with sarcasm in 1899, "I should have been much more appreciated in my native State!" Weeks's decision to sell his valuable collection of North Caroliniana in fragments instead of contributing it en masse to a library seriously retarded its use by early researchers.[6]

The increasing emphasis on primary sources in the study of slavery was especially apparent in the works of two early twentieth-century figures. In 1907 Alfred Holt Stone, a planter from Dunleith, Mississippi, wrote to William E. Dodd seeking information on "documentary manuscript and other materials bearing particularly on the ante bellum and earlier post bellum aspects of" southern blacks. Stone was collecting information for a projected book, "The Negro in Slavery and Freedom." He believed that a great deal of manuscript material on slavery was available but too widely scattered for use by historians, and was mainly in the hands of private families or individuals. Requesting names of families with manuscripts dealing with slavery, Stone informed Dodd:

> I am in search of all forms of sugar, rice, tobacco, indigo and cotton plantation records,—such as journals, diaries, account books, account sales, cotton picking records, instructions to overseers.... In fact, I want anything which will throw the least light upon the economic side of the institution of slavery, as it existed at various... places in the Southern and border states. This would of course include all other forms of economic activity in which the negro was employed before the war as well as that of the plantation.

Two years later the reform journalist, Ray Stannard Baker, made a similar request. Planning several articles "on slavery as it existed," Baker had already accumulated much primary source material "both in the way of personal experiences and documents." He still desired Dodd to offer hints on additional sources of materials, unpublished documents, pictures, and pamphlets.[7]

Most students of the history of slavery at this time, however, lacked any real way of gaining access to the records of the South's past. For years southern scholars had recognized the seriousness of the region's archival problems. A reviewer in the *Sewanee Review* in 1892 summarized the urgency by declaring that "a true history" of the southern people ought to be written before the materials for that history had vanished. The following year a correspondent advised Herbert Baxter Adams, in whose famous Johns Hopkins seminar many of the students of slavery were trained, to begin a study of southern blacks. "I earnestly hope that you will," wrote Lynn R. Meekins, then literary editor of the Baltimore *American*, because "this is an important dividing line between generations and valuable material will soon be slipping away."[8]

Too often manuscripts pertaining to the South were either lost or hoarded in attics and were "fast disappearing because of a lack of knowledge of their value as historical evidence." To help correct this, J. Franklin Jameson, the first editor of the *American Historical Review*, planned an extensive manuscript search throughout the South in 1905. Albert Bushnell Hart, professor of history at Harvard, advised him that the region's famous families held the key to uncovering the South's manuscripts. J. G. de Roulhac Hamilton, who had assembled the South's greatest archival collection at Chapel Hill by the 1930's, accurately recalled how in 1906 the South lacked any "great collections of historical manuscripts." Philip M. Hamer, when chief of Accessions of the National Archives, said that the preservation of sources such as plantation records, which could have been valuable to researchers of slavery, was generally "the result of chance and less the result of foresight." Had southern families preserved rather than destroyed their papers, large caches of slave owners' records might have been available to early researchers. Those saved were usually located in such informal repositories as corncribs and outbuildings.[9]

Historians widely lamented this lack of sources. Dodd asserted in 1904 that students of southern history were limited because "only one first rate library of reference," probably referring to the Library of Congress, existed in the entire South. A year earlier Professor Jameson had warned southern historians that "a hundred years from now inquiring minds will be eagerly seeking for knowledge of American slavery as an actual institution and for an understanding of the social system which was bound up with it, but now is the golden time to collect the data, before it is too late." Worthington C. Ford, a pioneer archivist at the Boston Public Library and the Library of Congress, regretted that, although the South had possessed abundant historical sources early in its history, they had been wasted. "Now that the trained historian is ready," he added, "the material is wanting." Professor Eugene C. Barker of the University of Texas believed that the absence of sources in the South had allowed New Englanders to dominate the writing of southern history. Walter Lynwood Fleming, then professor of history at Louisiana State University, complained that the university library lacked the materials necessary "to form a basis for an adequate course in Southern history." Fleming even doubted whether an acceptable course on any phase of southern history could be offered below Mason and Dixon's line. As late as 1923 William H. Kilpatrick, a Georgian transplanted to Columbia University, spoke of the dreadful condition of the South's primary sources.[10]

Despite these complaints, the South was a pioneer in the establishment of state archival programs. Led by Thomas M. Owen, Alabama in 1901 founded its Department of Archives and History. The state's decision to collect systematically its documents of the past was hailed as "the most far reaching step yet taken in the South looking to the support of historical work and research." Owen, described by historian Ulrich B. Phillips as "an extremely valuable and attractive man," was a national leader in state archival management and the dominant figure in a region lacking "an overplus of active men in the historical field." In 1903, according to Phillips, the Alabama Department of Archives and History joined only two other libraries in the United States—the Library of Congress and the Wisconsin State Historical Society—as depositories of primary materials for the writing of southern history. Owen took pride that Alabama was the first state to recognize the importance of caring for and preserving its archives by establishing a separate state agency. Nonetheless he had noted in a report on manuscripts in 1900 the conspicuous absence of plantation materials and other records of slavery, and six years later had to acknowledge that he could not locate "any manuscript material. . . on slave insurrections" when asked for citations.[11]

Following Owen's lead, Dunbar Rowland and Franklin L. Riley worked for a Mississippi Department of Archives and History, which was established in 1902. A decade later Frederic Bancroft, an expert on the domestic slave trade, praised the department as "perhaps the most civilizing influence in Mississippi." By 1911 its collections contained records highly useful to students of slavery, including slave auction lists and emancipation petitions. Similarly, North Carolina in 1903 chartered its Historical Commission. Directed by R.D.W. Connor it quickly acquired valuable manuscript collections with useful information on slavery. The Jonathan Worth Papers, for example, contained material on slave treatment, slave sales, and slave law. Researchers on slavery also had access to the Manuscript Division of the Library of Congress, which had been established in 1897. Within eight years the Division held over 120,000 manuscripts pertaining to many aspects of southern history. As early as 1815 the Library had acquired the Thomas Jefferson manuscripts containing primary materials on slavery. Also obtained during the Library's first years were its "Slave Papers," including slave appraisals, mortgages, and birth certificates of bondsmen. In 1899 an important collection of "Plantation Reports" was contributed by Richard West. But as late as 1914 Bancroft complained of the weak collection of plantation records at the Library of Congress—it contained only "a few plantation-books." Not until well into the twentieth century were there collections of records adequate for the writing of a satisfactory history of slavery.[12]

One scholar, however, Ulrich B. Phillips (1877-1934), overcame this paucity of sources. A native Georgian, Phillips studied with both Frederick Jackson Turner and William A. Dunning before embarking on a teaching career on the faculties of Wisconsin, Tulane, Michigan, and Yale. Phillips was a prolific author. In addition to more than a score of articles, his two best known books—*American Negro Slavery* (1918) and *Life and Labor in the Old South* (1929)—earned him a reputation as the foremost historian of slavery of his day. Not until the publication of Kenneth M. Stampp's *The Peculiar Institution* (1956) was Phillips dislodged as the master of slave historiography.[13]

Although historians' evaluations of Phillips's writings on slavery have undergone cyclical revision, they agree that he merits praise as the dominant figure in the collection and use of plantation materials. These became fundamental sources in Phillips's paternalistic interpretations of American slavery. Despite his racism and his overdependence on the records of large planters, Phillips revolutionized the study of slavery. He uncovered new sources of evidence, analyzed the profitability of slavery on a cost basis, and examined relationships between bondsman and master which existed under the slave regime.[14]

Phillips's role as a pioneer in the use of plantation records and a variety of other sources is an important factor in his reputation as a "scientific" historian and as one of the South's foremost scholars. The Georgian was the only student of slavery in the early twentieth century to exploit planters' letters, diaries, ledgers, and pamphlets on a large scale, and use census statistics in conjunction with such records. He paved the way in the extensive use of southern newspapers and of correspondence between masters and overseers and gleaned much statistical information for numerous charts and graphs from city directories, bills of sale, slave price quotations, slave ship manifests, and cotton factors' account statements. By popularizing the use of such sources, he anticipated the major sources employed by many of his successors. He made an additional contribution by identifying the location of plantation documents and encouraging their preservation, and undoubtedly possessed a broader understanding of the value of plantation materials than did any of his peers. He believed it was the historian's obligation to utilize those sources which served to reconstruct "the old system [of slavery] as an organic whole."[15]

Phillips believed strongly in plantation records because he looked upon them as unconscious sources for the study of slavery. To evaluate objectively the peculiar institution, always a topic charged with emotion, required, in Phillips's opinion, special sources. "The most reliable source of knowledge," he said, "and the source least used thus far," were plantation records—"documents written with no thought of reaching the public eye, writings whose purpose is to give the plain facts and nothing else." Phillips was convinced that the hostile attitude of northern writers toward slavery and the South resulted largely from their unfamiliarity with the region's primary sources. Writing in 1909, Phillips explained, "Original material for Southern history has been so scarce at the centres where American historiographers have worked, that the general writers have had to substitute conjecture for understanding in many cases when attempting to interpret Southern developments."[16]

From the time of his experiences as assistant librarian while in the graduate school at the University of Georgia, Phillips appreciated the value of books and documents. Even after his appointment in 1902 as instructor of history at the University of Wisconsin, he proposed an arrangement in which he would spend half of each year teaching at Madison and half as librarian for the Georgia Historical Society. In his opinion, "the two kinds of work" were "really supplementary in character." With much the same kind of fervor as that of such pioneer southern archivists as Alabama's Owen or Mississippi's Rowland, Phillips argued that if southern history was to become a serious research field, the region's manuscripts and other primary sources had to be preserved. In 1903, for example, he lamented that so little had been accomplished in Georgia for the maintenance of the state's records, that important documents in the State House were being devoured by rats. Similarly, he found the town records of his hometown, Milledgeville, Georgia—poorly arranged and cared for—"some... damaged by mice, and all... exceedingly dusty and disagreeable to use." Three years later Phillips admonished his friend Yates Snowden of the University of South Carolina to guard the plantation records which he was collecting. "For God's sake," implored Phillips, "keep 'em in a fire-proof vault."[17]

As a young historian, Phillips scoured the South for all types of plantation records and located important groups in city, state, and local archives. Many of his most noteworthy discoveries, however, came from private collections, access to which he gained through such personal contacts as Georgia planter John C. Reed. It was through Reed that he obtained the papers of Robert Toombs. Phillips relied heavily on these manuscripts for his biography of the Georgia fire-eater.[18] Summer appointments at several universities granted him the opportunity to investigate southern records much more thoroughly. At the Virginia State Library, for example, he uncovered 1,300 vouchers of bondsmen convicted of capital crimes. These served as the basis of Phillips's "Slave Crime in Virginia" published in 1915 in the *American Historical Review.*[19]

Besides supplying him with valuable primary sources for his books, Phillips's position as the authority on southern manuscript collections brought him other rewards. Several of the more valuable sources which he uncovered were published in their raw form as edited documents. In such works as "The Correspondence of Robert Toombs, Alexander H. Stephens, and Howell Cobb" (1913) and *Plantation and Frontier* (2 vols., 1909), he made important manuscript materials available for the use of other scholars. Phillips also gained appointments to the AHA's Public Archives and Historical Manuscripts Commissions. Throughout his career he continued to extol manuscripts as the most important sources in the study of southern history.[20]

Between 1903 and 1906 Phillips contributed articles to the AHA's *Annual Reports* which offer a glimpse into his conception of the limitless value of manuscripts to the student of slavery. In two of these essays, analyses of Georgia's public and local archives, Phillips emphasized the importance of property inventories and manuscript census returns. He considered them instruments in compiling numbers and values of slaves on farms and plantations over specific periods of time. From such information, Phillips said, plantation tendencies—such as average slave and land holdings—could be determined.[21]

The Georgian claimed that information in town and county records was of special value in the study of the economics of slavery. Local archives, he argued, contained vast amounts of significant material in contrast to the printed sources on the subject, which were "scanty and fugitive, and often unreliable." Phillips added: "The county records of appraisements and sales of estates at auction comprise the chief source from which knowledge may be had of the rise and fall of slave prices. A comparative study of data of this sort... will be essential as a basis for any definitive economic history of slavery in America." Such raw materials as wills, oaths, court minutes, and local slave ordinances joined plantation records as important sources used in Phillips's writings. He predicted that as these sources became increasingly available to researchers, they would replace the generally "fallacious" antebellum travelers' accounts.[22]

Phillips's correspondence reveals his great dependence on personal and professional contacts to locate and gain access to the various plantation records which he used in his writings. Through adventuresome manuscript hunts in the South with agricultural historian Herbert Anthony Kellar and others, Phillips acquired a rich collection of pamphlets, journals, and manuscripts. The buying, selling, and trading of these sources became for him a hobby closely related to his historical work. And Phillips was generous with his rare books and manuscripts. Many of his former colleagues and graduate students recalled how he shared with them his prize archival finds. When visiting the Phillips home at Ann Arbor, Avery O. Craven admired one of his host's rare volumes. Upon returning to his own residence Craven discovered that Phillips had slipped the volume secretly into his suitcase as a gift.[23] According to Fred Landon, Phillips possessed "the same zest for manuscripts that a fisherman might have for a trout stream." Not surprisingly, Phillips warmly recommended in 1928 that funds be allocated to help establish the Southern Historical Collection at the University of North Carolina. J.G. de Roulhac Hamilton—founder of the collection and longtime friend of Phillips—guaranteed the Georgian first crack at a "most wonderful body of plantation material." Hamilton explained that this was "a reward of virtue," but no doubt it was influenced by Phillips's endorsement of the funding of the collection.[24] Such personal connections and his affluence enabled Phillips to become the leading figure in the use of plantation materials. These sources were not easily obtained and Phillips's rise within the historical profession was attributable partly to his unusual access to them.

Among the papers of Herbert Anthony Kellar (1887-1955), Phillips's friend and fellow manuscript collector, is a valuable and entertaining document which illustrates the lengths to which Phillips and other early southern historians had to go to procure plantation manuscripts. A native Nebraskan and educated at Chicago, Stanford, and Wisconsin, Kellar served as director of the McCormick Historical Association in Chicago for almost four decades. He was a resourceful and energetic collector of manuscripts and at the McCormick Library developed one of the best collections of colonial and nineteenth century agricultural materials in the United States. Like Phillips, he enjoyed uncovering manuscripts—especially those pertaining to the farm and plantation. During the 1920's the two historians exchanged letters in which they discussed the location and value of sundry manuscript collections. At different times Phillips and Kellar exchanged or sold historical materials to each another.[25]

Kellar's unpublished "Notes on Trips to Virginia with Ulrich B. Phillips in Search of Manuscripts" is a charming reminiscence of a manuscript expedition in Virginia's Shenandoah Valley in the spring of 1926. Collecting materials for his projected *Life and Labor in the Old South*, Phillips joined Kellar in Lexington, Virginia, on April 17 after a number of stops at archival repositories in the lower South. Joining the two historians was James Rion McKissick (1884-1944), a South Carolina journalist who later served as president of the University of South Carolina. McKissick shared his colleagues' interest in manuscripts and was an avid collector of historical materials relating to the Palmetto State.[26]

The trio embarked on their manuscript-hunting trip through rural Virginia armed with a thirst for uncovering virgin manuscripts and fortified by two quarts of bootleg whiskey which the resourceful McKissick had acquired. On the first day they traveled by bus from Lexington to Greenville, located in Augusta County, about twenty-four miles away. They next rented an automobile and drove to the home of Kellar's acquaintance George W. Armentrout, a farmer antiquarian who several times previously had invited Kellar to examine his collection of old documents. Upon reaching Armentrout's farm the three researchers were stunned when the Virginian's elderly sister informed them that her brother had been dead for three years. Not to be denied their opportunity to look through the Armentrout collection, Phillips, McKissick, and Kellar persuaded their hostess to take them to one of her late brother's farms, then inhabited by a tenant. As Kellar later wrote in his recollection of the trip, "because the roads were rough, and our own car none too reliable, we accepted an invitation to ride in her Ford." Kellar described the remainder of this journey as only a participant could.[27]

> After Ulrich, McKissick, George's sister, and myself had gotten into the car, together with a boy to drive, we had a rather full load, but we did not care for adventure lay ahead. The ride was not all it might have been for the wind was cold and raw and we were half frozen before we reached our destination. Ulrich with his long arms vainly

attempted to hold down the curtains of the car to keep out the cold wind. Eventually descending into a deep valley, we stopped at the edge of a bawling creek, where the Ford disgorged its passengers, and we made preparations to cross a rickety foot bridge of the suspension type—the house was set back a few yards from the bank on the other side. The bridge did not look particularly trustworthy, but McKissick bravely volunteered to try it first. Our apprehensions proved correct for McKissick almost fell into the water, but finally to the accompaniment of free advice, he crossed safely and profiting by his example we quickly followed.

At the house George's sister knocked on the door and the wife of the tenant appeared. In answer to a request for George's papers, the woman nodded an assent and presently reappeared dragging a large and disreputable looking gunny sack. Like feasters at a banquet we eagerly gathered around the sack and opened it. At once we perceived that it was full of old letters and papers. Digging down into the mass, I pulled out a letter and looking at it found that it was dated 1732. I asked the woman if there were any more bags, and eventually she brought out four other sacks similar to the first. By this time Phillips and McKissick, not to mention myself, were becoming quite excited. Tying the sacks on the fenders and on the top of the car, and presenting a most bizarre appearance to anyone who might happen to meet us on the road, we started back to the… Armentrout house. On the way Phillips whispered to me: "I think we ought to get this material if we can." I replied in the affirmative, and suggested we make an offer. Phillips then wanted to know what I thought would be proper, and I said, "Well, suppose we offer $5.00 a sack, sight unseen." To our surprise and gratification, George's sister accepted the proposition and we promptly paid over the twenty-five dollars.

At the Armentrout house we transferred the treasure to our own car and as quickly as we decently could, made our departure, fearing all the while that the sister might change her mind about letting us have the material. As it turned out our fears were quite unfounded, because she was delighted to be able to obtain the amount stipulated in order to clear up some matters in connection with her brother's estate, of which she was the administratrix.

Reaching Greenville we found that the train, which ran to Lexington once a day, was due shortly, and accordingly decided to travel by that means since it would make it easier to carry our newly acquired possessions. At the station we bought tickets and turned over the sacks to the agent, asking him to express them with us to Lexington.

A few moments later the agent came up to me with a puzzled expression on his face and regretfully imparted the information that he could not accept the bags for shipment. Upon asking the reason, he said that he looked all through his express schedules and could find no designation which covered the content, which he had been told were old papers. I then told him that if he could not accept our papers, we would take them with us in the coach. The agent kindly, but firmly, said that this could not be done. In this impasse the agent suddenly had a brilliant idea, and asked if we objected to his shipping them as "corn shucks." So corn shucks they were and Phillips gravely paid out thirty cents to ship five sacks of corn shucks from Greenville to Lexington.

Upon arrival at our destination we hired a taxi and proceeded to the Dutch Inn. The guests in that somewhat sedate establishment were greatly astonished to see two colored boys, bending and staggering under the weight of five huge gunny sacks, proceeding through the front door, solemnly followed by three scholars, disheveled in appearance, but with the light of victory glowing in their eyes. An ominous pause ensued, but Mrs. Louise Owen, the proprietress, who is used to my vagaries, gallantly rose to the occasion and rented us a room for the gunny sacks.

Thereupon for two days and two nights with the aid of the major portion of the two quarts of whiskey and the enthusiasm of the quest for the unknown, Phillips, McKissick and myself proceeded to examine the twenty-five thousand or more documents contained in the gunny sacks. Befitting our enterprise and belief in cooperation, the arrangement that we made was practical and efficient. Taking one bag at a time, each of us selected a goodly portion for inspection. After due industry each had two piles, one of large proportion which was chaff, and one of smaller size which was wheat. In the course of our endeavor Phillips found about two thousand slavery items; I found several thousand iron furnace papers and McKissick, curiously enough, a few South Carolina items. When Phillips and McKissick finished, I still had three documents to go through. One turned out to be worthless. The second proved to be an iron furnace item. The third, the last document of the twenty-five thousand to be examined, nearly gave me apoplexy. I read it through once and then passed it to Ulrich with the remark "Do my eyes deceive me?" Ulrich took one look at what I handed him and let out a whoop of joy in which he was soon joined by McKissick. The document was a contract in the handwriting of Daniel Boone and signed by him, in which he accepted some several hundred pounds from a Mr. Johnson of Augusta County in return for which Boone proposed to locate a large tract of land for Johnson on his next trip to Kentucky. We voted that the occasion was dramatic and called for the finishing of the second bottle, which we did.[28]

The cache of documents uncovered by Phillips, Kellar, and McKissick is impressive even when contrasted with the large volume of plantation and slavery-related materials now readily available to researchers. But the 1920's was a different era both in the development of southern archives and in the serious study of southern history. It was the start of what one scholar has recently termed the "take-off point" of southern historiography.[29] Modern archivists, conditioned to think in terms of records managers, data banks, and endowment grants, frequently fail to appreciate the problems under which their forebears labored. Men such as J.G. de Roulhac Hamilton of the University of North Carolina and William K. Boyd of Duke University were successful collectors because they possessed uncanny abilities for ferreting out manuscripts from a variety of obscure places. Historians accustomed to the rich collections of plantation manuscript materials at Chapel Hill, Durham, and other southern repositories also should recall the barriers which their predecessors faced in locating sources. Even when Phillips and his contemporaries had the luxury of examining archival materials in the confines of a library, rarely were the documents carefully arranged and catalogued.

Owen, Rowland, Hamilton, Phillips, Kellar, and Boyd—to mention only a few of the better known pioneer historians and archivists—performed several vital functions for southern archival development. They educated southerners in the importance of preserving past records and they helped establish the nuclei of important manuscript libraries which today rank among the nation's best. Through their writings they further helped advance the scientific and objective study of the southern past. Following Laprade's suggestions early students of slavery helped solve the South's archival problems. Their efforts form a key chapter both in archival history and the historiography of slavery.

Notes

1. William Thomas Laprade, "Newspapers as a Source for the History of American Slavery," *South Atlantic Quarterly*, 9 (July, 1910), 230-38 and "Some Problems in Writing the History of American Slavery," *ibid.*, 10 (April, 1911), 134-41.

2. "Some Problems in Writing the History of American Slavery," 134. Laprade's interest in slavery is evident in his unpublished manuscript, "The Legal Status of the Negroes in the District of Columbia Previous to the Abolition of Slavery, 1800-1862," [1911], William Thomas Laprade Papers, Duke University Archives.

3. See John David Smith, "The Formative Period of American Slave Historiography, 1890-1920" (unpublished Ph.D. dissertation, University of Kentucky, 1977).

4. "Three Centuries of Southern Records, 1607-1907," *Journal of Southern History*, 10 (Feb., 1944), 23-25; Mrs. Granville T. Prior to John David Smith, 13 Feb. 1975, in possession of the author.

5. *Southern Historical Society Papers*, 1 (Jan., 1865), 41; "Historical Sketch of the Association,"*Publications of the Southern History Association*, 1 (Jan., 1897), 5-6; E. Merton Coulter, "What the South Has Done About Its History," *Journal of Southern History*, 2 (Feb., 1936), 27; George P. Garrison to Franklin L. Riley, 26 Dec. 1907, Franklin L. Riley Papers, Southern Historical Collection, University of North Carolina.

6. Winsor, "Manuscript Sources of American History—The Conspicuous Collections Extant," *Papers of the American Historical Association*, 3 (May, 1887), 19, 22, 27; Wendell Holmes Stephenson, "The South Lives in History: A Decade of Historical Investigation," *The Historical Outlook*, 23 (April, 1932), 153; William P. Trent, *William Gilmore Simms* (Boston, 1892), v; "The Study of Southern History," *Publications of the Vanderbilt Southern History Society*, 1 (1895), 16; Weeks to Thomas M. Pittman, 24 Dec. 1899, Thomas Merritt Pittman Papers, Southern Historical Collection, University of North Carolina.

7. Stone to Dodd, 10 July 1907, Baker to Dodd, 23 June 1909, William E. Dodd Papers, Manuscript Division, Library of Congress.

8. Review of Thomas Nelson Page, *The Old South; Essays Social and Political*, in *Sewanee Review*, 1 (Nov., 1892), 90; Meekins to Adams, 10 April 1893, Herbert Baxter Adams Papers, The Johns Hopkins University Library.

9. Stephenson, "The South Lives in History," p. 153; Jameson to Thomas M. Owen, 14 Jan. 1905, Jameson to Hart, 12 Jan. 1905, Hart to Jameson, 23 Jan. 1905, J. Franklin Jameson Papers, Manuscript Division, Library of Congress; Hamilton, "History in the South—A Retrospect of Half A Century," *North Carolina Historical Review*, 31 (April, 1954), 177; Hamer, "The Records of Southern History," *Journal of Southern History*, 5 (Feb., 1939), 9; Hamilton, "Three Centuries of Southern Records, 1607-1907," 16; Coulter, "What the South Has Done About Its History," 6.

10. Dodd, "Some Difficulties of the History Teacher in the South," *South Atlantic Quarterly*, 3 (April, 1904), 121; Charles H. Haskins, "Report of the Proceedings of the Nineteenth Annual Meeting of the American Historical Association," *Annual Report of the American Historical Association For The Year 1903* (2 vols.; Washington, 1904), I:29; Ford, "Manuscripts and Historical Archives," *Annual Report of the American Historical Association For the Year 1913* (2 vols; Washington, 1915), I:78; Barker, letter to the editor, *The Nation*, 99 (2 July 1914), 15; Fleming to Barker [30 Dec. 1912], copy in Wendell Holmes Stephenson Papers, Duke University Library; *New York Times*, 7 Sept. 1924, clipping in Dodd Papers; Kilpatrick, *Preserving Southern History Material: An Address Before the Southern Club of Columbia University, July 31, 1923* (New York, 1923).

11. "Report of the Mississippi Historical Commission," *Publications of the Mississippi Historical Society*, 5 (1902), 75; Phillips to Yates Snowden, 13 Jan. 1905, Yates Snowden Papers, South Caroliniana Library, University of South Carolina; Owen to William K. Boyd, 22 Nov. 1907, William K. Boyd Papers, Duke University Archives; Montgomery (Ala.) *Journal*, 23 Dec. 1903, clipping in Thomas M. Owen Papers, Alabama Department of Archives and History; Owen, ed., "Report of the

Alabama History Commission to the Governor of Alabama," *Publications of the Alabama Historical Society*, 1 (1900), *passim*; Owen to W.G. Leland, 1 September 1906, Jameson Papers.

12. Bancroft to Rowland, 22 March 1912, Frederic Bancroft Papers, Columbia University Library; Carl A. Ray to John David Smith, 6 Feb. 1975, in possession of the author; Hamer, "The Records of Southern History," 12; Connor, "The North Carolina Historical Commission," *Publications of the North Carolina Historical Commission*, 1 (1907), 9-10; Paul P. Hoffman to John David Smith, 7 Feb. 1975, in possession of the author; J.D. Rodeffer, "The South's Interest in the Library of Congress," *South Atlantic Quarterly*, 4 (October, 1905), 319, 322; John C. Broderick to John David Smith, 27 Feb. 1975, in possession of the author; John McDonough, "Manuscript Resources for the Study of Negro Life and History," *The Quarterly Journal of the Library of Congress*, 26 (July, 1969), 136; Bancroft to Theodore D. Jervey, 8 Dec. 1914, Bancroft Papers.

13. Smith, "The Formative Period of American Slave Historiography, 1890-1920," chapters 9 and 10.

14. *Ibid*.

15. *Ibid*.; Phillips to Andrew C. McLaughlin, 10 Dec. 1904, Jameson Papers.

16. Phillips, unpublished and untitled manuscript beginning, "The field of Southern history is so rich," [1904?], Ulrich B. Phillips Collection, Yale University Library, "The South Carolina Federalists, I," *American Historical Review*, 14 (April, 1909), 529.

17. Phillips to George J. Baldwin, 5 May 1903, Phillips to Lucien H. Boggs, 23 Feb. 1903, Ulrich B. Phillips Papers, Southern Historical Collection, University of North Carolina; Phillips, "The Public Archives of Georgia," *Annual Report of the American Historical Association For the Year 1903* (2 vols.; Washington, 1904), I:467; Phillips to Snowden, 31 March 1906, Snowden Papers; Phillips, "Plantation Records in General," in Phillips and James David Glunt, eds., *Florida Plantation Records* (St. Louis, 1927), 1-5.

18. Phillips, *The Life of Robert Toombs* (New York, 1913).

19. Phillips to J. Franklin Jameson, 20 Nov. 1905, Jameson Papers; Phillips to Jameson, 10 Oct. 1907, *American Historical Review* Editorial Correspondence, Manuscript Division, Library of Congress; Phillips to Frederick Jackson Turner, 12 July 1903, Frederick Jackson Turner Correspondence, University of Wisconsin Archives; Phillips to Jameson, 24 Dec. 1912, Phillips to Waldo G. Leland, 16 Jan. 1905, Phillips to Andrew C. McLaughlin, 17 Feb., 27 April 1904, Jameson Papers.

20. Phillips to J. Franklin Jameson, 8 July 1905, *American Historical Review* Editorial Correspondence; Phillips to Yates Snowden, 26 Sept. 1909, Snowden Papers; *The Galveston* (Tex.) *News*, 31 Jan. 1929, clipping in Phillips Scrapbook, Phillips Collection.

21. Phillips, "The Public Archives of Georgia," 439-74, and "Georgia Local Archives," *Annual Report of the American Historical Association For the Year 1904* (Washington, 1905), 555-96.

22. Phillips, "The Public Archives of Georgia," 464; "Documentary Collections and Publications in the Older States of the South," *Annual Report of the American Historical Association For the Year 1905* (2 vols.; Washington, 1906), I:203-4.

23. "Some Historians I Have Known," *The Maryland Historian*, 1 (Spring, 1970), 11.

24. Landon, "Ulrich Bonnell Phillips: Historian of the South," *Journal of Southern History*, 5 (August, 1939), 367; J.G. de Roulhac Hamilton to Phillips, 27 Oct. 1928, Dexter Perkins to Hamilton, 7 Jan. 1929, J.G. de Roulhac Hamilton Papers, Southern Historical Collection, University of North Carolina.

25. On Kellar see: Margaret C. Norton, "Herbert Anthony Kellar, 1887-1955," *The American Archivist*, 19 (April, 1956), 151-53; William B. Hesseltine and Donald R. McNeil, eds., *In Support of Clio: Essays in Memory of Herbert A. Kellar* (Madison, 1958), iii-viii, 41-43, 140.

26. Phillips to Kellar, 15 Feb., 1, 9, 24 March 1926, and Kellar to Phillips, 17 March 1926, Herbert Anthony Kellar Papers, State Historical Society of Wisconsin.

27. Kellar, "Notes on Trips to Virginia with Ulrich B. Phillips in Search of Manuscripts," 1-4, Kellar Papers.

28. *Ibid.*, 4-9.

29. James P. Hendrix, Jr., "From Romance to Scholarship: Southern History at the Take-Off Point," *Mississippi Quarterly*, 30 (Spring, 1977), 193-211.

15

U. B. Phillips, Unscientific Historian

W. K. Wood

The central theme of U.B. Phillips's career as a historian, or so we have been told, was his espousal of the scientific-critical method. As he himself wrote in his first published book, "Georgia and State Rights":

> I have made little use... of the historical imagination. The method is that of the investigator rather than the literary historian. The work is intended to be a thorough scientific treatment of its subject. No pains have been spared in obtaining exhaustive and accurate information.

Accuracy, objectivity, and thoroughness in research, these then were the watchwords that would guide him in his many writings on southern history. For Phillips, there were to be no bold generalizations about the past, only the facts painstakingly gathered, scientifically analyzed, and objectively reported. "Generalities have mostly been avoided," he declared in "Plantation and Frontier." Only "the facts are simply and plainly stated...."[1] At least that was the ideal. As numerous critics have pointed out over the years, Phillips was anything but a scientific historian. Phillips, they have noted, limited his investigations to upland Georgia and South Carolina and informed his judgments with a belief in the inherent inferiority of the Negro. Moreover, he selected evidence, cited some sources incompletely and ignored others. In short, basic subjective influence and fundamental methodological errors seriously compromised his view of slavery in the South.[2]

Further evidence of Phillips's unscientific methods can be found in *A History of Transportation in the Eastern Cotton Belt to 1860*, which was published in 1908.[3] Many of the same methodological and analytical shortcomings that marred his later studies of slavery—such as his neglect of important source materials, his misuse of evidence, and his misinterpretation of facts—also appear in this earlier work. Considering Phillips's central role in the writing and interpretation of southern history, not to mention the fact that *A History of Transportation* has yet to be critically examined, it is important that historians recognize these various shortcomings, for they raise anew the old debate over his reputation as a historian and the value and validity of his works. This is especially true in view of renewed interest in Phillips and efforts to revive his opinions on slavery and race. As one historian has observed, "Phillips remains a prominent historian who deserves consideration in any treatment of the Old South" and "even after the revisions of recent scholarship... we are left with important insights into the mechanics of the southern economy and society." Hopefully, the analysis presented here will not only remind us that Phillips's works are not the definitive studies on their respective subjects, but in the process help resolve the long-standing controversy concerning the accuracy and objectivity of his writings on the Old South.[4]

The basis for this critical analysis of Phillips's methodology is the author's own research into the antebellum history of the Georgia Railroad and Banking Company, one of the railroads included in *A History of Transportation*. It was while researching the voluminous records of this venerable old company, which date back to 1834 and nearly all of which are extant, that deficiencies in Phillips's research and discrepancies in his analysis were first realized. Most notable in this respect was Phillips's failure to exploit the extensive manuscript records of the company themselves. These include the following volumes for the antebellum period: "Minutes of the Board of Directors of Ga. R.R. & B. Co. [at Athens], March 10, 1834-May 11, 1840"; "Minutes of the Board of Directors of Ga. R.R. & B. Co. [at Athens], July 14, 1840-May11, 1842"; "Minutes of the Board of Directors of Ga. R.R. & B. Co. [at Augusta], June 7, 1836-March 23, 1842"; "Minutes of the Board of Directors of Ga. R.R. & B. Co. [at Augusta], May 18, 1841-May 10, 1871"; and "Minutes of the Stockholders of Ga. R.R. & B. Co., May 11, 1835-May 12, 1868." As far as this writer knows, these records were available for Phillips's use at the time he wrote his study of transportation; at least this writer was given complete access to them by company officials.[5]

Another key source that Phillips neglected in his account of the Georgia Railroad and Banking Company was the Augusta *Chronicle*, extensive files for which were available for the period he studied (1833-1860). In view of the importance of Augusta in the history of this company, this valuable primary source should have figured more prominently in his analysis. Phillips nevertheless relied almost exclusively upon the Athens *Southern Banner*. A check of the footnotes in his chapter on the Georgia Railroad and Banking Company reveals thirty-two citations to the *Banner* and only one to the *Chronicle*, and that one was quoted from the former paper. Beyond this much quoted source, Phillips seems to have relied primarily upon the *Memorial History of Augusta* by Charles C. Jones, Jr. and Salem Dutcher. As

Phillips wrote, "the history of the road...[had] already been well treated by Mr. Salem Dutcher."[6]

Phillips also ignored the Augusta City Council Minutes which date back to 1804.[7] While these records are not nearly as important as the *Chronicle*, they provide valuable information about the internal improvements craze and the railroad mania that followed in the years after 1830. They also reveal the important role that cities like Augusta played in the promotion and funding of transportation projects.[8] For that matter, Phillips can be said to have overlooked Augusta completely both as a repository of useful information and as a center of trade, commerce, and culture.[9] Phillips, for example, did not mention the Augusta Canal; nor did he recognize the contributions of Augustans in the field of business. Three individuals in this regard come readily to mind: William Longstreet, father of the humorist Augustus Baldwin Longstreet and steam-boat builder (some say inventor); John P. King, U.S. Senator and president of the Georgia Railroad and Banking Company from 1841 to 1878; and Henry Harford Cumming, father of the Augusta Canal.[10]

It should not be supposed that Phillips's neglect of primary source materials was limited solely to Augusta and the Georgia Railroad and Banking Company. He also ignored or only used sparingly similar records for the other railroads included in *A History of Transportation*. In the case of the Central of Georgia Railroad, Phillips only referred to company reports for 1838-1841, 1844-1848, 1855, and 1857-1860, although annual reports and other records were available for the entire antebellum period. As described by Jefferson Max Dixon and James F. Doster in their respective studies, these include one bound volume of legal documents (charter, deeds, leases, mortgages), annual reports of the presidents, engineers-in-chief, and superintendents, and three manuscript volumes of directors' minutes. The same complaint can be made about Phillips's use of records for the South Carolina Railroad with only twelve references to company records being recorded. Similarly under-utilized were the voluminous records of the Western and Atlantic Railroad. Phillips cited reports only for 1839, 1841, 1848, and 1855-1864.[11]

In addition to these company materials, there were other antebellum newspapers and town records that Phillips could have used but did not. Examples of the former include the Augusta *State Rights' Sentinel*, the Charleston *Mercury*, the Greenville (S.C.) *Mountaineer*, the Macon (Ga.) *Messenger*, and the Savannah *Daily Georgian*.[12] In the latter category, the eastern cotton belt towns to Atlanta, Macon, Milledgeville, and Savannah all have town records or minutes that go back to the antebellum period.[13] Newspapers are invaluable sources, containing as they do both straight news reporting as well as editorial opinion and conflicting views about the issues of the day. As new vehicles of conveyance, railroads received extensive press coverage, much of it in opposition to their introduction, at least in the formative years (which aspect of antebellum railroading Phillips did not investigate). Municipal records, on the other hand, could have been used to identify rail leaders as well as to study the financing of rail projects, their impact upon communities, and the opposition they engendered.[14]

Beyond these more local materials, there were still other primary sources that escaped Phillips's attention. Of special interest here are the report of the Select Committee on Southern Railroads during the second session of the Fortieth Congress (1867-1868) and four railroad directories that antedate *Poor's Railroad Manual* begun in 1868: [James W.] *Low's Railway Directory for 1858*... (New York, 1858); the *Low & Burgess Railroad Directory* (New York, 1858-1865); *Burgess' Railway Record* (New York, 1861-1868); and [A.H.] *King's Railroad Directory* (New York, 1867-1869). In addition to identifying antebellum southern rail leaders, the congressional study of "Southern Railroads" contains useful statistical data on the property value of selected rail companies, their length in miles, principal termini, and their indebtedness to the U.S. government for railway materials received. As for the railroad directories, the one edited by James W. Low exhibits "a correct list of all the officers and directors of the railroads in the United States and Canada... together with their financial condition."[15] The other directories provide information about "most railways in [the] U.S. and Canada" with lists of officers and directors, financial data, length, and location.[16] Similar information can be found in *Appleton's Companion Handbook of Travel* (1860), which Phillips also failed to cite.[17]

Another category of studies that Phillips overlooked includes technical treatises and engineering manuals such as *Appleton's Cyclopedia of Applied Mechanics* (New York, 1889); the *Illustrated Catalogue of Locomotives* (Philadelphia, 1881) by the Baldwin Locomotive Works; *Locomotives and Locomotive Building in America; being a brief Sketch of various improvements in locomotive building... together with a history of the origin and growth of the Rogers Locomotive and Machine Works...* (New York, 1876); Stephen H. Long, *Rail Road Manual, or, A Brief Exposition of Principles and Deductions Applicable in Tracing the Route of a Rail Road* (Baltimore, 1829); Earl Thomas, *Treatise on Rail-Roads and Internal Communications* (Philadelphia, 1830); William M. Gillespie, *Manual of the Principles and Practices of Road-Making* (New York, 1853); George L. Vose, *Handbook of Railroad Construction* (Boston, 1857); John Weale, *Elementary and Practical Instructions on the Science of Railway Construction*...(London, 1861); and Charles Paine, *The Elements of Railroading* (New York, 1895).[18]

Although Phillips cannot be blamed for not employing oral history in his study, it is regrettable that he did not do more with personal interviews since many of the southern rail leaders were still living at the time Phillips wrote his study. Some possibilities here include Algernon Buford (1826-1911), John C. Calhoun (1843-1918), Patrick Calhoun (1856-1943), William P. Clyde (1839-1923), William W. Gordon (1834-1923), Harry B. Hollins

(1854-1938), Thomas M. Logan (1840-1914), Charles H. McGhee (1828-1907), William G. Raoul (1843-1913), and Richard T. Wilson (1831-1910). Oral history was not as popular then as it is today; nevertheless, the effort could have yielded additional information about railroads in the South, their leaders, and their operations. More important, in the process of identifying and interviewing these personalities, Phillips might have discovered other valuable sources such as letters, diaries, and reminiscences.[19]

Phillips's neglect of the various sources, not to mention a plethora of secondary works, is all the more surprising when it is considered that he either knew about them directly or was more than likely aware of their existence. Phillips in fact had cited issues of the Augusta *Chronicle* in an earlier chapter of *A History of Transportation* and his first published study, "Georgia and State Rights," was based on extensive research in Georgia newspapers. He also referred to a file of annual reports of the Georgia Railroad that had been acquired by the Wisconsin Historical Society and, from previous studies, was aware of the extensive archives of the Western and Atlantic Railroad. At the same time, Phillips was probably familiar with an article by Julia A. Flisch in which she mentioned the Augusta City Council Minutes. His own articles, "The Public Archives of Georgia" and "Georgia Local Archives," had appeared in earlier volumes of the *Annual Report of the American Historical Association* for 1903 and 1904, respectively. As a research fellow with the Carnegie Institution of Washington, D.C. from 1904 to 1906, Phillips was in a position to know about research in progress and to have access to the available bibliography. Finally, Phillips had the opportunity to investigate town minutes and railroad records during his visits to southern cities.[20]

The point to be made here is that Phillips should have at least made the effort to seek out all pertinent sources and to use them in his study. After all, one of the first duties of a historian is to discern the best available sources for the subject at hand. As the *Harvard Guide to American History* has expressed this obligation:

> He [the historian] is thus committed, above all else, to the rigorous and unrelenting scrutiny of historical evidence. This commitment distinguishes his trade from that of the novelist, the propagandist, the prophet. Evidence is the only means by which to establish a historical fact; facts are the bricks out of which the structure of historical interpretation is erected. If there are not enough of them, the structure will collapse.

In the words of Homer C. Hockett, "the historian, no less than the scientist, must utilize evidence resting on reliable observation" and "the first step in the production of a historical work is naturally the gathering of the data pertinent to the topic." While it is true that the conditions of travel were not the best at the beginning of the twentieth century, it was not impossible to reach Atlanta, Augusta, Columbia, Charleston, Savannah, or other cities as demonstrated by Phillips's own frequent forays southward in search of historical materials. Besides, Phillips had at his disposal numerous reference works and finding aids to which he could have turned to identify sources as well as the extensive secondary literature about railroads that had been built-up in the years after 1880.[21]

Whatever the reason, Phillips did not comply with his own standards of the scientific-critical method, a failure that not only does little for his reputation as a historian but further detracts from the value and validity of A History of Transportation. By not researching the subject more fully than he did, Phillips overlooked important aspects of antebellum southern railroads that would have given him greater insights into their nature, operations and performance. To cite one example, Phillips would have discovered that the first railroads (North and South) were in the beginning very limited, local, and conservative enterprises and nothing like the railroads of the postbellum era which Phillips used as his standard of measure in evaluating pre-Civil War southern rails. In similar fashion, he would have realized that railroads in the South compared favorably in terms of construction, efficiency of operations, and management with their northern counterparts and thus were not inferior as he believed they were. Finally, Phillips would have observed that railroads in the South contributed in numerous and positive ways to the economic development of the region as a whole and did more than just carry cotton or extend slavery and the plantation system.[22]

In other words, had Phillips conducted more extensive research, he might have written a different book altogether. As it is, Phillips simply dismissed antebellum southern railroads for not being like those of the postbellum or modern era. Instead of being extensive in length and unified, southern railroads before 1860 were randomly located and conformed to no real system. Rather than transforming the economy and society of the Old South, as he believed they should, they only led to the intensification of plantation agriculture and the system of slavery. In short, railroads in the South were "sources of weakness and a failure" as well. More important, thus convinced that all railroads in the South were failures, Phillips saw little need to investigate the subject any further. As far as he was concerned, the history of railroads in the South was the simple story of failure repeated numerous times in the case histories of the rail companies included in A History of Transportation.[23]

If Phillips overlooked key historical materials, he also misinterpreted aspects of the Georgia Railroad and Banking Company's antebellum history. A case in point is his treatment of the removal of the company's principal office from Athens to Augusta in 1842. As he described it, from a pro-Athenian point of view, Augusta "had wrested the control of the corporation from Athens" with the implication being that the affair was a simple matter of politics and that underhanded tactics were somehow employed to effect the change. As it turns out, the decision to transfer the company's central office was more complex and less dramatic than implied by Phillips. In the first place, the decision itself was voted upon by the stockholders in convention as part of an amendment to the original charter of 1833 which had located the company's original headquarters in Athens. In the second place, little political acrimony accompanied the decision. (Newspapers in Athens and Augusta made little reference to the whole affair.) In the third place, the decision was related less to politics than to more practical considerations such as the years of financial crisis between 1837 and 1842 and the corresponding need for retrenchment. There was also the matter of Athens' isolated position vis-a-vis Augusta and the fact that the latter city served a larger population area in addition to being the receiving station for materials to construct the railroad.[24]

Phillips also misinterpreted the nature and function of the banking department of the Georgia Railroad and Banking Company. As he put it, the company "became almost as prominent in banking as in transportation, and in the long run throve so greatly in its banking that when at length the company leased its road to the Central of Georgia Railroad and retired from railroad operation, it continued its banking business. It is now [1908] one of the strongest banks in the South, and certainly one of the most luxurious- ly housed of all." Here Phillips seems to have projected backward his postbellum view of the Georgia Railroad's banking department which before the Civil War was merely an adjunct operation to the railroad. As John P. King, president of the company, remarked in 1858, "The Bank has not been mostly valued as a safe place of deposit and for the convenience it affords the operation of the [rail] Road... ." Nor did the company retire from its railroad operations after the lease of 1880. The company continued to operate the railroad as it still does today.[25]

Phillips's faulty methodology is further evident in his use (or misuse) of a letter written in 1854 to document what he thought was a long record of poor service by the Georgia Railroad to the town of Athens. As implied by Phillips, this neglect was a matter of company policy (owing to Augusta's supposed dominance of the board of directors) and dated back to 1842 when the company's principal office was removed from Athens to Augusta. "Thenceforward," Phillips wrote, "Athens had grievances to nurse, with little chance of redressing them." In actuality, the 1854 letter was related to a more recent and temporary problem, namely, an acute shortage of railroad cars. The junction of several railroads at Marthasville (later Atlanta) re- quired more facilities and equipment there than at Athens and other points along the line of the Georgia Railroad. As Superintendent George Yonge observed in April, 1854, the company was then temporarily "short of a proper outfit of cars" despite efforts to correct the situation which was "diverting trade from the line of the Georgia Railroad." In other words, the particular grievances referred to in the letter were neither long-standing nor the result of settled policy by Augusta-oriented officials. Rather they were related to a booming demand for railroad services that the Georgia Railroad was unable to provide at the moment.[26]

What Phillips did here in effect was to use evidence out of context. Instead of ascertaining the real nature of the letter itself or the circumstances that gave rise to it, he simply connected it with the act of the removal in 1842 to build a case for continued bad treatment on the part of the Georgia Railroad and Banking Company. The end result was an exaggerated account of the Athens-Augusta rivalry as well as a distorted picture of internal company politics and the excellent service record compiled by the company. As Phillips himself admitted, "the management... continued into the war time to live up to its reputation of conservatism, far-sightedness, and efficiency" and the "common report along the route has it at this day that the Georgia Railroad has always been so careful and capable in its operation that no passenger has ever lost his life on one of its trains".[27]

Phillips's use of this anonymous 1854 letter also points up another deficiency in his analysis of the Georgia Railroad and Banking Company and that is his pro-Athens bias. Instead of looking at Augusta's side of the story or considering the larger problems and priorities that confronted the company's directorate, Phillips simply accepted at face value the Athens' sources upon which he relied so heavily. Had he investigated the subject more thoroughly, he would have realized the facts related above and thus presented a more accurate and objective account of the company's antebellum history. He would have also realized that the letter in question represented more than just one anonymous Athenian's pique against the Georgia Railroad. Rather, it underscored the larger realization that Athens would not be the dominant commercial center in Georgia. In sum, Athens was not so much being neglected as it was being overshadowed by the rise of Atlanta.[28]

In retrospect, Phillips was not the scientific historian that he made himself out to be. If anything, the evidence presented here points to the opposite view of Phillips as a somewhat careless researcher who, far from conducting exhaustive research, happened to use the most readily available sources for his study of southern transportation. Nor can it be said that Phillips eschewed generalization given the highly interpretative nature of *A History of Transportation*. The purpose of that study in fact was not so much to provide a comprehensive history of transportation in all of its aspects but to present an account of the coming of the railroad and its failure to transform the economy and society of the Old South.[29] In this sense, Phillips's book must be viewed for what it really is and that is a very subjective work that tells us as much about Phillips's own view of what southern railroads should have been and done as it does about their actual nature and operations. Phillips's "fancy," it appears, was not "restricted by the records" after all and like Pegasus he preferred to soar as well as to delve.[30]

Notes

1. Ulrich Bonnell Phillips, "Georgia and State Rights: A Study of the Political History of Georgia from the Revolution to the Civil War, with Particular Regard to Federal Relations," in the *Annual Report of the American Historical Association for the Year 1901* (Washington, D.C., 1902), 5-6. The second quote is from "Plantation and Frontier: Documents, 1649-1863, Illustrative of Industrial History in the Colonial and Ante-Bellum South," in John R. Commons, et al., eds., *Documentary History of American Industrial Society*, 10 vols. (Cleveland, 1910-1911), I: 97. As Phillips would add later: "What must be sought is the absolute truth, whether creditable or not." (Quoted in Wendell Holmes Stephenson, *The South Lives in History: Southern Historians and Their Legacy* [Baton Rouge, 1955], 58.) According to Wood Gray, "the real source of his strength lay in his mastery of materials. Perhaps he, more than any other man who has worked in the field of southern history, succeeded in gaining this thorough familiarity with its sources." See Gray, "Ulrich Bonnell Phillips," in William T. Hutchinson, ed., *The Marcus W. Jernegan Essays in American Historiography* (Chicago, 1937; New York, 1958), 368. For other historians' praise of Phillips's scholarship and objectivity, see Stephenson, *The South Lives in History*; Fred Landon, "Ulrich Bonnell Phillips: Historian of the South," *Journal of Southern History*, 5 (August, 1939), 364-71; Phillip C. Newman, "Ulrich Bonnell Phillips—The South's Foremost Historian," *Georgia Historical Quarterly*, 25 (September, 1941), 244-61; and Harvey Wish, "Ulrich B. Phillips and the Image of the South," in *The American Historian* (New York, 1960), 236-64.

2. See Richard Hofstadter, "U.B. Phillips and the Plantation Legend," *Journal of Negro History*, 29 (April, 1944), 109-24; Kenneth M. Stampp, "The Historian and Southern Negro Slavery," *American Historical Review*, 57 (April, 1952), 613-24; Stephenson, *The South Lives in History*, 59-60, 72, 75, 81, 83-85; Ruben Kugler, "U.B. Phillips' Use of Sources," *Journal of Negro History*, 47 (July, 1962), 368-80; Gray, "Ulrich Bonnell Phillips," 369, 371; and Sam E. Salem, "U.B. Phillips and the Scientific Tradition," *Georgia Historical Quarterly*, 44 (June, 1960), 172-85. Included in Kugler's article cited above are references to earlier critical reviews of Phillips's studies by Carter G. Woodson, W.E.B. Du Bois, and Frederic Bancroft.

3. *A History of Transportation* was published in 1908 by the Columbia University Press. Page citations are to the 1968 reprint edition by the Octagon Press, Inc. of New York. So far as this writer knows, *A History of Transportation* has never been critically examined by scholars or used in any analysis of Phillips's life and works. See Wood, "*A History of Transportation*: One of U.B. Phillips's Early Works and Its Significance" (forthcoming).

4. See James M. McPherson, "Slavery and Race," *Perspectives in American History*, 3 (1969), 460-73, especially 463. See also Robert E. Shalhope, "Race, Class, Slavery, and the Antebellum Southern Mind," *Journal of Southern History*, 38 (November 1971), 557-74. Phillips's most enthusiastic latter-day supporter is Eugene D.

Genovese who edited a collection of Phillips's articles in 1968 published by the Louisiana State University Press: Ulrich Bonnell Phillips, *The Slave Economy of the Old South: Selected Essays in Economic and Social History*. See also his *In Red and Black: Marxian Explorations in Southern and Afro-American History* (New York, 1971) which contains two articles on Phillips. Other recent reevaluations of Phillips are: William L. Van Deburg, "Progress and the Conservative Historian," *Georgia Historical Quarterly*, 55 (Fall, 1971), 406-16; Allan M. Winkler, "Ulrich Bonnell Phillips: A Reappraisal," *South Atlantic Quarterly*, 71 (Spring, 1972), 234-45; John H. Roper, "A Case of Forgotten Identity: Ulrich B. Phillips As A Young Progressive," *Georgia Historical Quarterly*, 60 (Summer, 1975); Ruth H. Crocker, "Ulrich Phillips: A Southern Historian Reconsidered," *Louisiana Studies*, 15 (Summer, 1976), 113-30; and John David Smith, "The Historiographic Rise, Fall, and Resurrection of Ulrich Bonnell Phillips," *Georgia Historical Quarterly*, 65 (Summer, 1981), 138-53.

5. See W.K. Wood, "Conservative Banking During Crisis: The Georgia Railroad and Banking Company, 1836-1842," *Richmond County History*, 3 (Spring, 1971), 37-52; "The Georgia Railroad and Banking Company," *Georgia Historical Quarterly*, 57 (Winter, 1973), 544-61; "A Note on Pro-Urbanism and Urbanization in the Ante-Bellum South" Augusta, Georgia, 1820-1860," *Richmond County History*, 6 (Winter, 1974) 23-32; and "Henry Harford Cumming, 1799-1866: A Case Study of Republicanism and Civic Virtue in the Old South," *ibid.*, 9 (Winter, 1977), 5-9. The author would like to thank Dr. Darcy Jones of the Georgia State Archives for informing him that the records of the Georgia Railroad and Banking Company have now been acquired by the Georgia Historical Society. They were previously housed in the offices of the Georgia Railroad Bank and Trust Company in Augusta. The only other historians to make use of this valuable collection are Mary G. Cumming, *Georgia Railroad and Banking Company, 1833-1945: An Historic Narrative* (Augusta, Ga., 1945) and James F. Doster, "The Georgia Railroad & Banking Company in the Reconstruction Era," *Georgia Historical Quarterly*, 48 (March, 1964), 1-32.

6. Phillips, *A History of Transportation*, Chap. IV. The quote is from page 246.

7. These records, now located in the mayor's office, are briefly described by Julia Flisch in "Archives of Augusta, Ga., and of Richmond County," *Annual Report of the American Historical Association for the Year 1906* (Washington, D.C., 1908), 159-64. A more detailed analysis can be found in the inventory prepared by the Works Project Administration in 1939.

8. One of the standing committees of council in 1820, was that on "Roads." See the entry for 3 June 1820, in "Augusta City Council Minutes, 2 November 1816-24 May 1823" (ms. volume, mayor's office, Augusta, Georgia). For the city's expenditures on its river bank and wharves and its purchase of Georgia Railroad stock, see the statements of receipts and expenditures in *ibid.*, 12 April 1831-11 November 1837 (entries for 12 April 1834 and 10 April 1835) and *ibid.*, 21 April 1852-6 July 1855 (entry for 6 November 1852). For Augusta's interest in transportation and its efforts to promote itself, see *ibid.*, 21 April 1852-6 July 1855 and *ibid.*, 14 April 1857-21 March 1861 (entries for 12 November 1852; 7 May, 6 June, 8 August 1853; 14 April, 20 May, 8 July 1857; and 24 April 1858).

9. It would not be incorrect to state here that Augusta is one of the most overlooked cities in antebellum southern history despite the fact that it was a leading

commercial center (first with the Indian trade and later with tobacco and cotton) and later a sizeable manufacturing and transportation center. Augusta was also important in publishing circles with numerous newspapers and magazines being printed there during the antebellum period. Many of its citizens, moreover, made important contributions in law, medicine, business and the military. In addition to the *Memorial History of Augusta*, see Herbert Wender, *Southern Commercial Conventions, 1837-1859* (Baltimore, 1930); William T. Couch, ed., *Culture in the South* (Chapel Hill, 1934); Henry Prentice Miller, "The Life and Works of William Tappan Thompson" (Ph.D. diss., University of Chicago, 1942); Ray Dempsey, "The History and Influence of Major Southern Literary Magazines Prior to the Civil War" (M.A. thesis, University of Georgia, 1947). See also the description by George White in his *Statistics of the State of Georgia...* (Savannah, 1849): While "monuments of their enterprise and benevolence are seen in every direction," Augusta could also "boast of men profoundly versed in the various departments of learning.... . In no place in the United States, have we met with gentlemen more extensively read in polite literature, and more deeply learned in the professions of law, medicine, and theology than Augusta." (*Ibid.*, 501, 507.)

10. The Augusta Canal was begun in 1845 "for the purpose of affording an adequate supply of water for manufacturing and other purposes with a view of increasing the population and enhancing the value of real estate...." (Entry for 24 April 1858, in "Augusta City Council Minutes, 14 April 1857-21 March 1861.") The operations of the canal can be followed in the reports of its commissioners in the Augusta City Council Minutes, 1845-1861. William Longstreet's exploits as an inventor and entrepreneur are recounted in Jones and Dutcher, *Memorial History of Augusta*, 146, 166. Biographical information about John P. King can be found in *ibid*, and in the *Biographical Dictionary of the American Congress*, while his economic and political views are expressed in the *Register of Debates*, 1833-1837, and in the records of the Georgia Railroad and Banking Company, 1841-1878. An extensive collection of Cumming Family Papers is housed at the South Caroliniana Library at the University of South Carolina. A smaller collection of Thomas Cumming Papers is at the Georgia Historical Society in Savannah. Thomas Cumming was the first mayor of the city of Augusta (1798), a prominent banker and merchant, and father of Henry Harford Cumming. See Wood, "Henry Harford Cumming, 1799-1866" and Wood, ed., *A Northern Daughter and A Southern Wife: The Civil War Letters and Reminiscences of Katharine H. Cumming, 1860-1865* (Augusta, 1976).

11. See Jefferson Max Dixon, "The Central of Georgia Railroad, 1833-1892" (Ph.D. diss., George Peabody College for Teachers, 1953) and James F. Doster, "The Georgia Railroad & Banking Company in the Reconstruction Era." As described by Samuel M. Derrick, extant records of the South Carolina Railroad in 1930 included annual and semi-annual reports of the president and directors (1828-1843), by-laws, directors' and stockholders' minutes (1835-1841), and reports by its chief-engineer, Horatio Allen. Also available were annual reports of the Louisville, Cincinnati, and Charleston Railroad (1837-1843) and the South Carolina Railroad (1843-1880). See *Centennial History of South Carolina Railroad*. The voluminous records of the Western & Atlantic Railroad are described in Record Group 18, Georgia State Archives. The author would like to thank Dr. Darcy Jones of that repository for providing a copy

of the Western & Atlantic inventory and Mr. Eggerton of the Southern Railway for loaning him a copy of Jefferson Max Dixon's study.

12. See Winifred Gregory, comp., *American Newspapers, 1821-1936* (New York, 1937). Microfilm copies of these newspapers are located at the University of Georgia, the University of Texas, the South Caroliniana Library of the University of South Carolina, and the Georgia Historical Society, respectively.

13. For descriptions of these records, see John C. Butler, *Historical Record of Macon and Middle Georgia* (Macon, 1879); Thomas C. Gamble, Jr., *History of the City Government of Savannah* (Savannah, 1900); U.B. Phillips, "Historical Notes of Milledgeville, Ga.," *Gulf States Historical Magazine,* 20 (November, 1903), 161-71; and Richard H. Haunton, "Law and Order in Savannah, 1850-1860," *Georgia Historical Quarterly,* 56 (Spring, 1972), 1-24.

14. For examples of studies in this vein, see Thomas C. Cochran, *Railroad Leaders, 1845-1890* (New York, 1953); Maury Klein, *The Great Richmond Terminal: A Study of Businessmen and Business Strategy* (Charlottesville, Va., 1970); George D. Greene, *Finance and Economic Development in the Old South: Louisiana Banking, 1804-1861* (Stanford, 1972); and Robert W. Fogel, *Railroads and American Economic Growth: Essays in Econometric History* (Baltimore, 1964). The standard study of anti-railroad sentiment is William Van Metre, *Early Opposition to the Steam Railroad* (New York, 1924). See also Lewis Haney, *A Congressional History of Railways in the United States to 1850* (Madison, Wis., 1908).

15. "Southern Railways," *House Reports,* 40 Cong., 2d Sess., 1868, No. 3, Part I, 1-130.

16. These directories as well as many of the other works cited in the text are identified in Henrietta Larson, ed., *Guide to Business History: Materials for the Study of American Business History and Suggestions for Their Use* (Cambridge, Mass., 1950). See *ibid.,* 711, 713. This invaluable work, according to the introductory note by Prof. N.S.B. Gras, "was begun about 1931."

17. This work was edited by T. Addison Richards. A copy can be found in the Thomas Cooper Library at the University of South Carolina.

18. See Larson, *Guide to Business History,* 214-15, 230-37, 678-702.

19. These men are described in Klein, *The Great Richmond Terminal,* Chap. II. Manuscript material cited by Klein includes the David Schenck Diary (Southern Historical Collection, University of North Carolina), William Raoul Letterbooks (Emory University), Charles M. McGhee Papers (Lawson-McGhee Library, Knoxville, Tennessee), E. Porter Alexander Papers (SHC-UNC), Edward C. Anderson Papers (SHC-UNC), William W. Gordon Papers (SHC-UNC), and Henry Grady Papers (Emory University).

20. References to the *Chronicle,* the annual reports of the Georgia Railroad, and to the Executive Manuscripts in the Georgia State Library can be found in *A History of Transportation,* 73, 86, 101, 117, 246, 294, and 313. Phillips's research trips are described in Stephenson, *The South Lives in History,* 63, 138 and in "Plantation and Frontier," I, 22, 103. See also Phillips's letter to Yates Snowden, 20 September 1904, in which he states that "I have been diligently exploring for material for four or five years." (Yates Snowden Papers, South Caroliniana Library, University of South Carolina.)

21. Oscar Handlin, et al., eds., *Harvard Guide to American History* (Cambridge, Mass., 1954), 22; Homer C. Hockett, *The Critical Method in Historical Research and Writing* (New York, 1955), 8, 13. See also Jacques Barzun and Henry F. Graff, *The Modern Researcher* (New York, 1977) and Deborah L. Haines, "Scientific History as a Teaching Method: The Formative Years," *Journal of American History*, 63 (March, 1977), 892-912. Reference works available for Phillips's use were: *Biographical Directory of Railway Officials of America* (Chicago, 1895); the *Scientific American* (begun in 1845); Frederick J. Teggart, *Catalogue of the Hopkins Railway Library* (Palo Alto, Calif., 1895); *Poole's Index to Periodical Literature*; the *Annual Magazine Subject Index*; Roswell's *American Newspaper Directory*; N.W. Ayer and Son, *American Newspaper Annual and Directory*; and Alice B. Kroeger, *Guide to the Study and Use of Reference Works* (Chicago, 1902).

22. See Wood, "U.B. Phillips and Railroads in the South Reconsidered" (forthcoming) and "U.B. Phillips and Antebellum Southern Rail Inferiority: The Origins of A Myth," *Southern Studies* 26 (Fall, 1987) 173-87. For a favorable comparison of antebellum southern railroads with those in the North, see the *Annual Report* of the Georgia Railroad and the Banking Company for 1848. The original view of the railroad is presented in the works by Fogel and Klein cited above.

23. For Phillips's negative conclusions, see *A History of Transportation*, 19-20, 388-90. See also Wood, "U.B. Phillips and Railroads in the South Reconsidered."

24. Phillips, *A History of Transportation*, 238; Wood, "Conservative Banking During Crisis: The Georgia Railroad and Banking Company, 1836-1842"; and Ernest C. Hynds, *Antebellum Athens and Clarke County, Georgia* (Athens, Ga., 1964). As the *Banner* reported on 13 May 1842: "We understand that the reports made to the Convention were highly satisfactory" and that "the amendment to the charter... was accepted, and the principal Bank will consequently be located in Augusta hereafter." A year later the *Banner* noted without a hint of prejudice that "a train will leave Athens on Saturday next at 6:30 a.m. and arrive in Augusta at 3:30 p.m. for the convenience of stockholders wanting to attend the annual convention." (*Ibid.*, 15 May 1843.) For the Georgia Railroad and Banking Company's response to the financial crisis of 1837-1845, see Wood, "Conservative Banking During Crisis: The Georgia Railroad and Banking company, 1836-1842." Phillips was correct in his view that Augusta was reluctant at first to support the proposed Georgia railroad since only fifteen hundred shares were assigned to commissioners there. (*A History of Transportation*, 224.) By 1836 Augusta had changed its mind as seen in the distribution of stock for that year which shows 3,632 shares for Richmond County (Augusta) and 3,618 for Clarke County (Athens). Charleston, by the way, only had twenty shares, a figure that does not support Phillips's claim of Charleston's great influence upon company affairs. See the Cashier's Report, 1836, in "Stockholders' Minutes, 9-11 May 1836."

25. Phillips, *A History of Transportation*, 231; "President's Report," in [Annual] *Reports of the Directors &c., of the Georgia Rail Road and Banking Company to the Stockholders in Convention, May 11, 1858* (Augusta, Ga., 1858), 7-8. The original purpose for securing banking privileges was to facilitate the financing of the railroad. See "Directors' Minutes [at Athens]," 24 October 1835. The lease to William Wadley of the Central of Georgia Railroad was assigned in April 1881, not 1880.

Wadley then offered a half-interest to the Louisville and Nashville Road and the other half to the Central on 1 June 1881. See Klein, *The Great Richmond Terminal*, 148-49. See also James F. Doster, "The Georgia Railroad & Banking Company in the Reconstruction Era," 27-28. The lease itself is in "Directors' Minutes, April 12, 1881," pp. 314-22.

26. Phillips, *A History of Transportation*, 238-239; "Superintendent's Report," in [Annual] *Reports of the Directors &c., of the Georgia Rail Road and Banking Co., to the Stockholders in Convention, May 9th, 1854* (Augusta, Ga., 1854), 8.

27. Phillips, *A History of Transportation*, 251.

28. On the rise of Atlanta, see Works Project Administration, *A City of the Modern South* (New York, 1942); Walter G. Cooper, *Official History of Fulton County* (Atlanta, 1934); and Franklin M. Gannett, *Yesterday's Atlanta* (Miami, Fla., 1974).

29. See Wood, "*A History of Transportation*: One of U.B. Phillips' Early Works and Its Significance" (forthcoming) and "U.B. Phillips and Antebellum Southern Rail Inferiority: The Origins of a Myth." For that matter, the central theme of all of his works was nothing less than the all-pervasive and totally negative impact of slavery upon the economic, social, and political development of the Old South. See Wood, "Ulrich Bonnell Phillips," in Clyde N. Wilson, ed., *Dictionary of Literary Biography* (Detroit, 1983), 350-63.

30. The quote is a reversal of Phillips's statement that "only when the wind is in a rare quarter would I give rein to Pegasus if I could. In the main I am content to delve rather than to try to soar." (*Life and Labor in the Old South*, viii.)

V

THE SOCIAL AND ECONOMIC HISTORIAN

U. B. Phillips's writings in the areas of social and economic history rank among his foremost contributions. As the essays in this section make clear, social and economic issues were inseparable in Phillips's work and neither were ever far from the center of his careful focus. Significantly, Phillips's two most important books—*American Negro Slavery* and *Life and Labor in the Old South*—interpreted the South's plantation system as a framework for both the region's social organization and its economic operation. These selections are also those which, because of the reputations of either their authors or the works from which they are drawn, have attracted far more attention than most critiques of Phillips. As a result, they have been extremely influential in shaping his reputation within the profession.

Among the best examples of such influential statements is the first essay in this section. Richard Hofstadter's landmark 1944 article appeared exactly ten years after Phillips's death, and was the first open challenge to his reputation by a white scholar. Hofstadter attacked both Phillips's methodology and his conclusions and, in so doing, touched on many of the themes echoed and further expounded upon by critics during the civil rights era. Had Hofstadter been more explicit in challenging Phillips's claim to a scientific approach to his work, this well-known piece would have fit just as well into the preceding section of this collection. But its inclusion among this set of essays serves to point up the fact that, despite its negative assessment, Hofstadter's description of Phillips's method provides a revealing look at how he approached his work as a social historian.

Two pieces from the 1960s accentuate Phillips's contribution to our social and/or economic understanding of the antebellum South. In an excerpt from his 1961 essay, "The Enigma of the South," David M. Potter, who studied with Phillips at Yale University, put Phillips within the context of the long-standing debate over the basis of southern distinctiveness. Potter underscored Phillips's tendency to vacillate between biracialism (social) and agrarianism (economic) as the dominant themes of his interpretation of the antebellum South, an ambivalence adapted by many subsequent scholars as well. Five years later, as part of his extended campaign to revive Phillips's reputation, Eugene D. Genovese edited a collection of Phillips's essays entitled *The Slave Economy of the Old South*. In his introduction to that 1968 volume, Genovese provided a perceptive, but very different, analysis of how Phillips portrayed the social and economic functions of the plantation system. Genovese's treatment is also an appreciation of Phillips's sense of perspective in acknowledging how integral each function was to the other.

In *Time on the Cross*, their controversial 1974 reinterpretation of the economics of slavery, economic historians Robert William Fogel and Stanley L. Engerman challenged the economic aspects of Phillips's work. Unlike other critics, they placed Phillips's writings squarely within the mainstream of historians of slavery—all of whom, according to Fogel and Engerman, had failed to recognize slavery's economic realities. Fogel and Engerman noted that Phillips's critics—including Hofstadter and Kenneth M. Stampp—were so preoccupied with challenging Phillips's neglect of slavery's abuses that they missed fundamental flaws in Phillips's economic analysis. Like Phillips, charged Fogel and Engerman, scores of other historians had erred in evaluating slave labor as inefficient and thus unprofitable. Fogel and Engerman's own challenge to that assumption ranked among the most central themes of *Time on the Cross*.

Finally, in an important 1977 essay, Daniel J. Singal made an even broader assessment of Phillips's career. Though his title reflects the thematic logic Singal assigned to much of Phillips's work—basically, a chronological continuity and an affinity of values between the Old and New Souths—he was also more explicit than other critics in delineating a major shift in Phillips's thought. It was only toward the end of his career, Singal maintained, that the conservatism many saw in the full body of Phillips's work actually became apparent.

16

U. B. Phillips and the Plantation Legend

Richard Hofstadter

"We are concerned with Southern civilization and its cherishing."

—U. B. Phillips

No single writer has been more influential in establishing patterns of belief about the plantation system of the Old South among scholars and teachers than the late Ulrich Bonnell Phillips. His *American Negro Slavery* and *Life and Labor in the Old South* are the most widely read scholarly studies of the slave system, and have become classic sources of information and propaganda about antebellum southern life.[1] Professor Phillips's interest was clearly centered in the planter class; so much so that his popular study of *Life and Labor in the Old South* gives only casual attention to those classes, slaveholding and non-slaveholding small planters and farmers, which comprised the vast majority of the white population of the antebellum South.[2] It is also significant that while one of the chapters of *American Negro Slavery* is entitled "Types of Large Plantations," there is no serious effort anywhere in the book to compare large and small plantations nor any mention of the necessity of such a comparison. While Phillips certainly did not originate the plantation legend of the Old South, he did his best to continue it.

Even as a study of the plantation system, there is a flaw in Phillips's method that has drawn too little comment. It rests essentially in the fact that he gave no thought to the technique of sampling and that his picture of slavery and slaveholders in the rural South was drawn chiefly from the types of plantations that were not at all representative of the common slaveholding unit. The precise importance of this failure for the study of the slave system cannot be stated until much more investigation has been done in the great realm that Phillips chose to ignore; but in the meantime, it is fair to say that his portrait of the Old South is not drawn from the whole of life. It is the purpose of this essay to show: first, that Phillips's data are inadequate and misleading as a sample of Southern slaveholding or slaveholders because of their almost exclusive emphasis on the plantation-sized unit; second, that they are not even a good sample of the plantation unit itself (under any reasonable definition of the plantation)[3] because of the extent to which they draw for their most critical data upon atypical plantations of the largest size; and third, that we have no assurance that the data he used could have given an adequate account of slave management and slave conditions because the vast majority of slaves did not live on plantations of this order.[4]

There is an obvious pragmatic reason for drawing one's evidence from such non-representative plantations which should be acknowledged: the sources for the larger units are much better preserved. Indeed, the materials on small plantations and slave farms of sub-plantation size may prove on full investigation to be so limited that an adequate historical account of them can never be given. This, on the other hand, should not be used to justify projecting the picture of the large plantation onto the southern scheme of things entire. If the vital chapters of books which purport to describe American Negro slavery as a whole, or life and labor in the Old South as a whole, are based almost exclusively upon a parade of evidence taken from extraordinary types of plantations, their effect is bound to be somewhat misleading, regardless of the author's intention. The task of portraying the large plantations and their slave system is in itself worth doing, but its significance for the whole story should not be exaggerated. It does an historian no harm to know precisely what he is talking about.

It is not too difficult to discover from what sort of plantation units Professor Phillips drew his materials on the slave system. He had a strong, and understandable, preference for manuscript plantation records when they were available, and for the case method.[5] While he made some use of farm journals, newspapers, and the considerable travelers' literature about conditions in the Old South, his descriptions of plantation life and plantation management are generally compounded from source records of specific plantations. Usually these plantations are identified.[6] A sample of the identifiable planters or plantations he cited, with an eye to learning something of their economic size and importance, enables us to determine roughly how representative his data were. The most important chapters describing plantation life and management in *American Negro Slavery* are numbered from XII to XV inclusive, and entitled respectively, "The Cotton Regime," "Types of Large Plantations," "Plantation Management," and "Plantation Labor."[7] The results of a survey of their materials can be best put in tabular form.

Figures are here available on the slaveholdings of twenty-nine out of the forty-one planters listed. Among the others there are nine on whom information is readily available to show that they were anything but common

American Negro Slavery	Planter or Plantation	State	Number of Slaves	Number of Plantations
209	Levin Covington	Miss.	46 [12]	
210, 262	J.W. Fowler	Miss.	51 [13]	
216	James H. Hammond	S. Ca.	300 [14]	2
218	Martin W. Philips	Miss.	66 [15]	
229	George Mason	Va.	300 [16]	
229	James Mercer	Va.	103	4
230	Philip St. George cocke	Va.	125	7 [17]
232	Samuel Hairston	Va.-N.Ca	1600	many
233	David R. Williams	S. Ca.	500	4
234	Col. Wade Hampton [18]	S. Ca.		
234	Senator McDuffie	S. Ca.	147	
234, 257	Alexander Telfair	Ga.	126 [19]	several
239, 262	Joseph A.S. Acklen [20]	Miss. or La.		8
240	Planter interviewed by F.L. Olmsted	Miss.	135	
240-41	Planter interviewed by F.L. Olmsted	Miss.	400	4
242	Valcour Aime	La.	231	
244	Dr. John P.R. Stone	La.	101	2
246	Duncan F. Kenner [21]	La.		
246	John Burnside [22]	La.	1000	4
249	Nathaniel Heyward	S. Ca.	2087	17 [23]
250	Pierce Butler	S. Ca.	678 [24]	
251	William Aiken	S. Ca.	700	
254	Charles Manigault	S. Ca.	90 [25]	2
259	Thomas Parker	S. Ca.		
261	P.C. Weston [26]	S. Ca.		
261	Richard Corbin	Va.	5 [27]	
274	Henry Laurens [28]	S. Ca.		many
276	John Taylor [29]	Va.		6
277	Robert Collins	Ga.		
278	"N.B.P." [30]	Ala.	150	
282	A.H. Pemberton	S. Ca.		
283	George Washington	Ca.	401 [31]	several
288	John B. Lamar [32]	Ga.		6
294	Z. Zingsley [33]	Fla.	50	
296	Joseph Davis [34]	Miss.	355	
296	Jefferson Davis	Miss.	113	
297	Charles C. Pinckney	S. Ca.	221 [35]	2
298	Howell Cobb	Ga.	90 [36]	
299	E. Tanneret	La.	73 [37]	
300	Magnolia Plantation	La.	138	
308	"Mr. Mickle"	S. Ca.		

small slaveowning farmers. There are three—Parker, Pemberton, and Mickle—on whom there is no ready information.

The average holding of twenty-six of the twenty-nine planters—such freaks as the Heyward, Hairston, and Burnside holdings are not counted because they would distort the average—is 218.8. The figure, which is a conservative one because several of the planters had more slaves than are indicated, bears out the suggestion that Phillips in the chapters surveyed was studying an extremely non-representative minority. Even in 1860 there were only 312 planters who had over 200 slaves. It is also noteworthy that none[38] of the twenty-nine planters were owners of less than 50 slaves, while the census of 1860 shows that over 97% of the slaveholders were in that class.

Between the publication of *American Negro Slavery* and *Life and Labor in the Old South*, Phillips published an article which shows that he was well aware of the fact that large slaveholders were very few and that a great mass of slaves lived on small farms. He pointed out that there was a great variety in details of regulation even on prosperous plantations, and added:[39] "It is regrettable that data descriptive of small plantations and farms are very scant. Such documents as exist point unmistakably to informality of control and intimacy of white and black personnel on such units. This is highly important in its bearing on race relations, for according to the census of 1860, for example, one-fourth of all the slaves in the United States were held in parcels of less than ten slaves each, and nearly another fourth in parcels of ten to twenty slaves."

Phillips's preoccupation with the large plantation, however, did not come to an end. *Life and Labor in the Old South* celebrates notable planters in almost ninety pages and contains but a fourteen-page chapter on "the plain people" which does not even deal with the small slaveholders among them.[40]

Applying the above system of tabulation to the relevant chapters[41] of the later book—and omitting all duplicated material from the earlier one—one finds a similar story.

Of the twenty plantations listed, there are thirteen for which we have figures. Among the seven on which no definite figures have been secured, there is information to show that all but two were something other than common small planters. The remaining two—A.H. Bernard and Richard Hugg King—are unclassified. Three of the twelve planters had less than 100 slaves; of these, two had less than 50.

The average number of slaves on the plantations for which figures have been listed—and it should be noted once again that many of the figures are incomplete—is 199.2, a figure approximately the average for the earlier book.

A glance at the states in which the plantations from both of Phillips's volumes are distributed reveals another interesting fact: they are taken

Life and Labor	Planter or Plantation [9]	State	Number [10] of Slaves	Number [11] of Plantations
197	James Hamilton, Jr. [42]	S. Ca.	7	
198	Pringle Plantation [43]	S. Ca.	400	3
199	Thomas Spalding [44]	Ga.	421	
200	A.H. Bernard	Va.		
215	Richard Hugg King	N. Ca.		
225	Robert Carter	Va.	509	
228	Hill Carter	Va.	106	
232	John Selden [45]	Va.	60	
235	William Bolling [46]	Va.	3	
240	William Massie [47]	Va.	139	5
252	Josiah Collins, II[48]	N. Ca.		
253	Henry & Thomas Burgwyn [49]	N. Ca.	100	
267	George Noble Jones	Ga.-Fla.	183 [50]	3
274	Charles & James Tait [51]	Ala.	275	2
282	Benjamin Fitzpatrick [52]	Ala.		
284	Thomas S. Dabney [53]	Miss.	200	5
290	John Palfrey [54]	La.	49	
300	James F. Perry	Texas	23 [55]	
302	William Hugg King [56]	Tenn.		
304	Mark R. Cockrill [57]	Tenn.-Miss.	125	2

almost entirely from Virginia, North Carolina, South Carolina, Georgia, Alabama, Louisiana, and Mississippi. (There are two references to Florida and Tennessee planters and one to a Texas planter.) Excluding Delaware, there are four of the older slave states—Maryland, Missouri, Kentucky, and (with two minor exceptions) Tennessee—that did not come within the scope of Phillips's central chapters as important sources of information on rural slaveholding. The census of 1860 shows that a total of 703,322 slaves were held in these states—or 17.9% of all slaves. It was precisely in these states that the largest plantations were most seldom to be found; there were only 74 planters in all of them who had more than 100 slaves in 1860. It was also in these states that the greatest numbers of slaves were owned in very small parcels. These four states had 36.5% of the South's owners of one slave, 34.5% of its owners of two slaves, and 33.5% of its owners of three slaves, etc. His neglect of these states, then, is a partial explanation of Phillips's failure to make a more adequate sample. The task of studying the deep South was so great that the omission of these border states is quite understandable, for a scholar's years are limited; but it should not be overlooked that their omission contributed to Phillips's overemphasis on the large plantation.

In order to appreciate the narrowness of Phillips's sample, it is desirable to take notice of the familiar figures from the census of 1860 on slaveholding. These figures do not under-represent the large plantation class, because they came at the end of a decade of concentration in slave ownership.[58]

SLAVEHOLDING IN 1860

Owners of 1 slave	76,670
2 slaves	45,934
3 slaves	34,747
4 slaves	28,907
5 slaves	24,225
6 slaves	20,600
7 slaves	17,235
8 slaves	14,852
9 slaves	12,511
Owners of 10-14 slaves	40,367
15-19 slaves	21,315
20-29 slaves	20,789
30-39 slaves	9,648
40-49 slaves	5,179
50-69 slaves	5,217
70-99 slaves	3,149
100-199 slaves	1,980
200-299 slaves	224
300-499 slaves	74
500-999 slaves	13
1,000 and over	1
Aggregate number of slaveholders	383,637
Total number of slaves in 1860	3,950,513

The figures show that 906,537 slaves—which is 22.9% of all slaves—belonged to owners of *less than ten*. Turning to the upper brackets, which unfortunately are not taken down so specifically, we notice that even on a somewhat inflated estimate[59] slightly less than 25% of all the slaves in the states were owned in parcels of more than 50 and that only 10% were owned in parcels of more than 100.

Insofar, then as Phillips drew his picture of the Old South from plantations of more than 100 slaves, he was sampling about 10% of all the slaves and less than 1% of all the slaveholders. It would be too much to say that he was studying the upper crust. For the most part, he was concentrating upon the upper crust of the upper crust.

The historian is often tempted to study an institution or a civilization through those sources which are most readily available or most graphic, whether or not they prove to be most representative. We must nevertheless acknowledge that our understanding of the antebellum South is unsatisfactory without fuller information about its numerous small farmers and planters and their slaves. Unfortunately such persons were not in the habit of keeping records. Frank L. and Harriet C. Owsley have remarked on the "almost complete lack of personal letters and farm records of the non-slaveholder, the small slaveholder, and even the small planter."[60] They believe, however, that a diligent use of county records and court records of both the state and federal governments will go a long way to make up for the lack of personal materials, and that the affairs of these classes can be recreated from them. The travelers' literature on the Old South can be used to supplement such sources. Frederick Law Olmsted, in particular, made a practice of traveling off the main river lines and the regular avenues of communication into those parts of the South in which alone, he asserted, it was possible to observe the smaller farm units in great numbers.[61] Professor Phillips distrusted Olmsted as an observer because he believed that Olmsted had an uncontrollable animus against the South.[62] For a close reader of Olmsted to share that distrust today is impossible. Another southerner has remarked, "The real question is, did the writer tell the truth? There is a transparent candor in every line Olmsted wrote."[63] Olmsted was not only an honest but an unusually acute observer, and I believe that a fuller and more accurate knowledge of the late antebellum South can be obtained from the volumes of Olmsted than from Professor Phillips's own writings. Phillips might even have taken from Olmsted a treatment of the small plantation and small slave farm that could have been highly congenial to his purpose. For Olmsted was convinced, on the basis of personal observation and interviews with southerners from various regions and walks of life, that slaves were in important respects better off on the small units where their status was much like that of a familiar hired laborer than on the large plantations which were so often owned by absentee landlords and run by harsh overseers. Although physically "less well provided for and more neglected in every way," they enjoyed privileges, he believed, "and are less liable to severe labor or excessive punishment than the majority of those belonging to wealthy proprietors, who work on large plantations under overseers."[64]

Olmsted was also convinced of the presence of cruelty on the large plantations and believed that it was inherent in the institution as a whole. It was presumably for this that Phillips spurned him as a reporter. The way of thinking which underlay Phillips's work needs no elaboration here. He was a native of Georgia, to whom the southern past always appeared in a haze of romance.[65] His conception of the Negro was characteristically southern, and his version of slavery has been moderately described by a relatively impartial historian as "friendly."[66] His books can best be placed in the course of our intellectual history when it is realized that they represent a latter-day phase of the pro-slavery argument.

In the course of a lifetime's work Phillips handled a truly extraordinary mass of original source material which he used to great advantage. But he used it in accordance with principles of selection governed by his personal bias. A materially different version of the slave system will doubtless emerge when scholars animated by a counter-bias, or perhaps, if it is not too much to hope for, by a far greater spirit of detachment, have subjected the system to a similarly intense study.

Phillips chose to portray the Negro slave as a singularly contented and docile "serio-comic" creature. His casual treatment of the slave's resistance to slavery and in particular of slave revolts was accordingly inadequate, and highly misleading, not merely as to the character of the slave but also upon critical aspects of race relations. A recent student has found records of no less than 250 slave revolts and conspiracies which took place on the present soil of the United States from the beginnings of the institution.[67] Furthermore, although Phillips was given to stressing the give-and-take process between master and slave, he never appreciated the extent to which the easement of the slave's condition came not from the master's benevolence but from the slave's resistance to extreme exploitation.[68] Phillips's approach to the subject of slave care on the plantation was likewise questionable. It was his practice to draw in large part upon ideal rules set down in planters' manuals and essays and instructions to overseers and to assume that the care of the slaves on the average plantation was as good as the rules on the subject published to the world by planters who may very well have been exceptionally able and who in some cases are known to have been unusually kind.[69] Phillips's conception of slave health, which was for the most part an exceedingly rosy one, was arrived at without reference to some of the best testimony available—that of southern white physicians—and the result was considerable distortion.[70] His ability to handle such a mass of evidence without feeling impelled to write so much as a page on the important subject of miscegenation is also striking testimony to Phillips's great powers of intellectual resistance.[71]

But whatever shortcomings are charged against Professor Phillips, there is one important thing that must be said on his behalf: so thorough was his work that, granted the same purpose, the same materials, and the same methods, his treatment of the Old South is unlikely to be altered in fundamental respects. New facts, minor variations may appear, but the pattern in historiography that he set will hardly be changed by anyone who shares his limitations. There is, however, nothing inevitable about his point of view or his technique. Let the study of the Old South be undertaken by other scholars who have absorbed the viewpoint of modern cultural anthropology, who have a feeling for social psychology (a matter of particular importance in the study of a regime in which status was so vital), who will concentrate upon the neglected rural elements that formed the great majority of the southern population, who will not rule out the testimony of more critical observers, and who will realize that any history of slavery must be written in large part from the standpoint of the slave—and then the possibilities of the Old South and the slave system as a field of research and historical experience will loom larger than ever.

Notes

1. U.B. Phillips, *American Negro Slavery* (New York, 1918); *Life and Labor in the Old South* (Boston, 1929). The latter volume has been reprinted seven times. See also his collection of documents, *Plantation and Frontier*, 2 vols. (Cleveland, 1909).

2. See Chapter XVII, "The Plain People."

3. Phillips defines the plantation roughly as a unit having twenty or more slaves. This workable definition is in general accord with the usage of the Old South. See *Life and Labor*, 339.

4. Phillips himself did not discuss this problem, although he was aware of it. *Ibid*, 207.

5. For a statement by Phillips of his preference for plantation records and his objection to travelers' accounts see *ibid.*, pp. 218-19.

6. There are many casual references to planters who cannot be identified in any way from the text, but such references form an unimportant part of Phillips's sources on the plantation.

7. The other nineteen chapters deal with such topics as the foreign and domestic slave trade, the historical development of the sugar islands and the rice coast, slavery in the northern colonies, the westward movement in the South, town slaves, free Negroes, "slave crime," attitudes on the profitability of slavery, and legal and business aspects of the institution. The adequacy of these parts of *American Negro Slavery* is not under discussion here.

8. These pages give the first reference to each planter in the chapters covered and if necessary any other pages giving information used in the table; on some planters there are many other references in the volume.

9. These are the specific planters or plantations referred to at any length in chapters XII to XV, whenever they are identifiable either as to persons or numbers of slaves, as almost all of them are. They embrace cotton, tobacco, rice, and sugar planters of the eighteenth and nineteenth centuries.

10. These figures are in many cases incomplete. I have listed minimal figures for planters who had larger numbers, when these larger numbers were not available. If different figures for different times are available, the largest is used. This accounts for a few deviations from the figures given by Phillips. Figures generally include slaves of all ages. When no source for the number of slaves or plantations is indicated in footnotes, the information is from *American Negro Slavery*.

11. Absence of a figure in this column does not necessarily mean that the planter had only one plantation.

12. This is a minimal figure, including only those engaged in cotton picking in 1844.

13. This is a minimal figure, including only those engaged in cotton picking in 1859.

14. *Dictionary of American Biography* (hereafter *D.A.B.*), VIII:208.

15. Philips was noted for his agricultural experimentation and his essays.

16. Charles A. Beard, *An Economic Interpretation of the Constitution* (New York, 1913), 128.

17. This planter had 125 slaves on one plantation alone—Belmead in Virginia. The *D.A.B.* lists him as the owner of "extensive plantation interests in Virginia and Mississippi." IV:254.

18. This Wade Hampton (1791-1858) was the father of the Wade Hampton of Reconstruction fame. He owned 2,400 acres; his father, the first Wade Hampton (1751 [or 52]-1835), was reputed at his death to be "the wealthiest planter in America." *D.A.B.*, VIII:212.

19. Telfair had 90 slaves on one of his plantations and 30 on another; undoubtedly this figure represents only a portion of his holdings.

20. Although no figure on Acklen's slaves is available, he is described by Phillips as "one of the greatest proprietors in that region (i.e., the Mississippi Valley)." (Page 239.) For the number of his plantations see L.C. Gray, *History of Agriculture in the Southern United States to 1860* (Washington, 1933), I:538.

21. Kenner was a great sugar planter. A plantation in Ascension Parish owned by him produced 710 hogsheads of sugar in 1851-2. This was the second largest output in a very rich parish. See P.A. Champiomier, *Statement of the Sugar Crop Made in Louisiana, 1851-2* (New Orleans, 1852), 13-14.

22. Burnside was a millionaire merchant, the owner of at least 6,000 acres of sugar cane, and the employer of "a staff of overseers." See Phillips, and L.C. Gray, *op. cit., History of Agriculture,* p. 538.

23. For full information see Duncan Clinch Heyward, *Seed from Madagascar* (Chapel Hill, 1937). This writer is the source (p. ix) for the number of plantations owned by his grandfather, whose slaveholdings, he believes, once ran as high as 2,500. The figure in the table is from Phillips.

24. See Ralph B. Flanders, *Plantation Slavery in Georgia* (Chapel Hill, 1933), 79.

25. This figure is probably much too low. Manigault's property, including slaves, was once valued at over $100,000. *Life and Labor,* 256.

26. Weston's was a rice plantation; he evidently had, in addition to his overseer, a plantation nurse, several drivers, watchmen, caretakers (for sluice valves), etc. His instructions to his overseer give evidence of a very considerable estate. *Plantation and Frontier,* I:115-122.

27. Five plantations are mentioned by Corbin to his overseer. *Ibid.,* I: 111-112.

28. Laurens, a rich merchant, owned about 20,000 acres. "20,000 sterling would my negroes produce if sold at auction tomorrow," he wrote during his later years. D.D. Wallace, *Life of Henry Laurens* (New York, 1915), 446.

29. I found no clear statement of the number of Taylor's slaves at any time. His importance in the history of American agriculture and in Jeffersonian politics is a familiar story. His will, drawn in 1824, which is somewhat unclear, indicates the

possession of at least six plantations. H.H. Simms, *John Taylor* (Richmond, 1932), 223-226.

30. "N.B.P." is identifiable as N.B. Powell of Chunneneggee, Alabama. See R.B. Flanders, *Plantation Slavery in Georgia,* 155.

31. This was the number of slaves owned by Washington in the year of his death. *The Writings of George Washington* (Washington, 1940), XXXVII:268.

32. Lamar administered six large estates, some of which were his own, others of which belonged to his brother-in-law, Howell Cobb. According to Phillips, he managed hundreds of slaves, all told.

33. The figure is probably minimal, for Kingsley gives it as the number of his slaves at the beginning of his plantation enterprise. He was an unusually benevolent planter, and the author of *A Treatise on the Patriarchal System of Society as it Exists... under the Name of Slavery* (n.p., 1834).

34. The Davises allowed their slaves an unusual amount of initiative and self-control. The figures on their slaves are in Charles S. Sydnor, *Slavery in Mississippi* (New York, 1933), 43.

35. See *Plantation and Frontier,* I:203.

36. This figure is probably much too small. Cobb had at least 90 slaves of *working age* in 1847. *Ibid.,* I:178.

37. The figure is minimal, since it includes only slaves over the age of fifteen.

38. The only apparent exception is one in which the full number of slaves is not given. See footnote 12.

39. "Plantations with Slave Labor and Free," *American Historical Review,* XXX (July, 1925), 743; see also *Life and Labor,* 218; *American Negro Slavery,* 226; "The Origin and Growth of the Southern Black Belts," *American Historical Review,* XI (July, 1906), 798-816.

40. *Life and Labor,* 218-304, 339-353.

41. Chapters XI, XII, XIII, and XIV, entitled respectively "Life in Thraldom," "Some Virginia Masters," "Southeastern Plantations," and "Planters of the Southwest."

42. James Hamilton, Jr. owned five rice and two cotton plantations and was active in other businesses, including railroads and land speculation. One of the founders of the Bank of Charleston, he became governor of his state. *D.A.B.,* VIII:188.

43. The plantation of John Julius Pringle. The figure of 400 slaves is minimal. *D.A.B.,* XV:238.

44. For figures see Flanders, *Plantation Slavery in Georgia,* 80.

45. John Selden bought the old estate of William Byrd at Westover.

46. Bolling regularly planted 100,000 tobacco plants and about 900 acres in wheat, according to Phillips.

47. Phillips also gives some account of this planter's wealthy father; see pp. 238-9.

48. Collins, a wheat planter, owned at least 1,400 acres and a rather elaborate establishment.

49. The Burgwyns had at least 2,550 acres and raised chiefly corn and wheat. See Guion G. Johnson, *Antebellum North Carolina* (Chapel Hill, 1937), 485.

50. The figure is minimal. Jones had two plantations in Florida and the record shows 85 slaves on the smaller, Chemonie, in 1852, and 98 on the larger, El Destino,

two years later. There was another plantation in Georgia. See U.B. Phillips and J.D. Glunt, *Florida Plantation Records* (St. Louis, 1927), 547-550.

51. The figure is minimal. James alone owned 275 Negroes in 1841. See Charles S. Davis, *The Cotton Kingdom in Alabama* (Montgomery, 1939), 72.

52. Fitzpatrick was at one time Governor of Alabama and a sizable planter in the Alabama River Valley. *D.A.B.*, VI:439.

53. Dabney owned one plantation and managed four others. His own consisted of about 4,000 acres. See *American Negro Slavery*, 179.

54. John Palfrey, a New Englander, is one of Phillips's few instances of a moderately situated and ultimately unsuccessful planter.

55. Large plantations were rare in Texas and Perry's seems to have been one of the larger ones. The largest list of cotton-picking hands in his record shows 23, but Perry hired the slaves of others in small lots on occasion and the scale of his operations seems to have been considerable. See Abigail Curlee in Eugene C. Barker, *Readings in Texas History* (Dallas, 1929), 417 ff.

56. King was at times a preacher, planter, miller, lumberman, boat builder, and schoolmaster. He owned a sawmill and a grist mill and planted corn, wheat, oats, tobacco, flax, and cotton, and built flatboats. He was a planter for only four years.

57. Cockrill owned a plantation in Mississippi and a very large stock farm in Tennessee.

58. The average slaveholding per slaveholding family in 1850 was 9.2; in 1860 it was 10.2. All figures are from Eighth Census of the U.S., vol. III, *Agriculture of the U.S. in 1860*, 247. Figures for 1850 are also given, 248. The 1860 figures are conveniently available in R.S. Cotterill, *The Old South* (2nd ed. rev., Glendale, 1939), 274-5.

59. There is a table giving the per cent distribution of slaves by size of holding in 1860 in each of the states in Gray, *History of Agriculture*, I:530. Only 8.5% of all the slaves were held in parcels of over 100 in 1850.

60. "The Economic Basis of Society in the Late Ante-Bellum South," *Journal of Southern History*, VI (February, 1940), 26. Francis Lieber, during his residence in South Carolina, was astonished to learn how little record-keeping was practiced, even among the planters. A cashier in a Columbia branch bank assured him "that not 5 men out of the 500 who have business with the bank know what they owe or keep proper books." I am obliged to Dr. Frank Freidel for this reference from Lieber's scrapbook on slavery.

61. *A Journey in the Back Country* (London, 1860), 158.

62. See Broadus Mitchell, *Frederick Law Olmsted, A Critic of the Old South* (Baltimore, 1924), 90. Mitchell believes Phillips's judgment on Olmsted was unjustified. See pp. 68-73.

63. Thomas H. Clark, "Frederick Law Olmsted on the South, 1889," *South Atlantic Quarterly*, III (January, 1904), 12.

64. *A Journey in the Seaboard Slave States* (New York and London, 1856), p. 620. For other references to the difference between large and small units in the treatment of slaves, see *ibid.*, 391, 447, 487; *A Journey in the Back Country*, 55, 58, 64-5, 123, 158, 202, 220, 226-7; for similar conclusions see Gray, I:460, 470, 489, 518, 519, 520. Phillips seems to have been quite uncertain as to whether small farmers dealt more harshly

or more easily with their slaves; the only evidence he cites is in favor of the large plantation. *Life and Labor*, 207.

65. For Phillips's background see the essay by Wood Gray in William T. Hutchinson (ed.), *The Marcus W. Jernegan Essays in American Historiography* (Chicago, 1937), pp. 354-373. For a frank and revealing statement of Phillips' social attitudes, see his essay, "The Historic Civilization of the South," *Agricultural History*, XII (April, 1938), 142-150.

66. Allan Nevins, *The Gateway to History* (New York, 1938), 39.

67. Herbert Aptheker, *American Negro Slave Revolts* (New York, 1943), 162 ff. Also relevant is the slaves' reaction to freedom. See Bell Irvin Wiley, *The Southern Negroes* (New Haven, 1938).

68. Frederick Law Olmsted pointed to a common and effective check. When the day's task had become fixed, he noted, it often became extremely difficult for the master to increase it. "If it should be systematically increased very much, there is a danger of a general stampede to the 'swamp'—and a danger the slave can always hold before his master's cupidity." *Seaboard Slave States*, 435-6. See also Raymond A. and Alice H. Bauer, "Day to Day Resistance to Slavery," *Journal of Negro History*, XXVII (October, 1942), 388-419.

69. See *American Negro Slavery*, chap. XIV. Phillips's method in this respect is followed by many other students. Sometimes these published rules themselves give evidence of miserable conditions. See Aptheker, *American Negro Slave Revolts*, 126.

70. Felice Swados, "Negro Health on the Antebellum Plantations," *Bulletin of the History of Medicine*, X (October, 1941), 460-72, has the most satisfactory review of the evidence. See also Richard Shryock, "Medical Practice in the Old South," *South Atlantic Quarterly*, XXIX (April, 1930), 172-5.

71. There is a short paragraph on miscegenation in *Life and Labor*, 205. On miscegenation see A.W. Calhoun, *A Social History of the American Family* (Cleveland, 1917-19), II, Chap. XII; E. Franklin Frazier, *The Negro Family in the United States* (Chicago, 1939), Chap. IV. For the importance of miscegenation in the social psychology of the South, see W.J. Cash, *The Mind of the South* (New York, 1941), 84-7, 128; John Dollard, *Caste and Class in a Southern Town* (New Haven, 1937); and Hortense Powdermaker, *After Freedom* (New York, 1939), all of which have illuminating material on the theme.

17

The Enigma of the South

David M. Potter

Although a whole generation of writers have made this tempting equation between southernism and agrarianism, it requires only a limited analysis to see that in many respects the southern economy and the southern society have not been agrarian at all; in fact, have embodied almost the antithesis of agrarianism. Agrarianism implies an escape from the commercialism of the money economy, but southern cotton and tobacco and sugar cultivators have consistently been agricultural businessmen producing for market and for cash income. Agrarianism implies production for use rather than production for sale, and therefore diversification rather than specialization, but the southern agriculturist stuck to his one crop system in the past as tenaciously as he clings to segregation at the present. It implies the independence of a husbandman who looks to no one else either for his access to the land or for the necessities of his living, but the southern cultivator has been historically either a slave or a sharecropper, without land and often without opportunity even to grow his own turnip greens in a garden patch. Meanwhile the southern landowner, whether an absentee planter or a mortgage-holding bank, frequently failed to follow the ennobling agrarian practice of laboring in the earth. To one who is impressed by these aspects, it may seem realistic to regard Calhoun rather than Jefferson as the typical leader of the South; the plantation producing raw materials for the textile industry, rather than the subsistence farm producing for use, as the typical economic unit; hierarchy rather than equality as the typical social condition; and conservatism rather than radicalism as the typical mode of thought.

One man who was long the leading historian of the South saw the region to some extent in these terms. This was Ulrich B. Phillips, who began his career around the turn of the century with studies of southern political history and the history of southern transportation. But wherever his investigations began, they always led him, as he himself said, back to one feature of life in the South which was constant both before emancipation and after, namely the presence of Negroes and whites whose destinies were inextricably intertwined but whose paths in life were separated by a biracial system. Accordingly, Phillips gave only slight attention to the agrarian theme. Instead he concentrated on the staple-crop economy with its plantation units and its slave labor. With supreme thoroughness in research, he made what remains the basic study of slavery as a system of labor (*American Negro Slavery*, 1918). Later he developed an artistry in writing which matched his soundness in research, and he achieved a felicitous conjunction of both talents in a study of the society and economy of the antebellum period (*Life and Labor in the Old South*, 1929).

When Phillips looked at the southern economy, the image which seemed visible to him was not an independent husbandman laboring in the soil, but a Negro field hand picking cotton. The persistence of this figure, either as a slave or as a sharecropper, and the persistence of the system which kept him in his subordinate role led Phillips, five years before his death in 1934, to write an essay, "The Central Theme of Southern History," in which he stated what he found at the core of distinctive southernism. This was not some agrarian ideal, but rather a fixed purpose on the part of the southern whites to preserve biracialism, or, as he said, in unvarnished terms, to assure that the South "shall be and remain a white man's country."

Although Phillips's stature is still recognized even by his critics, liberal historians have been reluctant to accept his views. Kenneth Stampp has written a new account of slavery (*The Peculiar Institution*, 1956) which emphasizes, as Phillips never did, the harsh and exploitative aspects of the system; Richard Hofstadter has criticized Phillips for giving too much attention to the plantation, and not enough to the slaves held in small holdings; and at least two writers have questioned the "Central Theme."

It is in some ways ironical for liberals, concerned as they are with the "sick South," to reject a formula which explains so cogently the chronic nature of the illness. But what they found fault with was not in fact the accuracy of Phillips's conclusion; it was rather the lack of moral indignation in his statement of it. By asserting that the policy of biracialism is and will continue to be a central aspect of southernism, without personally repudiating this policy, he made it difficult for liberals to identify with him. When Harry Ashmore, more recently, said in *An Epitaph for Dixie* (1958) that the South will cease to be the South when it ceases to be segregated, the statement was almost identical with that of Phillips, but liberals could accept Ashmore's because he expects the South, in the old sense, to vanish (hence "an epitaph"), whereas they could not accept Phillips's, because he seemingly expected the South to survive, with the implied corollary that efforts at integration must fail.

Moreover, in the case of liberals who want to love the South, as some do, but who find it psychologically impossible to love an embodiment of biracialism, the only recourse is a resort to Dodd's original formula: dispose of the factor which is troublesome (in this case the biracialism) by treating it as a great aberration. Here even so excellent a book as Vann Woodward's *Strange Career of Jim Crow* (1955) is a case in point, for though it was intended to emphasize a thoroughly valid observation—namely, that the patterns of biracialism have varied and are not immutable—it lends itself to being read as a statement that caste does not have very deep roots in the South. The preface to the paperback edition (1957) showed that Woodward was himself concerned that his work had been taken too much in this way.

18

Ulrich Bonnell Phillips as an Economic Historian

Eugene D. Genovese

For Ulrich Bonnell Phillips the economy formed only one part of the slave regime of the Old South. It never occurred to him to try to study it apart from ideology, politics, and social structure. He would have had no trouble in understanding Gunnar Myrdal's impatient dismissal of the conventional division of historical factors into economic and noneconomic; for Phillips, as for Myrdal, the only question for an economic historian concerned the extent to which economically rational decision-making was probable in daily life. He wasted little time in applying economic models, for he saw clearly what many of his critics have missed, that standards of rationality developed to study the capitalist marketplace would break down at too many points. Certainly, he understood the essentially capitalistic nature of that system of commodity production to which the South was committed, and one of his great contributions was the exploration of many of its mechanisms. He also understood—in his own terms—the countertendencies thrown up from within the plantation regime itself, specifically the attitudes, policies, and exigencies rooted in the peculiar labor system. Throughout his work there is an implicit distinction between that which might be considered economically rational in a free-labor economy and that which was socially rational (necessary for the maintenance of a special form order and class rule) for the slave system.

The social essays at the beginning and end of this collection stress the race question and offer the concern for white hegemony as the "central theme." Yet, these and the more narrowly economic essays may be read somewhat differently, as revealing the process by which a specific form of class hegemony arose, grew, and collapsed. For Phillips, the persistence of the race question proved that slavery itself was not central to southern history, but we might take issue sharply with his attempt to separate the southern ethos of paternalism and patriarchal responsibility from the master-slave relationship. This debate might more appropriately be pressed elsewhere. For our immediate purposes, it is enough that he strove with such determination and with such an impressive degree of success to develop a social framework within which the economy could be studied.

Chapters XVIII and XIX of Phillips's *American Negro Slavery* form an indispensable part of his contribution to southern economic history as narrowly defined. The first, "Economic Views of Slavery: A Survey of the Literature," constitutes an excellent review of the subject as of 1918 and retains great value. Few new arguments have been added to the debate on such questions as the productivity and costs of slave labor. New techniques of measurement have been advanced, most skillfully by Alfred H. Conrad and John R. Meyer, but even if, as we may hope, they prove to be long strides toward the solution of old problems, they have added few new ideas or arguments. After half a century Phillips's survey remains useful as an introduction to the subject in general as well as to the specifics of the debate down to World War I. The second, "Business Aspects of Slavery," offers a good account of Phillips's views, and supplements, corrects, and occasionally supersedes those earlier articles which are included in Part Two of this volume. The concluding paragraph of the chapter brings out two of his main points—that slavery cannot properly be understood in economic terms alone and that, whatever limited economic advantages of slave labor to planters, the broader effects on the economy as a whole were largely negative:

> The slaveholding regime kept money scarce, population sparse and land values accordingly low; it restricted the opportunities of many men of both races, and it kept many of the natural resources of the Southern country neglected. But it kept the main body of labor controlled, provisioned and mobile. Above all it maintained order and a notable degree of harmony in a community where confusion worse confounded would not have been far to seek. Plantation slavery had in strictly business aspects at least as many drawbacks as it had attractions. But in the large it was less a business than a life; it made fewer fortunes than it made men.

These and other chapters from *American Negro Slavery* have not been included in this volume because the book is again in print and available in a paperback edition. Those who wish to understand Phillips's thought must consult it and its sequel, *Life and Labor in the Old South*. This collection, however useful it may prove to be, ought to be read together with those books.

In a larger sense *American Negro Slavery, Life and Labor in the Old South*, these essays, and almost everything Phillips wrote form a massive contribution to the political economy of the slave regime. Harold D. Woodman, in his excellent historiographical article, "The Profitability of Slavery: A Perennial," has shown that two questions have become intertwined and sometimes confused in the secular debate on the economics of slavery. The first concerns the returns to individual producers, the second, the impact on regional economic growth and stability. As Woodman has pointed out, Phillips's primary interest lay in the second, and much of his finest work was done on its range of problems. Since Phillips saw plantation slavery as a pervasive social institution, its continued existence never presented itself to him as proof of economic viability. So long as the system could pay its way—in this sense any system is proven economically viable by the fact of its being—its preservation would rest on its usefulness as a means of social control.

He stressed the racial component: the presence of an inferior race, undisciplined to sustained labor, required a stern regime. Early in his career, as "The Plantation as a Civilizing Factor" especially makes clear, he viewed slavery as a special case in a general plantation condition. From this probe to the sophisticated "Central Theme of Southern History" he insisted on the primacy of the race question. While slavery seemed the best, and to some the only, means of controlling Negro labor, the system would continue regardless of its glaring economic faults. But there were limits. Past a certain point, he argued, the economic question could no longer be ignored, and the regime would evolve toward a form of serfdom or specially controlled "free" labor.

This viewpoint, which he linked to the thesis on the natural limits of slavery expansion most commonly associated with Ramsdell, contains serious difficulties. Unless Phillips thought that the system would become absolutely unprofitable—a dubious assumption to say the least—he came close to self-contradiction. He could rescue himself only by arguing that, in time, the specific attractiveness of slavery as a system of racial control would yield to the general attractiveness of the plantation system. To this line of argument several objections may be made. First, Phillips himself pointed out repeatedly, and Conrad and Meyer have underscored, that slavery made possible the degree of labor mobility required for the successful operation of the plantation system. Second, conversion to free labor, even if peaceably effected, would have required enormous capital investments that, as Phillips untiringly maintained, could not have come from within the South. It would therefore have opened the way to northern penetration and domination. Phillips took great pains to demonstrate that the southern regime created men of a special type—proud, tough, independent, and jealous of their prerogatives. It is therefore strange to confront his insistence that they ever would have faced such extraordinary threats to their hegemony and sensibilities with equanimity.

From one point of view, which I have developed elsewhere, Phillips's work may be read as an effort to lay bare the history and sociology of the slaveholders as a ruling class. His impressive article, "The Origin and Growth of the Southern Black Belts," is simultaneously a contribution to southern political economy and an impressive introduction to the formation of social classes, especially the planter class. He analyzed the process by which capital became concentrated in relatively few hands but also considered the various countertendencies that prevented the process from running its full course. In his elegantly constructed "Transportation in the Antebellum South: An Economic Analysis," which first appeared in the *Quarterly Journal of Economics* and then served as the opening chapter of his important monograph, *A History of Transportation in the Eastern Cotton Belt to 1860,* he wove economic geography and politics into a discussion of transportation and thereby added another dimension to the history of the slaveholding class. Ordinary economic interest compelled certain kinds of projects rather than others, but once developed, those projects reinforced the existing social regime and deepened the economic commitments beyond anything originally intended or perhaps thought advisable.

Phillips wrote little about town life and the middle classes but apparently retained considerable interest in them throughout his life. His personal papers, deposited at Yale University, contain a great many notes on these subjects, and one of his earliest articles dealt with urban history. His "Historical Notes of Milledgeville, Ga.," published in the short-lived *Gulf States Historical Magazine,* demonstrated what could be done with existing source materials on local history, but, more important, it drew attention to certain essential features of antebellum southern town life.

Phillips saw Milledgeville as a typically unprogressive town overshadowed by the plantation-studded countryside. Essentially a cotton-collecting and political center, it accumulated businessmen, lawyers, politicians, and planters, all of whom in one way or another lived off the countryside or its proceeds. His brief but suggestive discussion of the leading classes goes to the heart of the urban dimension of southern life. The country intruded itself into the town; when those who commanded the rural regime and its economy did not strangle the urban bourgeoisie at birth, they bent it to their lifelong will; and the plantation, its deals and temper, dominated the consciousness of the townsmen. These few pages offer, in addition to their revealing material on slave life, strong hints for further work, which still needs doing after half a century, and provide, in a burst of youthful insight, a firm grasp of the quality of life under the old regime.

In his accounts of transportation, town life, and the plantation system itself, economic problems and developments are treated as an integral part of the social regime. However much we may quarrel with Phillips's specific formulations or wish to revise his priority of race over class in the interpretation of southern history, there can be little doubt that he posed the difficult questions, advanced stimulating hypotheses, and kept the consideration of economics where it belongs—in the context of an integrated human history.

19

Toward an Explanation for the Persistence of the Myth of Black Incompetence

Robert William Fogel and Stanley L. Engerman

The principal cause of the persistence of the myth of black incompetence in American historiography is racism. Perhaps no single history book written during the twentieth century has had a greater impact on the interpretation of slave life than U. B. Phillips's *American Negro Slavery*. To point out that this volume was deeply marred by its author's adherence to the proposition that Negroes were racially inferior to whites would hardly evoke controversy among historians today. This point is now emphasized not only by the critics of Phillips but also his defenders.

How different the situation was when *American Negro Slavery* was published in 1918. Of the principal reviewers of the book, only two attacked Phillips's treatment of the historical profession as it was then constituted. One of these reviewers was W. E. B. Du Bois, the director of publicity and research for the N.A.A.C.P. and the editor of its journal, *Crisis*. Du Bois found *American Negro Slavery* "curiously incomplete and unfortunately biased."

> The Negro as a responsible human being has no place in the book. To be sure individual Negroes are treated here and there but mainly as exceptional or as illustrative facts for purposes outside themselves. Nowhere is there any adequate conception of "darkies," "niggers" and "negroes" (words liberally used throughout the book) as making a living mass of humanity with all the usual human reactions....

> Mr. Phillips recurs again and again to this inborn character of Negroes: they are "submissive," light-hearted" and "ingratiating" (p. 342), very "fond of display" (pp. 1, 291), with a "proneness to superstition" and "acceptance of subordination" (p. 291); "chaffing, and chattering" (p. 292) with "humble nonchalance and a freedom from carking care" (p. 416). From the fourteenth to the twentieth century Mr. Phillips sees no essential change in these predominant characteristics of the mass

of Negroes; and while he is finishing his book in a Y.M.C.A. army hut in the South all he sees in the Negro soldier is the "same easy-going amiable serio-comic obedience," and all he hears is the throwing of dice (pp. viii, ix). Even the few exceptional Negroes whom he mentions are of interest mainly because of their unexpected "ambition" and not for any special accomplishment (p. 432). The fighting black maroons were overcome by "fright" (p. 466), and the Negroes' part in the public movements like the Revolution was "barely appreciable" (p. 116); indeed his main picture is of "inert Negroes, the majority of whom are as yet perhaps less efficient in freedom than their forbears were as slaves" (p. 396)!

Brilliant as it was, Du Bois's critique fell largely on deaf ears. It could hardly have been otherwise during an era when the pseudoscientific racial theories which still dominated anthropology were widely accepted in scholarly circles. Indeed, more than two decades elapsed before scholars in the mainstream of the history profession began to press the theme enunciated by Du Bois.

While not unanticipated by others, the flag of general revolt against the Phillips school was raised by Richard Hofstadter in a 1944 paper entitled "U. B. Phillips and the Plantation Legend." Hofstadter attacked Phillips for exaggerating the paternalistic impulses of the planter, for painting too "rosy" a portrait of the material conditions of slave life, and for depicting the Negro as "a singularly contented and docile 'serio-comic' creature." The real nature of the treatment of slaves, said Hofstadter, was far more cruel than admitted, and slaves were more often left to the mercy of harsh overseers by their absentee owners than Phillips admitted. Hofstadter also charged Phillips with having underestimated the extent, and having distorted the nature of, "the slave's resistance to slavery." He chided Phillips for stressing a benign type of "give-and-take process between master and slave," for failing to appreciate "the extent to which the easement of the slave's condition came not from the master's benevolence but from the slave's resistance." Hofstadter ended his essay with a call for the rewriting of the history of slavery from the "viewpoint of modern cultural anthropology"; by this he meant the new view on race, pioneered by Franz Boas, which held that racial factors were unimportant in determining intellectual capacity.

Hofstadter's rebellion was far less sweeping than might appear. Hofstadter did not challenge Phillips on the general profitability and viability of slavery. Neither did he take issue with him on the quality of slave labor, on the economic efficiency of slavery, or on the effect of slavery on southern economic growth. Indeed, Hofstadter confined his attack to just four of the twenty-three chapters of *American Negro Slavery*, specifically excluding from consideration those which dealt with the issues of profitability, efficiency, and growth.

The limited nature of Hofstadter's attack on Phillips is not difficult to explain. Like so many others, Hofstadter's conception of slavery was developed largely from his reading of Olmsted. Hofstadter excoriated Phillips for not having made greater use of the work of this witness and critic. "Olmsted was not only an honest but an unusually acute observer," said Hofstadter, "and I believe that a fuller and more accurate knowledge of the late antebellum South can be obtained from the volumes of Olmsted than from Professor Phillips's own writings." But Phillips, despite his mistrust for the man, had read Olmsted with care and made great use of him. On the issues of the profitability and efficiency of slavery, as well as on the quality of slave labor and the effect of slavery on southern economic growth, Phillips was pure Olmsted. And on some of these issues Phillips merely paraphrased Olmsted. (Olmsted: "slaves thus get a fictitious value like stocks 'in a corner.'" Phillips: "When the supply [of slaves] was 'cornered' it was unavoidable that the price should be bid up to the point of overvaluation.")

Despite Phillips's pretensions to a revolutionary break with James Ford Rhodes, the dominant historian in the interpretation of southern slavery at the time Phillips was a graduate student, and despite Hofstadter's claims to a revolutionary break with Phillips, all three men — and the schools of historical writing on the antebellum South which they symbolize — were adherents to what we have termed the "traditional interpretation" of the slave economy. That interpretation is the one which emerged from the economic indictment of slavery described in chapter 5 of *Time on the Cross*. It consists of five main propositions. These are: 1, that slavery was generally an unprofitable investment, or depended on a trade in slaves to be profitable, except on new, highly fertile land; 2, that slavery was economically moribund; 3, that slave labor, and agricultural production based on slave labor, was economically inefficient; 4, that slavery caused the economy of the South to stagnate, or at least retarded its growth, during the antebellum era; 5, that slavery provided extremely harsh material conditions of life for the typical slave.

Phillips accepted all of these propositions except the last. When he claimed he was revolutionizing the interpretation of the antebellum South, he was referring only to point five, the harsh treatment of slaves, and to the shadow which that treatment cast on the character of slaveholders. Phillips did not have to overturn Rhodes on the character of blacks and the quality of their labor. Rhodes's views on the character of slaves and on the quality of their labor were fully congenial to Phillips. Rhodes described slaves as "indolent and filthy"; their expression was "besotted and generally repulsive"; on their "brute-like countenances...were painted stupidity, indolence, duplicity, and sensuality"; their labor was "stupid, plodding, machine-like"; licentiousness and indifference to chastity were "a natural inclination of the African race" which was further fostered by slavery; as women displayed "an entire lack of chastity," the men displayed "an entire lack of honesty"; and slave women yielded "without objection, except in isolated cases, to the passion of their master." In Rhodes's view the error of southern apologists was not in the claim that blacks were inferior, but in the manner in which they sought to cope with the problem created by this inferiority. "So long as Southern reasoners maintained that the negro race was inferior to the Caucasian, their basis was scientific truth, although their inference that this fact justified slavery was cruel as well as illogical."

The irony of Hofstadter's call for a rejection of the Phillips position on treatment, without a simultaneous attack on the other four points, is that it led in the direction of the re-establishment of the pre-Phillips or "pure" version of the traditional interpretation of the economics of slavery. As long as historians remained locked in combat on the issue of treatment, explicitly accepting all other aspects of the economic indictment of slavery, the myth of Negro incompetence continued to reign supreme—just as it had in the antebellum era when critics of slavery and apologists debated over whether slavery had exacerbated or ameliorated the "natural" inferiority of blacks.

We do not mean that Hofstadter, or that scholars who responded to his call, aimed to re-establish the theories of the racial inferiority of Negroes as they existed in Rhodes or as in Henry Clay, Hinton Rowan Helper, and Olmsted. Quite the contrary, as both Hofstadter and those who rallied to his banner have made clear, their aim was the unequivocal and complete rout of the racist myths that lingered on in the historiography of the antebellum South. What they failed to appreciate was that these racist myths drew sustenance not merely from one of the five points in the traditional interpretation of slavery but from each of them.

This was true even of Kenneth Stampp who... went further than any other post-Phillips scholar, except perhaps Lewis C. Gray, in rejecting the traditional interpretation of slavery. In *The Peculiar Institution*, Stampp argued that investments in slaves were quite generally profitable, indeed, highly profitable for most planters. He also rejected the contention that economic forces would by themselves have led to the demise of slavery, even in the upper South. Nor did Stampp find any evidence to support the claim that slavery prevented industrialization and economic growth. He pointed to "innumerable experiments" which "demonstrated that slaves could be employed profitably in factories," arguing that slaveholders preferred to operate in agriculture because, for the South, agriculture "seemed to be the surest avenue to financial success."

Stampp even expressed doubts about the fourth proposition in the traditional interpretation — that slavery was less efficient than an economic system based on free labor. "Slavery's economic critics overlooked the fact," he said, "that physical coercion, or the threat of it, proved to be a rather effective incentive, and that the system did not prevent masters from offering tempting rewards for the satisfactory performance of assigned tasks."

At this point, however, Stampp faltered. He hesitated to go on to the conclusion that slaves were equal to free men in the efficiency of their labor. He conceded that slave productivity was sharply reduced by "the slave's customary attitude of indifference toward his work, together with the numerous methods he devised to resist his enslavement." Stampp was able to hold on to his contention that slavery was profitable only by arguing that there were other "advantages" which "more than compensated for whatever superiority free labor had in efficiency." These "advantages" included longer hours of work, more complete exploitation of women and children, and lower real wages for slaves than for free men.

Why did Stampp, who broke with so much of the traditional interpretation and who came so close to rejecting the myth of the incompetence of slave labor, fail to do so? Why did he, as it were, pull back just as he seemed about to do so?

The answer lies in Stampp's preoccupation with the refutation of Phillips on point five, the nature of the treatment of slaves. Surely Phillips's idyllic portrait needed correction. In reacting against the Rhodes treatment of plantations as houses of immorality and unmitigated terror run by men who were not only brutal but corrupt, Phillips substituted a near-paradise—at least as much of a paradise on earth as was reasonable to expect from a "primitive" race whose "savage" instincts had to be kept in check and which had to be trained to overcome a "natural ineptitude" and "indolence." In Phillips's reconstruction, planters emerged not merely as good men but, to use Du Bois's word, as supermen. Slavery became "less a business than a life." The objective of planters was not so much to make a profit as to make men.

Recoiling from such apologetics, Stampp provided testimony that cruelty was indeed an ingrained feature of the treatment of slaves. The cases of cruelty which Phillips regarded as unusual, as outside the unwritten rules of the master class, emerged as a common pattern of which behavior in *The Peculiar Institution*. Cruelty, Stampp said, "was endemic in all slaveholding communities"; even those "who were concerned about the welfare of slaves found it difficult to draw a sharp line between acts of cruelty and such measures of physical force as were an inextricable part of slavery." For Stampp, cruelty arose not because of the malevolent nature of the slaveholders but because of the malevolent nature of the system—because a master could brook nothing less from his slave than "perfect" submission. To achieve that goal masters were impelled, regardless of their humanity in other respects, to develop in the Negro "a paralyzing fear of white men," to "impress upon him his innate inferiority," and to "instill in him a sense of complete dependence." While Stampp did not employ the concentration camp analogy later set forth by Stanley Elkins, his plantation strongly suggested a prison with cruel wardens.

From this point the argument could have gone—and did in fact go—in two directions. One was the direction taken by Elkins, who argued that a system as cruel as the one described by Stampp must have had a devastating impact on the personality of slaves. No one could live under so brutal a regime without succumbing to it. Negroes were not supermen, any more than were the Jews in Hitler's concentration camps. Although plantations were not concentration camps, the masters who ran the plantations had as much absolute power over slaves as Hitler's gauleiters had over the Jews and as much determination to crush their spirit. What emerged from the process was "Sambo, the typical plantation slave... docile but irresponsible, loyal but lazy, humble but chronically given to lying and stealing." Sambo's "behavior was full of infantile silliness" and his "relationship with his master was one of utter dependence and childlike attachment."

Stampp decided to move in a direction that, on the surface, appears quite different from the one Elkins chose. He argued that slaves did not succumb; they resisted. Resistance did not generally take the form of revolution or strikes. Such open forms of resistance were sheer suicide. There were no rebellions among U.S. slaves comparable to those in Jamaica or Brazil; there was no protracted guerilla warfare. Resistance in the U.S. took a much more subtle form; it came in guises so innocent that masters and overseers failed even to recognize it. The participants in this resistance movement "were the meek, smiling ones whom many thought were contented though irresponsible."

> They were not reckless rebels who risked their lives for freedom; if the thought of rebellion crossed their minds, the odds against success seemed too overwhelming to attempt it. But the inevitability of their bondage made it none the more attractive. And so, when they could, they protested by shirking their duties, injuring the crops, feigning illness, and disrupting the routine. These acts were, in part, an unspectacular kind of "day to day resistance to slavery."

What, of course, is common to both Stampp and Elkins is agreement on the characteristic of slave behavior: slaves lie, steal, feign illness, behave childishly, and shirk their duties. Indeed, this characterization has been one of the enduring constants in the literature on slavery. By whatever path they moved, writers on slavery usually returned to the theme of the inferiority of slave labor. To Olmsted, Rhodes, and Phillips the inferiority was due to racial factors. To Cairnes, inferiority was sociological in origin. To Elkins, the cause was psychological. To Stampp, the inferiority was due to "day to day resistance." Paradoxically, it was the slaveholders who were least inhibited in acknowledging that blacks were better workers than whites, although they attributed this superiority to themselves rather than to their bondsmen.

Stampp hesitated to make the leap required to recognize the superior quality of slave labor because he remained too enmeshed in the debate between the critics of slavery and the apologists, and he overestimated the cruelty of the slave system. The logic of his position made it difficult to acknowledge that ordinary slaves could be diligent workers, imbued like their masters with a Protestant ethic, or that, even though they longed for freedom, slaves could strive to develop and improve themselves in the only way that was open to them.

Still, Stampp came remarkably close to discovering the true nature of the slave system, the true advantage of bondage to the agricultural capitalists who dominated antebellum society. What was crucial to the system was not cruelty but force. Force could, and often did, lead to cruelty, but not as much cruelty as Stampp then believed. For what most planters sought was not "perfect" submission but "optimal" submission. These are two very different concepts. If Stampp blurred the distinction, it was because, like so many before him, he tended to confuse rhetoric with reality. "Perfect" submission was the rhetorical position of the master class, not its practical objective. The shrewd capitalistic businessmen who ran the slave plantations were not usually psychological perverts who gloried in the exercise of unlimited force for its own sake. They generally used force for exactly the same purpose as they used positive incentives — to achieve the largest product at the lowest cost. Like everything else, they strove to use force not cruelly, but optimally.

20

Ulrich B. Phillips: The Old South as the New

Daniel Joseph Singal

Most readers nowadays regard Ulrich B. Phillips as the epitome of Old South Bourbonism. Phillips, they say, was a fine historical craftsman who mastered his manuscript sources thoroughly, but whose manifest racism and overwhelming bias toward the planter class irretrievably marred his conclusions. The attack began in 1943 with Richard Hofstadter. "While Phillips certainly did not originate the plantation legend of the Old South," Hofstadter charged, "he did his best to continue it." A "reverence for the values and standards of the old planter class" pervaded Phillips's life and work, agreed Stanley Elkins. Even Wendell Holmes Stephenson, a writer on southern historiography highly sympathetic to Phillips, described him as one who "surveyed the southern scene from the hospitable atmosphere of the 'big house'; a patrician who saw only fringes of friction on a tranquil tradition."[1]

There is much truth to this view. Phillips's insistence on dedicating his second book "TO THE DOMINANT CLASS OF THE SOUTH," despite the strong objections of his publisher, gives ample evidence of his affections. Yet a close study of Phillips suggests that his critics have overlooked the most persistent theme of his work—his desire to place the South in the vanguard of progress. Most of all, they have failed to interpret Phillips within the context of his times. When Phillips is seen in historical perspective, as Eugene D. Genovese has pointed out, his social viewpoint is "neither nostalgic, nor reactionary, nor unreconstructed, but... cautiously forward-looking, humanely conservative, and deeply committed to social and racial justice." With his progressive outlook, Phillips was prepared to turn a critical eye on the Old South when necessary. Young southern intellectuals in the 1920s looked to him, not as a bulwark of the old guard, but as an exemplar of what southern scholarship could produce at its finest. In brief, Phillips was a far more complicated thinker than his liberal detractors have usually depicted him; his role in the South's intellectual history warrants reassessment.[2]

To begin with, his bias toward the plantation system notwithstanding, Phillips deserves to be included among the New South school of historians who held sway over the field of southern history during the first two decades of this century. Led by Philip A. Bruce and Holland Thompson, these men spent much of their prose celebrating the supposed arrival of full-scale industrialization in the South, but, as Paul Gaston notes, their foremost concern lay always with the question of moral character. Ruefully they admitted that antebellum planters had made a cult of leisure, until the entire region had acquired a reputation for urbane inactivity. Now, they insisted, all that had changed. The South's great success in rebuilding its economy after the war along the lines of northern industry had proved, once and for all, that southerners were just as capable of hard work, thrift, and enterprise as other Americans. "Most of the real Southern colonels are dead," Thompson assured his readers, "and the others are too busy running plantations or cotton mills to spend much time discussing genealogy, making pretty speeches, or talking about their honor." The old affability was gone, he reported; these new captains of southern industry were "cold, hard, and astute, for the New South has developed some perfect specimens of the type whose natural habitat had been supposed to be Ulster or the British Midlands... ."[3]

This approach to southern history posed one major problem. In their effort to destroy the myth of the lazy South, writers in this vein were forced to disown the whole antebellum period as an unfortunate aberration from the South's true development. Slavery, they believed, had been the main culprit. Unscrupulous Yankee traders had fastened the slave system on the South, leaving southerners with the unhappy alternatives of either continuing slavery or coping with the dire racial dilemmas associated with an immense population of emancipated blacks. Reluctantly, according to the New South historians, the planters had chosen the former course and had been partially corrupted as a result. Thus, the typical New South account would condemn slavery, castigate Old South indolence, add an obligatory compliment to antebellum "grace and charm," half-apologize for secession, and then proceed as if the real history of the South began in 1880.[4]

Phillips's achievement was to reverse this historiographic process by showing that the antebellum period could be interpreted within the framework of New South values. His exhaustive research in plantation archives had convinced him that the Old South did not deserve its stigma as a land of industrial slackness and that the plantation system in particular had been badly maligned. He did not see the plantation as a latter-day version of the feudal manor, but rather as a highly efficient economic unit where southerners practiced "the application of manufacturing or capitalistic methods to agricultural production." Far from being an idle aristocrat, the antebellum planter had been a veritable captain of industry, a man whose primary claim to distinction rested not on his pedigree but on his remarkable skill as a manager. Phillips thus carried the New South argument about southern character to its utmost limits by applying it not only to the New South but also to the Old South as well. The old regime in his hands turned into the embodiment of traditional Yankee virtues.[5]

In this way, although he surely had no such intention, Phillips became the first major southern intellectual to challenge the Cavalier myth. Like other New South writers, Phillips felt a keen sense of sectional chauvinism; and his emotional ties to the myth were strong. His books are strewn with the standard references to "the graciousness and charm of the ante-bellum civilization." Nevertheless, his vision of the Old South stood at odds with the myth at several key points. The efficiency-minded capitalist Phillips depicted at the center of plantation society, whatever his merits, could not be construed in any fashion as a romantic, devil-may-care aristocrat; nor did he eschew the profit motive at all times as did the planter of legend. Phillips may well have done his best to continue the plantation legend, as Hofstadter contends, but the net effect of his work in the long run was to help undermine it.[6]

Phillips was born in 1877 to a middle-class family in the small Georgia farming town of La Grange. His early years appear to have been uneventful. In 1891, however, his parents, evidently recognizing his intellectual gifts, sent him to a special preparatory school at Tulane. He attended the University of Georgia, where he received both his B.A. and M.A. under the aegis of John T. McPherson, a disciple of Herbert Baxter Adams. McPherson endowed Phillips with a life-long zeal for "scientific history." For his doctoral studies, Phillips chose Columbia University and its acknowledged master of southern studies, William Archibald Dunning. Phillips chafed under Dunning's preoccupation with political history and much preferred the social and geographical approach of Frederick Jackson Turner, whom he had encountered during a summer session at the University of Chicago in 1898. Turner's concept of sectionalism, he believed, was far more useful than Dunning's staid constitutionalism in making sense of the South's distinctive development. Still, his prize-winning dissertation, *Georgia and States Rights*, clearly bears Dunning's stamp.[7]

With his doctorate in hand Phillips in 1902 made a fateful decision. Rather than returning to his native region or remaining in one of the conservative academic citadels of the Northeast, such as Columbia, Phillips plunged himself into a hotbed of progressivism by accepting an offer from the University of Wisconsin. The presence of Turner, along with the sizable collection of materials on southern history available at Wisconsin, seem to have been the chief attractions.[8]

For a supposedly unreconstructed Bourbon, Phillips had no trouble whatever adjusting to Wisconsin's liberal environment. He immediately struck up friendships with the high priests of progressivism assembled there, including John R. Commons, Richard T. Ely, Charles McCarthy, and, of course, Turner. These friendships were as much professional as personal: Phillips shared many intellectual interests with these men, especially their concern for "industrial history." To the progressives, that term meant something far broader than the study of factory production. How men worked—their routines, techniques, and relative efficiency—was thought to be among the most important ingredients in establishing their styles of life. Above all, the goal was to get away from the conventional emphasis on political and legal events, which the progressives regarded as mere surface manifestations, and to find the true economic and social wellsprings of American life. To this end, Phillips collaborated with Commons and several other reform-minded economists in editing the ten volume *A Documentary History of American Industrial Society*. His own *Plantation and Frontier Documents*, the first two volumes of the series, was designed to show how the new methods could be applied to the study of the South. Although he never fully adopted his colleagues' sympathetic view of trade unions and labor legislation, Phillips, while at Wisconsin, was open to the most advanced thought of his day. The progressive theories acquired during his stay there would remain with him for the rest of his career.[9]

Phillips conducted his fervent defense of the antebellum plantation system along such progressive lines. He began by rejecting the standard portrait of Old South life, which had centered on shiftless, ill-trained slaves performing their tasks in haphazard fashion while their helpless masters looked on in kindly indulgence. For Phillips, the key word was "routine." Antebellum southerners may not have exhibited the frantic pace of the Yankee peddler, he argued, but they did understand the need for routinized labor practices, the very basis of modern industrial efficiency. "Just as in the case of the factory system, which of course is entirely analogous as regards labor organization, the success of industry [on the plantation] depended upon its regularity and the constant repetition of similar tasks," he wrote. Over and over he quoted the maxim of Richard Corbin, a Virginia planter Phillips especially admired, who put the matter succinctly: "'The ways of industry... are constant and regular, not to be in a hurry at one time and do nothing at another, but to be always usefully and steadily employed.'" In other words, southerners were not naturally slow of tempo or adverse to hard work, as the legend of their supposed laziness had it; they merely knew how to pace themselves for maximum productivity.[10]

Phillips implied that the Old South, in industrial matters, had been not backward but ahead of its time. It had in fact succeeded in anticipating Frederick W. Taylor's concept of scientific management by nearly a century. For example, Phillips often spoke of the plantation slave-gang system as a species of "time-work" and the task system as "piece-work." With obvious relish he swooped down on a series of articles in the *Southern Planter* in 1842 by H.W. Vick, whose "analysis of stance and movement" savored "of the most advanced industrial study in the twentieth century." Indeed,

Phillips claimed, it was the incredible "routine efficiency" of the system which proved its undoing when the resulting overproduction periodically glutted the cotton market.[11]

Phillips emphasized this point by including lengthy, detailed descriptions of plantation work routines in all his books. As these passages wind on, occupying scores upon scores of pages, the list of chores to be done becomes almost staggering:

> From the end of May until as late as need be in July the occurrence of every rain sent all hands to setting the tobacco seedlings in their hills at top speed as long as the ground stayed wet enough to give prospect of success in the process. In the interims the corn cultivation was continued, hay was harvested in the clover fields and the meadows, and the tobacco fields first planted began to be scraped with hoe and plow. The latter half of June was devoted mainly to the harvesting of small grain with the two reaping machines and twelve cradles; and for the following two months the main labor forces was divided between threshing the wheat and plowing, hoeing, worming and suckering the tobacco, while the expert Daniel was day after day steadily topping the plants. In late August the plows began breaking the fallow fields for wheat. Early in September the cutting and housing of tobacco began, and continued at intervals in good weather until the middle of October.... Two days in December were devoted to the housing of ice; and Christmas week, as well as Easter Monday and a day or two in summer or fall, brought leisure.[12]

This account of a tobacco plantation in Virginia was repeated for each major southern staple, leaving the reader with the clear impression that life on a typical southern plantation consisted of continuous regulated motion with free time always a rarity.

Although he realized how thoroughly labor intensive plantation practice actually was, Phillips tried to show that the Old South had kept in step with technological advance. He seized every chance to point to the planters' use of machinery, often straining to make his point and lavishing far more attention on the subject than it deserved. The chapter on cotton cultivation in *American Negro Slavery*, for example, begins with a page and a half description of the gin house and baling press, which Phillips terms "the outstanding features of the landscape" on the upland plantation. However, only on the rice and sugar plantations, with their elaborate irrigation systems and refineries, could he find truly convincing evidence of a commitment to technology. Here he could discuss sluice gates, pounding mills, clarifiers, retorts, vacuum pans, and similar equipment to his heart's content, crushing all doubt that the antebellum captains of industry could cope with the most sophisticated apparatus of their era when necessary.[13]

Phillips found the old plantation system so modern and attractive, in fact, that he recommended it as a prime cure for the South's twentieth-century ills. Allowing the former slaves to shift for themselves as tenant farmers or sharecroppers after Reconstruction had been a dreadful mistake, he believed, since the "ignorance, indolence, and instability" of the average black would always "prevent him from managing his own labor in an efficient way." This pernicious arrangement was the root cause of postwar southern poverty in Phillips's view: "It is a dead loss for a good manager to have no managing to do. It is also a dead loss for a laborer who needs management to have no management." The only solution he could foresee was to restore the plantation on the basis of Negro wage labor secured through long-term contracts—"voluntary indenture," as he called it. If someone had charged that this proposal sounded suspiciously like a return to slavery, Phillips would doubtless have answered that his plan would at least raise southern blacks out of their current state of slothful penury into steady and gainful employment.[14]

This last point suggests one additional Old South virtue, which Phillips commended to his own age—the tradition of plantation paternalism. Genovese, indeed, maintains that it was the patriarchal ethos above all that Phillips wished to preserve in southern life, that capitalism to him was no more than an adjunct to paternalism. Certainly Phillips placed great emphasis on the planters' observance of *noblesse oblige*. Equally certain, that pre-capitalistic set of customs, which held the master responsible for the welfare of his sick and aging workers, undercut the kind of tough business practice Phillips wanted the South to follow. How can this apparent contradiction be explained?[15]

The answer is that Phillips saw no antagonism whatsoever between the patriarchal ethos and the profit motive. Rather, for him paternalism was indispensable to the proper functioning of plantation capitalism. Adopting a fatherly concern for one's slaves was the only feasible method of labor control available to antebellum planters, if they wished to preserve the morale of their work force. Phillips constantly repeated his formula: the "successful management" of slaves necessitated "a blending of foresight and firmness with kindliness and patience." Everything depended on the correct "blending." "The ideal in slave control," he wrote, "may perhaps be symbolized by an iron hand in a velvet glove. Sometimes the velvet was lacking, but sometimes the iron. Failure was not far to see in either case." Those masters who performed this task well were rewarded with few disciplinary problems and great prosperity; those who did not met with continual instances of slave resistance and runaways, which could eventually lead to bankruptcy. Implicit in this view, of course, was Phillips's belief that blacks were inherently child-like in their dispositions and would respond according to paternal treatment.[16]

To Phillips, this balancing act between firmness and kindness was close-ly akin to an art form. He would appraise the managerial skills of those planters and overseers whose records he examined with the eye of a connoisseur. There is the pointed story of John Palfrey of Louisiana, whose plantation account book revealed frequent whippings, truancies, and recur-rent financial disasters during his first ten years as a master. Ultimately, however, Palfrey found the right touch. In Phillips's words, his eventual economic success "plainly tells that Palfrey had learned to be a much more considerate and effective master than the record of his runaways indicates for his first Louisiana decade." By contrast, a Georgia overseer, Rufus King, drew Phillips's praise from the start for his discretion in meting out punish-ments, his use of varied incentives, and his genuine concern for his workers' health, all of which resulted in a "brisk and will performance" by the slaves. Phillips also liked to cite the example of Thomas S. Dabney, an "ideal" master, whose "continued prosperity proved his benign discipline effec-tive."[17]

Nor was this advocacy of paternalism incompatible with Phillips's commitment to progressive reform. Like others of his generation, Phillips was troubled by labor violence and the worst abuses of the factory system. Paternalism, by stressing the mutual obligations between employer and worker, seemed to speak directly to these problems. Labor relations in the old plantation regime, he delighted in reminding his readers, did not suffer from "that curse of impersonality and indifference which too commonly prevails in the factories of the present-day world...." But whether or not the rest of the world chose to adopt these lessons, Phillips believed the racial make-up of the region's unskilled work force made them "essential" for the South.[18]

Thus Phillips's position came full circle: to place southern agriculture on a modern business basis, the captains of southern industry must resort to paternalism. To realize its most cherished objectives, the New South must recapture the values of the Old South. That, Phillips thought, was the only sure path to progress and reform.

Item number one on the liberals' bill of charges against Phillips has always been his benighted stand on race. Throughout his career, Phillips's attitude toward blacks remained highly condescending, if indulgent. As he wrote in 1904: "The average negro has many of the characteristics of a child, and must be guided and governed, and often guarded against himself, by a sympathetic hand." To his critics such a statement supplied incontrover-tible proof that Phillips was at best a bigoted Old South Bourbon bent on resurrecting slavery.[19]

To judge Phillips this way is to ignore the historical environment in which he worked. Despite the impulse for reform which arose during the Progressive era, that period also witnessed the most virulent display of racism in American history. Nor was that display limited to the South—the anti-black pronouncements and calls for immigration restriction which issued from certain "respectable" circles in New York and Boston sounded almost as shrill a note as those heard in Dixie. To most reformers of that age racism did not necessarily violate the spirit of progressivism. As they saw it, the campaign for racial purity was itself a reform. Keeping the Negro and others of dubious skin color at the margins of American life was indispensable to realizing the progressive vision of a wholesome, homogeneous society.[20]

Moreover, until the mid-1920s, the notion of racial inequality represented conventional wisdom in academic circles as well. Categorical statements on Anglo-Saxon superiority appeared regularly in the works of the liberal economists Phillips collaborated with at Wisconsin, as well as in scientific journals, textbooks, and doctoral dissertations. Within the discipline of American history, highly regarded northern writers like James Ford Rhodes, John W. Burgess, and Dunning may have evaluated the Civil War and Reconstruction from a pro-Union standpoint, yet each made clear his belief that blacks were genetically inferior to whites and that no evil could match the loss of white control over southern society. The anti-Negro bias so apparent in Phillips, then, was no more or less than the standard fare of his time. In fact, when compared to his fellow southerners in this respect, Phillips comes out looking much like a reformer.[21]

Far from being "solid" in its attitudes, the white South during most of this period was divided into two main camps on race, the bitter-end extremists and the New South liberals. The extremists, who usually held the upper hand until World War I, consisted of three groups: political demagogues, who made racism their bread and butter; survivors of the old planter class; and a number of highly vociferous polemical writers obsessed with the need for race purity, including Thomas Dixon, Ernest Sevier Cox, and Charles Carroll. These men believed that the very social fabric of the South stood in mortal danger as a result of emancipation and its aftermath. Blacks, they assumed, harbored intense animal passions, which could easily be aroused by political agitators or sexual temptation, leading to general chaos. The strict controls of slavery had in their view effectively prevented that dire possibility, but, with slavery gone, the door was left open to black criminality and aggression. To counter this threat the extremists took upon themselves the task of warning other southerners of the Negro's true nature; mounting, as George Fredrickson puts it, "an evangelical effort to transform the stereotype of the Negro" from the kindly image of Uncle Tom to the menace of the black beast. In addition, they advocated the strongest conceivable methods, including lynching, to keep the dread "beast" in his place.[22]

To a large extent, the "moderate-liberals," as Phillips preferred to describe them, found their voice on this issue in response to the extremists. Beginning with New South prophets like Henry Grady and J.L.M. Curry and continuing down to progressive activists such as Edgar Gardner Murphy and W.D. Weatherford, they chose to emphasize the black man's purported child-like qualities, focusing on the first half of the traditional child-beast dichotomy. In general, their program was built on an updated version of paternalism in which whites would offer blacks help, guidance, and protection in exchange for a commitment to the New South values of thrift and hard work, as well as a continued subservience. While often divided on the question of disfranchisement, the liberals all vigorously condemned lynching, supported Tuskegee-style industrial education, and promised economic opportunity for blacks with special talents. If pressed for a long-range prognosis, most liberals would have predicted a very gradual uplifting of the Negro race, although they would have quickly added that blacks would never attain full equality with whites. Regardless of the final outcome, however, they wanted racial peace and harmony for the present, not the constant turbulence stirred up by the extremists.[23]

Hence the starting point of all Phillips's writings on race was the Negro's supposedly child-like temperament. "Typical negroes," he claimed, "are creatures of the moment, with hazy pasts and reckless futures" who, under suitable discipline, would respond to commands with an "easy-going, amiable, serio-comic obedience." Although "dilatory" and "negligent" when left to their own devices, when set to work they became "robust, amiable, obedient, and contented." This combination of traits, which had made them "the world's premium slaves" in the past, suited them perfectly for industrial exploitation in the present. Accordingly, Phillips insisted, it was time the South regarded its black population as an important economic asset rather than as a powderkeg.[24]

If these assumptions about the Negro's personality were true, it also followed that southern whites had little to fear from their black neighbors, despite the alarms of the extremists. Phillips frequently served up historical evidence designed to establish this very point. He suggested on several occasions that antebellum southerners who saw slaves as a potential source of mass violence either did not comprehend the black personality or lacked the ability to discriminate fact from rumor. A great number during that regime had "held the firm belief that the negro population was so docile, so little cohesive, and in the main so friendly toward the whites and so contented that a disastrous insurrection by them would be impossible." In his opinion, those few revolts which did occur were often blown out of proportion by overanxious southern newspapers.[25]

Although Phillips generally upheld the orthodox New South position on race, he did introduce one important modification. Southerners had long explained the black man's distinctiveness just as they had answered all other basic questions—in Biblical terms. They had assumed that God had shaped the Negro's physical and emotional makeup at the beginning of existence and rendered him forever inferior to whites. But Phillips was too heavily steeped in social science empiricism to accept such a vague, mythological explanation. Instead, he adopted a quasi-Darwinian theory, highly popular among contemporary anthropologists, which traced the racial characteristics of the Negro to his adaptation to the African environment. It was the hot, stultifying climate of Africa, according to this theory, which had arrested the Negro's evolutionary development, even as the comparatively cool climate of northern Europe had stimulated Anglo-Saxons to achieve higher and higher levels of civilization. "To live where nature supplies Turkish baths without the asking," Phillips wrote, "necessitates relaxation"; such an environment "not only discourages but prohibits mental effort of severe or sustained character." In this fashion Phillips planted, without intending to, a seed of Darwinian doubt which would in time prove fatal to the South's traditional racial views.[26]

Indeed, his adoption of environmentalism as an explanatory devise often posed problems for Phillips himself, especially in regard to his cherished notion of how the antebellum plantation served as a "school" for its slaves. As he argued in a 1904 article entitled, "The Plantation as a Civilizing Factor," blacks had been "heathen savages" when they first arrived in America, with their animal impulses always in danger of "breaking forth." To fit them "for life in civilized, Christian society," they had to be drilled, educated in a manner, and controlled." The plantation was ideal for this purpose, Phillips contended, functioning much like a modern social settlement house by providing its residents a close-hand view of American life at its best, only in this case it was a master and his family who set the example for the newcomers, rather than trained social workers. Since Negroes possessed a natural "imitative faculty" as part of their racial heritage, they were able to learn quickly. Thus the Old South succeeded by environmental means in transforming the African savage into the dependable, contented plantation "darkey."[27]

There are, however, some troublesome questions. If the plantation had been so effective in altering the black man's personality, why then did the South still require a thoroughgoing system of racial control in the twentieth century? Why were not blacks at least partially civilized? Phillips had no real answers, except to toy with words. In *American Negro Slavery*, for example, he claimed that the African's nature was "profoundly modified but hardly transformed by the requirements of European civilization." At times he seemed to be saying that blacks had made considerable progress and were becoming more like whites, at other times he described them as "still in the main as distinctive in experience, habit, outlook, social discipline and civilian capacity as in the color of their skins or the contour of their faces." His dilemma became especially keen when dealing with the so-called "exceptional negroes," the "high-grade, intelligent, self-reliant negroes, mulattoes, and quadroons" for whom Phillips felt genuine sympathy. The failure of the slave regime to find a place for these "graduates" of the plantation school constituted its major defect, according to Phillips, and, like other southern progressives, he strongly urged that the New South avoid a similar mistake. But again he left the main question unanswered: if these exceptional blacks had adapted so well to the American environment, why need they be segregated?[28]

To escape this logical thicket, Phillips fell back on the old child-beast dichotomy and its parent formulation, the radical Victorian distinction between savagery and civilization. Caucasians, he asserted, were innately civilized; they carried the germs of civilization in their blood as a matter of "natural inheritance." Negroes, however, could acquire civilized ways only by imitating whites. Accordingly, Negroes had to renew their acquisition in each generation or stand in danger of "lapsing back into barbarism." In Phillips's estimate, these racial differences were so great that blacks could not even transmit such "lessons" to each other: "To contend that the educated negro is the best source of guidance and enlightenment for the average negro in American system is to argue that the reflected light of the moon is brighter and more effective than the direct rays of the sun." Since the savagery in the Negro's blood could never be fully tamed, Phillips concluded, areas like the South which harbored large black populations would always require a permanent system of racial control, regardless of the economic or moral cost entailed.[29]

Many writers on Phillips have tended to see a mellowing of his sectional attitudes in his later years, as if the simple passage of time and his continued residence in the North had brought him closer to the revised national consensus on race. In fact, just the opposite was true. When environmental theory began to displace scientific racism in the various social science disciplines after World War I, Phillips became increasingly strident in his defense of southern policy. He appears to have realized that his primary values were under attack and that his strategy of accounting for racial distinctions on environment as well as genetic grounds was rapidly falling apart. Little more was heard of the steam baths of tropical Africa. Instead, in "The Central Theme of Southern History," his famous essay of 1928, he adopted a new and far harsher tone on racial matters. What bound the white South together, he wrote, was "a common resolve indomitably maintained—that it shall be and remain a white man's country. The consciousness of a function in these premises, whether expressed with the frenzy of a demagogue or maintained with a patrician's quietude, is the cardinal test of a Southerner and the central theme of Southern history." The very fact that Phillips had broken with his previous practice of shunning generalization to offer up a "central theme"—and that he was willing to link himself as a southerner with political extremists like James Vardaman and Coleman Blease—indicates the degree of desperation he had come to.[30]

In sum, Phillips's environmentalist strategy did not work. Tying the orthodox southern position on race to evolutionary theory may have lent it intellectual respectability for a while, but such an expedient also let the genie of environmentalism out of the bottle. Likewise, Phillips's emphasis on the Negro's childlike qualities and his downplaying of black criminality could suggest a very different racial policy for the South from the one Phillips advocated. Assuming that blacks were indeed harmless, or at least that they posed no special threat to southern society, a new generation of southern liberals in the late 1920s would start to view the shackles of segregation as cruel and unnecessary and call for some to be removed. Assuredly Phillips did not join them. By that time he was already beginning to appear a conservative.

A parallel shift from a liberal to a conservative stance marked Phillips's general approach to Old South history during the last years of his career. When Phillips first came on the scene around the turn of the century, he had found his field of study dominated by the "Lost Cause" spirit. Those late nineteenth-century southern writers who were venturing into antebellum territory did so with a high degree of chauvinism. The South, they thought, needed loyal sons and defenders, not critics; for them, the sole function of a southern historian was to keep alive the South's memories of glory. Phillips, of course, had no use for this sentimentalism. He dismissed the work of what he called the "thick-and-thin champions of everything Southern," such as the United Daughters of the Confederacy, as "in keeping with the futility of propagandist efforts by patriotic societies in general." It was time, he thought, for the region to regard its history through the eyes of a detached professional scholar who could point to the defects along with the glories. Thus, although he never relinquished his allegiance to the Cavalier myth, Phillips often took on the role of critic of the old regime. And since he kept wishing the Old South had really been the New South, he had much to criticize.[31]

The chief target of his critical remarks was slavery. As Phillips saw it, chattel labor had made some economic sense through the period of initial settlement when workers of any kind were scarce, and it had been essential in gearing blacks to plantation routine when they first arrived from Africa. But afterwards slavery soon became that worst of all sins, a "clog upon material progress." It had tied up the region's capital, prevented the diversification of the southern economy, blocked the introduction of advanced machinery into southern agriculture, forced the South to base its entire industrial system on the crudest sort of labor, and trapped the planters into a cycle of chronic speculation over slave and land prices. In keeping with his New South penchant for technology, Phillips summed up the results with an image drawn from mechanics:

The system may be likened to an engine, with slavery as its great fly-wheel—a fly-wheel indispensable for safe running at first, perhaps, but later rendered less useful by improvements in the machinery, and finally becoming a burden instead of a benefit.... This great rigid wheel of slavery was so awkward and burdensome that it absorbed the momentum and retarded the movement of the whole machine without rendering any service of great value.

Slavery, the South's foremost historian of the subject concluded, was "out of place in the modern, competitive world."[32]

Phillips lodged still further charges against the slave system. He repeatedly condemned the way it restricted opportunity for nonslaveholding whites, who, "whether farmers, artisans, or unskilled wage earners, merely filled interstices in and about the slave plantations." He also faulted it for scaring immigrants away from the South (a common New South complaint) and for depleting the soil through wasteful methods of cultivation. In addition to these "industrial" flaws, Phillips deeply regretted the check slavery placed on freedom of speech in the Old South due to the need to guard against insurrection. He accounted the "death of southern liberalism" in the 1830s as one of the major costs of maintaining the peculiar institution. Clearly, then, Hofstadter was wrong in describing Phillips's presentation of slavery as "a latter-day phase of the pro-slavery argument." To Phillips slave labor was a usage "civilized people had long and almost universally discarded as an incubus: whose sole value to the South lay in the area of racial control. He never really wavered from that judgment.[33]

Alongside his critique of slavery, Phillips also began to formulate an analysis of the plantation's impact on southern society similar to that put forth by writers such as Edgar T. Thompson in the later 1930s. This was a wholly different matter from slavery, since the antebellum plantation represented the very model Phillips wished to use in revitalizing the modern South. Phillips nonetheless could see its defects. "Unfortunately," he noted, "the plantation system was in most cases not only the beginning of development, but its end as well. The system led to nothing else." This had happened as a result of the system's inherent tendency to too rapid expansion, which had kept the population in most black belt countries "too sparse to permit a proper development of schools and the agencies of communications." He fully understood that the speculative finance he abhorred stemmed not only from slavery, but from the very nature of the plantation itself, and that the consequent reliance on distant markets put the South in a quasi-colonial relationship with the North and Europe from which it had yet to obtain release. This willingness to acknowledge the more serious failings in a system he dearly loved indicates how objective a scholar Phillips at the height of his career could be, and how far he had advanced from Bruce.[34]

Furthermore, given his interest in putting to rest the myth of planter indolence, Phillips on occasion could even directly contradict the Cavalier legend. Leisure had almost no place in his version of Old South existence. The haughty rice nabobs of South Carolina, so often depicted as the ultimate in antebellum decadence, appeared in Phillips's pages as men who "deliberately and constantly preferred the career of the useful captain of industry to the life of the idle rich." His typical planter was usually portrayed as a diligent, unostentatious businessman, more interested in what was "plain and comfortable" than in fancy display. Nor did he put much stock in the storied "big house" of plantation romance. While a few such colonnaded mansions did exist, he reported, many planters lived in virtual log cabins; and the usual plantation domicile—as his own travels around the South had taught him—had been "commodious in a rambling way, with no pretense to distinction without or luxury within." Attacking another aspect of the myth, Phillips cautioned his readers about plantation size, reminding them that "slave industry was organized in smaller units by far than most writers, whether of romance or history, would have us believe."[35]

However, such departures from traditional southern mythology remained the exception, never the rule. Despite Phillips's efforts to eradicate the image of Old South leisure, he could not resist upholding the planter's pretension to gentility. Periodically he would speak of the "fine type of the Southern gentleman of the old regime," or those "considerate and cordial, courteous and charming men and women" of the antebellum South with their "picturesque life" who represented "the highest type of true manhood and womanhood yet developed in America." Later his critics would focus on these passages in their attempts to label him a Bourbon.[36]

Most often such compensatory gestures to the Cavalier hovered in the background in Phillips, to reappear in full force at the conclusion of his books. Equally striking is the way the space alloted the myth tended to increase as his career progressed. In American Negro Slavery, for example, it required only the final paragraph to reinstate the gentleman as the centerpiece of southern history, while ten years later, in Life and Labor in the Old South, Phillips devoted the full concluding chapter to an adoring description of "The Gentry." The effect of this arrangement was curious. Clearly the graceful, learned, temperate aristocrats he portrayed in his conclusions bore little or no relation to the hard-driving, competitive managers and speculators who occupy the stage through most of his work. Phillips might suggest in epigrammatic fashion that running a slave plantation was "less a business than a life" and that "it made fewer fortunes than it made men," but all the elaborate evidence he had marshalled to establish the planter as a "high-grade captain of industry" indicated just the contrary. It was almost as if, having proved his case that the Old South was actually the New South, Phillips wanted to take it all back in the end.[37]

The tightening of the myth's hold over Phillips was especially apparent in his treatment of the frontier, always a good touchstone for judging the power of the Cavalier on a southern writer's imagination. Initially Phillips had accepted the theory of his mentor, Turner, who saw the frontier as the wellspring of American democratic virtue. In his 1909 introduction to *Plantation and Frontier Documents*, Phillips argued that the plantation and frontier had been of equal significance in shaping southern character, with the frontier operating along Turnerian lines. In *American Negro Slavery*, published in 1918, he still spoke of the frontier in terms of "self-sufficing democratic neighborhoods" where the challenges of daily existence forced the inhabitants to develop the spirit of innovation and enterprise, along with a healthy taste for hard work. The frontier, in other words, was seen as a moulder of New South values. As late as the 1850s, he observed, "the whole South was virtually still in a frontier condition."[38]

By 1928, Phillips had shifted his views decidedly. He contended that the southern frontier had been "tamed with considerable speed." A good thing, too. "Pioneers here as elsewhere," he explained, "left most of the apparatus of law and culture behind them when they plunged into the forest." Thankfully, though, the old aristocracy came swiftly to the rescue. Certain households headed by transplanted Virginians soon began "to radiate refinement instead of yielding to rough mediocrity; and the stratification of society facilitated the recovery of culture by those who had relinquished their grasp." Here was the Cavalier myth in its most dramatic form—the gentleman planter, that bulwark of civilization in the wilderness, redeeming his society from barbarism and possible dissolution. As for those backwoodsmen who escaped the planters' civilizing touch, Phillips now described them as "listless, uncouth, shambling refugees from the world of competition." No longer, it seems, did the frontier automatically instill the spirit of enterprise.[39]

Even the element of southern chauvinism—the one component of Lost Cause mythology Phillips had always successfully resisted—ultimately came to the fore in *The Course of the South to Secession*, an unfinished manuscript published by one of Phillips's friends after his untimely death by cancer in 1934. It is possible that Phillips might have revised this work heavily had he lived. It is true, in addition, that he had left behind the more neutral field of "industrial history" to write of the sectional conflict directly. Nevertheless, one cannot imagine the younger Phillips ever penning such an extended diatribe against the North. The strategy throughout was to turn the tables on New England by accusing it of all the evils the abolitionists had once heaped upon the South. Yankees were presented as religious fanatics, just as southerners had been called fanatics on slavery. Southern nationalism was seen as a defensive response to "predominant Northern selfishness." If a solid South existed, it had been called forth by an equally "solid North," which had used its power to undo the Missouri compromise and the Compromise of 1850, cheat in Kansas, aid and abet John Brown, and array itself in a "phalanx" to crush the unoffending South. Whatever the merits of correcting the pro-northern bias in American historiography, this book plainly overstepped the bounds of objective scholarly debate.[40]

By the 1930s, when his fellow southern historians were just beginning to explore the insights of his earlier work, Phillips was beating a hasty retreat back to the nineteenth century. While others muted the race issue, "rediscovered" the southern frontier, analyzed the economics of slavery, charted the scope of Old South entrepreneurship, and generally played down the political antagonisms that led to the Civil War, Phillips was re-fighting the war, disowning the frontier, and passionately defending segregation.

Since so few of Phillips's personal papers have survived, the reasons for this retreat may never be fully known. However, the available evidence does suggest one likely explanation. In the sharp, assertive, occasionally bitter tone Phillips sustained in his last publications, a reader detects a pained reaction on his part to the intellectual changes then underway in the country, which brought him in turn to a fervent affirmation of those values under challenge. In addition to the mounting environmentalist attack on southern racial policy which he responded to in his "Central Theme" essay, Phillips could not have helped but notice the inclination of so many postwar writers within the South to question regional pieties. While it was true Phillips himself had contributed to the launching of that rebellion by using progressive standards to gain perspective on antebellum society, he had done so against a cultural backdrop in which the old verities of Cavalier and "Lost Cause" had been secure. The values and beliefs attached to those myths had remained intact at the deepest level of his mind, ready to make their customary reappearance in his conclusions. Now, with a new group of southern writers starting to tear those pieties apart, Phillips could only react by rushing to defend his heritage.[41]

It is in this sense that Phillips must be seen not as a true reactionary, but as a southern post-Victorian, as part of that sizable contingent of intellectuals who became caught midway in the transition from nineteenth- to twentieth-century thought. Coming of age just after 1900, he had peered through the doorway of modernism and, at first, liked what he saw. Attempting to bring the South's past into line with the new era, he had emphasized as best he could the continuity of the region's commitment to capitalism, technology, efficiency, and the work ethic, along with the velvet glove of paternalism in racial matters. But the progressive movement— especially as Phillips understood it—was never more than a halfway station to the modern world. So many of the virtues progressives championed, like industrial efficiency, really belonged to the high tide of Victorianism. Accordingly, when the main forces of change became apparent following World War I, Phillips started to pull back. His position on race hardened into a stern defense of the iron hand of segregation, while traditional southern mythology occupied a larger and larger place in his work.

In the end he arrived at the impasse which has always been implicit in his thought. On the one hand, Phillips desperately wanted his antebellum planters to appear as forerunners of modern businessmen; on the other hand, he did not have the slightest desire to dislodge the Old South myth. It was a dilemma which would have troubled him profoundly had he ever acknowledged it.

Notes

1. Richard Hofstadter, "U.B. Phillips and the Plantation Legend," *Journal of Negro History*, XXIX (April, 1944), 109-10; Stanley M. Elkins, *Slavery: A Problem in American Institutional and Intellectual Life* (Chicago, 1959), 10; Wendell Holmes Stephenson, *The South Lives in History: Southern Historians and Their Legacy* (Baton Rouge, 1955), 75.

2. Eugene D. Genovese, "Race and Class in Southern History: An Appraisal of the Work of Ulrich Bonnell Phillips," *Agricultural History*, XLI (Oct., 1967), 345, 355. For the dispute over the dedication of *Transportation in the Eastern Cotton Belt*, see William H. Carpenter to Ulrich B. Phillips, Oct. 16, 1907, Ulrich B. Phillips Papers (Southern Historical Collection, Chapel Hill).

3. Paul M. Gaston, "The New South," Arthur S. Link and Rembert W. Patrick, eds., *Writing Southern History: Essays in Honor of Fletcher M. Green* (Baton Rouge, 1965), 318-19, 321-22; Holland Thompson, *The New South: A Chronicle of Social and Industrial Evolution* (New Haven, 1920), 203-04. See also Philip A. Bruce, *The Rise of the New South* (Philadelphia, 1905).

4. Gaston, "The New South," 320; Bruce Clayton, *The Savage Ideal: Intolerance and Intellectual Leadership in the South, 1890-1914* (Baltimore, 1972), 68-70.

5. Ulrich Bonnell Phillips, "The Economics of the Plantation," *South Atlantic Quarterly*, II (July, 1903), 232.

6. Ulrich B. Phillips, "Conservatism and Progress in the Cotton Belt," *South Atlantic Quarterly*, III (Jan., 1904), 7.

7. Ulrich Bonnell Phillips, *Life and Labor in the Old South* (Boston, 1929), 123; Stephenson, *South Lives in History*, 60-64; Wood Gray, "Ulrich Bonnell Phillips," in William T. Hutchinson, ed., *The Marcus W. Jernegan Essays in American Historiography* (Chicago, 1937), 355-57; Ulrich Bonnell Phillips, "Georgia and States Rights: A Study of the Political History of Georgia from the Revolution to the Civil War, with Particular Regard to Federal Relations," *Annual Report of the American Historical Association* (2 vols., Washington, 1902), II, 3-224.

8. Wendell Holmes Stephenson, *Southern History in the Making: Pioneer Historians of the South* (Baton Rouge, 1964), 179; Phillips to Henry [?], Feb. 27, 1903, Frank L. Owsley Papers (Joint University Libraries, Nashville).

9. Gray, "Ulrich Bonnell Phillips," 357; Phillips, Introduction to *Plantation and Frontier Documents*, John R. Commons, Ulrich B. Phillips, Eugene A. Gilmore, Helen L. Sumner, and John B. Andrews, eds., *A Documentary History of American Industrial*

Society (10 vols., Cleveland, 1910-1911), I:3, 5. On Phillips as a progressive, see the introduction by C. Vann Woodward to Ulrich B. Phillips, *Life and Labor in the Old South* (Boston, 1963), iii-iv; and Genovese, "Race and Class," 355.

10. David Bertelson, *The Lazy South* (New York, 1967), 180; Ulrich B. Phillips, "The Origin and Growth of the Southern Black Belts," *American Historical Review*, XI (July, 1906), 803-05; Ulrich Bonnell Phillips, *American Negro Slavery: A Survey of the Supply, Employment and Control of Negro Labor as Determined by the Plantation Regime* (New York, 1918), 273; Phillips, *Life and Labor*, 366.

11. Phillips, *American Negro Slavery*, 228, 398; Phillips, *Life and Labor*, 132-33.

12. Phillips, *American Negro Slavery*, 232. For additional passages of this sort, see *ibid.*, 205-60; and Phillips, *Life and Labor*, 112-31.

13. Phillips, *American Negro Slavery*, 206-07, 167, 249-52; Phillips, *Life and Labor*, 116-18, 121-23.

14. Phillips, "The Economics of the Plantation," 233-36; Ulrich B. Phillips, "Plantations with Slave Labor and Free," *American Historical Review*, XXX (July, 1925), 750.

15. Genovese, "Race and Class," 349-51, 357-58. In his various pieces on Phillips, Eugene Genovese claims Phillips saw the antebellum regime as one in transition from an essentially "capitalistic enterprise" to a genuine "paternalistic community." According to Genovese, Phillips understood that the planters were rapidly becoming a full-fledged "ruling class" in the pre-bourgeois sense of the term, with their paternalistic ideology shaped by the obligations of the master-slave relationship rather than the ethos of profit making. To be sure, Genovese is aware that Phillips never engaged in such analysis explicitly, but he argues that the evidence Phillips marshalled and the manner in which he presented it all lead unmistakably in this direction. "If he [Phillips] failed to draw the necessary conclusions from his extraordinary lifetime efforts," Genovese maintains, "we are under no compulsion to follow suit." Genovese is also aware that Phillips tried hard "to prove the Old South a capitalistic society," but this, he believes, was mainly a tactical maneuver—the only way Phillips could get the ear of his generation for his espousal of patriarchal values.

My disagreement with this reading of Phillips is chiefly one of emphasis, although a crucial emphasis. Genovese thinks Phillips viewed capitalism as an accessory to paternalism, but in fact the opposite was true. Phillips exulted in depicting his southerners as hard-nosed, ambitious managers, not as models of benevolence; he saw them primarily as captains of industry, not "Lords of the Manor." Genovese himself is forced to acknowledge this fact on several occasions, as when he notes with surprise how Phillips, "having told us...that the Southern regime produced men of a special, high-spirited type,...proceeded to insist that their ultimate decisions would flow from economic calculation of the crassest sort." Most of all, I would contend that the focus must rest on Phillips's concern for efficiency and the discipline of work, and not on capitalism or paternalism as such, since that was always uppermost in Phillips's own mind, at least until the latter part of his career.

See *ibid.*, 347, 349, 353-54, 357, as well as Genovese's introduction to the paperback edition of Ulrich Bonnell Phillips, *American Negro Slavery: A Survey of the Supply,*

Employment and Control of Negro Labor as Determined by the Plantation Regime (Baton Rouge, 1966), vii-xxi.

16. Phillips, *American Negro Slavery*, 301, 287, 385; Phillips, "Plantations with Slave Labor and Free," 742; Kenneth M. Stampp, "Reconsidering U.B. Phillips: A Comment," *Agricultural History*, XLI (Oct., 1967), 366-68.

17. Phillips, *Life and Labor*, 293-96, 260-61, 285.

18. Phillips, *American Negro Slavery*, 307; Ulrich Bonnell Phillips, "The Plantation as a Civilizing Factor," *Sewanee Review*, XII (July, 1904), 264. By the late 1920s, when he began to come under the spell of southern mythology, Phillips's portrait of paternalism came much closer to the plantation legend. Now he spoke of how slaves were "cherished" as "loving if lowly friends" and of how "benignity" was taken "somewhat as a matter of course." This sort of language does not appear in his earlier writings. See Phillips, *Life and Labor*, 214.

19. Phillips, "The Plantation as a Civilizing Factor," 264.

20. I.A. Newby, *Jim Crow's Defense: Anti-Negro Thought in American, 1900-1930* (Baton Rouge, 1965), xi, 58-59; Elkins, *Slavery*, 11-13. For an extended treatment of progressive racism, see John Higham, *Strangers in the Land: Patterns of American Nativism, 1860-1925* (New York, 1955), 131-93.

21. Newby, *Jim Crow's Defense*, 29, 49, 64-65, 70-79; George M. Fredrickson, *The Black Image in the White Mind: The Debate on Afro-American Character and Destiny, 1817-1914* (New York, 1971), 314.

22. Newby, *Jim Crow's Defense*, ix, 69, 130; Fredrickson, *Black Image*, 221-22, 262, 275-81.

23. Phillips, "Conservatism and Progress in the Cotton Belt," 9; Fredrickson, *Black Image*, 210, 283-95.

24. Ulrich Bonnell Phillips, *The Slave Economy of the Old South: Selected Essays in Economic and Social History*, Eugene D. Genovese, ed. (Baton Rouge, 1968), 43; Phillips, *American Negro Slavery*, vii-ix, 8.

25. Phillips, *Slave Economy*, 60; Phillips, *American Negro Slavery*, 449, 474-76, 484.

26. Phillips, *American Negro Slavery*, 3-4; Newby, *Jim Crow's Defense*, 27-29.

27. Phillips, "The Plantation as a Civilizing Factor," 257-67; Phillips, *Slave Economy*, 26; Phillips, *American Negro Slavery*, 342-43; Phillips, *Life and Labor*, 199-200.

28. Phillips, *American Negro Slavery*, 291; Phillips, *Life and Labor*, 163, 195; Phillips, *Slave Economy*, 51, 248-49.

29. Phillips, "The Plantation as a Civilizing Factor," 258, 265-66. Phillips's use of the savage/civilized dichotomy was not limited to race relations. The imagery appears scores of times throughout his writings in a wide variety of contexts. For example, he refers to early seventeenth-century Virginia settlements along the James River as "a ribbon of civilization thrown into a continent of barbarism." Phillips, *Life and Labor*, 26. The metaphor, and the mode of perception it represented, were fundamental to Phillips's intellectual makeup.

30. Ulrich Bonnell Phillips, *The Course of the South to Secession*, E. Merton Coulter, ed. (New York, 1939), 152, 165.

31. Stephenson, *South Lives in History*, 17-18; Phillips, *American Negro Slavery*, 202; Phillips to Carl R. Fish, May 19, 1926, Phillips Papers.

32. Genovese, "Race and Class," 350; Phillips, *American Negro Slavery*, 395-97; Ulrich B. Phillips, "The Economic Cost of Slaveholding in the Cotton Belt," *Political Science Quarterly*, XX (June, 1905), 264-69, 271-75; Phillips, *Slave Economy*, 146, 150.

33. Phillips, *American Negro Slavery*, 337-39; Phillips, "Conservatism and Progress in the Cotton Belt," 3-4; Hofstadter, "U.B. Phillips," 122.

34. Phillips, *Slave Economy*, 274-49; Phillips, *Life and Labor*, 99-101; Phillips, *American Negro Slavery*, 399; Ulrich B. Phillips, "Transportation in the Ante-Bellum South: An Economic Analysis," *Quarterly Journal of Economics*, XIX (May, 1905), 451.

35. Phillips, *American Negro Slavery*, 289-90, 309, 314, 384; Phillips, *Slave Economy*, 438; Phillips, *Life and Labor*, 207.

36. Stephenson, *South Lives in History*, x; Phillips, "The Economics of the Plantation," 236; Phillips, *American Negro Slavery*, 514; Phillips, "Conservatism in the Cotton Belt," 3.

37. Phillips, *American Negro Slavery*, 514, 401; Phillips, *Life and Labor*, 354-66; Phillips, *Slave Economy*, 34.

38. Commons, Phillips, Gilmore, Sumner, and Andrews, eds., *American Industrial Society*, I:4-7; Phillips, *American Negro Slavery*, 78, 331, 512.

39. Phillips, *Life and Labor*, 107-11, 348, 351. For the planter as a civilizing force in southern mythology, see William R. Taylor, *Cavalier and Yankee: The Old South and American National Character* (Garden City, N.Y., 1963), 301-02.

40. Phillips, *Course of the South to Secession*, 3-4, 31, 72, 95-97.

41. *Ibid.*, 165.

VI

THE POLITICAL HISTORIAN

In the light of the continuing impact and controversy surrounding Phillips's major works on slavery, it is easy to overlook the fact that both his first and last books, as well as his dissertation and numerous other writings, focused on political history. Indeed nineteenth-century southern politics ranked among the most enduring of Phillips's interests. He was intrigued by the nature and the course of antebellum politics both in Georgia and the South, and devoted much thought and analysis to their roles and that of key individuals as causal factors in the sectional crisis and the Civil War. The broad scope of Phillips's first book, *Georgia and State Rights* (1902) is suggested by its weighty subtitle, *A Study of the Political History of Georgia from the Revolution to the Civil War, with Particular Regard to Federal Regulations.* This book, awarded the Justin Winsor Prize by the American Historical Association, earned Phillips a reputation as a most promising young historian, and has been reprinted in new editions both in 1968 and 1983. But Phillips's subsequent work in political history, particularly his posthumous *The Course of the South to Secession*, published in 1938, remains virtually overlooked by the historical profession. Curiously, none of Phillips's work on southern politics has attracted the serious or lasting attention accorded his two major books on the plantation South, *American Negro Slavery* and *Life and Labor in the Old South*.

All of the essays and excerpts included in this section assess favorably Phillips's achievement as a political historian. It is fitting that the first comprehensive look at his career, that by Wendell H. Stephenson in one of his three 1955 Walter Lynwood Fleming Lectures in Southern History, was among the earliest to acknowledge what he called Phillips's "genuine interest and modest achievement in political history." The two brief excerpts from that published lecture focus on the scope of that work and on the predominant themes they embodied.

In introducing the 1968 edition of *Georgia and State Rights*, Louis Filler brought renewed appreciation for not only the scope of the material Phillips gathered and interpreted, but also for the complexity and detail with which he treated the political history of his native state in his first book. It is striking to note how fully developed Phillips's themes were so early in his career. In comparing Filler's assessment with Merton L. Dillon's 1985 analysis of Phillips's final work, one is struck as well by the endurance and the consistency of those themes over the course of a vastly broadened career, the focus of which expanded from Georgia to the South as a whole. Dillon, in his recent biography of Phillips, viewed his subject's political theories in terms of both his posthumous book and articles and on several lectures he gave on the topic in the months and years before his death in 1934.

These selections demonstrate the value of viewing Phillips's political history as an important facet of his historiographical contribution. For as Dillon astutely observed, Phillips's greatest accomplishment was that he advanced the study of the South "from a polemical to an analytical stage," thus demonstrating that "southern politics was not to be understood by narration but by linking event with economic and social change."

21

U. B. Phillips on Southern Politics, Politicians, and Civil War Causation

Wendell Holmes Stephenson

Phillips's productive record was impressive, whether in quantity or quality. A zealous promoter of agricultural reform in the early years of the twentieth century, he published a score of pieces in Georgia newspapers; but the role of advocate, in which he exhibited considerable talent, seemed less inviting than the lure of scholarship. He wrote six volumes and edited four others; contributed more than fifty articles to professional journals, association reports, collaborative works, dictionaries, and encyclopedias; and reviewed forty-seven books. The pages Phillips wrote and edited during a period of little more than three decades serve as a monument to his industry.

Southern politics as a field of research appealed to Phillips at the threshold of his career as a productive scholar. His dissertation, *Georgia and State Rights*, an antebellum political subject with emphasis on federal relations, won the Justin Winsor prize in American history. He returned to a political theme to edit *The Correspondence of Robert Toombs, Alexander H. Stephens, and Howell Cobb*, an assemblage of documents which provided much of the evidence incorporated in the *Life of Robert Toombs*. Eventually he began a study of the Old South's public policy as a companion volume to *Life and Labor*; the fragment appeared posthumously as *The Course of the South to Secession*. A few of Phillips's contributions to *The South in the Building of the Nation* were political in nature, but his most significant articles in this area were "The South Carolina Federalists" and "The Southern Whigs," published respectively in the *American Historical Review* and *Essays in American History Dedicated to Frederick Jackson Turner*. Sketches of John C. Calhoun, William H. Crawford, Robert Y. Hayne, Alexander H. Stephens, and Robert Toombs appeared in the *Dictionary of American Biography*; of Jefferson Davis, Stephen A. Douglas, and Toombs in the *Encyclopaedia of the Social Sciences*. Phillips lamented to Allen Johnson that he had no talent for political biography, but the editor of the *Dictionary of American Biography* justifiably commended the sketch of Calhoun in warmest terms. Indeed, his brief biographies of southern statesmen were gems of perfection.

In his Wisconsin period Phillips assembled considerable material on Crawford with biographical intent, but paucity of private papers prompted abandonment of the project. Perhaps kind fate intervened; the historian's method of treatment and style of writing did not lend themselves easily to character delineation. That he lacked skill in comprehensive portraiture is indicated by the biography of Toombs. Phillips saw him as a product and a type rather than an individual, and he sought to use the Georgian's life as a focal point in presenting state and regional problems and policies. The biographer concluded "that Toombs was primarily an *American* statesman with nationwide interests and a remarkable talent for public finance, but the stress of the sectional quarrel drove him, as it had driven Calhoun before him, into a distinctly *Southern* partisanship at the sacrifice of his *American* opportunity." Frederick Jackson Turner and Justin H. Smith penned laudatory comments; the Harvard professor, who had watched his former colleague attain "a higher level each time" he wrote, commended him for making "a real person" of Toombs; and Smith, who violated a lifelong rule by reading several chapters on the train, thanked him for revealing the man as well as the debater and legislator. Actually, Phillips did not succeed in making Toombs live again, for the Georgian was relegated to a "shadowy background" by political detail, the book's major contribution. The biography lacked "portraiture," said Nathaniel W. Stephenson; it neglected Toombs's personality, asserted William K. Boyd.

Despite genuine interest and modest achievement in political history, Phillips concluded that he could not understand that thread until he examined the South's social and economic structure.

❖ ❖ ❖ ❖ ❖

While Phillips confined most of his research and writing to the ante-bellum period, an occasional article of his early years dealt with problems of the New South; of his later years with the cause of secession and civil war. He made it abundantly clear in his lectures on the Old South that a paucity of statesmanlike leadership in the last antebellum decade led to the disastrous culmination of 1860-61, but his clearest published statement of causation appeared in a Memorial Day address delivered in 1931 at Yale University. Eloquent in phrase and succinct in thought, the speech of less than seven hundred words summarized the conclusions of a mature student of southern society. In his own Southland the commemoration came earlier, for April rather than May yielded flowers "in fullest bloom"; but the southern spirit was not essentially different from that which prevailed in the North: "a resolve in grief that the flower of American youth, a long lifetime ago, shall not have been killed or crippled in vain; that national peace, nobility, justice and wisdom shall be drawn from that carnage."

The cause of the carnage? "With every passing year of thoughtful research a belief grows wider and stronger that the war of the 'sixties was not an irrepressible conflict but a calamity of misguided zeal and blundering." Slaves in Kansas Territory, reduced to two on the eve of secession, sparked the crisis. In that vast area "two slaves were in plain purport the equivalent of none. But in the politics of the time they were the equivalent of two thousand or two million. In heated controversy they and the law concerning them had become a symbol, a portent, a touchstone."

Why did a nonexistent problem become a symbol of portentous magnitude? Southern-rights advocates sought a share of the national territory as a gesture that the North did not intend to overturn the South's scheme of life. Without the token, acquiescence "would bring a sequence of aggressions until an overpowering North would impose a fanatical will, carrying industrial paralysis and social chaos." Northern champions, "deeming these fears to be groundless and suspecting a conscious exaggeration, refused the token. Peacemakers, in a desperate effort which is now wellnigh forgotten, failed to find any formula for solution or postponement."

The result? "Secession came, and the denial of its validity; Fort Sumter and the choice of dread evils by the states of the Upper South; the panoply of war, the dust and mud and heat and cold and hunger and thirst of marching men, the fumes and roar of battle, the shock of bullet and shell, the groan and gasp of the dying, amputation in rough hospitals, misery beyond the telling in prison camps, anxiety and anguish of loved ones at home. There was invasion and grim devastation; and at long last Appomattox, as an end yet not an end."

Not an end because "war's objective is peace, but war's cult of hatred persists beyond the laying down of arms and set the peace askew. The victor is prone to fix the terms at his own will and whim, to grind the face of the prostrate foe. "Reconstruction ["The Hell that is Called Reconstruction" Phillips had said a quarter of a century before] is imposed; but an imposed reconstruction will not fit the case, for it is uninformed, ill-considered, and arbitrary. It must be painfully remodeled before a workable regime is attained again and a normal course of policy resumed. Thus if war chances to settle one problem it raises a host of others in its train." The conflict "came through default of statecraft, it imperilled the nation on doubtful occasion, and, to the general detriment, it diverted public notice then and for years afterward from genuine to false issues. The memories of its heroism are a pride; the thought of its cost is a sorrow."

22

Ulrich B. Phillips:
A Question of History and Reality

Louis Filler

There are certain curious facts about our historical writing, and if our affairs should show possibilities of improvement we might yet understand some of them. For example, our present era has seen disturbances in Negro-white relations, and not a little done, officially and otherwise, to augment the status and opportunities of Negroes. It is not surprising, therefore, that there has also been official effort to add elements of Negro history and biography to school and college curricula, in some institutions, at least. Negro historians have been conscientiously added to northern faculties as part of a general drive to build racial balances of one sort or another.

Yet in such a time, a historian of the Old South who never repudiated its values and, if anything, defended them with new vigor and strategy, continues to exert influence—and influence not only on the intellectual South, where he is considered perhaps its greatest historian, but on the intellectual North as well. Ulrich B. Phillips died in 1934. As Professor of History at Yale University, he had directly affected everywhere—that is, North and South—attitudes toward the South and toward such associated topics as slavery and anti-slavery.

One unacquainted with the field might imagine the reverse: that his fame and works would disappear in an efflorescence of "new" liberal history. This has not happened. His major works are alive and very much in print, and mainly through northern publishers. Several of his writings have been re-issued in more editions than one; this is true of his posthumous *The Course of the South to Secession* (1939), which was edited by a distinguished professor of the University of Georgia, E. Merton Coulter, a sometime student and teacher at the University of Wisconsin.

But Phillips's works have not been honored solely by his sectional or spiritual compatriots. *Life and Labor in the Old South*, his most famous and widely-read work, received a prize award from the Boston publishers Little, Brown & Company when first issued in 1929, and has been reprinted many times since then. In 1963 it was also accorded paperback distribution and a new introduction by the latest in the line of Phillips's successors at Yale University, C. Vann Woodward, himself a native of Arkansas. This biographer of the notorious Georgia racist Tom Watson, in his introduction to Phillips's book, admitted various charges levelled by "new" northern historians against Phillips. But Woodward argued that Phillips merited at least the attention which might be properly accorded a "friendly" historian of the Old Regime in France or in Russia, "assuming one of equivalent learning, grace, and elegance." In addition, Woodward noted that "much of what Phillips wrote has not been superseded or seriously challenged and remains indispensable."

Woodward did not, in his introduction, wonder why Phillips had not been superseded by more "enlightened" historians. It is perhaps interesting that Woodward, though surely not a racist and perhaps no aristocrat—the major charges against Phillips—is no more than Phillips a friend of abolitionists, and has actually been quick to to accept a derogatory, utterly unfounded legend—accepted by no responsible historian in the field—that there had been no underground railroad![1]

Briefly, Woodward believes that the abolitionists, in their moral zeal, had hurt not only the nation, but even the practical cause of helping Negroes improve their lot. It needs to be kept in mind that such a view does not seriously separate him from Phillips. It represents no more than a kind of modernization of Phillips who, like other southerners, had believed that his South had been the truest friend of southern Negroes: much more so than abolitionists. This thesis offered many possible variations for both southerners and northerners. For example, one of Phillips's influential northern admirers had been the late Professor Gilbert H. Barnes, who dedicated his *The Anti-Slavery Impulse* (1934) to Phillips, "whose teaching first moved me to begin this study and whose unwearying faith and help encouraged me to continue through the ensuing years." Barnes had distinguished between allegedly rational abolitionists, like one Theodore D. Weld, and irrational and otherwise distasteful ones like William Lloyd Garrison. Barnes had patently distorted facts in pursuit of his thesis—a deed for which Phillips himself, of course, cannot be directly held responsible.

As striking a phenomenon as the Woodward endorsement of Phillips has been that by none other than Professor Eugene D. Genovese, who recently achieved considerable publicity as vigorous dissenter from consensus, and whose *Political Economy of Slavery* (1965) was a worthwhile effort in the field. In his 1966 introduction to Phillips's other major work, *American Negro Slavery* (1918), Genovese asserted that Phillips had come as close to greatness "as any historian this country had produced." Genovese was puzzled to explain how a man of such primitive views as Phillips on what Genovese called "fundamental social questions"—how such a man "could write such splendid history." A stronger investigation than

Genovese's would probably also wish to ask why persons of more "advanced" views so often write worthless history.

For the moment it suffices to note that, according to Genovese—no friend of Phillips or Phillips's people—the historian from Georgia had "asked more and better questions than many of us still are willing to admit [sic], and he carried on his investigations with consistent freshness and critical intelligence.... *American Negro Slavery* is not the last word on its subject; merely the indispensable first." Merely.

Georgia and State Rights was Phillips's first ambitious writing. It would be inaccurate to see it simply as a monograph. Properly viewed, it comes immediately out of the category of special subjects and affects some of our most vital thoughts.

Phillips had no other interest except to write about his beloved South, and he studied and wrote freely on its literature and life, its humors and discontents. The South's politics was his first love. Its details fascinated him from his earliest days as a graduate student and Fellow at Columbia University, where he took his Ph.D. He pursued its study as a professor at the University of Wisconsin, at Tulane University, and, for many years before he joined the Yale faculty, at the University of Michigan. But the wider social scene grew on him. He pored happily through newspapers, publications of every sort, and manuscript materials searching for the exciting detail which would illuminate his own pages. Certainly, his disinterestedness was qualified by his love for Georgia. How did this affect his studies?

The problem lies in distinguishing between Phillips's skill as a historian, and the desirability of particular Georgia policies. If Georgians believed in a certain position, Phillips was bound to state this as a fact; there will be no argument on that score. But if he agreed with them, does that impugn the truth of his statement? History is first of all a matter of fact, or it is nothing. What constitutes a fact is often debatable.

Phillips worked to acquire facts. Still, any close student of his work is bound to discover that his frame of reference sometimes consciously, sometimes unconsciously (as in his choice of particular words) built up a pattern which for him made up the history of Georgia, and, by implication, of the South as a whole.[2] Professor Genovese dreams of counter-history which would in effect refute Phillips's history. But what of the fact that Phillips has put in our hands the means for understanding Georgians *as Georgians understand themselves,* for understanding southerners *as southerners understand themselves?*

Northerners tend to think of their southern neighbors in terms of one question. It takes only a moment's thought to realize that southerners themselves are involved in a larger spectrum of interests. I recall the late Professor Charles S. Sydnor, who had written authoritatively on slavery in Mississippi, telling me that he was tired of the subject. What interested him in his last years were details of early political elections: how southerners voted, in what patterns, according to what regulations. What was the mechanism, for example, by which Thomas Jefferson was raised to various offices, including Governor of Virginia and President of the United States? The point is that even if you believe that the question of Negroes in southern society is one of unqualified priority, you must still recognize that other factors beside the Negro factor entered into the development of state attitudes and policies.

Take early Georgia, before the Revolution: it built up strong state loyalties, even in opposition to other southern states, as when it resisted South Carolina's desire to absorb her. On the other hand, Georgians, in their distrust of the British, the Spanish, and the Indians encouraged the colonial drive to separate from the British Empire. Later, Georgia opposed wiping out the foreign slave trade in the new Federal Constitution, but note: not because it favored that trade. Its statesmen apparently expected to abolish it without help from the central government. They were trying to avoid giving the new nation more power than it needed or ought to have.

Phillips has many other pieces of evidence which suggest that there is more to know about Georgia than its stand on slavery. Phillips maintains an independent tone, distributing praise and criticism as he thinks the evidence warrants. Observe that he questions Governor George Matthews's good faith in dealing with the Creek Indian—this is in 1794—and is critical of the pompous Georgian justices of the peace who supported harsh measures against the Creeks.[3]

But more often than not Phillips approves his state's early policies. Its population was small, he says, but its swift endorsement of the Constitution accelerated acceptances of it by the larger and more cautious states. Fighting for her sovereignty, Georgia denied the right of individuals to sue states, and gave us all the Eleventh Amendment to the Constitution which erases the privilege. Loyal to the Union and its program of limited state power and authority, Georgia gave up land claims which could have taken its borders to the Mississippi River.

But what of the Negroes? What of the Negroes? May I interrupt that question to ask some attention for the Indians? It seems useful here to remark differences between the two major tribes which concerned Georgia. Creeks were not Cherokee. The day may come when the differences seem more important to Americans than they do today. Some day we may wish to rediscover the fact that social wrong is indivisible, and that if we concentrate on one class of need at the expense of the other classes, all of them must suffer. I realize very well that to too many people this will sound like just words. We will continue to be in incomprehensible trouble until it does not.

The Cherokee became classic in their resistance to expulsion by Georgians from their ancient tribal lands. They became Christians. They produced Sequoyah, an American genius who created a Cherokee alphabet. They demanded their rights under treaties with the United States government which, when broken, raised questions about what might be called its "credibility gap." Not a little of Phillips sounds quite modern when read with fresh eyes.

To Phillips, "friendly Indians" are Indians who made concessions. The phrase reflects a curious American use of language which involves not only Phillips, but almost all Americans who are not Indians down to the very present.

Phillips' attitude is not his alone. It can be found in the related historical writings of Woodrow Wilson. It can be found in the works of William E. Dodd of North Carolina, a professor of history at the University of Chicago. Dodd was not only Wilson's biographer; he wrote on *Statesmen of the Old South* (1911) and *The Cotton Kingdom* (1919). Later he became our Ambassador to Germany under Franklin D. Roosevelt. Phillips's attitude can be found in many other southern-born historians who were trained and who taught in the North.[4]

They took what they believed to be a realistic position respecting the true meaning of American history—one which all Americans, whether northerners or southerners, and to some extent whether Negro or white, actually accepted, no matter what they said they believed. These historians described with interest and sympathy the rugged, individualistic, ambitious character of their white southern predecessors. They recognized that their determination to grab land, make money, and suppress competitors who, like the Indians, were, in their view anachronisms resulted in rough and illegal actions. But they felt that it also resulted in "progress."

The white men were superior, they believed, and were not to be stopped by mere formalities. The entire movement of western expansion was inevitable. It is interesting to note that Phillips was inspired in his work by Frederick Jackson Turner of the University of Wisconsin—the historian of the frontier—and that Phillips believed himself to be contributing to an understanding of the true functions of democracy.

It is crucial to history and reality to determine how the tale Phillips tells in *Georgia and State Rights* would differ from that which could be told by northerners. Senator Theodore Frelinghuysen of New Jersey denounced Georgia for its treatment of the Cherokee. He appealed for a humane approach to the Civilized Tribes, and for keeping treaties which involved the honor of the United States. But how had Indians in the North been regarded? How had they been handled? Phillips does not underscore the sad answer, but you know it, and it would help us all to attain perspective by spelling it out for ourselves and then striking a balance between northern and southern experience. We are all implicated in Georgia's decisions, and cannot get away from them by seizing on one detail at the expense of others and hammering away at it like shyster lawyers.

There are other aspects of this matter which merit notice here. But Americans find it psychologically hard to concentrate on Indians, and easier to give and receive impressions about Negroes. Phillips's chapters on the growing sectional crisis can be read with particular concern not only for the light they throw on pre-Civil War debates, but also on the more obscure struggle which in our own era goes on day after day.

It is often difficult for what used to be called North Americans to realize that the southerner lives with the Negro problem all the time, without holidays or pauses for station announcements. A northerner whose attention was riveted by an event in Little Rock, Arkansas, or New Orleans, or Atlanta, but whose attention is diverted so that his sense of what has gone before or what is going on becomes fuzzy, is at a disadvantage. It is, of course, well known that the South cherishes its history much more than the North does, and treats it with a greater sense of its intrinsic reality. This fact has today made the *Journal of Southern History*, for example, one of the most varied and resourceful professional journals in the country, its pages solicited by northern and Negro historians.[5]

It would help understanding if the northerner especially realized that race perspectives in the South are affected not solely by economic factors or other simplistic motivations, but by congeries of attitudes deriving from the times of which Phillips writes. In 1902, when Phillips prepared the following history, Georgia had come free of its failure at civil war. Phillips was himself a symbol of that victory, as was his success at winning national acceptance of his work. *Georgia and State Rights* was a prize-winner when first issued under the imprint of the American Historical Association.

The time which saw Phillips's entrance into the historical profession also saw the rise of Progressivism and the organization of the N.A.A.C.P. It seems worthwhile keeping this fact in mind and to see it as it really was. Woodward, in the introduction mentioned before, goes out of his way to claim that "Northern Progressives took Phillips to their heart," and explains this "fact" by judging racism to have been an ingredient of Progressivism "wholly compatible with its brand of reform."

This is tricky language since Woodward, of course, has first of all in mind Tom Watson, who was a sometime southern Progressive. But were all Progressives racists? Was David Graham Phillips, who made a Jewess the heroine of one of his novels? Was Charles Edward Russell, who denounced our Philippine War, and glorified Filipino leaders? Was Oswald Garrison Villard, one of the founders of the N.A.A.C.P.? Were Lincoln Steffens, Finley Peter Dunne, Norman Hapgood? Does Woodward know of any movement anywhere which was wholly composed of angels who loved to fly around and do nothing but good?

The fact is that some Progressives were more or less conscious of race, with racial implications, and some were not. Senator A.J. Beveridge was a racist, and so was Theodore Roosevelt. Woodward may be willing to dump

T.R. from our annals, but I am not. Nor am I willing to turn my back on Upton Sinclair, though he was probably, being a southern Progressive, weak in faith respecting Negro potentials.

The truth is that we are all, being Americans, Negro and white, mixtures of every kind of background and preference, and need to be used efficiently, in terms of social strength and virtues rather than our weaker characteristics. At this moment in time, for example, we are all struggling with aspects of Negro racism, especially in the North. It defends itself speciously—and is defended by weak-minded sympathizers—by claiming that it is calling the needs of the Negro community to the attention of the larger American public. I for one am not impressed by this argument. "Burn, baby, burn" will never produce any historians, let alone great ones. So much is certain. We would be prudent, I think, to study the great ones, and attempt to emulate their great qualities.

There are numerous matters in *Georgia and State Rights* which could be analyzed for insight into southern life and viewpoints and into our own larger psychology. I like Phillips's treatment of the Troup-Clarke factions, for example, because it reminds me that all Georgians do not look alike, and that it would be false merely to sum them up as "Whitey." The slavery issue distinguished these two factions not in terms of moral considerations, but as politics and economics. Slaves were property. (So, in a real sense, were children, by the way.) Slaveholders were property-holders and as such different from non-property-holders. I have no doubt that there are other distinctions between Georgians today. Intelligent and far-sighted Americans, not self-hypnotized with their own rhetoric, can probably find some use for these distinctions.

Phillips writes of Whigs and Democrats. We could today profitably muse about differences between Democrats and Republicans. Phillips recalls (what non-Georgians easily forget) that his state had been settled by idealists. They had soon been overcome by their own human nature, as uplift movement after uplift movement has in our own time. History is humbling, but it need not be discouraging. Phillips's examination of slavery as an institution is precise, and on occasion he notes the barbarity of some Georgian law, like that which provided a reward for the scalps of escaped slaves. Whether or not there is "progress" may be debated, but the world does move on. We can emulate Phillips's fearlessness in facing facts, whether we plan to use them for him or against him.

We will not solve our problems by avoiding them or by clinging to shallow formulas. Southern historians have been learned and clear about what they wished to say. They have had programs. Some of them have been recently more or less under attack, but alternative programs have been hazy, when spelled out at all. It will help us to downgrade rhetoric and evasions, to say nothing of funny-book history. My own commitment, for what it is worth, is to a national program which will serve us all. I don't believe it can be attained without a respect for history and reality.

Georgia and State Rights is a testament to a state whose history affects all Americans, if only by way of its two Senators in the Congress of the United States. No one can hope to deal competently with Georgians who cannot cope with this work.

Notes

1. "The Antislavery Myth," *American Scholar*, (Spring, 1962), 312 ff. The thesis indicated above was one of a number of anti-abolitionist theses sponsored by the late Professor William B. Hesseltine, at the University of Wisconsin.

2. To illustrate, Phillips, at one point speaks of "self-respecting negroes" who despise "poor white trash." He distinguishes the latter from the "hardworking poor man." With a little care and attention, Phillips's scale of social values can be readily constructed.

3. See pages 45 and 47 of *Georgia and State Rights*.

4. See W. H. Stephenson, *The South Lives in History: Southern Historians and their Legacy* (1955), and the formidable collection of essays in historiography prepared in honor of Fletcher M. Green and edited by A.S. Link and R.W. Patrick, *Writing Southern History* (1965).

5. In the absence of any revived sense of the abolitionists as positive contributors, it will be interesting in the coming period to observe the rate at and the historical stance by which Negro historians who have "made it" support the anti-abolitionist viewpoint.

23

U. B. Phillips: Revisionist of the 1930s

Merton L. Dillon

Earlier in his career [Phillips] had written several successful essays on discrete topics in southern politics, including his dissertation, but dealing with the entire subject presented a challenge of a different order. Its "quirks... often give me pause and still more pause," he admitted. "How the hell shall I make their cloudiness clear?" If full treatment of the political history of the antebellum South would not now be within his reach, he could at least sketch out an interpretation. This he did in a series of lectures delivered at Northwestern University over the period of a week in the spring of 1932. Out of necessity these were somewhat hastily done. "I must get the last of my lectures in shape after arrival," he told [Herbert A.] Kellar, "and husband my strength somewhat at all times."[1]

Some of the ideas presented at Evanston had been foreshadowed in earlier essays and books but now were placed in a political context. In tracing the establishment and growth of English colonial settlement, for example, he discerned not one but several Souths, socially and economically diverse but united in loyalty to self-determination. When "blundering" British officials upset traditional power relationships, they precipitated rebellion. Americans fought the revolution to defend the liberty of communities, not to establish the liberty of individuals. In orthodox progressive mode, Phillips insisted that concrete interest rather than abstract ideals led southerners toward independence. He denied that liberal ideals, sometimes taken to be the expression of American purpose, furnished the motive for rebellion. Their assertion was merely "justificatory of what was being done." Home rule itself was the central issue. "Theoretical rights of all men as individuals were used for what they were worth as "fundamental principles," which means a philosophical gloss, in a campaign for community interests." It follows, then, that those who found in slavery a betrayal of the principles of the revolutionary generation falsified the history of the time by mistaking rhetoric for reality.[2]

This does not mean that no one in early America questioned slavery. Private antislavery protest, he speculates, probably appeared with arrival of the first blacks, for the "kind-hearted and the neurotic" were ever revolted by scenes of coercion. But well-adjusted, practical people took such incidents as matters of course, and these kinds of men governed. "From Florida to Canada" slavery came to be accepted as part of the existing order. The black revolt in Santo Domingo—momentous in setting attitudes toward both race and slavery—brought drastic change by thrusting the black population into view as a source of public danger.[3]

Meanwhile even in the South some were applying the "philosophical gloss" of revolutionary rhetoric to slavery. The lower South remained nearly immune to such influence, but in Virginia the conscience-stricken freed their slaves, and others talked of doing so. Always, however, more general emancipation proposals were tied to colonization, for nearly all agreed with Jefferson that large numbers of blacks and whites could not live peaceably together if both were in a state of freedom. Colonization proving unfeasible, emancipation projects were abandoned. At the same time, colonization lost the support of northern extremists, who called instead for the revolutionary program of emancipation without emigration. At several points in his lectures Phillips portrayed abolitionists as abnormal men and women subject to "ecstasy," fanatics whose activities were encouraged from England. He assumed, perhaps, that a program so ill considered and destructive as theirs could not have flourished unaided on wholesome American soil.[4]

Slavery entered national politics, Phillips continued, when northern politicians during the Missouri controversy used antislavery propaganda to cast an idealistic cloak over sectional ambitions aimed at checking southern influence in national affairs.[5]

In consequence southerners for the first time found it necessary to defend slavery from outside governmental interference. They did so by resorting to the same theories of particularism that generations earlier had justified resistance to England. At stake was economic interest, but the fate of Santo Domingo demonstrated that social survival was at issue as well. Thus, to "a question of ethics" raised by the North, the South responded with "an answer of race." In the 1850s, coincident with the continued growth of antisouthern, antislavery attitudes among an increasingly large northern electorate, the fire-eaters appeared, to agitate the formation of a separate southern nation in which slavery—racial controls—could be made secure and perpetuated.[6]

Obviously, much of this will not withstand scrutiny, and little in it accords with current interpretation. But the historiographical scene was different in 1932. The dominant progressive historians offered materialistic explanations for historical development with which Phillips's views did not strikingly clash. They, too, found little room for the force of ideas.

Further, neither abolitionists nor slaves found many champions in American history as it then was written. Phillips's version of southern political history was in harmony with more prevailing assumptions than it challenged.

Presented to an audience consisting mostly of Chicago-area faculty and students, Phillips's lectures received little professional notice at the time and were not published until after his death. Even when they appeared as articles in the *Georgia Historical Quarterly* and in book form in 1939, they commonly were viewed as being for the most part predictable, a repetition of ideas the author had advanced earlier. *The Course of the South to Secession* was not welcomed as a notable addition to this life and work.[7]

The book reflected at least in spirit the thesis of his controversial paper, "The Central Theme of Southern History," presented at the AHA's Indianapolis meeting in 1928. There he asserted his understanding that the theme uniting the white population of the South was "a common resolve indomitably maintained—that it shall be and remain a white man's country. The consciousness of a function in these premises, whether expressed with the frenzy of a demagogue or maintained with a patrician's quietude, is the cardinal test of a Southerner and the central theme of Southern history." This was history reaching into the present, a comment intended for 1928 as much as it was an observation about the past. The paper provoked lively discussion from historians unwilling to accept race as the sole determinant in southern history. Some scholars, less deterministic than Phillips, argued that the racial adjustments that then prevailed might have been different had Reconstruction been managed more adroitly. Some found the interpretation too sweeping, too oblivious to exception and variation. Still others objected to the exclusion of factors other than race that contributed to southern distinctiveness. At Indianapolis, Phillips treated the contrary views with respect, but privately he afterward wrote them off. The paper "made a sprightly session, especially while one bounder and two cranks had the floor (under a five-minute rule, praise be)."[8]

His paper of 1928 and the lectures of 1932 conveyed nearly all Phillips was able to say about southern politics and as much as he ever would accomplish of what was to have been the second volume of his comprehensive history. He would no doubt have expanded upon these interpretations and refined them; yet, enough is known about his position to suggest that fuller expression of it would have done little to enhance his long-range reputation. It is apparent that he stood with the revisionists of the 1930s who advanced the argument that the Civil War concerned no fundamental issue but had resulted from the mistakes of a "blundering generation." The war was fought over unreal issues created by agitators and cynically used by politicians for personal and party advantage.

He had not always held precisely to that view. In *The Life of Robert Toombs*, published in 1913, he asserted that "no man could then nor can any man now hereafter be sure that it was by human means avoidable." But he had come to believe otherwise. By 1931 in his Memorial Day address at New Haven he could assert that "with every passing year of thoughtful research a belief grows wider and stronger that the war of the 'sixties was not an irrepressible conflict but a calamity of misguided zeal and blundering." Southern-rights advocates on the one hand and abolitionists on the other produced the crisis. The political disputes of the 1850s—preludes to secession and war—concerned only phantom issues. To both North and South, slaves in Kansas Territory, of whom there were but two in 1860, "had become a symbol, a portent, a touchstone." At stake in their defense of slavery in the territories, men at the time believed, was survival of the South itself, for failure to resist Republican exclusionary policy "would bring a sequence of aggressions until an overpowering North would impose a fanatical will, carrying industrial paralysis and social chaos." In one portentous sentence Phillips conveyed his mature interpretation of the Civil War era and its consequence. This war "came through default of statecraft, it imperilled the nation on doubtful occasion, and, to the general detriment, it diverted public notice then and for years afterward from genuine to false issues."[9]

Phillips made that appraisal in May of 1931. A few weeks later in a speech at Blacksburg, Virginia, he distributed guilt impartially. The war had been "a fruit of excessive and misguided zeal by fervid partizans of the North and South," he said. But there is little doubt that in his mind abolitionists bore the greater share of responsibility. Zealous southern fire-eaters defended the southern interests as they understood them. They did so, however, in response to northern-based attack. Abolitionists were malicious as well as mad, and they were recalcitrant in error. "Disproof had failed and would fail again to cure the wilful ignorance or silence the aspersions of these fanatics," he told a North Carolina audience in 1931 in paraphrase of sentiments first voiced by the South Carolina partisan Robert J. Turnbull in 1827.[10]

Notes

1. Phillips to Fairfax Harrison, December 1, 1931, in Fairfax Harrison Papers, Virginia Historical Society; Phillips to Herbert A. Kellar, April 8, 1932, State Historical Society of Wisconsin.

2. Phillips, *The Course of the South to Secession* (New York, 1939), 18, 19, 22, 86.

3. *Ibid.*, 59, 84, 100-101.

4. *Ibid.*, 86-87, 93-95, 111-13, 114.

5. *Ibid.*, 95-99.

6. *Ibid.*, 128-49.

7. William B. Hesseltine, Review of Phillips's *Course of the South to Secession*, in *Mississippi Valley Historical Review*, XXVII (1940), 298-99; Charles S. Sydnor, Review

in *American Historical Review*, XLVI (1940), 230-31. The book was not reviewed in the *Journal of Southern History*.

8. Phillips, "The Central Theme of Southern History," *American Historical Review*, XXXIV (1928), 31; American Historical Association, *Annual Report... for the Years 1927 and 1928*, 144-45; Phillips to Nathaniel W. Stephenson, January 1, 1929, in Ulrich B. Phillips Papers, Southern Historical Collection, University of North Carolina, Chapel Hill.

9. Phillips, *Life of Toombs*, 102; Stephenson, *South Lives in History*, 90-92; New York *Times*, May 31, 1931, p. 23.

10. Phillips, "The Historic Civilization of the South," *Agricultural History*, XII (1938),146; Phillips, "The Historic Defense of Negro Slavery," December 4, 1931, manuscript in Ulrich B. Phillips Collection, Yale University. Phillips also uses the quotation in his *Course of the South to Secession*, 104.

BIBLIOGRAPHIES:

The Major Writings of Ulrich Bonnell Phillips

Manuscripts

University of Georgia, Hargrett Rare Book and Manuscript Collection: Ulrich Bonnell Phillips Papers

University of Michigan, Michigan Historical Collections: Ulrich Bonnell Phillips Papers [duplicates of papers in Southern Historical Collection (see below)]

University of North Carolina at Chapel Hill, Southern Historical Collection: Ulrich B. Phillips Papers

Yale University, Sterling Library Manuscript Division: Ulrich Bonnell Phillips Collection

Books

American Negro Slavery; a Survey of the Supply, Employment, and Control of Negro Labor, as Determined by the Plantation Regime. New York: D. Appleton, 1918.

Georgia and State Rights; a Study of the Political History of Georgia from the Revolution to the Civil War, with Particular Regard to Federal Relations. American Historical Association Report for the Year 1901, Vol. 2. Washington: Government Printing Office, 1902.

A History of Transportation in the Eastern Cotton Belt to 1860. New York: Columbia University Press, 1908.

Life and Labor in the Old South. Boston: Little, Brown, 1929.

The Life of Robert Toombs. New York: Macmillan, 1913.

The Course of the South to Secession; an Interpretation. New York: D. Appleton-Century-Crofts, 1939.

Edited Works

The Correspondence of Robert Toombs, Alexander H. Stephens, and Howell Cobb. Annual Report of the American Historical Association for the Year 1911, Vol. 2. Washington: Government Printing Office, 1913.

Florida Plantation Records from the Papers of George Noble Jones. (co-edited with James D. Glunt). St. Louis: Missouri Historical Society, 1927.

Plantation and Frontier Documents, 1649-1863; Illustrative of Industrial History in the Colonial and Antebellum South: Collected from MSS. and Other Rare Sources. 2 Volumes. Cleveland: A. H. Clark, 1909.

Articles

"An Antigua Plantation, 1769-1818." *North Carolina Historical Review,* 3 (July, 1926): 439-45.

"Azandeland." *Yale Review,* 20 (December, 1930): 293-313.

"Black Belt Labor, Slave and Free." In *Lectures and Addresses on the Negro in the South.* Charlottesville: University of Virginia Press, 1915, pages 29-36.

"The Central Theme of Southern History." *American Historical Review,* 34 (October, 1928): 30-43.

"Conservatism and Progress in the Cotton Belt." *South Atlantic Quarterly,* 3 (January, 1904): 1-10.

"The Decadence of the Plantation System." *Annals of the American Academy of Political and Social Sciences,* 35 (January, 1910): 37-41.

"The Economic and Political Essays of the Antebellum South." In *The South in the Building of the Nation,* 12 vols. Richmond: Southern Historical Publication Society, 1909, vol. 7, pages 173-99.

"The Economic Cost of Slaveholding in the Cotton Belt." *Political Science Quarterly,* 20 (June, 1905): 257-75.

"The Economics of the Plantation." *South Atlantic Quarterly*, 6 (June, 1903): 231-36.

"The Economics of Slave Labor in the South." In *The South in the Building of the Nation*. 12 vols. Richmond: Southern Historical Publication Society, 1909, vol. 5, pages 121-24.

"The Economics of the Slave Trade, Foreign and Domestic," In *The South in the Building of the Nation*. 12 vols. Richmond: Southern Historical Publication Society, 1909, vol. 5, pages 124-29.

"Financial Crises in the Antebellum South." In *The South in the Building of the Nation*. 12 vols. Richmond: Southern Historical Publication Society, 1909, vol. 5, pages 435-41.

"Georgia in the Federal Union." In *The South in the Building of the Nation*. 12 vols. Richmond: Southern Historical Publication Society, 1909, vol. 2, pages 146-71.

"Georgia Local Archives." *Annual Report of the American Historical Association for the Year 1904*. Washington: Government Printing Office, 1905, pages 555-96.

"The Historic Civilization of the South." *Agricultural History*, 21 (April, 1938): 142-49.

"Historical Notes of Milledgeville, Georgia." *Gulf States Historical Magazine*, 2 (November, 1903): 161-71.

"A Jamaica Slave Plantation." *American Historical Review*, 19 (April, 1914): 543-48.

"The Literary Movement for Secession." In Walter Lynwood Fleming and J.G. de Roulhac Hamilton, eds. *Studies in Southern History and Politics*. New York: Columbia University Press, 1914, pages 33-60.

"New Light on the Founding of Georgia." *Georgia Historical Quarterly*, 6 (December, 1922): 277-84.

"The Origin and Growth of the Southern Black Belts." *American Historical Review*, 11 (July, 1906): 798-816.

"The Overproduction of Cotton and a Possible Remedy." *South Atlantic Quarterly*, 4 (April, 1905): 148-58.

"The Plantation as a Civilizing Factor." *Sewanee Review,* 12 (July, 1904): 257-67.

"Plantations East and South of Suez." *Agricultural History,* 5 (July, 1931): 93-109.

"Plantations with Slave Labor and Free." *American Historical Review,* 30 (July, 1925): 738-53.

"Racial Problems, Adjustments, and Disturbances." In *The South in the Building of the Nation.* 12 vols. Richmond: Southern Historical Publication Society, 1909, vol. 4, pages 194-241.

"Railroads in the South." In *The South in the Building of the Nation,* 12 vols. Richmond: Southern Historical Publication Society, 1909, vol. 5, pages 358-67.

"Railway Transportation in the South." In *The South in the Building of the Nation.* 12 vols. Richmond: Southern Historical Publication Society, 1909, vol. 6, pages 305-16.

"The Slave Labor Problem in the Charleston District." *Political Science Quarterly,* 22 (September, 1907): 416-39.

"The Slavery Issue in Federal Politics." In *The South in the Building of the Nation.* 12 vols. Richmond: Southern Historical Publication Society, 1909, vol. 4, pages 382-422.

"The South Carolina Federalists, Parts 1 and 2." *American Historical Review,* 14 (April and July, 1909): 529-43, 731-43.

"The Southern Whigs, 1834-1854." In *Essays in American History Dedicated to Frederick Jackson Turner.* New York: Henry Holt, 1910, pages 203-29.

"State and Local Public Regulation of Industry in the South." In *The South in the Building of the Nation.* 12 vols. Richmond: Southern Historical Publication Society, 1909, vol. 5, pages 475-78.

"The Traits and Contributions of Frederick Jackson Turner." *Agricultural History,* 19 (January, 1945): 20-35.

"Transportation in the Antebellum South: An Economic Analysis." *Quarterly Journal of Economics,* 19 (May, 1905): 434-58.

Historical Analyses of Ulrich Bonnell Phillips and His Work, 1934-1989

1934   Landon, Fred and Edwards, Everett E. "A Bibliography of the Writings of Professor Ulrich Bonnell Phillips." *Agricultural History*, 8 (October, 1934): 196-218.

1934   [Malone, Dumas.] "Ulrich B. Phillips." *American Historical Review*, 39 (April, 1934): 598-599.

1934   Potter, David M., Jr. "A Bibliography of the Printed Writings of Ulrich Bonnell Phillips." *Georgia Historical Quarterly*, 18 (September, 1934): 270-282.

1937   Gray, Wood. "Ulrich Bonnell Phillips." In Hutchinson, William T., ed. *The Marcus W. Jernegan Essays in American Historiography*. Chicago: University of Chicago Press, 1937, pages 354-373.

1939   Coulter, E. Merton. "Introduction." In Phillips, Ulrich B. *The Course of the South to Secession*. New York: D. Appleton-Century Co., 1939, pages vii-ix.

1939   Landon, Fred. "Ulrich Bonnell Phillips: Historian of the South." *Journal of Southern History*, 5 (August, 1939): 364-370.

1941   Newman, Philip C. "Ulrich Bonnell Phillips—The South's Foremost Historian." *Georgia Historical Quarterly*, 25 (September, 1941): 244-261.

1944   Coulter, E. Merton. "Ulrich Bonnell Phillips." In Harris E. Starr, ed. *Dictionary of American Biography*, Vol. XXI, Supplement 1. New York: Charles Scribner's Sons, 1944, pages 597-598.

1944   Hofstadter, Richard. "U.B. Phillips and the Plantation Legend." *Journal of Negro History*, 29 (April, 1944): 109-124.

1947   Kellar, Herbert A. "The Historian and Life." *Mississippi Valley Historical Review*, 34 (June, 1947): 3-36.

1952   Stampp, Kenneth M. "The Historian and Southern Negro Slavery." *American Historical Review*, 57 (April, 1952): 613-624.

1954   Pressly, Thomas J. "Ulrich B. Phillips." In *Americans Interpret Their Civil War*. Princeton: Princeton University Press, 1962, pages 265-272.

1955   Stephenson, Wendell H. "Ulrich B. Phillips: Historian of Aristocracy." *The South Lives in History: Southern Historians and Their Legacy*. Baton Rouge: Louisiana State University Press, 1955, pages 58-94.

1957   Stephenson, Wendell H. "Ulrich B. Phillips: The University of Georgia and the Georgia Historical Society." *Georgia Historical Quarterly*, 41 (June, 1957): 103-125. Reprinted in Stephenson, *Southern History in the Making: Pioneer Historians of the South*. Baton Rouge: Louisiana State University Press, 1964, pages 165-183.

1959   Doyle, Michael A. "The Life and Labor of Ulrich Bonnell Phillips." B.A. thesis, Yale University, 1959.

1959   Elkins, Stanley M. *Slavery: A Problem in American Institutional and Intellectual Life*. Chicago: University of Chicago Press, 1959, pages 9-15.

1960   Salem, Sam E. "U.B. Phillips and the Scientific Tradition." *Georgia Historical Quarterly*, 44 (June, 1960): 172-185.

1960   Tindall, George B. "The Central Theme Revisited." In Charles G. Sellers, Jr., ed. *The Southerner as American*. Chapel Hill: University of North Carolina Press, 1960, pages 104-129.

1960   Wish, Harvey. "Ulrich B. Phillips and the Image of the Old South." *The American Historian: A Social-Intellectual History of the Writing of the American Past*. New York: Oxford University Press, 1960, pages 236-264.

1961   Potter, David M. "The Enigma of the South." *Yale Review*, 51 (Autumn, 1961): 142-151. Reprinted in Potter, *The South and the Sectional Conflict*. Baton Rouge: Louisiana State University Press, 1968, pages 3-16.

1962   Kugler, Ruben F. "U.B. Phillips' Use of Sources." *Journal of Negro History*, 47 (July, 1962): 153-168.

1963   Woodward, C. Vann. "Introduction." Ulrich B. Phillips. *Life and Labor in the Old South*. Boston: Little, Brown and Company, 1963, pages iii-vi.

1966   Genovese, Eugene D. "Ulrich Bonnell Phillips & His Critics." [Introduction to] Ulrich Bonnell Phillips. *American Negro Slavery: A Survey of the Supply, Employment and Control of Negro Labor as Determined by the Plantation Regime*. Baton Rouge: Louisiana State University Press, 1966, pages vii-xxi.

1967   Elkins, Stanley M. "Class and Race: A Comment." *Agricultural History*, 41 (October, 1967): 369-371.

1967   Genovese, Eugene D. "Race and Class in Southern History: An Appraisal of the Work of Ulrich Bonnell Phillips." *Agricultural History*, 41 (October, 1967): 345-358.

1967   Potter, David M. "The Work of Ulrich B. Phillips: A Comment." *Agricultural History*, 41 (October, 1967): 359-363.

1967   Stampp, Kenneth M. "Reconsidering U.B. Phillips: A Comment." *Agricultural History*, 41 (October, 1967): 365-368.

1968   Filler, Louis. "Ulrich B. Phillips: A Question of History and Reality." [Introduction to] Ulrich B. Phillips. *Georgia and State Rights: A Study of the Political History of Georgia from the Revolution to the Civil War, With Particular Regard to Federal Relations*. Yellow Springs: Antioch Press, 1968, pages v-xiv.

1968   Genovese, Eugene D. "Ulrich Bonnell Phillips as an Economic Historian." [Introduction to] Ulrich Bonnell Phillips. *The Slave Economy of the Old South: Selected Essays in Economic and Social History*. Baton Rouge: Louisiana State University Press, 1968, pages vii-xiv.

1969   Mathis, G. Ray, ed. "Ulrich Bonnell Phillips and the Universities of Georgia and Wisconsin." *Georgia Historical Quarterly*, 53 (June, 1969): 241-243.

1970   Craven, Avery O. "Some Historians I Have Known." *The Maryland Historian*, 1 (Spring, 1970): 1-11.

1971   Van Deburg, William L. "Ulrich B. Phillips: Progress and the Conservative Historian." *Georgia Historical Quarterly*, 55 (Fall, 1971): 406-416.

1971   Wilson, James D. "The Role of Slavery in the Agrarian Myth." *Recherches Anglaises et Americaines*, 4 (1971): 12-22.

1972   Kugler, Ruben F. "U.B. Phillips' Use of Sources." *Pan African Studies Journal*, 1 (Summer, 1972): 41-47.

1972   Smiley, David L. "The Quest for the Central Theme in Southern History." *South Atlantic Quarterly*, 71 (Summer, 1972): 307-325.

1972   Winkler, Allan M. "Ulrich Bonnell Phillips: A Reappraisal." *South Atlantic Quarterly*, 71 (Spring, 1972): 234-245.

1974   Crowe, Charles. "Historians and 'Benign Neglect': Conservative Trends in Southern History and Black Studies." *Reviews in American History*, 2 (June, 1974): 163-173.

1974   Fogel, Robert W. and Engerman, Stanley L. *Time on the Cross: The Economics of American Negro Slavery*. Boston: Little, Brown and Company, 1974, pages 223-232.

1975   Wood, Peter H. "Phillips Upside Down: Dialectic or Equivocation?" *Journal of Interdisciplinary History*, 6 (Autumn, 1975): 289-297.

1976   Crocker, Ruth H. "Ulrich Phillips: A Southern Historian Reconsidered." *Louisiana Studies*, 15 (Summer, 1976): 113-130.

1976   Roper, John Herbert. "A Case of Forgotten Identity: Ulrich B. Phillips as a Young Progressive." *Georgia Historical Quarterly*, 60 (Summer, 1976): 165-175.

1977   Roper, John Herbert. "Ulrich Bonnell Phillips: His Life and Thought." Ph.D. dissertation, University of North Carolina at Chapel Hill, 1977.

1977   Singal, Daniel Joseph. "Ulrich B. Phillips: The Old South as the New." *Journal of American History*, 63 (March, 1977): 871-891.

1977   Smith, John David. "The Formative Period of American Slave Historiography, 1890-1920." Ph.D. dissertation, University of Kentucky, 1977.

1978   Smith, John David. "Ulrich B. Phillips and Academic Freedom at the University of Michigan." *Michigan History*, 62 (Spring, 1978): 11-15.

1979   Smith, John David. "An Old Creed for the New South—Southern Historians and the Revival of the Proslavery Argument, 1890-1920." *Southern Studies*, 18 (Spring, 1979): 75-87.

1979   Smith, John David. "'Keep 'em in a fire-proof vault'—Pioneer Southern Historians Discover Plantation Records." *South Atlantic Quarterly*, 78 (Summer, 1979): 376-391.

1980   Smith, John David. "Du Bois and Phillips—Symbolic Antagonists of the Progressive Era." *The Centennial Review*, 24 (Winter, 1980): 88-102.

1981   Smith, John David. "Historical or Personal Criticism? Frederic Bancroft vs. Ulrich B. Phillips." *Washington State University Research Studies*, 49 (June, 1981): 73-86.

1981   Smith, John David. "The Historiographic Rise, Fall, and Resurrection of Ulrich Bonnell Phillips." *Georgia Historical Quarterly*, 65 (Summer, 1981): 138-153.

1982   Smith, John David. "Ulrich Bonnell Phillips: The Southern Progressive as Racist." *Yale University Library Gazette*, 56 (April, 1982): 70-75.

1982   Wood, W. K. "U.B. Phillips, Unscientific Historian: A Further Note on His Methodology and Use of Sources." *Southern Studies*, 21 (Summer, 1982): 146-162.

1983   Wood, Kirk. "Ulrich B. Phillips." In Clyde N. Wilson, ed. *Dictionary of Literary Biography, Twentieth-Century American Historians*. Detroit: Gale Research, 1983, pages 350-363.

1983 Wood, W. K. "Rewriting Southern History: U.B. Phillips, the New South, and the Antebellum Past." *Southern Studies*, 22 (Fall, 1983): 217-243.

1983 Roper, John H. "Progress and History: A Southern Dialectic on Race." *Southern Humanities Review*, 17 (Spring, 1983): 101-120.

1983 Roper, John Herbert. "Phillips, Ulrich Bonnell." In Kenneth Coleman and Charles S. Gurr, eds., *Dictionary of Georgia Biography*. 2 vols. Athens: University of Georgia Press, 1983, volume 2, pages 793-794.

1984 Roper, John Herbert. "Introduction." Phillips, Ulrich B. *Georgia and State Rights*. Macon: Mercer University Press, 1984, pages vii-xxxv.

1984 Roper, John Herbert. *U.B. Phillips: A Southern Mind*. Macon: Mercer University Press, 1984.

1984 Wood, W.K., ed. "'My Dear M. Snowden': U.B. Phillips' Letters to Yates Snowden of South Carolina College, 1904-1932." *South Carolina Historical Magazine*, 85 (October, 1984): 292-304.

1985 Dillon, Merton L. *Ulrich Bonnell Phillips: Historian of the Old South*. Baton Rouge: Louisiana State University Press, 1985.

1985 Morgan, James C. *Slavery in the United States: Four Views*. Jefferson, N.C.: McFarland and Co., 1985, Chapter II.

1985 Smith, John David. *An Old Creed for the New South: Proslavery Ideology and Historiography, 1865-1918*. Westport: Greenwood Press, 1985, Chapter 8.

1985 Smith, Mark C. "Southern History and Myths: Ulrich Bonnell Phillips Reconsidered." *Journal of the American Studies Association of Texas*, 16 (1985): 9-13.

1986 Smith, John David. "The Life and Labor of Ulrich Bonnell Phillips." *Georgia Historical Quarterly*, 70 (Summer, 1986): 254-272.

1987 Filler, Louis. "Phillips, Ulrich B." In Filler, ed. *Dictionary of American Conservatism*. New York: Philosophical Library, 1987, page 248.

1987 Pyron, Darden Asbury. "U. B. Phillips: Biography and Scholarship." *Reviews in American History*, 15 (March, 1987): 72-77.

1987   Wood, W. Kirk. "U.B. Phillips and Antebellum Southern Rail Inferiority: The Origins of a Myth." *Southern Studies*, 26 (Fall, 1987): 173-87.

1989   Crowe, Charles. "Black Culture and White Power: Notes On the History of Historical Perception." *Georgia Historical Quarterly*, 73 (Summer, 1989): 250-277.

1989   Smith, John David. "The Historian as Archival Advocate: Ulrich Bonnell Phillips and the Records of Georgia and the South." *The American Archivist*, 52 (Summer, 1989): 320-331.

1989   Smith, Mark. "Phillips, U. B." In Charles Reagan Wilson and William Ferris, co-eds. *The Encyclopedia of Southern Culture*. Chapel Hill: University of North Carolina Press, 1989, page 297.

Index

Abolitionists, 68, 100, 120, 229, 242, 248 n.5, 250-52
Absentee ownership of slaves, 93, 139
Adams, Henry, 25
Adams, Herbert Baxter, 26, 155, 217
Advertisements for slaves, 96
Africa, Phillips on, 135, 224
African survivals, 38
Agrarianism, 199-200
Agrarians: *See* "Twelve Southerners"
Agricultural History Society, 37
Agricultural reform in Georgia, 41-42, 49-51
Alabama Department of Archives and History, 156-57
American Bureau of Industrial Research, 60
American Historical Association, 37, 154, 159
American Negro Slavery (Phillips), 2-4, 24, 37, 65, 97, 103, 121, 131-32, 135, 139, 144, 146-49, 185-86, 204, 207-9, 219, 224, 229, 242-43; reviews of, 83-89
American Revolution, Phillips on, 244, 250-51
Andrews, E. A., 146-47
Aptheker, Herbert, 6, 13 n.30, 94
Armentrout, George W., 161
Ashmore, Harry, 200
Athens, Ga., railroad rivalry with Augusta, 174-76, 181 n.24
Atlanta *Constitution*, 48-50, 53
Atlantic slave trade. *See* Slave trade, Atlantic
Augusta, Ga., 178-79 n.9,10; railroad rivalry with Athens, 174-76, 18l n.24

Autobiographies, slave, 96

Baker, Ray Stannard, 39, 155
Baldwin, William H., Jr., 18
Bancroft, Frederic, 4, 5, 157
Banks, Enoch Marvin, 45 n.25
Barker, Eugene C., 156
Barnes, Gilbert H., 242
Beard, Charles, 109
Becker, Carl, 109
Beveridge, A. J., 246
Blake, W.O., 144
Blassingame, John W., 1
Boone, Daniel, 163-64
Boyd, William K., 164, 238
Bremer, Fredricka, 144-45
Brewer, William M., 4-5
Brown, Joseph E., 132
Bruce, Philip Alexander, 3, 4, 216, 227
Burgess, John W., 23, 97, 222
Buxton, Thomas, 144

Calhoun, John C., 199, 237-38
California, University of, 76 n.25
Camp Gordon, Ga., 25
Capitalist economy of Old South, 63-66, 74 n.14, 203-5, 213, 220
Carnegie Institution, Phillips as research fellow, 173
Carroll, Charles, 222
Cartwright, Samuel, 94
Cavalier myth: *See* Plantation myth
"Central Theme of Southern History," (Phillips), 28, 29, 47, 68, 76 n.29,77 n.35, 115, 119, 122, 125, 134, 200, 203, 205, 225, 230, 251

Charleston, S.C., 5
Cherokee Indians, 244-45
Chicago, University of, 217
Civil rights, anticipated by Phillips, 141
    n.16, 246
Civil War causation, Phillips on, 2, 6, 38,
    66-68, 237-39, 246, 251-52
Clay, Cassius M., 119
Climate, 29, 98, 114
Columbia University, 21, 23, 48, 59-60,
    217
Commager, Henry Steele, 3
Commons, John R., 60, 217
Conrad, Alfred H., 204-5
Connor, R.D.W., 157
Correspondence of Robert Toombs,
    Alexander H. Stephens, and Howell
    Cobb (Phillips), 159, 237
Cotton production, 77 n.31, 137; in Geor-
    gia, 50-53
Coulter, E. Merton, 241
Course of the South to Secession (Phillips),
    66-67, 119, 229-30, 237, 241, 251; *See*
    also Secession
Cox, Ernest Sevier, 222
Craven, Avery O. , 70, 160
Crawford, William H., 237, 238
Creek Indians, 244-45
Curry, J.L.M., 58-59, 222

Davis, Jefferson, 237
DeRenne, Wymberly Jones, 24
Dew, Charles B., 6
Dew, Thomas R., 98
Dictionary of American Biography,
    Phillips's contributions to, 237-38
Dillon, Merton L., 9, 10; essay by, 249-53
Dixon, Thomas, 222
Dodd, William E., 9, 26, 74 n.15, 127
    n.32, 155, 156, 200, 245
Domestic slave trade. *See* Slave trade,
    domestic
Douglas, Stephen A., 237
Du Bois, W.E.B., 4, 83; reviews *American*
    Negro Slavery, 4, 84-86, 133, 207-208;
    essay by 17-18
Dunning, William A., 23, 26, 39, 73 n.9,
    103, 217, 222

Economics of slavery. *See* Slavery,
    economics of
Elkins, Stanley, 212-13, 215; essay by, 103-8
Ely, Richard T., 60, 217
Engerman, Stanley L., essay by, 207-13

Environment: *See* Slavery and environ-
    ment; Phillips, as environmentalist

Farm tenantry, 41-42
Federal Writers Project, 96
Filler, Louis, 38, essay by, 241-48
Fire-eaters, 66, 68, 121, 250, 252
Fiske, John, 97
Fitzhugh, George, 97, 119, 121
Flanders, Ralph, 106
Fleming, Walter L., 26
Fogel, Robert W., essay by, 207-13
Fredrickson, George, 222
Free blacks, 136
Frelinghuysen, Theodore, 245
Frontier, Phillips on, 62-63, 229

Galloway, E.H., 49
Garrison, William Lloyd, 121, 242
Gaston, Paul M., 71 n.2, 216
Genovese, Eugene D., 3, 6-7, 13 n.26, 14
    n.39, 58, 70 n.1, 215, 232 n. 15, 242-43;
    essays by, 113-28, 203-6; *See also*
    Paternalism, plantation
Georgia: agricultural reform of, 41-42,
    49-52; archival resources of, 159-60;
    educational reform of, 49-50; politics
    in, 244-45
Georgia, University of, 20, 22, 158, 217;
    Phillips wishes to reform, 41, 48-49
Georgia and State Rights (Phillips), 22, 37,
    39, 68, 217, 237, 243, 245-48; intro-
    duction to by Louis Filler, 241-48
Georgia Railroad and Banking Com-
    pany, 174-77
Georgia Historical Quarterly, 251
Georgia Historical Society, 19, 48, 159
Georgia's Indian Removal policy,
    244-45
Goebbels, Joseph, 13 n.30
Govan, Thomas P., 5, 99
Grady, Henry W., 58-59, 75 nn. 21, 22,
    222
Gray, Lewis C., 5, 93, 99, 210
Gray, Wood, 133
Gutman, Herbert C., 4, 10

Hamer, Philip M., 156
Hamilton, J.G. de Roulhac, 3, 154, 156,
    160, 164
Hammond, James Henry, 61
Harper, Roland M., 20
Hart, Albert B., 103, 156
Hayne, Robert Y., 237

Health, slave. *See* Slave health
Hill, Walter B., 49, 50
History of the People of the United States
(McMaster), 20
*History of the United States from the Com-
promise of 1850* (Rhodes), 20
*History of Transportation in the Eastern
Cotton Belt to 1860* (Phillips), 65, 117,
119, 173-77, 206
Hofstadter, Richard, 5, 31, 92, 133, 138,
200, 208-11, 215; essay by, 185-98
Holland, Edwin C., 119
Hooker, Edward, 150
Howell, Clark, 29, 48-54
Hughes, Henry, 119

I'll Take My Stand, 122-23
Immigration, to South, 105, 227
Imperialism, 97, 110
Indian policy, Georgia's, 244-45
Inman, Hugh T., 52
Interviews, slave, 96

Jameson, J. Franklin, 156
Jefferson, Thomas, 157, 244
Johns Hopkins University, 26, 154, 155
Journal of Southern History, 246

Kellar, Herbert A., 160-64, 249
Kemble, Fanny, 148
Kilpatrick, William H., 156
Kugler, Ruben, essay by, 143-52

LaFollette, Robert, 49
La Grange, Ga., 15, 20, 217
Landon, Fred, 108 n.8, 160
Laprade, William Thomas, 153
Laurens, Henry, 154
Library of Congress, 157
Life and Labor in the Old South (Phillips),
4, 21, 26, 39, 97, 109-11, 121, 131-32,
135, 185, 188, 241-42; introduction to
by C. Vann Woodward, 109-11
Life of Robert Toombs (Phillips), 76 n.29,
133, 237-38, 251
"Lost Cause" myth, 69, 134, 226, 229-30
Lowell, James Russell, 100
Leverages, slave, 2

Master-slave relationship: See Paternalism, plantation; and Slave treatment
Matthews, George, 243
McCarthy, Charles, 217

McCormick Historical Association, 161
McKissick, J. Rion, 70 n.1, 161-64
McMaster, John Bach, 20
McPherson, John H.T., 2, 217
McWhorter, Hamilton, 49
Meekins, Lynn R., 155
Memorials of a Southern Planter (Smedes),
20
Mercer College, 50
Meyer, John R., 204-205
Michigan, University of, 243
Milledgeville, Ga., 73 n.12, 159, 206
Miscegenation, 114
Mississippi, black labor in, 17-18
Mississippi Department of Archives
and History, 157
Morrill Land Grant College Act, 48
Murphy, Edgar Gardner, 223
Myrdal, Gunnar, 203

National Archives, 156
National Associatio.. for the Advance-
ment of Colored People, 246
Natural limits of slavery expansion
thesis, 68, 205
"New History," 3, 59, 241
Newman, Philip, 108 n.8
New Orleans, La., 5
New South, 8, 29, 57, 122-24, 216-17, 223
Nonslaveholders: *See* Plain folk
North, slavery in, 27
North Carolina Historical Commission, 157
Northwestern University, Phillips lec-
tures at, 142 n.35, 250
Nuttall, Elijah F., 119

Olmsted, Frederick Law, 25, 93, 138,
139, 145-46, 149, 191-92, 209-10
O'Neall, Judge J.B., 148
Osgood, Herbert Levi, 23
Overseers, 3, 93, 139, 221
Ovington, Mary White, 4; reviews
American Negro Slavery, 89
Owen, Thomas M., 156-57
Owsley, Frank L., 5, 93, 191
Oxford College, 50

Page, Thomas Nelson, 74 n.15, 105
Parrington, Vernon Louis, 109
Passing of the Great Race, The (Grant), 105
Paternalism, plantation: Genovese on,
7, 14 n.39, 114, 117-18, 121, 122, 124,
220, 232 n.15; Phillips on, 2, 3, 38, 104,
109, 135, 137, 220-21

Peabody, George F., 49, 50
Peculiar Institution, The (Stampp), 6, 7, 146
Percy, William Alexander, 31-32
Phillips, Alonzo Rabun, 20, 30
Phillips, Jessie Elizabeth Young, 20, 30
"Phillips School," 4, 105
Phillips, Ulrich Bonnell: as agricultural reform advocate, 41, 50-53, 60, 237; Albert Kahn Fellow, 24, 37, 126 n.10; ancestry and early life, 20-23, 30-31, 103, 157, 217; as biographer, 237-38; at Columbia University, 22-23, 48, 59; conservatism of, 40, 42-43, 47, 124, 133; education of, 21-23, 37, 158-59; as educational reform advocate, 49-50; environmentalism of, 224-26; geographical determinism of, 24, 39; historical methodology of, 132-33, 138, 144-50; awarded Justin Winsor prize, 37; liberalism of, 41; awarded prize by Little, Brown and Company, 12 n.13, 38, 241; as New South spokesman, 58-62; personality, 9; as progressive, 8, 30, 31, 38-40, 47-48, 58-60; as racist, 3, 5-6, 8-11, 13 n.30, 31, 38, 40, 47, 83-84, 96, 103, 110, 134-36, 207-13, 221-24, 246-47; religious views of, 50; research fellow at Carnegie Institution, 173; romanticism of, 47; as scientific historian, 40, 138-39, 143, 158-61; sectional biases of, 15-16, 20, 25-27, 28, 62, 69; at University of Chicago, 22; at University of Georgia, 20-22, 41, 48; at University of Wisconsin, 48, 59-60, 217-18, 241; writing style, 11, 31; at Yale University, 7, 238, 241. Works of: See individual titles
Plain folk, 3, 5, 64, 115, 116, 227, 248 n.2
Plantation and Frontier Documents (Phillips), 24, 60, 218, 229
Plantation paternalism: See Paternalism, plantation
Plantation records: as historical sources, 155-57; Phillips's use of, 23, 25, 37, 104, 110, 139, 143, 158-61, 186-92
Plantation Slavery in Georgia (Flanders), 106
Plantations, 2, 8, 120, 137-138, 140; Phillips favors reestablishment of, 41-42, 44-45 n. 25, 51, 66, 134-35, 220, 227; as concentration camp analogy, 211-12; as factory analogy, 41-42, 62,

216-17, 218-19; as school analogy, 2, 37, 75 n.23, 97, 104, 106, 110, 118, 143, 224-25; as settlement house analogy, 123; myth of, 185-92, 217, 226, 228-31; size of, 185-91, 228
Planters: See Slaveholders
Politics: Georgia, 244-25; southern, 243-48
Pollard, Edward A., 120, 121
Populists, 104-5
Potter, David M., essay by, 199-201
Pressly, Thomas J., 71 n.2, n.4
Progressive movement, 104-5, 107 n.5, 109-10, 122, 217-18, 221-22, 230, 246; and racism, 38-40, 221-23, 246-47; See also Phillips, as progressive

Racial inferiority, myth of, 207-13, 220-21
Racism: See Phillips, as racist
Railroads, southern, Phillips on, 61-62, 73, 173-77
Ramsdell, Charles W., 205
Ranke, Leopold von, 131-32, 136-37, 140
Ransom, John Crowe, 108 n.8
Reconstruction, 239, 251
Revolutionary War: See American Revolution
Rhett, Robert Barnwell, 119
Rhodes, James Ford, 20, 37, 103, 106, 108 n.8, 209-11, 222
Riley, Franklin L., 157
Robinson, James Harvey, 3, 23, 59-60
Roosevelt, Theodore, 53, 246-47
Roper, John Herbert, 7-8, 9; essays by, 29-33, 47-55
Rowland, Dunbar, 157
Russel, Robert R., 5, 99
Russell, William H., 25

Salem, Sam E., essay by, 131-42
Santo Domingo, slave revolt in, 250
Savannah News, 51-52
Schevill, Ferdinand, 22
Scientific history, 10, 40, 91, 131, 138, 140, 143
Segregation, Phillips's defense of, 230-31
Secession, 66-68, 76 n.26, 119, 120, 238-39, 251-52; See also Course of the South to Secession
Seligman, Edwin R.A., 59-60
Sheehan, Donald, 143
Simms, William Gilmore, 154

Sinclair, Upton, 247
Singal, Daniel J., 8, 58; essay by, 215-34
Slave artisans, 5
Slave breeding, 4, 146
Slave codes, 26, 148
Slave health, 98
Slave labor, efficiency of, 63-66, 120, 209-11, 218-19, 226-27, 232 n.15
Slave leverages: *See* Leverages, slave
Slave ownership: *See* Slaveholders
Slave population, 190-91
Slave prices, 5, 89, 95, 146, 209
Slave rebelliousness, 4, 212, 250
Slave resistance, 6, 94, 192, 208, 212
Slave testimony, 83, 96
Slave trade, Atlantic, 137, 144, 243
Slave trade, domestic, 89, 147
Slave treatment, 93-94, 104, 124, 138, 139, 192, 211-13, 220-21
Slave women, 88, 118
Slaveholders: large, 93, 120-21, 185-91, 205-6, 228; small, 93
Slavery: and environment, 224-26; demographics of, 186-91; economics of, 2, 5, 17-18, 98-100, 120, 203-6, 210-11; natural limits of, 68, 205; in North, 217; origins of, 98, 137, 223-24, 225, 250; profitablity of, 2, 5, 98-88, 205, 209-11; source material on, 2-4, 8, 10, 11, 23-24, 93, 96, 103-4, 138, 139, 186-92
Slavery (Elkins), excerpt from, 103-8
Slavery in Mississippi (Sydnor), 106, 243
Sloane, William M., 23
Smith, Hoke, 53
Smith, John David, essays by, 1-14, 153-67
Smith, Justin H., 238
Smith, Rembert, 50
Smith, Robert W., 5, 99
Snowden, Yates, 70 n.1, 159
Social Relations in our Southern States (Hundley), 20
Soil exhaustion, 99
South Carolina Historical Society, 154
South in the Building of the Nation series, Phillips's contributions to, 237
South Lives In History (Stephenson), excerpts from, 19-28, 237-39
Southern Historical Collection (UNC), 156, 160
Southern Historical Society, 154
Southern history as research field, 19, 25, 153-55
Southern History Association, 154

Southern Oral History Collection (UNC), 7
Southern Planter, 218
Stampp, Kenneth M., 6, 7, 10, 200, 210-13; essay by, 91-101; *See also The Peculiar Institution*
State rights, 68, 119, 238-39
Stephens, Alexander H., 237
Stephenson, Nathaniel W., 238
Stephenson, Wendell H., 115, 131, 139, 154, 215; essays by, 19-28, 237-39
Stone, Alfred H., 18, 155
Sydnor, Charles S., 106, 243

Tannenbaum, Frank, 114
Taylor, Frederick W., 218
Terrell, Joseph M., 49
Terry, Benjamin S., 22
Testimony, slave: *See* Slave testimony
Thompson, Edgar T., 227
Thompson, Holland, 216
Time on the Cross (Fogel and Engerman), excerpt from, 207-13
Toombs, Robert, 9, 76 n.29, 133, 159, 237-38
Transportation, in Old South, Phillips on, 61, 117, 172-77, 206; *See also History of Transportation in the Eastern Cotton Belt*; and Railroads, southern
Travel accounts as sources on antebellum South, 25, 27, 93, 104, 139, 144-47, 150, 191-92
Trent, William P., 74 n.15
Tulane Preparatory School, 21
Tulane University, 243
Turner, Frederick Jackson: 3, 26, 31, 38-39, 60, 73 n.9, 74 n.16, 109, 113, 238; influence on Phillips, 22, 60, 217-18, 245
"Twelve Southerners," 108 n.89, 123

U.B. Phillips: A Southern Mind (Roper), 7-8; excerpt from, 29-33
Ulrich Bonnell Phillips: Historian of the Old South (Dillon), 9; excerpt from, 249-53
University of Chicago: *See* Chicago, University of
University of Georgia: *See* Georgia, University of
University of Michigan: *See* Michigan, University of
University of Virginia: *See* Virginia, University of

University of Wisconsin: *See* Wisconsin, University of
Urban South, Phillips on, 206

Van Deburg, William L., essay by, 37-45
Van Hise, Charles R., 49
Virginia, manuscript collecting trip to, 24, 161-64
Virginia Polytechnic Institute, Phillips lectures at, 40
Virginia State Library, 159
Virginia, University of, 17

Wall, Bennett H., 70 n.1
Washington, Booker T., 53, 105
Watson, Tom, 242, 246
Weatherford, W.D., 223
Weeks, Stephen B., 154-55

Weld, Theodore D., 242
Wigfall, Louis T., 69-70
Wilson, Woodrow, 26, 245
Winsor, Justin, 154
Wisconsin, as model for Georgia, 48-50
Wisconsin, University of, 19, 48, 59-60, 217-18, 241, 243
Wisconsin State Historical Society, 173
Women, slave: *See* Slave women
Wood, W. K., essays by, 57-78, 169-82
Woodman, Harold D., 204-5
Woodson, Carter G., 4; reviews *American Negro Slavery*, 86-88
Woodward, C. Vann, 9, 70 n.1, 107 n.4, 111, 201, 242, 246; essay by, 109-11

Yale University, 7, 238, 241-43
Yancey, William L., 132

About the Contributors

MERTON L. DILLON is professor of history at Ohio State University. A leading authority on the American abolitionist movement, his works include biographies of Elijah P. Lovejoy (1961) and Benjamin Lundy (1966) and *The Abolitionists: The Dissenting Minority* (1974). The selection in this volume is drawn from *Ulrich Bonnell Phillips: Historian of the Old South* (Baton Rouge: Louisiana State University Press, 1985), 158-162.

W.E.B. DU BOIS received his Ph.D. from Harvard University in 1895, the first black to receive this degree from an American university. He wrote several of the most influential historical and sociological studies of blacks in the twentieth century, including *The Philadelphia Negro* (1899); *The Souls of Black Folk* (1903); and *Black Reconstruction in America* (1935). From 1910 to 1934 Du Bois edited *The Crisis*, the organ of the National Association for the Advancement of Colored People. His editorial "The Experts" appeared in *The Crisis* 5 (March, 1913), 239-240. His book review of *American Negro Slavery* appeared in the *American Political Science Review* 12 (November, 1918), 722-726.

STANLEY M. ELKINS is professor of history at Smith College and co-editor with Eric McKitrick of *The Hofstadter Aegis: A Memorial* (1974). He is represented here by an excerpt from his book, *Slavery: A Problem in American Institutional and Intellectual Life* (Chicago: University of Chicago Press, 1959), 9-15.

STANLEY L. ENGERMAN is professor of economics and history at the University of Rochester. He is co-editor of *The Reinterpretation of American Economic History* (1971) and *Race and Slavery in the Western Hemisphere: Quantitative Studies* (1975). With Robert W. Fogel, he wrote *Time on the Cross: The Economics of American Slavery* (Boston: Little, Brown and Company, 1974), from which the selection in this volume is taken (pp. 223-232).

LOUIS FILLER is professor emeritus of American Civilization at Antioch College. His many works include *Crusaders for American Liberalism* (1939); *A Dictionary of American Social Welfare* (1963); *A Dictionary of American Conservatism* (1987); and *Crusade Against Slavery: Friends, Foes and Reforms, 1820-1860* (1960). His article, "Ulrich B. Phillips: A Question of History and Reality," served as the introduction to the paperback reprint of Phillips's *Georgia and State Rights* (Yellow Springs, Ohio: The Antioch Press, 1968), v-xiv.

ROBERT W. FOGEL is professor of economics at the University of Chicago. He is the author of *The Union Pacific Railroad* (1960); *Railroads and American Economic Growth* (1964); and *Without Consent or Contract: The Rise and Fall of American Slavery* (1989). He is the co-author, with Stanley L. Engerman, of *Time on the Cross* (see above).

EUGENE D. GENOVESE is professor of Arts and Sciences at the University of Rochester. Among his many writings on slavery are *The Political Economy of Slavery* (1967); *The World the Slaveholders Made* (1969); *Roll, Jordan, Roll* (1974); and *From Rebellion to Revolution* (1979). His article "Race and Class in Southern History" first appeared in *Agricultural History* 41 (October, 1967), 345-358. His article "Ulrich Bonnell Phillips as an Economic Historian" served as the introduction to an anthology of essays by Phillips edited by Genovese, *The Slave Economy of the Old South: Selected Essays in Economic and Social History* (Baton Rouge: Louisiana State University Press, 1968), vii-xiv.

RICHARD HOFSTADTER ranked as one of the most influential intellectual historians and cultural analysts of the twentieth century. His major publications include *Social Darwinism in American Thought* (1944); *The Age of Reform* (1955); and *Anti-Intellectualism in American Life* (1963). His article "U.B. Phillips and the Plantation Legend" appeared in the *Journal of Negro History* 29 (April, 1944), 109-124.

RUBEN F. KUGLER taught at Los Angeles State College. The selection "U. B. Phillips's Use of Sources" is a condensation of his article in the *Journal of Negro History* 47 (July, 1962), 153-154, 159-168.

MARY WHITE OVINGTON, a pioneer social worker and reformer, published *Half a Man: The Status of the Negro in New York* (1911). She forcefully refuted racist theories and championed equal opportunities for blacks. Her review of Phillips's *American Negro Slavery* appeared in *The Survey* 40 (September 28, 1918), 718.

DAVID M. POTTER studied with U. B. Phillips at Yale University, receiving his Ph.D. in 1940. Among his earliest publications was a bibliography of Phillips's writings that appeared in the *Georgia Historical Quarterly* in 1934. Potter's books include *Lincoln and His Party in the Secession Crisis* (1942); *People of Plenty* (1954); and *The Impending Crisis, 1848-1861* (1976) (completed and edited by Don E. Fehrenbacher). "The Enigma of the South" is drawn from Potter's *The South and the Sectional Conflict* (Baton Rouge: Louisiana State University Press, 1968), 9-12. It first appeared in the *Yale Review* in 1961.

JOHN HERBERT ROPER is associate professor of history at Emory and Henry College. His latest book is *C. Vann Woodward, Southerner* (1987). The selection "U. B. Phillips: A Southern Mind" comes from Roper's first book, *U. B. Phillips: A Southern Mind* (Macon, Ga.: Mercer University Press, 1984), 1-2, 5-6, 165-167. His article "A Case of Forgotten Identity" first appeared in the *Georgia Historical Quarterly* 60 (Summer, 1976), 165-175.

SAM E. SALEM worked on his Ph.D. in history at Western Reserve University and lectured at Case Institute of Technology. His article "Ulrich B. Phillips and the Scientific Tradition" was published in the *Georgia Historical Quarterly* 44 (June, 1960), 172-185.

DANIEL JOSEPH SINGAL is associate professor of history at Hobart and William Smith Colleges. He is the author of *The War Within: From Victorian to Modernist Thought in the South* (1982). His article "Ulrich B. Phillips: The Old South as the New" appeared in the *Journal of American History* 63 (March, 1977), 871-891. The author has made minor revisions in the version that appears here.

JOHN DAVID SMITH is co-editor of this volume. Earlier versions of his introduction appeared in the *Georgia Historical Quarterly* 65 (Summer, 1981), 138-153, and 70 (Summer, 1986), 254-272. His essay "'Keep 'em in a fire-proof vault'" was published in the *South Atlantic Quarterly* 78 (Summer, 1979), 376-391.

KENNETH M. STAMPP is the Morrison Professor of History Emeritus at the University of California at Berkeley. Among his many writings are *The Peculiar Institution* (1956); *The Causes of the Civil War* (1959); and *The Era of Reconstruction, 1865-1877* (1965). His article "The Historian and Southern Negro Slavery" appeared in the *American Historical Review* 57 (April, 1952), 613-624.

WENDELL HOLMES STEPHENSON studied with Phillips at the University of Michigan, earning his Ph.D. in 1928. His books include biographies of Alexander Porter (1934) and Isaac Franklin (1938), and *Southern History in the Making: Pioneer Historians of the South* (1964). Stephenson was the first historian to locate and use Phillips's unpublished correspondence in historiographical analysis. His essays in this volume are drawn from *The South Lives in History: Southern Historians and Their Legacy* (Baton Rouge: Louisiana State University Press, 1955), 58-65, 70-72, 76-83, 90-94.

WILLIAM L. VAN DEBURG is professor of Afro-American Studies at the University of Wisconsin. He is the author of *The Slave Drivers* (1979) and *Slavery and Race in American Popular Culture* (1984). His article on Phillips appeared in the *Georgia Historical Quarterly* 55 (Fall, 1971), 406-416.

W. K. WOOD is dean of graduate studies at Alabama State University. Both of his selections in this volume were published in longer versions in *Southern Studies.* "U.B. Phillips, Unscientific Historian" appeared in vol. 21 (Summer, 1982), 146-162; and "Rewriting Southern History" appeared in vol. 22 (Fall, 1983), 217-243.

C. VANN WOODWARD is Sterling Professor of History Emeritus at Yale University. His many books on southern history include *Tom Watson, Agrarian Rebel* (1938); *Origins of the New South* (1951); *The Burden of Southern History* (1960); and *Mary Chesnut's Civil War* (edited, 1981). His selection on Phillips served as the introduction to a 1963 edition of Phillips's *Life and Labor in the Old South* (Boston: Little, Brown and Company), iii-vi.

CARTER G. WOODSON followed W.E.B. Du Bois as the second black scholar to earn a Ph.D. in America. He received the degree in 1912, also from Harvard. He established the Association for the Study of Negro Life and History in 1915 and a year later began editing the *Journal of Negro History.* His books include *The Education of the Negro Prior to 1861* (1915) and *The Negro in Our History* (1922). His review of Phillips's *American Negro Slavery* appeared in the *Mississippi Valley Historical Review* 5 (March, 1919), 480-482.

About the Editors

JOHN DAVID SMITH is associate professor of history and director of the M.A. in Archival Management program at North Carolina State University. He has published widely on U. B. Phillips and the historiography of slavery. His books include *Window on the War: Frances Dallam Peter's Lexington Civil War Diary* (1976); *Black Slavery in the Americas: An Interdisciplinary Bibliography, 1865-1980* (2 vols., 1982); *An Old Creed for the New South: Proslavery Ideology and Historiography, 1865-1918* (1985); and *The Dictionary of Afro-American Slavery* (1988).

JOHN C. INSCOE is editor of the *Georgia Historical Quarterly* and assistant professor of history at the University of Georgia. He is the author of *Mountain Masters, Slavery, and the Sectional Crisis in Western North Carolina* (1989), and of articles on slavery and early twentieth century race relations that have appeared in the *Journal of Southern History; Civil War History; South Atlantic Quarterly; North Carolina Historical Review; Slavery & Abolition;* and the *Virginia Magazine of History and Biography*.